The Value of Popular Music

Alison Stone

The Value of Popular Music

An Approach from Post-Kantian Aesthetics

Alison Stone
Lancaster University
Lancaster, UK

ISBN 978-3-319-83539-6   ISBN 978-3-319-46544-9   (eBook)
DOI 10.1007/978-3-319-46544-9

Cover design by Fatima Jamadar

Printed on acid-free paper

This Palgrave Macmillan imprint is published by Springer Nature
The registered company is Springer International Publishing AG
The registered company address is: Gewerbestrasse 11, 6330 Cham, Switzerland

PERMISSIONS

Quotations from Michaels (2012), Morley (2014), Savage (2008), Simpson (2013) and Simpson (2014) are reproduced courtesy of Guardian News & Media Ltd., under Guardian Open License terms.

The quotation from Katy Guest in *The Independent*, 29 July 2012, is reproduced by permission of the Evening Standard.

COLLECTED POEMS by Rimbaud, translated by Sorrell (2009), 8 lines from p. 127, are reproduced by permission of Oxford University Press.

ACKNOWLEDGEMENTS

Many people have generously helped me as I wrote this book. Several people read drafts of the material at various stages. They include Alexander Bird, Emily Brady, James Connelly, Dan DeNicola, Robin Downie, Andy Hamilton, Susanne Hermann-Sinai, Max Paddison, Chris Partridge, Richard Stopford, and Bob Stern, as well as anonymous readers. My colleague Brian Garvey deserves particular thanks for reading the whole book in draft form and providing many detailed and helpful comments and suggestions.

I thank Lancaster University both for providing the sabbatical leave during which I did much of the writing and for funding research assistance through the Research Incentivisation Fund within my department, Politics, Philosophy, and Religion. This paid for Richard Leadbeater to read the whole draft manuscript with a musicologist's eyes, picking up inadequacies in my notation, improving descriptions of songs' stylistic features, and prompting me to reconsider parts of my song analyses. I am especially grateful to Richard on all these counts.

My greatest thanks of all go to my partner John Varty, with whom I have discussed every song analysis in this book. John has helped me to pick out what is happening in particular songs and suggested many examples and comparisons. Thanks, too, to James Lord for answering some musical queries that came out of my and John's discussions.

The book is dedicated to John, to our daughter Elinor, and to the memory of my parents Hannah and Patrick Stone.

CONTENTS

LIST OF FIGURES

LIST OF TABLES

Introduction: In Defence of Popular Music

Popular Music, Value, and the Body

In this book I argue that popular music of the era since the Second World War——since the emergence of rhythm-and-blues and rock-'n'-roll——is a form of culture that has aesthetic value. Its value is to affirm the central importance of materiality and the body, challenging the Western tradition of ranking reason and the intellect above all things corporeal. It might sound as if that is an ethical value, or an epistemic one, but it is aesthetic too. For post-war popular music affirms the priority of materiality to the intellect not by making explicit statements about that priority but rather by *enacting* or embodying this priority in how this music is typically organised. Post-war popular music *shows* us the primacy of what is material and bodily in how its components are arranged, thereby presenting us with a truth about the importance of materiality in an embodied and implicit manner——a mode of presentation that is characteristic of aesthetic phenomena, I will claim, following Hegel.

In putting forward this thesis I focus on popular music as it has evolved since, roughly, the early 1950s in Anglo-American contexts. Popular music in this post-rock-'n'-roll setting is only part of the still broader field of popular music, taking that to be music made in a commercial setting for entertainment and enjoyment. From the 1800s onwards, such music has been defined against both 'art' and 'folk' music, the latter regarded as pre-modern or made outside the monetary economy.[1] Increasingly, music that is identifiable in broadly these terms as being 'popular' rather than 'folk' is made across the ever-more globalised world. But for manageability's sake I focus on the West.

I do not claim that every single piece of popular music of the post-rock-'n'-roll era has aesthetic value, but neither do I selectively uphold the merit of certain genres, albums, or songs. Rather, I argue that post-war popular music, for all its breadth and variety, is nonetheless a unified cultural form, and that it is intrinsic to this form to affirm the body's importance, an affirmation that has aesthetic value. Popular songs, albums, or genres, then, can have aesthetic value *as* instances of the post-rock-'n'-roll form of music, not *despite* belonging to it. These songs might have value on other grounds too——folk-rock songs might have value by participating in the form of folk music as well as that of rock. But, crucially, the post-rock-'n'-roll form is a source of aesthetic value in music, not aesthetic disvalue. Given the hugely varied character of post-rock-'n'-roll popular music, this claim that it is a unitary musical form may seem dubious or false. Nevertheless, I'll argue that post-rock-'n'-roll popular music——hereafter 'popular music' for short——*does* have a level of unity that is compatible with its variety, hybridity, and porous boundaries.

An account of popular music's aesthetic value is needed because, despite this music's ubiquity, assumptions that it has little or no aesthetic worth remain widespread. Supposedly it is banal, salacious, formulaic, trivial, disposable, ephemeral, produced merely for profit to appeal to the 'lowest common denominator', and so on. Such assumptions have a long history. Critics condemned the Beatles' 'She Loves You', with its 'yeah, yeah, yeah' refrain, for its banality and decadence; the eminent Marxist historian Eric Hobsbawm was confident that the Beatles would be forgotten 30 years later (Maconie 2013: 58–59).[2] Popular music has risen in cultural standing since then. The Beatles' oeuvre now has a high aesthetic standing, as do those of, say, The Velvet Underground, David Bowie, and U2. Yet many who rate these bodies of work highly do so by distinguishing them from branches of popular music that are deemed formulaic and unimaginative. Listeners often valorise 'rock' over 'pop'——or, in another variation, US radio station WBUS proclaims 'No rap, no crap', instead offering 'timeless music from the 50s to the 90s'. So even if relatively few people today dismiss popular music outright, most people still discriminate *within* this field using the same criteria——authenticity *versus* triteness, originality *versus* formulae, integrity *versus* commerce——by which earlier critics condemned this whole field.[3]

An alternative view is that divisions between high and low culture have collapsed, replaced by the stance of the omnivore whose tastes range eclectically over all of culture.[4] But there are various ways to interpret the omnivore. If she holds all cultural products to be equal or thinks that cultural judgements just reflect personal taste, then popular culture has not obviously risen in status; instead all cultural products have been levelled. If the omnivore likes popular culture *as* 'trash'——feeling cultured enough to 'slum it'——then older hierarchies remain intact. Or maybe the omnivore judges that some popular culture really has as much aesthetic worth as some high culture. But on what grounds? If the grounds derive from the history of avant-garde aesthetic practices——if, say, The Prodigy's 'Firestarter' is valued for being transgressive, shocking, assaulting our senses——then older aesthetic categories and hierarchies may still be supplying the grounds of judgement. In sum, we still need to clarify the grounds on which popular culture can be valued *as* popular.

Furthermore, not everyone is an omnivore; traditional aesthetic hierarchies have not wholly disappeared.[5] Explicit condemnations of popular music have issued, for instance, from Allan Bloom (1987), Julian Johnson (2002), Roger Scruton (1997, 1998)——as, earlier, they issued from Theodor Adorno. His attack on the 'culture industry' still cannot be ignored, for it continues to feed, however indirectly, into many evaluations of popular music, for instance when counter-cultural 'rock' is valorised over mere commercial 'pop'. The terms on which Adorno condemns the culture industry——as a branch of capitalism——continue to frame many evaluative contrasts of this kind.

It is against this uneven background that I uphold the positive value of popular music as a unified cultural form, and locate this value in popular music's affirmation of materiality.[6] I am not alone in linking popular music and materiality; this connection has often been made. To give just one example, John Sinclair, the manager and spokesperson for the rock band the MC5, declared: 'The MC5 will make you feel it. ... The MC5 will drive you crazy out of your head into your body. The MC5 is rock and roll. Rock and roll is the music of our bodies, of our whole lives—— the resensifier' (Sinclair 2011: 28–29). Ironically, some opponents of rock hold similar views. For Allan Bloom, rock is rhythm-based and 'has the beat of sexual intercourse' (1987: 73). As such, Bloom laments, rock is void of intellectual content and is part-and-parcel of a cultural decline in which Mick Jagger and his ilk have assumed the authority once reserved for truly significant figures. Bloom writes on the back of a long tradition of condemning rock-'n'-roll for being savage, primitive, and mindless (on which, see Ehrenreich 2007: 1–9). For good or ill, then, popular music is widely seen as being linked to the body and affects.

However, some popular music theorists have criticised this view of popular music as 'body music'. In *Performing Rites* Simon Frith argues that the view rests on a racist logic that runs as follows: Africans and people of African descent are more primitive and 'natural' than Europeans, so African music must be more instinctual and bodily than European music; much African music prioritises rhythm, so rhythm must be the instinctual and bodily factor; and rock-'n'-roll too draws largely on black musical traditions and gives prominence to the 'beat', so rock-'n'-roll too is primitive and savage (Frith 1996: 127).[7] This *is* a problem with some versions of the body music view——including some of the celebratory versions, as when the (white) MC5 embraced the supposed raw primitivism of black masculinity as an alternative to an effete civilization. And they were not alone in doing so: popular music history is full of white appropriations of the alleged raw energy of black musical styles——as when Patti Smith sings 'Baby, baby, baby is a rock-'n'-roll nigger' (on *Easter*), embracing the 'outsider' location of black Americans as a way to challenge the hierarchies of white America (Duncombe and Tremblay 2011: 37). Indeed, such appropriation was fundamental in initiating rock-'n'-roll in the first place, as white musicians began to make music modelled on the rhythm-and-blues that black musicians were then producing.[8]

Further problems beset such 'body music' views. Sometimes those taking this view assume that popular music's rhythms, energies, dynamics, and sheer loudness force listeners back into their bodies in some kind of pure, pre-cultural, and non-intellectual state. Similarly the body is sometimes envisioned as a reservoir of energies repressed by civilisation but breaking out at times——at rock concerts, raves, music festivals, clubs. But actually our bodies are not pre-cultural: they participate in culture through and through; we take on the habits, gestures, and behaviours that are expected in the cultures around us, and our bodily activities thereby become infused with cultural meanings.

Despite these problems, I believe that popular music *does* have connections with the materiality of the body and that rhythm is important to these connections. I aim to make these connections without assuming that the body is natural, devoid of intelligence, or affected by popular music by brute causal impact. My view instead is that popular music presents us with a truth about the importance of bodily materiality in how it typically handles matter-form relations, rhythm, and meaning. To present this truth is to make an intelligent contribution to our collective thinking about human existence. And when we are drawn to move with the rhythms of popular songs, this is because our bodies are the sites of the practical, everyday intelligence with which we navigate the world. Rather than affecting the body with brute force, popular music reminds us that explicit intelligence is rooted in the latent intelligence of our bodies.

I'll focus on four ways in which popular music presents us with truths about the importance of bodily materiality, in how this music is typically organised.

1. Generally popular songs do not have the structure of a necessary musical progression. They are structured repetitively, not progressively; and their elements are contingently brought together then adapted until they coalesce into a whole. These songs' unity typically emerges *from* the interactions among their parts, rather than governing how the parts evolve out of one another from the outset. Songs' material components typically generate the form of the whole, not the other way around.

The idea of 'necessary musical progression' may seem puzzling. As I'll explain, necessary progression is something that some major music theorists——Adorno and Hanslick, for example——have valorised. On such theories, a piece of music exhibits a necessary progression if its elements (notes, chords and their groupings, with their rhythms and timbres) arise by explicating the harmonic and other relations embedded in earlier elements, ultimately going back to an initial motive, such as the famous 'short-short-short-*long*' motive that opens Beethoven's Fifth Symphony. Popular music is not organised by this type of developmental logic, but rather repetitively. Each element presented at each layer of sound is repeated a given number of times, their repetitions aligning with one another and comprising sections, which in turn are repeated to make up whole songs.

For its part, necessary progression is possible on condition that there is a set of background norms or rules of harmonic 'grammar' that specifies fairly closely what options for musical development are possible at given points. Popular music is not devoid of norms, but it is a particularly pluralistic and hybrid form. It draws on and brings together norms and practices from the blues, early jazz, folk, Tin Pan Alley pop, and pre-modernist classical music, while forging additional norms of its own. As a result, popular-musical norms regarding which musical elements can be put together, and how, are flexible. In any given song, there will typically be a range of musical elements that can be brought together, each option making roughly equal grammatical sense. This flexibility is increased further by the absence of a developmental programme. In a typical popular song, then, one of many possible sets of components is assembled and these components are then adapted into a unified ensemble: thus, the whole form arises out of material parts.

2. Rhythm is important in enabling these material parts to coalesce. Virtually all popular songs have explicit rhythm: a constant layer of unpitched (or, more precisely, indefinitely pitched) percussion. In relation to this layer, the rhythmic qualities of all the other layers of sound——vocals, melodies, chords, bass-lines, and so on——are heightened. For example, the bass guitar might emphasise different beats to the snare-drum so that their rhythms pull against one another. Rhythmic interrelations and tensions of this kind help to bind songs' layers of sound into a whole and to give songs a pronounced rhythmic character. This pertains to the body because rhythm has special connections with the body. We make sense of music's rhythmic dimension at a bodily level, by moving in response to it. This is not a matter of music having brute causal impact on us but of our engaging with its rhythms through the latent intelligence of our bodies. In giving central importance to rhythm, then, popular music implicitly affirms the body's centrality in our existence and encourages us to embrace that centrality by moving and dancing.

3. Just as popular songs' forms typically emerge out of their material parts, so do songs' overall meanings, including their emotional qualities, evocations of atmosphere, and articulations of social identities. These meanings arise as the connotations of the individual material parts of a popular song coalesce together. These are *semiotic* meanings, I'll argue, following Kristeva.

For Kristeva, the semiotic realm is where meaning emerges for the young infant, as its bodily energies and impulses becoming patterned through the routines, gestures, and interactions of everyday life, especially those unfolding between the infant and its main care-giver, usually the mother. The infant discerns structure in these interactions by apprehending relations——of similarity, contrast, causal expression, and other kinds——among the phenomena around it, centrally including the mother's speech. Pitched and rhythmic relations figure importantly here, as when an abrupt, high-pitched utterance by the mother conveys alarm. As the infant participates in these interactions, its energies become organised into affects——for example, a slowing-down of energy might comprise an affect or feeling of depression——where affects arise just as bodily energy come to be patterned and embody meanings. Thus, meaning first arises for the infant in the shape of affective patterns that embody, rather than state, meanings.

The semiotic realm persists throughout our lives as one mode in which meaning obtains around us. Advertisements; clothes; visual images; street furniture and architecture——all communicate meanings semiotically, that is indirectly, by how their components——say, the details of a sartorial style——figure into networks of relations, such as contrasts and similarities, with other details elsewhere. But music, including popular music, has particular continuities with the semiotic because of the additional role of pitch, rhythm, and affect in both domains. In sum, popular music's meanings typically arise through semiotic processes. This gives popular music pronounced continuities with the bodily-based realm of infancy, continuities that qualify it as material.

4. However, most popular music has lyrics. Doesn't that suggest that explicit verbal meaning shapes which material components are used in popular songs, so that these songs prioritise conceptual understanding over bodily-based, semiotic processes after all? I think not. Usually the content of lyrics is either treated as unimportant compared to the sounds of the words and music or, when lyrical content is given importance, this is because it is used to articulate meanings already embodied in the music and in the words *qua* sounds. Either way, explicit meaning is treated as secondary to semiotic meaning, and conceptual understanding as dependent on and emergent from material processes.

To clarify, then, I do not claim that popular music affirms materiality in the sense of giving primary importance to music's physical constituents——overtones, frequencies, the shapes and temporal properties of sound-waves, and suchlike. Nor does popular music affirm materiality in the sense that when we listen to it sound-waves have causal effects on our ears and the rest of our bodies——which is true of any auditory phenomenon. Rather, popular music affirms materiality in that (i) it gives organising primacy to the manifold *parts* of songs, which are material in contrast to the forms that unify songs; (ii) in that our bodies and their energies are invited into movement and creativity through popular music's *rhythmic* dimension; and (iii) in that popular songs' parts generate meaning in a specifically *semiotic* and thus material way——that is continuously with the processes by which affects and meanings first precipitate out of bodily energies during human infancy. What is affirmed here is that materiality has primary importance in human life relative to its explicitly intellectual aspects, partly because materiality and its processes are themselves generative *of* the explicit meanings with which the intellect is concerned.

Thus, popular music affirms materiality in a range of ways from more abstract to more concrete. In sense (i) 'materiality' is relatively abstract——as the manifold components of popular songs——while in sense (ii) 'materiality' is the concrete materiality of living, moving human bodies. In sense (iii) 'materiality' is somewhere in-between——a mode of meaning-generation with continuities with the concrete, bodily-based realm in which meaning emerges in human infancy. These several senses interconnect, in ways to be explored.

No doubt this schematic initial statement prompts many questions, some warranting immediate attention. One might object that, while popular music might have the typical *organising features* that I've identified, it does not follow that such music *affirms* anything at all, about materiality or anything else. An object might have organising features——for example my desk has four legs, a flat rectangular surface, and no adornment——but the desk does not thereby affirm any truths (one might say). I disagree: the desk *does* uphold certain principles just in its organisation: its parts are arranged to facilitate it functioning as my work-space; its sensory qualities are subordinated to its function. The desk is so organised that it effectively upholds the principle 'function over form', implicitly affirming its truth. An environment containing many such desks likewise tacitly upholds the principle 'function over form' in its spatial and physical organisation. This can be so even if the designers have never heard the Bauhaus slogan 'Form follows function' and only wanted their designs to work ergonomically or admit of cheap production. By analogy, popular songs can be so organised that they affirm the priority of materiality to the intellect, whether or not the individuals who wrote those songs took this view of matters. This is not to say that individual song-writers' intentions are never relevant to songs' meanings, but their intentions do not exhaust the meanings. And among these meanings, songs can, implicitly, affirm truths.[9]

One might now accept that popular music affirms a truth——that materiality is fundamentally important in human life including as the root of the intellect——but object that this gives popular music *epistemic* and not aesthetic value. Indeed, the value *is* epistemic, but it is aesthetic as well, under a particular understanding of the aesthetic which I derive from Hegel. For Hegel, works of art——'fine' art, but also popular-cultural artefacts in my extension——along with some natural things embody truths in a specifically aesthetic way, in that they do not state these truths but *present* them in how their materials are organised. These truths are presented, *dargestellt*, not represented, *vorgestellt*. Presentation of truth is the hallmark of the aesthetic, for Hegel. On this basis I will argue that popular music's value when it affirms bodily materiality is aesthetic: popular music is typically organised so as to embody a priority of materiality, thereby presenting the truth that that priority really obtains.

The aesthetic so understood is not the same as the semiotic, although, on my view, both aesthetic and semiotic phenomena convey meanings implicitly and their modes of operation overlap. Semiotic phenomena such as popular songs convey meanings of various kinds, through processes of a particular type, involving relations among micro-elements, including pitched and rhythmic relations, and generating meanings with an affective aspect (as explained above). For their part, aesthetic phenomena present truths——following Hegel, truths of significant scope and scale——and do so in how they are organised, that is how their part-whole relations are configured, including the relations between their different types of parts (e.g. verbal and non-verbal). The fact that popular music has semiotic meaning contributes to, but is not the same as, its aesthetic function of presenting truths about materiality. For since it is typical of popular songs *that* their meanings emerge through semiotic processes, this treatment of meaning forms part of popular music's typical organisation, through which the music, whatever songs' specific meanings, presents a global truth—that meaning fundamentally obtains at a material level prior to that of explicit concepts.[10]

One might have doubts about this picture of aesthetic value. Why should the value of popular music be located in its *meaning* at all, rather than in its materiality just as such? Some theorists of popular music, Robert Grossberg for one, maintain that popular music affects us in a directly corporeal, visceral way that short-circuits the intellect altogether, where this is valuable because it subverts——indeed reverses——the West's traditional hierarchy of mind over body (Grossberg 1990: 113). This is a sophisticated variant of the 'body music' position mentioned earlier. In contrast, my view is that popular music affirms the intelligence of the body: the implicit, practical intelligence of our bodies as the seat of our agency, and the role of our bodies as the source of more explicit, conceptually based forms of intelligence that arise out of and depend on its more implicit, corporeal levels.

Some might think that here I am still effectively presuming that intellect is superior to 'mere' materiality, and that this presupposition descends from Hegel. Indeed, Hegel's account of aesthetic value is often rejected, particularly on the grounds that he wrongly subordinates art to philosophy.[11] Nonetheless, I use Hegel's account, first, because I believe that he is right to connect art with truth——although this connection need not be confined to fine art, and by broadening it beyond fine art we can simultaneously avoid subordinating art to philosophy. Second, Hegel's account enables me to claim that when popular music affirms materiality this gives it aesthetic value. For many others have also claimed that popular music expresses the body and its pleasures, feelings, and energies. But this is not usually taken to be an *aesthetic* value of popular music, and so leaves unanswered critics who deem popular music low in aesthetic value, however 'useful' it is for our bodily self-realisation, social identity or sense of communal belonging.

Others might concur that popular music has (positive) aesthetic value but reject my understanding of what aesthetic value consists in. I make no claim to provide the only viable account of popular music's aesthetic value. I offer just one way of giving theoretical underpinning to broader convictions that this form of music has value, in the hope of opening up further possibilities for exploration along the way.

THEORETICAL SOURCES AND APPROACH

In developing my account of popular music I will draw on continental European aesthetics. As I've indicated, I draw on Hegel, despite the problems with his approach, and on Kristeva, again despite her condemnation of the supposed oppressive world of mere entertainment (Kristeva 2002: 101). I draw, too, on phenomenological treatments of the body by Simone de Beauvoir and Maurice Merleau-Ponty and, finally, on Adorno's work. For although he condemns mass culture, he offers an important critique of the Western trend for the intellect to dominate materiality, and an equally important account of how art can resist that domination.[12] Unfortunately, Adorno denies that popular music can contribute to that resistance, but we can use his own aesthetic theory to correct that misconception. Thus, with Adorno, Kristeva, and Hegel, I turn their ideas against themselves: these ideas provide intellectual grounds for valuing popular music, but only after critical transformation. We might wonder why I turn to their ideas at all if they require such overhaul. I do so because there is considerable merit in Kristeva's account of the semiotic, Adorno's stance on behalf of materiality and against the tyranny of the intellect, and Hegel's view that art is no mere adjunct to the serious business of life but *is* deeply important——even in play——because it presents truth.

The other body of scholarship on which I draw is popular music studies. Philosophers have so far contributed relatively little to this interdisciplinary field, with notable exceptions including Jeanette Bicknell (2015), Theodore Gracyk (e.g. 1996, 2001, 2007), Bruce Baugh (1993), John Andrew Fisher (1998, 2011), Bernard Gendron (1986, 2002), and Richard Shusterman (1991, 2000). Most academic philosophers, though, continue to focus on classical music, that is, the broad tradition of Western art music (see, e.g., Stock 2007).[13] That focus is either explicit or, more often, implicit——with philosophers concentrating on problems that have been shaped by engagement with classical music and where it is neither obvious nor discussed how those problems bear on other traditions of music. The problems principally concern (1) the ontological status of musical 'works', which is especially puzzling when they are notated and performed, (2) how music without words can be expressive of emotions, and (3) how listeners are emotionally aroused by such music and how this arousal relates to the music's expressiveness (see Kania 2014). Philosophical work on these questions may well bear on popular music. Nonetheless, I want to examine popular music directly, in its own right, so the literature with which I engage is largely drawn from popular music studies. I shall not address philosophy of music directly, except for philosophers who have tackled popular music explicitly.

In concentrating on popular music in its own right, I do not deny that it has continuities and overlaps with other musical forms——classical, jazz, folk, and so on. These arise not least because popular music is hybrid, drawing on and bringing together a plurality of traditions. Nor is popular music's value necessarily unique to it: the values of other musical forms may well overlap with those of popular music. Plausibly, for instance, emotional expression is central to all forms of music, even if its several forms achieve their expressiveness in characteristically different ways. These commonalities and differences lie beyond the scope of this book, although hopefully my study of popular music in its own right will provide useful material for such comparisons.[14]

Turning to non-philosophical scholarship on popular music, we find—with important exceptions including Frith (1996) and Hesmondhalgh (2013)—that theorists often bracket questions of value, doubt that objective value-judgements are possible, or approach evaluative practices sociologically, that is, as means by which some social groups assert or shore up their power or 'distinction' over others (informed by Bourdieu 1984).[15] Even so, contributors to popular music studies have a shared goal 'to rescue popular music from being treated as trivial and unimportant' (Hesmondhalgh and Negus 2002: 6). The whole enterprise of studying popular music rests on the conviction that at least some of this music has value and does so *as* popular music, not despite being popular. I aim to provide one line of philosophical support for that conviction.

Initially, much work in popular music studies drew on sociology and cultural studies with little musicological input. In response, some scholars including Richard Middleton (2000), Allan Moore (2001), Robert Walser and Susan McClary (1990) called both for more musicological engagement with popular music and more engagement with musicology from popular music scholars. As of 2015, much more scholarship of both types now exists, a development entwined with the rise of Critical Musicology during the 1990s. This family of approaches attends critically to how social power relations bear on music and the evaluative hierarchy among forms of music——roughly classical/jazz/folk/'world'/popular——rejecting musicology's traditional preoccupation with classical music (see, e.g., Griffiths 2010–11).

However, important questions that figured into the earlier stand-off between musicology and popular music studies deserve philosophical re-examination. Among them is the question of how popular music has meaning. Earlier on, popular music theorists tended to think that musicology could only analyse songs' formal properties without shedding light on what those properties mean. To access meaning, it was suggested, one must study interactions among audiences, musicians, industry practitioners, critics, and other parties——the musical 'texts' being only part of the story (see, e.g., Shuker 2001: x). The role of social mediations is particularly evident in popular music, given that recorded songs are produced and received along with videos, fashion and dance styles, and cultural and sub-cultural groupings and activities, which do much to differentiate popular music genres.[16] Others, though, re-affirmed the centrality of the 'primary text' (e.g., Moore 2001).

My argument will be that 'secondary' social mediations, such as audience responses, certainly come to bear on what songs and genres mean, but they do so in response to meanings already embodied in songs' 'primary' stylistic features.[17] Consider David Brackett's discussion of stylistic differences between two singles released in 1983: Michael Jackson's 'Billie Jean' and George Clinton's 'Atomic Dog'.

> 'Atomic Dog' presents a much denser texture with many more fragmented musical ideas overlapping with one another than 'Billie Jean'. While the beat and 'groove' are very clear in both examples, 'Billie Jean', due to its sparser texture, presents a 'cleaner', 'lighter' groove. The resulting groove in 'Atomic Dog' is 'heavier' and feels more complex. Listeners may experience 'Atomic Dog' as pulling them physically in several directions simultaneously, whereas 'Billie Jean' offers a more unilinear, straightforward pull. (Brackett 2002: 73)

In sum, 'Atomic Dog' contains a lot of syncopation, 'Billie Jean' only a modest amount. (Brackett defines syncopations as 'rhythms that produce tension against the basic background pulse' [75].) Brackett notes further differences in timbre, melody, and vocal delivery, but the rhythmic differences are central. Brackett then argues that these stylistic differences were significant factors in the songs achieving different levels of chart success. Both reached number one on the 'Black' chart (since renamed 'R&B/Hip-Hop') but only 'Billie Jean' crossed over to the Hot 100, reaching number one there too. Hence, 'the *sound* of "Atomic Dog" and "Billie Jean" is an important part of their story——how one remained in a musical ghetto while the other received an entrée to white, middle-class America' (79). For Brackett, then, stylistic details——for example levels of syncopation——contribute to the overall meanings that songs acquire in social contexts.

These details and their meanings——popular music's 'primary' layer of meaning——will be my concern in this book. To what extent do these features have their meanings by virtue of social conventions? Only partially so, I will argue; non-conventional factors also play a role. I'll explore this in relation to the processes by which songs' overall meanings precipitate from the connotations embedded in their material elements. When I speak of 'elements' I draw loosely on Philip Tagg's notion of 'musemes': 'basic units of musical expression' (Tagg, quoted in Björnberg 2000: 356). However, although I sometimes use the term 'museme' interchangeably with 'element', my sense of 'museme' differs from Tagg's. First, with Richard Middleton, I take it that 'the nature and size of the museme need to be regarded flexibly' (Middleton 1990: 189). Thus, an 'element' of a recorded song is any identifiably distinct component occurring at one of its constituent layers of sound. That component might be a bass-line, riff, phrase of melody, percussion rhythm pattern, or recurring sound. Such components are repeated many times over to make up a given layer of sound (its bass layer, for instance). The norm is that these various elements are brought together into a popular song contingently——they are not derived logically from one another. Second, Tagg takes it that these small-scale components always signify culturally and socially. While I agree with him that these components are significant and contribute to songs' overall meanings, I do not think that these meanings are entirely socio-cultural; non-conventional factors are also at work.[18]

Given this interest in how meaning emerges from stylistic details, I analyse some individual songs in detail——by Chuck Berry, the Beatles, the Supremes, Wire, Joy Division, Michael Jackson, U2, R.E.M., and Lady Gaga, among others. Rather than survey a vast range of popular songs, I discuss a few songs in some detail——hopefully still enough songs to support my general claims about popular music.[19] Indeed, musicologists may find my descriptions unnecessarily lengthy, but I think that it is important to provide such descriptions because non-musicologists often struggle to identify songs' stylistic features. Yet we need such description to provide a sound basis for interpretation. Again because I want to communicate with non-musicologists, I've tried to avoid technical terms and to explain basic musical concepts in endnotes. I have included some notation, based on my analysis of recordings, but sometimes informed by existing sheet music arrangements to an extent. However, most published sheet music arranges popular songs for performance on particular instruments rather than attempting to capture songs exactly as they sound on record. Furthermore, notation has limitations with respect to popular music (see Middleton 2000: 4). Western musical notation——which assumed more-or-less its modern form by the seventeenth century——is ill-equipped to deal with timbre or slight nuances of pitch and timing, which are often

crucial in popular music. Other important factors——modes of recording, mixing, and production, including how stereo sounds are distributed
spatially; sampling and intertextual reference——are not readily notated
at all. Above all, popular songs exist first and foremost as recordings, and
whenever we translate from that original medium——recording——into
another——notation——we inevitably interpret (see Cook 1989: 121–2).
Notwithstanding, it can be helpful to see songs represented visually; hence
I use notation, for all its imperfections.

Some might think some of the songs analysed (e.g. Wire's '1 2 X U')
are too simple to merit the attention. Yet popular entertainment has often
been dismissed for its supposed lack of complexity.[20] To do justice to
popular music, we need to suspend these hierarchical assumptions and be
open to the possibility that simple artefacts can have as much value as complex ones and that simple songs can still be rich in meaning and interest.
Rather than defend such songs by claiming that they harbour hidden complexities——which they may nonetheless do——we should allow that simplicity can have positive value in its own right and can also be a source of
meaning——for example by conveying directness, honesty, or confidence.

TERMINOLOGY AND CHAPTER OUTLINE

I have used 'popular music' as shorthand for 'popular music since the era
of rhythm-and-blues and rock-'n'-roll'. A possible alternative is 'rock', as
used in, among others, Stephenson's *What to Listen For in Rock*, Zak's
The Poetics of Rock, and Everett's *The Foundations of Rock*. Yet rock is a
set of genres *within* the broader field of post-war popular music. Rock
encompasses progressive rock, glam rock, hard and soft rock, indie rock,
punk rock, heavy metal, and many others. Borthwick and Moy therefore
label rock a 'metagenre' (Borthwick and Moy 2004: 3). Genres of rock
are connected because they descend from one another——albeit often by
reacting critically against one another——and because they share certain
features: the central role of the electric guitar; frequent use of riffs and distortion; self-positioning in opposition to 'pop', and sometimes to rap and
electronic dance music (EDM) too. Pop is another metagenre: although
pop is sometimes taken to contain all that escapes any other genre classification (e.g. by Frith 2001: 95), more commonly pop is subdivided itself,
into (say) soul, disco, synth- and electro-pop, girl group- and boy band
music, dance-pop, national varieties of pop, and so on. Arguably rap and

EDM are metagenres too. We might treat rhythm-and-blues as another metagenre encompassing 1940s and 1950s rhythm-and-blues, soul, reggae, funk, disco, and 'contemporary'——post-1980s——rhythm-and-blues. Calling all these metagenres 'rock' is problematic and produces ambiguities about exactly what music is being referred to.

Calling the whole field 'rock-'n'-roll' or 'pop' instead of 'rock' is problematic for similar reasons. Another alternative is 'pop-rock', as in Everett's *Expression in Pop-Rock Music* (2000a). 'Pop-rock' at least captures the continuities between pop and rock, but omits mention of other metagenres such as rap and EDM, falsely suggesting that the rock/pop continuum is the only central one.

One alternative option would be to speak of 'post-rock-'n'-roll music', but the disadvantages are that this is not an expression in everyday use; it risks privileging rock-'n'-roll over all that has come after it, and over rhythm-and-blues; and it is cumbersome. This leaves the alternative 'popular music'. Its advantage is that it does not falsely single out any genres or metagenres as if they exhausted the field. The problem is that 'popular music' is a broader category than the still vast array of genres that descend from rock-'n'-roll. Since the nineteenth century, 'popular music' has figured into a tripartite division. This is between (1) 'art' music, (2) 'folk' music, supposedly the traditional music of the people rather than the elite, stemming from rural and pre-modern contexts, and (3) 'popular' music, also non-elite but this time aimed at the urban masses in industrial, modern, commercial contexts. 'Popular' styles and practices have therefore included cabaret, music hall, vaudeville, minstrelsy, community bands, jazz, blues, and country (although arguably the last two originated as kinds of 'folk' while jazz and blues have since migrated into 'art'). The 'popular' has also included the mainstream pop of Tin Pan Alley and big band music. In sum, the post-rock-'n'-roll field by no means exhausts popular music. But for purposes of this book I simply stipulate that 'popular music' refers to that field. We can then benefit from the non-exclusiveness of this expression compared to 'rock', 'pop', and 'pop-rock'.

Further questions surround 'song', which I've treated as popular music's basic unit. First of all, this choice of word indicates that my focus will be exclusively on popular music as music, and in fact as recorded music. I will not be looking in any systematic way at popular music as it is performed live, or at its visual side——clothes, videos, sleeve art, posters——although these are inseparable from the music for many listeners. The reasons are that I take it that recording is prior to performance in popular music, as I'll explain; and that I regard the musical side of popular music as primary, which is not to deny that visual elements can contribute to the meanings of songs. But why focus on individual songs and not genres? Despite genres' undeniable importance, my aim is to identify popular music's overall form and positive value and to do so with reference to detailed concrete instances, that is individual songs. Hence I move directly between general claims about popular music and discussion of individual songs. Questions remain about how the overall form *popular music* becomes differently realised in different genres, but these are beyond my scope. Of course, it might seem over-ambitious or premature to theorise the whole form *popular music*. But if I upheld the aesthetic value of a single genre or group of genres then detractors could reply that the others still lack aesthetic value. I need to generalise about popular music, however provisionally, to defend its aesthetic worth as a form.

Another complication of 'song' is that ordinarily it means a vocal melody with or without accompaniment.[21] That meaning may seem to fit the bulk of popular music perfectly well: after all, most popular music has vocals and these vocals are usually melodic to some degree (although not always——rapped vocals can be wholly non-melodic). Instrumental tracks, too, generally have melodies, provided by the electric guitar or synthesiser. But are the other layers of sound rightly conceived as *accompanying* these melodies? Certainly melodies and/or vocals are often foregrounded in popular music. Nonetheless, I'll argue that typically all the layers of sound in popular songs interact with and qualify one another so that, in principle, each layer is equally integral to the whole. On this view, pieces of popular music are wholes to which melody and chords contribute without having a priori privilege over other components. It is these wholes that I call 'songs', using the term in an extended sense.

Others have rejected 'song' for the different reason that the term occludes the essential place of recording in popular music, whether on vinyl, cassette tape, compact disc, or digital audio file. Better alternatives to 'song' might be 'track', 'record', or 'recording'.[22] Yet 'track' and cognates don't mention *what* is recorded: music. A recording needn't contain only music; 'found sounds' (e.g. dogs barking, glass breaking, tyres screeching) are not uncommon, as are distortion, feedback, and other 'noise'. Nonetheless, the heart of these recordings is generally a composition of layers of sound——melody, chords, bass, percussion——which function under the musical parameters of pitch, rhythm, timbre, dynamics, and texture and are organised into a finite whole: a song.

Another complication is that in ordinary language musicians can re-record an existing 'song' with new instrumentation, mix the sound in a new way, and provide a new style of vocal delivery. Conventional wisdom has it that the result is not a new song but a new recorded version of an existing song. So perhaps we should distinguish tracks——particular recordings——from songs, where the latter are relatively abstract entities realisable in manifold ways. Thus Allan Moore identifies (1) *songs* by their metric and harmonic structures, melodies, and lyrics, arguing that songs are then (2) *performed* in the studio with those performances (3) recorded to constitute *tracks* (Moore 2012a: 15). Likewise Andrew Kania defines rock songs as 'very thin structures of melody, harmony, and lyrics' which are manifested in different ways in tracks (2006: 404). On such views a 'song' remains essentially a melody plus accompanying chords. I understand 'song' differently, to refer to the song-*as*-recorded——roughly equivalent to Moore's 'track' (see Chap. 4). This is not to deny that we can identify melodies and sets of chords that are common to, say, the different recordings of 'Always on My Mind' by Elvis and the Pet Shop Boys among others. But I am reluctant to identify those recurring elements with 'songs' lest that imply that melody and chords are the most fundamental part of any piece of popular music. In fact they are just part of the whole, I'll argue. Hence I prefer to use 'song' to refer to those wholes, although this usage deviates somewhat from ordinary language.

To outline the chapters to come: in Chap. 1 I expand on the pervasive and problematic impact that aesthetic values have had on the reception of popular music. I also identify some features common to popular music, thereby suggesting that it is a unified cultural form. In Chap. 2 I turn to the impact of aesthetic values on the making of popular music and especially on the division between 'rock'——supposedly serious, authentic, and creative——and 'pop'——supposedly manufactured, formulaic, and ephemeral.[23] Although aesthetics has had this problematic effect on popular music, the pervasiveness of its influence also means that we cannot set aesthetics aside. We need instead to find non-traditional ways to identify aesthetic value in popular music.

I begin this task in Chap. 3 with Adorno's aesthetic theory. This may seem an odd starting point given his critique of popular music, but, as I explain, Adorno powerfully criticises the dominance of intellect over materiality in the West. He locates resistance to this dominance in art, and this view extends to parts of popular culture, including popular music—— so that by his own standards Adorno should have valued it. He did not, though, but condemns popular songs for having the structure of a mechanical assemblage, in which interchangeable parts (e.g. chords, bass-lines, rhythmic cells, melodic fragments) are slotted into a fixed framework, with the whole dominating the material parts. Despite himself, Adorno helps us here to conceptualise popular songs' typical organisation: their structure is *repetitive* and not progressive; and it is typically a matter of *contingency*, not logical necessity, which elements are brought together in a given song. But, *contra* Adorno, this does not entail that those elements are interchangeable or the framework fixed; once contingently brought together, musical elements are adapted to coalesce into a whole to which each makes an integral contribution. The shape and significance of the whole thus emerges out of the interactions among particular material parts. I elaborate on this 'coalescent' unity of popular songs in Chap. 4.

In Chap. 5 I turn to rhythm, which plays an important organising role in popular songs. Moreover, due to the essential connection between bodily and musical rhythms, the pronounced rhythmic dimension of popular music means that it invites our bodies to move creatively. In this way too, as with its typical matter-form configuration, popular music gives priority to bodily materiality. I identify another way that it does so in Chap. 6, in which I look at how meanings emerge in popular songs semiotically. In Chap. 7 I explain how the centrality of the semiotic in popular music is consistent with most of it having lyrics: generally, the explicit meanings stated in lyrics are treated as being secondary to songs' deeper levels of semiotic meaning. To conclude, I tie these strands together to stress the importance of evaluating popular songs by the standards of the cultural form to which they belong, not by alien standards unsuited to them.

NOTES

1. On the art/folk/popular triangle see Tagg (1982: 42).
2. Hobsbawm wrote as Francis Newton in the *New Statesman* in 1963 (see Newton 2007).
3. Venrooij (2009) argues that these discriminations, especially between rock and pop, have weakened even within the popular field. Plausibly, though, these discriminations have actually been revitalised in reaction to competitions such as *Pop Idol* and *X Factor*.
4. On the 'omnivore', see Peterson (1997); on the 'no-brow', see Gendron (2002: 326–7); and on the postmodern 'degree zero' of

eclecticism, Lyotard (1984: 76). Peterson's omnivore thesis, which has spawned much debate, is pitted against Bourdieu's view (1984) that socially dominant groups affirm their cultural credentials and so power through their preference for high culture, especially in music.

5. Critics of the omnivore thesis——Bryson (1996), Washburne and Derno (2004), Savage and Gayo (2011)——have found that 'omnivores' continue to employ good/bad discriminations, often rejecting heavy metal, rap, and smooth jazz.

6. David Hesmondhalgh (2013) also examines music's value, but ultimately for him most of popular music's contributions are social and political: it offers lyrical commentary on sex and romance, fosters forms of sociability, and furthers processes of democratisation. Popular music also helps to integrate body, affect, and mind, for Hesmondhalgh, and I agree.

7. Criticising the MC5's logic, see Waksman (1999: ch. 6). Frith is criticising his own earlier view that 'Rock is ... primitive. ... Whereas Western dance forms control body movements ... with formal rhythms ... black music expresses the body, hence sexuality, with a directly physical beat and an intense, emotional sound—— the sound and beat are *felt* rather than interpreted via a set of conventions' (1981: 14–19).

8. For some (e.g. Shaw 1978) rock-'n'-roll just *is* rhythm-and-blues as practised by white musicians: the genre distinction here is basically racial. This raises a question about whether, in describing popular music as descending from rock-'n'-roll and not rhythm-and-blues, I'm already overplaying white musicians' contributions. Notwithstanding, I've stuck with 'rock-'n'-roll' because it is so standard to treat it as the start of a new musical era. Nor do I mean to imply that appropriation is necessarily objectionable——as the Patti Smith case shows, its politics are complicated (see Gracyk 2001). Philip Tagg (1989), however, cautions against classifying musical forms and genres as 'black' and 'white'. Yet in certain genres——for example soul, reggae, and funk——(1) many key practitioners have been black; (2) these genres have been important to the identities and political consciousness of black people; and (3) the principal stylistic reference points for musicians in these genres are other 'black' genres, for example gospel and rhythm-and-blues for soul musicians (those two in turn being 'black' in

terms of features 1–3). Along these non-essentialist lines we can identify certain genres as 'black' and others as 'white', relatively at least. Otherwise we risk making invisible the enormous contribution of black musicians to popular music's evolution.

9. To clarify, *one* way in which cultural artefacts can embody meanings or make tacit truth-claims over and above their makers' intentions is through semiotic processes, but semiotic processes do not exhaust the possibilities. That art- and cultural works can embody meanings beyond what their actual authors intended is widely accepted in the humanities today, often inspired by Barthes's 'The Death of the Author' (1977: 142–8). Notwithstanding the hyperbole in certain statements of the author's 'death', I assume that the general principle is well-established.

10. Presentation is somewhat heterogeneous for Hegel, just as there are different ways in which art-works can operate. They can offer a symbol or likeness of some content, or they can more directly put forth an item that instantiates or is an example of that content.

11. An alternative view of aesthetic value in the Anglo-American tradition is that things have aesthetic value based on their aesthetic qualities (e.g. gracefulness), which supervene on things' physical properties (e.g. the shape and arrangement of a deer's limbs and movements); see Sibley (1959), Brady (2003). On other Anglo-American positions on aesthetic value, see Stecker (2006).

12. Others might have doubts about such large-scale claims about Western thought. Certainly there are many counter-currents, but the dominant current has been to favour intellect and reason over body and affect, a bias visible even in the history of aesthetics (see Chap. 2).

13. Gracyk (2008) appraises the state of philosophical interest in popular music more positively, noting its growth and increasing legitimacy. One instance is the range of music books in Open Court's *Philosophy and Popular Culture* series covering, among others, U2, Bob Dylan, and rap (see, e.g., Darby and Shelby 2005, Harris 1993, Wrathall 2006). Yet the growth and legitimacy of philosophical study of popular music are still not at the levels one might expect given popular music's dominance in the contemporary world.

14. A stronger view is that no viable distinctions can be drawn between such putatively different forms as popular, jazz, classical, and so on. I argue against this view in Chap. 1.

15. On popular-musical preferences as matters of taste see, for example, Partridge (2014: 22–27) and Moy, for whom 'aesthetic judgements can never be objective' (2007: 83).

16. On popular music genres as distinguished by contextual as well as stylistic factors, see Borthwick and Moy (2004), Fabbri (1982), and Railton and Watson (2011: 41ff).

17. I allude to Lucy Green's distinction between 'inherent' and 'delineated' meanings in music, the latter conferred on stylistic details through the social processes of their reception (2008).

18. Nor do I understand the semiotic in the same way as Tagg. On Tagg's method for analysing how musemes signify see, *inter alia*, Tagg (2000), and, for critical comment, see Cook and Dibben 2010: 56–57; Middleton (1990: 180–3, 233–5). Middleton's looser view, to which my view is closer, is that popular songs are composed of a range of manifold musical elements, each drawn from prior networks of meaning (1990: 16).

19. However, I draw on the findings of De Clercq and Temperley (2011), Everett (2008), Moore (2001, 2012a), and Stephenson (2002), who do examine large bodies of popular songs.

20. Much twentieth-century art has likewise been simple in sensory appearance——Donald Judd's 'minimalist' sculptures, for example. But the valued trait of complexity remains, having migrated into the art-work's underlying concept. See Danto (1986).

21. Bicknell adds that song has *words* and that this distinguishes song from other kinds of music (2015: 1). However, she rejects the 'hybrid model' that songs are composites of words and music, arguing that sung words are already musical. I agree, but unlike Bicknell, I also want to shift the meaning of 'song' away from vocal melody.

22. On 'track', see *inter alia* Kania (2006), Moore (2012b), and Zak (2001), and, on 'recordings', Gracyk (1996).

23. I am by no means the first to criticise these hierarchies as they manifest themselves at once in aesthetics, popular music, and social power relations; so have Bannister (2006), Blacking (1981), Dettmar and Richey (1999a), Frith (2001), Frith and McRobbie (2007b), and Leach (2001), among others.

CHAPTER 1

Evaluation, Aesthetics, and the Unity of Popular Music

1 Introduction

In this chapter I aim to motivate my argument for popular music's aesthetic value and to begin to establish my framework. In Sect. 2, I expand on why popular music needs defence. In Sect. 3, I suggest that we need an account of the aesthetic value that is particular to popular music *as* popular music. We need not claim that every popular song has aesthetic value or that all such songs are equal in aesthetic value. Rather the cultural form *popular music* has aesthetic value in particular respects, value that individual songs can share in to varying degrees, depending on how they realise this form. In Sect. 4, I argue that, despite their immense variety, there is enough unity among the songs and genres that make up the popular music field that we can justifiably regard them as belonging to a unified cultural form——albeit one with porous boundaries and great internal diversity. In Sect. 5, I ask whether popular music's principal value is socio-political and not aesthetic. Aesthetic considerations tend to creep back into politically focused accounts of popular music's value, though. The question of its aesthetic value is thus unavoidable.[1]

2 Formulaic and Always the Same?

As I've noted already, one might think that popular music is so ubiquitous that it needs no defence. The vast majority of the music that is bought, listened to, and 'used' today is popular music. According to the British

© The Author(s) 2016
A. Stone, *The Value of Popular Music*,
DOI 10.1007/978-3-319-46544-9_1

Phonographic Industry, only 3–4 % of the albums sold from 2004 to 2014 were 'classical', whereas 'pop' commanded 31 % of the market share and 'rock' a further 33.8 % (BPI 2014).[2] Album sales aside, popular music provides the backdrop to much of our lives, and for many people, especially but not only in their teenage years, it is important in structuring their social relationships and identities.

For critics, the ubiquity and power of popular music are damaging, since the music is formulaic and homogeneous, providing entertainment but lacking real aesthetic value. A common line of critical thought——often informed, directly or not, by Adorno——is that the music industry churns out songs designed to sell. Accordingly they are made highly simplified, requiring no intellectual effort that would compromise their enjoyability. Each new product is purposely modelled on others that have already succeeded; hence the products become homogeneous, and consumers come to expect as much and to shun anything innovative or challenging. Thus the industry reduces culture to its basest level and trains people to respond to cultural artefacts in crude, unthinking, conformist ways.

Many people accept some aspects of this critical stance, as when the music industry is condemned for reducing rock-'n'-roll to 'the corporate spine of American entertainment' (Eliot 1996: 201). But often critics of the music industry, such as Chapple and Garofalo (1977), identify conflicts between the creative urges that inspire musicians and the economic constraints that the industry imposes. Relations between musicians and the music industry are thus taken to be antagonistic.[3] Even so, the implication remains that because of the financial imperatives driving the industry its products will *tend* to the homogeneous and formulaic, much as musicians may wish otherwise.

Such concerns about homogeneity are regularly voiced in the public domain. A media fanfare greeted an article published in *Nature* in 2012 by Joan Serrà and co-authors, 'Measuring the Evolution of Contemporary Western Popular Music' (Serrà et al. 2012). They begin: 'Isn't it always the same? This question could be easily posed while listening to the music of any mainstream radio station in a western country'. Serrà et al. then analyse data from 464, 411 songs spanning 1955–2010, obtained from the Million Song Dataset.[4] They identify three statistical tendencies. The first is towards increased intrinsic loudness in recordings——a result of the 'loudness war' between record labels since the 1990s, with albums engineered at increasing volume levels to better grab listeners' attention. Yet it is unclear why this tendency is problematic for Serrà et al., since they find no corresponding reduction in the average dynamic range within songs: intrinsic loudness has increased but dynamic range has been preserved (they claim).[5] Second, Serrà et al. find that the range of timbres used in popular music fell between 1965 and 1980 and, again, in the 2000s. Third, they find that since 1955 the most common transitions between pitches have become steadily more common while more unusual transitions have become even less frequent.

One problem with Serrà et al.'s analysis, noted by Stephen Graham (2014), is that they neglect rhythm, yet it is particularly central to the metagenres of rap and electronic dance music. To some extent, then, the focus of popular-musical innovation and experimentation has migrated from harmony to rhythm. Serrà's co-author Martin Haro overlooks this when, interviewed by Macrae, he says that 1950s and 1960s music was more artistic, experimented with sounds and harmony, and conveyed messages concerning politics, whereas contemporary music is for dancing and relaxation and focuses on energy and rhythm rather than experimentation (Macrae 2012). Here Haro neglects the possibility that rhythm has *become* the focus of experimentation and that this shift in focus might itself convey political messages, perhaps by re-orienting music towards 'black cultural priorities' (Rose 1994: 65).

Critics might reply that even if musicians' priorities have indeed shifted towards rhythm, popular-musical rhythms generally lack complexity compared to classical music, for the vast majority of popular songs are in 4/4 metre throughout (i.e., each measure is divided into four equal length parts or 'beats'). However, 4/4 metre is only a base on which an infinite variety of kinds of syncopation occur in popular music. If popular music tends to *metric* simplicity, this is not so of its *rhythms*. In any case, even when popular songs do have simple rhythms, we should remember that simplicity is not necessarily bad.

As Graham notes too, Serrà et al. neglect meaning and context, which can lead relatively small differences, say between timbres, to assume considerable significance. To give just one example: in the 1980s and 1990s Candida Doyle of the 'Britpop' band Pulp used a range of synthesisers and electronic organs that were by then obsolete——such as the Farfisa Professional, originally issued from 1968 to 1975. Doyle thereby created a deliberately 'cheap' and old-fashioned sound, tying in with the band's evocations of working-class life in Sheffield in the 1970s. But when the same Farfisa models were originally used they sounded futuristic and modern, as used by some 'Krautrock' bands for instance. Thus the same timbres can take on different, even opposed, connotations. So we cannot directly infer from a decreased range of timbres at a purely sonic level that there has been a corresponding shrinkage in popular music's range of meanings.

That Serrà et al. neglect these possibilities indicates another problem: although they present their findings as purely objective, they seem determined to portray popular music unfavourably. Thus they conclude that its volume dynamics are now 'potentially poorer'——by intimation, *already* somewhat impoverished——when their actual analysis is that, despite the loudness wars, no such impoverishment has yet occurred (Serrà et al. 2012: 5). Ultimately, Serrà et al. do not justify their conclusion that popular music is becoming increasingly homogeneous so much as presume that that conclusion is true all along.

Unsurprisingly, then, Serrà's finding about decreased variety of timbres and pitch transitions has been challenged (by Mauch et al. 2015). But why would it matter if popular music's harmonic and melodic vocabulary was becoming increasingly restricted? This might matter because it would mean that popular music's emotional range is shrinking, compared not only to earlier popular music but also to classical music. Or, at least, this would follow assuming that harmony is of primary importance for popular music's emotional expression. Yet arguably harmony does not have the same expressive primacy within popular music that it does in common-practice classical music. Rather (I'll argue in this book), harmony within popular songs typically generates emotional qualities, along with other meanings, in *co-operation* with popular songs' other elements and parameters. And since popular songs retain considerable diversity under these parameters——such as rhythm, texture, vocal style, production style, and so on——we need not fear restriction of their emotional palette.

To see this, let's consider the comedy song 'Four Chords' by the Axis of Awesome, released on video on YouTube in 2011 and quickly garnering millions of views. The band performs a succession of short passages from 47 songs, passages that all use the same chord sequence, I–V–vi–IV.[6] Thus 'Four Chords' simply cycles through this sequence over and over again. For some listeners, such as *Independent* journalist Katy Guest, this confirms that,

as Joan Serrà put it after analysing 55 years' worth of songs from the Million Song Dataset, 'We found evidence of a progressive homogenisation of the musical discourse'. This is nothing new, as shown by the band The Axis of

Awesome, who can demonstrate that 'all the greatest hits from the last 40 years just use four chords'. (Guest 2012)

Guest exaggerates greatly: a composite of parts of 47 songs is hardly telling about 40 years of greatest hits, let alone all the music that never reaches the charts. Moreover, the songs that Axis of Awesome excerpt do not share the same four chords in absolute terms, because those songs are in many different keys. Rather the excerpts share the same *relative* chords. For example, a song in the key of D major that follows the I–V–vi–IV sequence will move through the chords D-major–A-major–B-minor–G--major, while a song in the key of A♭ major following that sequence will move through A♭-major–E♭-major–F-minor–D♭-major. Axis of Awesome transpose all the songs that they use into the same key, D major, so that they can be seamlessly amalgamated.

The original songs included in 'Four Chords' are actually very diverse. We see this from one brief sequence in which Axis of Awesome render four measures of first John Denver's 'Country Roads, Take Me Home' (on *Poems, Prayers, and Promises* of 1971), then Lady Gaga's 'Paparazzi' (on *The Fame* of 2008), then U2's 'With or Without You' (on *The Joshua Tree* of 1987)——respectively from the genres country-folk, dance-pop, and rock, and conveying very different connotations. The first is warm and nostalgic, the second steely and metropolitan, the third anguished.

Even harmonically these songs differ significantly, as Table 1.1 shows. (A dash denotes no chord; straight lines mark divisions between measures.)

Table 1.1 Chord sequences in John Denver, 'Country Roads, Take Me Home', Lady Gaga, 'Paparazzi', and U2, 'With or Without You'

'Country Roads' acoustic guitar:	*'Paparazzi'* keyboard synthesiser:	*'With or Without You'* bass guitar:
(*verse*)	(*verse*)	(*throughout song*)
| I | I | vi | vi	| i | – | – | –	| I | V | vi | IV
| V | V | IV | I	| VI | – | i | –	
	| i | – | – | – | VI | – | iv | iv⁷	
(*chorus*)	(*chorus*)	
| I | I | V | V	| I | V | vi | IV	
| vi | vi | IV | IV	| I | V | vi | IV	
| I | I | V | V	| I | V | vi | IV	
| IV | IV | I | I	| I | V | vi | IV	

Thus 'Country Roads', which is in A major, actually follows I–V–vi–IV only in the first half of the chorus. 'Paparazzi' too only follows that progression in the chorus, in which each chord sounds at the start of each four-beat measure and the four-chord sequence is repeated four times. In 'Paparazzi's' verse, though, the chords are used much more sparingly and traverse a i–VI–i–VI–iv sequence in C minor, which ends by modulating to A♭ major for the chorus.

'Country Roads' and 'Paparazzi' differ in many further respects. Each chord in 'Country Roads' is maintained over two measures, presented in arpeggiated form by the acoustic guitar, and, after the first chorus, the banjo. Because it is acoustic and sounds clean and undistorted the guitar sounds 'natural', associated with US country and folk more than rock. The banjo and pedal steel likewise impart a natural, rural atmosphere. The sonic space becomes increasingly full as the track unfolds and successive layers of instrumentation——bass, banjo, pedal steel, increasing elements of percussion, and additional layers of male and female vocals——become woven in. This build-up of layers suggests a journey 'home', towards a place of emotional fullness and wholeness evoked by the sonic fullness that is reached. The relation between banjo and guitar, particularly, contributes to the sense of unity and harmony: one track of guitar plays arpeggiated chords while another plays brief solo passages woven around the vocals; but once the banjo comes in, it plays arpeggiated chords with further adornments, thereby mediating between and unifying the two tracks of guitar. These qualities of unity, harmony, and wholeness are projected onto an idealised US countryside. This is cast as the 'home' towards which the narrator and music are travelling by virtue of the rural and American connotations of the instrumentation, as well as by the lyrics.

The contrast with 'Paparazzi' could hardly be more pronounced. In 'Paparazzi's' chorus the synthesiser chords come in noticeably at the start of each measure, but their sound quickly fades, contributing to a sonic space much sparser than that of 'Country Roads'. This sparseness is even more evident in the verses, in which the chords are largely absent, replaced by a low-pitched synthesiser part making abrupt octave leaps. In the chorus the synthesiser plays simpler patterns but it retains its artificial quality; the percussion, including the hand-claps, sounds artificial too. These synthetic timbres and jerky rhythms evoke a modern city, while the rapidity with which the chords die out produces a sense of emotional coldness and harshness. In the verse, the alternation between the i and VI chords (i.e. C minor and A♭ major) hints at a possible transition to the A♭ major key of the chorus——but that transition is not yet made, so that the verse seems to grasp towards a fulfilment that does not come. This ties in with the way that Gaga's vocal melody seems to rise, lonely, above the cold and busy urban world. In the chorus her vocal melody sounds more hopeful—— partly due to the modulation to A♭ major, her brighter vocal delivery, and the smoother harmonic texture compared to the disjointed and angular one of the verse.[7] Overall, despite its harmonic overlap with 'Country Roads', 'Paparazzi' evokes a harsh urban world sharply opposed to the rural comfort of the former.

Unlike 'Country Roads' and 'Paparazzi', U2's 'With or Without You' is in D major and repeats the I–V–vi–IV sequence throughout. However, that sequence is only implied by the bass guitar, which plays eight eighth- notes on each root note in turn, pulsating through a steady 4/4 time signature. This driving, repetitive bass pattern powers the song forward, while the guitar presents a variety of riffs, melody lines, and chords, inter- woven to narrate an emotional journey from anguish towards reconcilia- tion. But at no point does guitarist. The Edge ever play the 'four chords' in sequence. So the four-chord pattern is not fully present in 'With or Without You' at all, only intimated. Yet when Axis of Awesome perform the excerpt from 'With or Without You' in 'Four Chords' they import into it a full chord progression——which disguises what is most original about 'With or Without You', its texture as it generates a narrative of emotional development. Far from 'Four Chords' revealing that popular music lacks imagination and innovation, then, actually 'Four Chords' misleadingly presents it in that light.

One might object that these differences between 'Paparazzi', 'Country Roads', and 'With or Without You' are mere superficial overlay upon underlying homogeneity at the deeper harmonic level. After all, despite their different instrumentation, timbres, textures, and rhythms, these songs *do* overlap in their harmonic make-up, and this harmonic make-up *is* important to their connotations. 'Paparazzi' illustrates the latter: the modulation from minor-key verse to major-key chorus is crucial to the song's form and meaning, conveying the ambivalence that the song is about, according to Gaga: 'Do I want fame or do I want love? Can you have both, or can you only have one?' (Gaga, quoted in Slomowicz 2008). The lyrics reflect this ambivalence: they are ambiguous as to whether the narrator is genuinely a paparazza chasing a star or whether the paparazza/ star image is merely a metaphor for a lover and beloved. As Ayah Rifai (2010) notes, the ambivalence is also conveyed by the abruptness of the

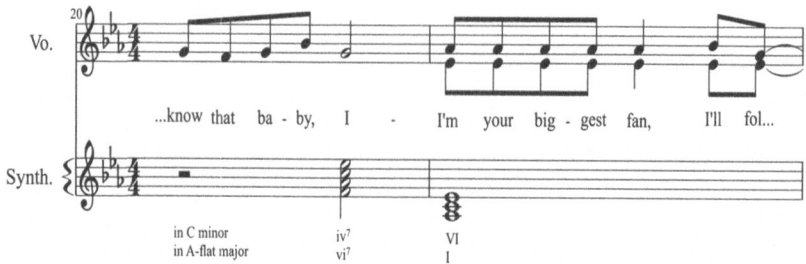

Fig. 1.1 Lady Gaga, 'Paparazzi', vocal melody and synthesiser, timing ca. 00:39–00:42

modulation: at the end of both verses it happens with no preparation when Gaga is in mid-sentence, splitting the word 'I' in two to convey a divided self (Fig. 1.1).

Harmony *is* important to the meaning of 'Paparazzi' as of our other two songs, then. But so are their rhythms, instrumentation, timbres, and textures. Without further argument it would be arbitrary to say that their harmonic features are *more* fundamental to these songs' meanings than their instrumentation, rhythms, and so on. As things stand, therefore, there is no reason to dismiss the differences between these songs as merely superficial. Their harmonic overlap indicates not that they are all basically the same but that the same harmonic materials can be re-employed and recontextualised to function in different ways and convey different meanings.

3   EVALUATION

Serrà and Guest's negative views of popular music rest on shaky grounds, yet these and similar views remain widely held. Many journalists endorsed Serrà's verdict uncritically——thus Sean Michaels in the *Guardian*: 'Pop music is too loud and it all sounds the same. That's the conclusion of scientists' (2012).[8] Such judgements continually resurface in new guises, however often their previous versions are refuted. This suggests that powerful background assumptions in our culture fuel these negative judgements. Plausibly these assumptions surround the contrasts between art and mere entertainment, works of aesthetic merit and mere commercial 'product'.

In this section, I want to sketch out the shape of these assumptions and indicate their roots in the history of aesthetic thought. My point is not that evaluation of popular music, or of any other kind of culture, is bad. On the contrary, I defend evaluation as a practice. The problem is the evaluative *criteria*, or *standards*, that people routinely use when judging popular music. These are problematic because they are biased against the popular field in the first place. We therefore need new standards, I'll suggest.[9]

To be sure, few people today repudiate popular music outright. Most people combine some level of negative judgement with some liking of popular music——perhaps admitting that they like music that they nonetheless rate aesthetically 'bad' or, most often, distinguishing *within* popular music between its 'good' and 'bad' parts. Often music is judged 'good' if its makers have pursued their artistic vision against the industry's commercial imperatives. Thus in the 1980s some British music listeners reviled music produced by Stock, Aitken, and Waterman while celebrating 'indie' rock by the Smiths, the Jesus and Mary Chain, and so on, released on independent record labels that allowed musicians greater artistic freedom. Here the underlying assumption is that popular music is aesthetically better the more it escapes its condition *as* popular music: the more it is obscure, requires specialist knowledge to be enjoyed, and (supposedly) escapes the context of commercial manufacture (Hibbert 2005: 56–59).[10] So when audiences distinguish 'good' from 'bad' popular music, they still tend to draw those distinctions using the art/commerce contrast and its ramifications. The resulting distinctions that are regularly drawn by music writers, critics, and journalists include the following:

(1) Earlier, 'good' popular music versus contemporary, 'bad' popular music——as when Martin Haro praises the artistic experimentation of 1960s musicians, allegedly abandoned today (Macrae 2012).

(2) 'Good' music that expresses artists' felt emotions or personal visions versus 'bad', soulless, uninspired music. Thus Lester Bangs: 'WE LISTEN TO MUSIC ... TO HEAR PASSION EXPRESSED' (1980: 70); and Jon Landau: 'the criterion of art in rock is the capacity of the musician to make a personal, almost private, universe and to express it fully' (Landau, quoted in Frith 1981: 53).

(3) 'Good' music that embodies musicians' artistic integrity and autonomy versus 'bad' music that merely reflects commercial

pressures. Thus music journalist Paul Morley: 'pop music is now a form of skilfully engineered product design, the performers little but entertainment goods ... whose ultimate job is to market phones, tablets, consoles, films, brands', not express ideas (Morley 2014).

(4) 'Good' music that innovates, breaks with conventions, and sounds new and unique versus 'bad' music that adheres to conventions, sounding formulaic and standardised.[11] Thus for Stephen Thomas Erlewine, reviewing Katy Perry's *Teenage Dream* on Allmusic (an extensive online music database and guide):

> Perry is smart enough to know every rule in pop but she's not inspired enough to ignore them, almost seeming nervous to break away from ... *de rigeur* [*sic*] lite club beats ... the music feels familiar, so Perry distinguishes herself through desperate vulgarity ... Perry's greatest talent is to be a willing cog in the pop machine, delivering sleek singles ... with efficiency. (Erlewine 2014)

In effect, Erlewine's charge is that Perry lacks genius, the artist's power to create new rules in inspired break with tradition. Lacking genius, Perry can only succeed by hard work: 'Working hard is Katy Perry's stock in trade'. And so she follows tried-and-tested rules, willingly complying with the industry's preference for formulae with proven commercial success. Yet if Perry's songs become totally indistinguishable from others, they will fail to stand out and sell. So they need a veneer of what Adorno calls 'pseudo-individuality', provided here by Perry's 'desperate vulgarity'——as in, say, her song 'Peacock': 'I wanna see your pea-cock, cock, cock'.

These four evaluative distinctions often combine. Erlewine faults Perry for lacking both originality and integrity——she willingly complies with the 'pop machine'. For others such as Leonard (2014), contemporary popular music is inferior to older music because the former is soulless and inexpressive. Morley too castigates contemporary pop for abandoning innovation and giving way to commercial dictates. The notion of authenticity often rolls these interconnected values together and so guides much evaluation of popular music (although it is often uncertain what 'authenticity' means and——as we'll see——it is a problematic value).

These interconnected values of originality, integrity, and so on derive——however indirectly——from the aesthetic tradition, particularly its Romantic branch as it mutated into modernism (see Knightley

2001; and on modernism's genesis from Romanticism, Taylor 1989). The English and German Romantics celebrated the figure of the genius who creates from spontaneous impulse. They insisted that art should express emotions and the kind of personal imaginative vision exemplified in Coleridge's dream-poem 'Kubla Khan'. The values of innovation and experimentation, too, descended through Romanticism into modernism. Both sets of values——those centred on authentic expression and on artistic innovation——have been pitted against the commercial realm ever since the nineteenth century, with mounting intensity in the early twentieth century when popular culture assumed 'mass' form, becoming manufactured for mass consumption by Hollywood and similar conglomerates.

Among mass culture's critics (critiqued in turn by Carroll 1998) was R.G. Collingwood. For Collingwood, making 'amusement art'——entertaining culture for a mass audience——is actually a craft (1958: 78–79). Its products are skilfully engineered using established rules and formulae to achieve a pre-defined purpose, that is, arousal and pleasurable discharge of the audience's emotions. Those emotions are pre-conceived——as horror, sexual pleasure, sadness, and so on——to be aroused using tried-and-trusted formulae——the stock tropes of horror films, pornography, or tear-jerkers. In contrast, art proper has no pre-set goal. Although the artist expresses his emotions in an art-work, what these emotions are only becomes clear through their expression and articulation. This is because the emotions finding expression are unique in each case, and so cannot be known in advance of their expression. Thus, whereas the entertainment arts aim to *arouse* stereotypical emotions in audiences, true art is authentically *expressive* of unique emotions (116).

The details of Collingwood's work are not widely known, yet the terms in which he criticises entertainment culture are widely accepted. Hence Morley complains that contemporary pop is the result of 'skilfully engineered product design' (2014)——that is craft——whereas Landau holds that rock can rise to become art if it expresses a unique vision. In short, criteria from the aesthetic tradition are widely used in relation to popular music, sometimes to criticise it overall, more often to discriminate within it. Social and political criteria are commonly used too, for instance when Owen Hatherley (2011) praises a line of popular musicians for expressing the standpoint of the 'working-class maverick'. But aesthetic values are consistently *among* the criteria by which popular songs are judged.

That said, many people believe that 'it's just a matter of taste'——each of us just happens to like music X and not Y, no consensus is possible, and nobody is right or wrong. Judgements and pleasures are indeed distinct; witness the phenomenon of guilty pleasures——I know that Lana del Rey's *Born to Die* has had negative reviews but I still enjoy it. But it would be rare and anomalous for enjoyment and judgement to be entirely disconnected. If my enjoyment of *Born to Die* is aroused by the album and not by some chance accompanying situation or associations, then that enjoyment arises in response to some features of *Born to Die*. As such, my enjoyment alerts me to valuable qualities in *Born to Die*, indicating that there *are* grounds to evaluate it positively, on account of these qualities. Pleasures, then, can outstrip our judgements——but in that case the pleasures are a pointer that the judgements need revision. Pleasure and judgement remain entangled, which may be why those who say 'it's just a matter of taste' usually persist in making evaluations anyway.

Aesthetic criteria pervade these evaluations, then. But the problem is that the evaluative criteria bequeathed by aesthetics are slanted against the popular field in the first place. These criteria can be used to canonise parts of this field as 'art'——the Beatles' later records, for instance—— but this is done by elevating them over other parts of the field. Moreover, such discriminations do not necessarily track the relative value that different branches of popular music really have. For there is a systematic pattern for the music that most clearly counts as 'popular' to be downgraded relative to the music that is thought to transcend the 'popular' condition. The inherited category *popular* includes the characteristics *commercial, standardised, manufactured, derivative*, and so on. Set against these are *authentic, original, innovative, artistic*, and similar qualities. Some parts of popular music may be more readily taken than others to have the latter traits, but the evaluative contrasts being employed are questionable in the first place, structured as they are around the contrast between genuine art and commercial entertainment.[12] If we are to do justice to popular music's value we cannot take for granted an evaluative framework that downgrades such music at the outset. We need a framework for evaluating how good particular songs and genres are *as* popular music, not *despite* being it.

Bruce Baugh makes a similar argument (1993). According to Baugh, traditional music aesthetics treats complex form as the chief source of musical value, a criterion that was formulated with reference to classical music but is not appropriate to 'rock'. I take it that by 'rock' Baugh means what I mean by popular music, although admittedly all Baugh's examples are from rock in the narrower sense——illustrating the frustrating ambiguities that can result from using 'rock' to refer to post-rock-'n'-roll music overall. Anyway, Baugh says, by the criterion of formal complexity rock counts as formally simple and uninteresting, which misses its distinctive merits. To appreciate those merits we need different criteria, ones formulated with reference to rock from the start.

Baugh proposes to create these criteria by reversing traditional formalist standards, so that what gives rock value is its sheer material sound, expressive qualities, and bodily effects on us. But most important here is the structure of Baugh's argument, not his specific criteria for judging rock.[13] That is: we should be evaluating popular songs as pieces of *popular music*, where certain values are characteristic of popular music *as a form*, which particular songs may exhibit to varying degrees. An analogy may help. Arguably, modernist paintings shouldn't be assessed by the standards appropriate to pre-modernist realism——lifelike representation of objects and persons, creating the illusion of three-dimensional space——but by criteria appropriate to the modernist project. This project, according to Clement Greenberg (1982), is to explore the possibilities intrinsic to the specific medium of painting as involving the application of paint to flat canvases. Having grasped this, we can judge that Manet's paintings (say) are good by the modernist standards that suit them, because Manet embraces rather than conceals the flatness of his canvases and the artificiality of his colours (their being made of paint).

A premise of the parallel argument regarding popular music, though, is that this *is* an identifiable form of music with particular characteristics and values. But one might object that popular music is too diverse to count as a single, unified form of music. In addition, we may think that its overlaps with and borrowings from other forms of music——classical, folk, jazz, blues——are so extensive that popular music has no clear boundaries.[14] In contrast, I believe that we can recognise the diversity and porous boundaries but still recognise popular music to be a unified cultural form. It has enough unity that we *can* claim that certain qualities and virtues characterise this form, which means that particular popular genres, albums, and songs (etc.) can have aesthetic worth *as* instances of popular music. Let's explore this unity.

4   The Unity of Popular Music

Some work in popular music studies examines the ambiguities of the concept *popular*. By revisiting these ambiguities, we can see whether we can salvage any coherence in the concept which might shed light on popular music's unity.

First, not all popular music is widely bought——most releases even on major labels fall flat. Especially in the long term, a few classical artists outsell most 'popular' artists and outstrip them in popularity. Yet, as I noted earlier, only 3–4 % of UK albums sold in the 2000s were classical. Of course, album sales give only a limited reflection of people's attitudes towards music, but still sales roughly indicate how the land lies. *Overall* market share qualifies popular music as 'popular', although many individual bands, albums, and genres belong to this field only because of their stylistic features and influences and not because they themselves are liked *en masse*.

Alternatively 'popular' can mean 'non-elite': emerging from below, not above. Yet much popular music seems to be manufactured by large corporations for mass consumption, being imposed upon listeners from above. Hence Adorno contrasted the 'culture industry' to a hypothetical culture that *would* be genuinely popular, emerging from below (1991: 98–105). Against Adorno, early practitioners of cultural studies excavated ways that mass-manufactured culture *is* after all 'popular', for those consuming it engage actively with records, fashions, and so on, and shape their meanings through everyday practices of interpreting and using these items——so that these cultural artefacts are, if not made, at least used, consumed, and interpreted from below. Theorists such as Frith (1981) and Negus (1992) further established that the music industry rarely if ever controls popular music's content in a top-down way. Even in major labels, complicated negotiations constantly unfold between musicians, producers, and other industry personnel. So mass-manufactured music *is* again 'popular' in being shaped by musicians' ongoing impact on record company processes——musicians who mostly lack specialised ('elite') training in European art music.

These considerations shed light on an initial feature of popular music:

(1) It is made in <u>capitalist modernity</u>, so that commercial as well as aesthetic factors generally bear on the making of popular songs.

Radiating out from this modern context, we can identify further features typical of popular music:

(2) It is <u>technological</u> music: its sound depends in multiple ways on technologies of electrical amplification and/or electronic processing. Recording is the central means of production and distribution, and so the music's reception is technologically mediated too, through radio, television, sound systems, computers, and so on.[15] From this:

(3) Pieces of popular music are essentially <u>recordings</u> (Gracyk 1996; Wicke 1982). Live performances remain important but in relation to recordings: when performing live, musicians generally either play songs that they have already recorded or try out songs with a view to recording them (or attracting record company interest in doing so). Self-evidently, performances in the studio are likewise conducted with a view to recording, which rarely simply captures a complete performance; more often recordings are composites of many partial performances, composites that are subject to all sorts of technological manipulation. As Kania puts it, live practices are 'asymmetrically dependent' on recorded practices (2006: 403): performances are oriented around recordings, not vice versa.

(4) From (2), historically, electrical amplification meant that small groups could generate volume levels that previously called for an orchestra, with vocalists still able to make themselves audible over the top (see Bradley 1992: 15; Durant 1984: 191). This is just one way in which technology is not merely an external condition of popular music's production but has been internally constitutive of the music's form. In this case the resulting small group set-up meant that popular songs came to have a <u>texture typically comprised of four layers</u>, as Allan Moore says: explicit beat, functional bass, melody, and 'harmonic filler' (2012a: 20–21; see too Tagg 2012: 475). Moore explains:

> The vast field that is popular music … exhibits a strong tendency to display four functional layers. Not all will be present in every example, not all will remain unchanging throughout a particular example. However, while one layer may be absent, or changes in these layers may occur in the course of a track, they do so against the background assumption of their presence. It is the principal norm of popular music.

For Moore, particular instruments enact each layer and certain instruments commonly perform certain roles——for example the bass guitar or synthetic bass usually provide the functional bass layer——but variations are always possible in which instruments serve which roles. Thus, functions or 'layers' of sound should be distinguished from the instruments that realise them. Let's look at these four layers:

(4i) <u>Explicit rhythm</u> (Gracyk's phrase; Moore uses 'explicit beat'). Most commonly this is provided by a drum-kit or drum-machine (or looped samples of the same), but other percussion media can serve too——handclaps, foot-stomps, tambourines, maracas, and so on. The rhythm that these instruments present is 'explicit' in that it is unpitched rather than being carried by pitched sounds (as it is when violins in an orchestra present phrases of melody to a rhythm). Usually in popular music the layer of explicit rhythm is constantly present throughout a song and consists of one or more 'cells'——say, a particular combination of beats played on the drums for a measure——that are repeated, with or without alterations, through an entire song or song section. Most commonly the drumbeats that are emphasised are on the 'back-beat'——that is, beats two (and four) in each measure when the metre is 4/4——'*back*-beat' because the European tradition is for beats one (and three) in 4/4 metre to be accented.

(4ii) <u>Bass</u>. Usually provided by the bass guitar or bass synthesiser, this layer integrates the explicit rhythm layer with the harmonic and melodic layers. The bass layer integrates them because it functions rhythmically and melodically at once, playing notes that tie in with the chords and melody but to a definite, usually repeated rhythm that locks in with the percussion. The bass's melodic function is usually fairly minimal (it might present merely the root notes of each chord in turn, or alternate root notes with octaves or fifths, or 'walk' up and down the pitches around each root note), which foregrounds both the bass's role of supporting the other pitched layers and its important rhythmic function.

(4iii) <u>Melody</u>. Often vocals provide a song's main melody but other instruments, such as 'lead' guitar or keyboard, may add further melody lines, or a song's melody can be entirely instrumental. Moreover, vocals can be more or less melodic, or entirely non-melodic in some rap music. Melodies not only provide a focus of attention——the 'tune'——but also contribute rhythmically and harmonically, the latter by implying or spelling out a song's key and tying in with the concurrent chords and chord progressions.

(4iv) '<u>Harmonic filler</u>' (Moore's phrase): normally chords 'fill in the "registral" space between [the] bass and treble layers' (2012a: 21). Guitar, piano, keyboards, and various other instruments can furnish this 'filler', which moreover need not consist only of chords: individual tones and noises can help to fill out a song's sound. Still, songs routinely include one or more chord sequences——such as I–V–vi–IV——which are repeated many times over to make up the harmonic layer. Various harmonic systems are in use: major and minor scales, pentatonic (five-tone) scales that descend from the blues, and modes such as the Dorian, Mixolydian, and so on. Indeed Moore holds that popular music harmony is best analysed in modal terms (e.g., Moore 1992, 2001, 2012a). Walter Everett (2004), however, proposes a mixed classification scheme which I find more helpful, on which the harmonic systems used in popular music include major and minor, blues-based, modal, and highly chromatic scales (making extensive use of all 12 notes of the octave) as well as compounds.[16]

(5) <u>Lyrics</u>. Most popular music has lyrics, uttered by the vocalist(s), whether or not their vocals are melodic.

(6) <u>Repetitive construction</u>. How are a song's four layers of sound co-ordinated into a whole? In a nutshell, this is effected through *repetition*. Each layer of sound is usually assembled through repetitions of a small unit of material or several such units: a rhythmic cell; a bass-line; a chord sequence; a particular phrase of melody. (One instance of the very common practice for a section of melody to be built of iterations of a single phrase is the verse of Lily Allen's 'The Fear'; see Fig. 7.7. Another instance is the verse of David Bowie's 'Life on Mars'; see Moore 2001: 37). Each 'unit' may last for less than a measure or extend over several measures. The repetitions of these several units are aligned with one another temporally: for example, a given section of song might consist of four four-measure lines of melody, each one aligned with one passage through a four-chord sequence, with each such passage in turn aligned with four repetitions of a one-measure bass-line and four repetitions of a one-measure rhythmic pattern on the drums.

(7) <u>Form</u>. At a higher level of organisation these sections of song are assembled into a whole following a range of 'templates' for how to vary, relate, and combine different sections. These 'templates' include contrasting and non-contrasting verse/chorus forms, AABA form, 12-bar blues, and numerous compounds and modifications (see Covach 2005). First, then, units (or 'musemes') are repeated to make up sections of song, then sections are repeated to make up whole songs. Following Richard Middleton, the former kind of repetition is 'musematic' repetition, the latter is 'discursive' repetition (1990: 269ff).

(8) <u>The organising role of rhythm</u>. Rhythm takes on a special role in popular music in several ways. (i) Usually, the elements presented at each layer of sound——not only the explicit rhythm layer——have pronounced rhythmic qualities. Chords are played to a definite rhythm; bass-lines operate rhythmically as much as melodically; and melody lines always have rhythm as well as pitch, with popular vocal styles tending to accentuate melodies' rhythmic aspects.[17] (ii) These qualities are accentuated by the fact that these elements are repeated many times over to constitute the

corresponding layers of sound. (iii) The rhythmic qualities of each layer of sound are highlighted further by their entering into relation with the explicit rhythm layer, pulling with or against it or both at different times. And (iv) those relations are again made possible by the repetitive construction of songs, whereby the repetitions of units at each layer of sound line up temporally with one another, so that their rhythms come to interweave in predictable, recurring ways (within which endless variations remain possible). Rhythm thus acquires a central role in binding popular songs together.

(9) <u>Contextual factors</u> also figure into whether a song is popular music or, say, jazz or folk. Beyond the overarching contexts of capitalist modernity and the record industry, these factors include the settings and practices in which popular music genres are received and 'used': discos, night-clubs, gigs, concerts; together with dance routines and activities, videos, fashions, and promotional materials; as part of or against the star system; in relation to the charts and to songs' use in advertisements, films, and television; and so on.

In what sense are features 1–9 'typical' of popular music? To be part of the popular music field a song need not have *all* the above features——although it might do so——and there is no single feature among the above that each and every song must have to count as a piece of popular music. A song might not have any percussion instruments providing explicit rhythm, one instance being The Beatles' 'Eleanor Rigby' (on *Revolver*). A song might have no chord sequences——just one chord figures in The Temptations' 'Papa Was a Rolling Stone'——or no chords whatever—— as in 'Paid in Full' by Eric B and Rakim, which essentially consists of a recurring drum pattern and bass-line over which a changing succession of samples and rapped passages is overlaid. That said, the bass-line in 'Paid in Full' *implies* a I–IV–V–I chord sequence, and the samples provide an alternative sort of sonic 'filler'. Songs may lack melody——say, when rapped vocals are not pitched——or songs may have no bass layer——Prince removed the bass from 'When Doves Cry' (on *Purple Rain*) to make the song sound more unconventional (see Starr and Waterman 2006: 264). Songs might not be electrically amplified, if a vocalist self-accompanies on acoustic guitar——although insofar as such songs are recorded they remain technologically mediated. And some songs never make it onto record, as when a band collapses before becoming signed to a record company——although such cases don't diminish the centrality of recording to popular music overall.

As we can see, it can often be difficult to say whether a song lacks typical features of popular music or retains those features but exemplifies them in unusual ways. Instruments can exchange their usual functions: the bass guitar can present chords (as does one of the two bass guitar parts in Lou Reed's 'Walk on the Wild Side', on *Transformer*) or passages of solo melody (as in The Who's 'My Generation'). Two instruments can share a single function, as when chords are presented on both piano and guitar. An instrument can swap between functions within a song: the guitar might move between playing solo passages and chords. Furthermore, a single functional layer of a song can be made up from more than one recorded track of instrumentation, as when vocals are double-tracked in a song's chorus or when samples from several drum parts are layered on one another to produce a very 'fat', full drum sound (Rose 1994: 79–80).

These permutations reflect the fact that each feature typical of popular music can be instantiated in many ways and to varying degrees. Take (8), the heightening of the rhythmic dimension. This occurs to greater or lesser degrees depending on how far the rhythmic qualities of a song's component layers of sound are accentuated——as they are, say, when vocals are rapped, when harmonic filler is relatively quiet and serves to support the bass and drums rather than vice versa, or when the bass guitar's rhythmic role is increased compared to its melodic role. Alternatively the rhythmic qualities can be diminished——say, if the vocals are highly melodic and heavily foregrounded, if the bass and drums take more of a background, supporting role, or if the bass guitar's melodic role is foregrounded. Such differences help to differentiate genres: schematically, rhythmic qualities tend to be accentuated more in 'black' than 'white' genres, albeit within a continuum across which rhythm remains central overall.

In sum, whether a song is part of the popular music field depends on how many of features 1–9 it exemplifies and to what degree it does so. Because songs can conform more or less closely to the typical form of popular music, ambiguous cases abound. Take Steeleye Span's 'Alison Gross' (on *Parcel of Rogues*): is it rock or folk? *Folk* is itself a contested category, but let's specify that typical features of folk song include: (i) origination among the 'common people', especially in rural communities, even if the broader society is urbanised; (ii) continuing roots in communal life, in which no sharp division of performers from audiences obtains; (iii) oral transmission, mediated by way of performances and not technologies; (iv) traditional material that has been passed down orally and is not composed by any identifiable individuals; (v) lyrics that have central importance, often relating a story or legend; (vi) strophic form (i.e. where each verse has different words but the music remains essentially the same); (vii) metre that is often irregular or uneven, reflecting the importance of the spoken words, as well as the spontaneous and improvised variations that occur in transmission; (viii) a primacy of vocal melody, often built on one of the modes, and not always accompanied; (ix) accompanying instruments that are acoustic when they are present.[18] 'Alison Gross' has features (i), (iv), (v), (vi), and (viii): it is a 'Child ballad', that is one of the traditional ballads collected by Francis James Child in the nineteenth century; it relates the narrator's persecution by the witch Alison Gross. However, Steeleye Span's version gives a prominent role to the electric guitar, modifies feature (vi) by adding a regularly recurring chorus, and, partly through the addition of the electric guitar, transports the song into the contexts of modernity and recording technology. The song exemplifies the forms of both folk and popular music to some degree, straddling the gap between them.

So the boundaries between popular music and other musical forms are not sharp (any more than are the boundaries between popular music genres). That popular music is not hermetically sealed is unsurprising given its constitutive hybridity, its borrowing from a wide range of pre-existing musical forms. Even so, we may distinguish musical forms——even when we cannot sharply separate them——because different sets of features are standard for different musical forms, as the above set of features of folk differs from that of post-rock-'n'-roll popular music.[19] That there are ambiguous cases, hybrids, and blurred boundaries therefore need not destroy the unity of popular music.

But aren't the differences *within* the popular music field as great as those *between* popular music and other musical forms? If so, then we should still not regard popular music as an identifiable and unified form. This is a matter of judgement, not one that any algorithm could settle, but my judgement is that these differences, vast as they sometimes are, still arise within popular music's overall unity. A good deal changes between, say, a quintessential rock-'n'-roll song such as Chuck Berry's 'Sweet Little Sixteen' (on *One Dozen Berrys*), Kraftwerk's electronic epic 'Trans-Europe Express' (on the album of the same name), and Dizzee Rascal's 'I Luv U' (on *Boy in Da Corner*), of the grime genre. Yet all three exemplify all of features 1–9 to an identifiable degree. Regarding (1) and (9), though, Kraftwerk began as practitioners of avant-garde electronic music, thus in an art music context deliberately opposed to commercial modernity. Increasingly, though, Kraftwerk's music came to be indebted primarily to popular music genres, especially the repetitive song-forms developed by Krautrock bands (see Stubbs 2014a). And subsequently Kraftwerk's immense influence on electronic dance music has further enfolded songs such as 'Trans-Europe Express' into the popular field. In 'I Luv U' the vocals are rapped, hence non-melodic, and there are no chords, the 'filler' being provided by fragments of synthesiser melody. Because of these features as well as the prominent, squelchy bass-line and the lop-sided, ungainly percussion rhythm the track exemplifies feature (8), the centrality of rhythm, to a high degree. But in this it has considerable continuity with 'Trans-Europe Express', which gives centrality to rhythm partly through its repetitiousness and partly through its key rhythmic figure, the percussive pattern that sounds like a travelling train rolling over tracks. In turn, 'Trans-Europe Express's' repetitive quality takes further a feature already present in 'Sweet Little Sixteen', which contains a good deal both of 'discursive' repetition (most of the verses repeat the same eight-chord sequence) and 'musematic' repetition (Berry generally plays the chords to the same eighth-note 'boogie' rhythm in each measure) (see Chap. 3, Ex. 3.4, for more detail).

Popular music, then, constitutes a unified form that different songs, albums, and genres instantiate in manifold ways. Schematically, this form consists of features 1–9, but this list is indicative, not exhaustive. Moreover, these features are not a mere aggregate: they interlock and have implications for one another. The technological mediation of popular music, specifically its reliance on electrical amplification, first made it possible for small groups to perform the set of sonic functions that have become normative, initially by distributing them across particular instruments——melody enacted by vocalist and lead guitar; chords enacted by rhythm guitar and/or piano; bass enacted by upright bass then bass guitar; explicit rhythm enacted by the drum-set. This distribution of functions gives each layer of song a level of independence with respect to the others——for instance, given a particular melody, a wide variety of bass-lines can be combined with it. Given this independence, repetition becomes the primary means for co-ordinating the layers of sound, which helps to make rhythm central to how songs are constructed. These are only some initial ways in which the features of popular music interrelate, but hopefully they show that these features are not a gerrymandered set but a cluster: each tends to foster the presence of the others so that they congregate together. This is only a tendency, though; it is not an invariant necessity that the features must always occur together.[20]

Just as we can distinguish the form *popular music* from the individual songs that instantiate it, likewise we can distinguish the value of the form from that of individual songs. Those songs may embody the value of their form more or less fully, depending on how they instantiate it. Because songs may instantiate other musical forms too, that can also give these songs value: for instance, one value of 'Alison Gross' is to transport a traditional song into the present day——arguably a value of the overall form *folk*. The values characteristic of different musical forms can overlap. Emotional expressiveness is probably a value that all forms of music share, although they realise it differently——primarily through harmonic progression in classical music of the common-practice era (c. 1600–1900), for instance, whereas harmonic progression is less important to popular music's expressiveness. These overlaps, though, are beyond this book's scope.

5   The Persistence of the Aesthetic

Assuming, then, that popular music has enough unity that it makes sense to consider what overall value the form has, does it make sense to look for its *aesthetic* value? After all, the aesthetic tradition bears much responsibility for people's negative views of some or all popular music. Perhaps it is self-defeating to look for aesthetic value in popular music when aesthetic values have been slanted against the popular domain.

Alternatively, we might see no problem in claiming aesthetic value for popular music. For one thing, this need not entail trying to show that popular music is art. Given our intellectual heritage art inescapably connotes *fine* art——what is superior to and more serious and important than mere entertainment. As Larry Shiner rightly says: 'We now usually speak simply of "art", not "fine art", but the capital "A" of fine art nearly always lurks within the small "a" of art in our twentieth-century usage' (2002: 12). Admittedly, this art/pop hierarchy faced countless challenges over the twentieth century. Artists exhibited urinals, mocked-up Brillo boxes, graffiti, and——less famously——a music video in which movie star Kirsten Dunst performs the Vapors' post-punk hit 'Turning Japanese'.[21] Artists have repositioned much that was once excluded from art *within* the art-world. From the other side of the divide, some popular musicians have claimed to make art: Lady Gaga stated that with her album *Artpop* she intended 'to put art culture into pop music, a reverse of Warhol. Instead of putting pop onto the canvas, we wanted to put the art onto the soup can'

(Strang 2013). And sometimes listeners praise particular pieces of popular music on the grounds that they are art or use the devices and techniques of classical music, or that their makers have been 'classically trained' (for these respective strategies see, e.g., Ansell-Pearson 2016; Tilden 2013; Youorski 2014). Yet these attempts to raise pop to art status presuppose that art status is desirable, presumably because art ranks higher than mere entertainment. Thus the art/pop hierarchy is inadvertently held in place——to the detriment of all the pop that remains just pop.

The Velvet Underground exemplify this problem. Their sponsor Andy Warhol wanted their music to be art in what he considered the only sense now legitimate: pop art——*not* high art, but something subversive of the art/pop divide. The band straddled that divide: John Cale came out of the avant-garde, whereas Lou Reed had worked as a staff songwriter churning out songs for Pickwick Records (see Cunningham 2014: 69). But because they mixed rock and avant-gardism the Velvet Underground have often been judged artistically superior to all the popular music that simply operates on the low side of the high/low divide. Subverting the art/pop divide is itself an avant-garde gesture——so that music that makes this gesture after all belongs with art, hence with the high and not the low. As Frith and Horne sum up, the Velvet Underground's 'importance turned out to be not quite what Warhol had intended: they became the model for an avant-garde *within* rock and roll' (1987: 112).

But perhaps the category of the aesthetic poses fewer problems than that of art, for the aesthetic domain reaches beyond art. Many things besides art have aesthetic qualities: human faces and bodies, animals, plants; everyday artefacts, houses, gardens, landscapes; food; tastes, smells, sounds; and much more, as proponents of 'everyday aesthetics' have explored (e.g. Saito 2010). So, one might argue, once we recognise that the aesthetic is broader than the artistic, then we need have no difficulty in classifying popular songs as aesthetic phenomena. If the tradition of aesthetic thought has nonetheless impeded us from savouring the aesthetic qualities of the everyday world around us, then that tradition is problematic on *aesthetic* grounds: it has diminished our access to aesthetic phenomena in their full wealth.

Yet this fault of the aesthetic tradition——that it has limited people's capacity to engage appreciatively with popular music as an aesthetic phenomenon——has made some popular music theorists wary of any concept of the aesthetic and inclined to locate popular music's value elsewhere. To make matters worse, the aesthetic tradition has devalued the popular domain in ways that have been integrally bound up with social and political hierarchies. One manifestation of this is that this tradition has tended to valorise refined, detached appreciation, hence the eighteenth-century practice of viewing picturesque landscapes through Claude landscapes and the custom of viewing paintings in a gallery from a respectful distance, preferably in thoughtful silence. This sort of cultivated appreciation has been understood in contrast to the supposedly raw, immediate, 'primitive' feelings that were often attributed to African peoples and their descendants——rock-'n'-roll thus being denounced for having 'been played in the jungle for centuries'.[22] The industrial working class, too, was routinely judged too coarse, too unrefined, to engage in aesthetic appreciation.[23]

Aesthetic categories, then——such as the notion of refined appreciation——have been entangled with social power relations. Recognising this fact, some popular music theorists have preferred to approach popular music's value in social and political rather than aesthetic terms (a trend noted by Hesmondhalgh and Negus 2002: 6). Simon Frith is representative: he insists that 'the bases for cultural evaluation are always social: what is at issue is the *effect* of a cultural product. Is it repressive or liberating? … The aesthetic question … is secondary' (1981: 55). To mention one instance of socio-political evaluation at work, Jeremy Gilbert (2014) condemns Britpop on the grounds that it is nationalist and racist, harking back to an imagined England devoid of ethnic diversity. Evaluation on socio-political grounds is also at work, less overtly, when theorists conceive popular music as a 'dynamic medium for the formation of identity', as Chris Partridge puts it (2011: 182)——providing a vehicle through which individuals and groups can articulate their personal and collective identities. By implication, popular music genres and songs have positive value when they enable individuals to articulate their identities in liberating ways, negative value when they subject individuals to oppressive versions of those identities.

However, aesthetic considerations often creep back into politically focused discussions. Take Simon Frith and Angela McRobbie's claim that Tammy Wynette's 'Stand by Your Man' is more progressive than Helen Reddy's 'I Am Woman'. Frith and McRobbie argue that Wynette's powerful, soaring vocal exudes 'country strength and confidence' and so conveys female authority, knowledge, and experience, in contrast to Reddy's 'cute, show-biz self-confidence' (Frith and McRobbie 2007: 42). Ultimately, then, Frith and McRobbie prefer 'Stand by Your Man', despite its seemingly conservative message, partly on the grounds that Wynette's vocal delivery embodies *aesthetically* valuable qualities of authenticity and integrity, qualities that connote female confidence and authority as well. On the other hand Frith and McRobbie take 'I Am Woman' to offer a mere 'commodity for consumption'——to be mere pop, inauthentic, and made for profit (53). These complaints are as much aesthetic as they are political: Reddy's song is condemned for the aesthetic faults of commercialism, banality, and insincerity.

To give another example, political evaluation shades into aesthetic terrain in Dick Hebdige's *Subculture: The Meaning of Style*, an important text in initiating popular music studies despite Hebdige's focus on subcultural fashions rather than music genres. Hebdige overtly distances himself from aesthetic evaluation, criticising positions that herald popular music as being 'at least as good as high art' (Hebdige 1979: 128). In contrast Hebdige values subcultural styles such as punk on the grounds that they scramble dominant semiotic codes, for instance when punks wore ripped clothes held together with safety-pins or engaged in pogoing: 'anti-dancing', a '*reductio ad absurdum* of all the solo dance styles associated with rock music' (108–9). Hebdige valorises this scrambling of semiotic codes for political reasons: it effects far-reaching and potentially revolutionary change in the tacit codes of meaning that regulate social life. Yet, as Hebdige says, 'both artistic expression and aesthetic pleasure are intimately bound up with the destruction of existing codes and the formulation of new ones' (129). In his own terms, then, code-scrambling functions aesthetically as well as politically. This is so both in the modernist sense that code-scrambling is innovative and creative and in the expressivist sense that it gives people's creative energies pleasurable expression and outlet. The aesthetic connection is confirmed when Hebdige explicitly likens punk practices to those of Dada and Surrealism (Hebdige 1979: 106–12).

One more instance: in *Studying Popular Music* Richard Middleton explicitly connects political and aesthetic considerations. He equates aesthetic responses with feelings of pleasure, defining aesthetics as 'the sphere of "I like it"' (Middleton 1990: 256), and he insists that these bodily and sensory pleasures should not be overlooked. He therefore suggests that Frith and McRobbie's preference for Wynette over Reddy probably in fact stems from their pleasure in the corporeal 'grain' of Wynette's voice (263).[24] But Middleton's view of the aesthetic belongs within a complicated theoretical framework. He argues that no musical style is a seamlessly coherent whole but that all are composed of multiple elements articulated together and ever-capable of 'being prised open and the elements rearticulated in different contexts' (16). These rearticulations can connect up with broader changes in social power relations. As an example Middleton considers how Elvis combined country, rhythm-and-blues, and mainstream pop. According to Middleton, Elvis combined a full, rich, precisely intoned vocal style untypical of the blues with a 'boogie-woogie'-style vocal rhythm: he tended to group notes into triplets and to put unexpected stress on the third note in each grouping. The effect is 'a bit jittery and absurd; the sensuality [conveyed by the rich vocals and romantic lyrics] seems almost out of control' (19). Elvis, then, took two elements of vocal style that had not been combined before and re-assembled them in a way that connected with the emerging youth culture——its mingled preoccupations with romance, sex, and rebellion——of which Elvis could then be seen as a representative.

Middleton relates this to aesthetics, saying that 'Presley offered an individual body, unique, untranslatable, outside the familiar cultural framework, exciting and dangerous' (1990: 262–3). Thus, for Middleton, it is when musical elements are rearticulated anew that spaces appear in which bodies in their individuality can come forward and be enjoyed aesthetically, and corporeal energies and pleasures can escape from the usual conventions under which they are bound. It is where conventional norms are transgressed and remade that political *and* aesthetic value arise. The political value comes from breaking open linkages that had been so entrenched as to appear natural, unquestionable, and unchangeable. The aesthetic value comes from the attendant outbreak of bodily pleasure, the liberation of bodies and senses from their everyday bonds. Indirectly, then, Middleton's picture of aesthetic value continues to descend from the aesthetic tradition, specifically its expressivist and modernist branches. For in Middleton's view popular music has aesthetic value when it is innovative and creative——bringing about new assemblages——and when it gives expression to bodily affects and pleasures.

Evaluative schemes that descend from the aesthetic tradition, then, seep into the work of popular music theorists whose focus is more political. This is not surprising, given that aesthetic values pervade popular music's reception generally. Since we cannot escape aesthetic evaluation, then, neither can we avoid thinking about what aesthetic value popular music may have.

Before I pursue this task, though, I want to substantiate further my claim that aesthetic ideas have had pervasive and problematic effects on popular music. After all, my picture of the history of aesthetic thought remains very general and I have only considered its impact on popular music's reception. But aesthetic values have also impacted on the *making* of popular music, becoming embodied in the stylistic details of many genres and structuring these genres' often hostile relations to one another. I turn to these matters next.

NOTES

1. To clarify, *aesthetic value* includes but is not confined to *cultural value*, for natural things can have aesthetic value too. In turn, cultural value includes but is not confined to *artistic value*, for cultural artefacts can have value without being art-works: a street-light may be no work of art but it can still improve our cultural life, over and above its utility in illuminating the street. This value is aesthetic insofar as it depends on the street-light's look and shape as they embody particular meanings. In these terms popular music can have cultural and so aesthetic value but not artistic value, assuming that the latter inescapably means the value of *fine* art.

2. Given such figures, Julian Johnson (2002) reasons that classical and not popular music needs defence: the former is beleaguered, being forced to compete on the terrain of entertainment when really it is art, as popular music is not. Johnson does, at least, give a frank statement of the aesthetic hierarchy that I oppose.

3. Howard Caygill likewise portrays musician-industry relations as antagonistic in his short piece on Syd Barrett (Caygill 2011: 42–45). In Caygill's view Barrett struggled to bring avant-garde concerns into pop music, could not cope with EMI's unsympathetic demands, and retreated, having failed to re-unite the 'torn halves' of art and pop.

4. See http://labrosa.ee.columbia.edu/millionsong/

5. Deruty (2011) agrees with Serrà et al. on this point, but see, however, Milner (2010: ch. 6). Arguably loudness itself can be a valuable quality anyway, enabling music to affect us corporeally (Baugh 1993), or enabling us to hear more of a recording's full sonic wealth (Gracyk 1996: ch. 4).

6. A chord is a group of pitches played simultaneously as a unit—— or, successively, as an arpeggio. The most basic kind of chord is a triad, containing a root note, a note above the root by the interval

of a third, and a note above the root by the interval of a fifth. What specific notes those are in a given case depends on the key in which the music containing the chord is built. The easiest key to understand is C major. The C major scale can be obtained by playing each white key on the keyboard from C through to the C an octave above, yielding C–D–E–F–G–A–B, with no sharps or flats. So, if our triad is in this key and its root note is C, then its middle note is E, its upper note G.

The whole series of intervals between the tones in the C major scale yields the major scale outline: tone–tone–semitone–tone–tone–tone–semitone. That is, on a keyboard, C and D are separated by a whole tone——there is a semitone, C♯, between them——but E and F are separated by only a semitone. The same outline is common to all major scales: if we take a new tone as the starting point (and thus the key-note or tonic)——say D——and apply the major scale outline, we get the tones comprising the D major scale, that is D–E–F♯–G–A–B–C♯. Or if we start with tonic C♯, its scale contains C♯–D♯–E♯–F♯–G♯–A♯–B♯ (E♯ is effectively F: they are 'enharmonically' equivalent, i.e. they differ in name only).

The natural minor scale outline is different, running tone–semitone–tone–tone–semitone–tone–tone. The other forms of the minor scale——melodic and harmonic——are rare in popular music, which by default uses the natural minor; so hereafter 'minor' means 'natural minor' unless otherwise stated. Each tone in every major or minor scale has a name that indicates its role——in particular, the first member is the 'tonic' or 'home' note; the fifth (e.g. G in the key of C major) is the 'dominant', the most important tone after the tonic; the fourth (e.g. F in the key of C major) is the 'subdominant', the tone directly below the dominant; and the seventh (e.g. B in C major) is the 'leading note', leading strongly back to the tonic. Scale degrees are numbered: thus first ($\hat{1}$), second ($\hat{2}$), and so on, degrees of the scale.

Chords are numbered correspondingly but using Roman numerals: that is if the root note of a triad is ($\hat{1}$) then the chord is I, if the root is ($\hat{2}$) then the chord is ii, and so on——where major triads have upper-case numerals, minor triads lower-case ones. A triad is major if its middle note is above the root by the interval of a *major* third (tone–tone) rather than a *minor* third (tone–semitone or semitone–tone). Thus in the key of C major, the iii chord (on

root note E) is a minor triad because its middle note G is above E
by semitone–tone, not tone–tone. In fact then, in major keys, triads ii, iii, and vi are minor and only I, IV, and V are major, while
vii° is diminished (symbolised °), that is the upper and middle
notes are both above the notes below them by only a minor third.
However, in popular music the vii° chord in major-key music is
often made into a major triad——made into bVII——by having its
root note flattened by a semitone, for example (if the key is C
major) to Bb rather than B (see Moore 1995). Regarding minor
keys, i, iv, and v are minor triads; III, VI, and VII are major; and ii°
is diminished.

Triads are not the only possibility. Often in popular music seventh chords are used, which comprise a root and the notes above
it by a third, a fifth, and a seventh (symbolised I^7, ii^7, etc.). Also
common in popular music are open perfect fifth intervals, containing just a root and the note above it by a perfect fifth (i.e. an interval of three tones and one semitone). Strictly speaking the latter are
not chords, which should usually contain at least three tones, but
in popular music contexts open perfect fifth intervals without a
third are generally identified and treated as chords and I shall
adhere to that practice. Such 'chords' are strictly neither major nor
minor, but we hear them as major or minor depending on the key
in which the music in which they occur is built. Suspended chords
also occur in popular music; in these the middle note is above the
root by the interval of a second or a fourth, not a third. Inverted
chords appear too; in first inversion (symbolised with lower-case b)
the chord's middle note——for example the E in a C major
chord——is moved to lowest (bass) position. In second inversion
(symbolised c) the chord's highest note——for example the G in a
C major chord——is moved to the bass. Third inversion (d) arises
only when the highest note of a seventh chord is moved to bass
position. Numerous other chord constructions are found in popular music: see Everett (2008: ch. 8) and Stephenson (2002: ch. 4).

Popular music also uses modes. Each mode has a distinct outline
obtained by beginning on a given note and playing all and only the
white-key notes up to the octave above. If we begin on C the
resulting mode, the Ionian, coincides with the major scale. The
Aeolian mode, obtained by commencing on A, coincides with the
natural minor scale. Other commonly used modes are Dorian,

Phrygian, Lydian, and Mixolydian. If we begin on D, for instance, we obtain the outline tone–semitone–tone–tone–tone–semitone–tone, which characterises the Dorian mode. But Dorian-mode music need not have D as the tonic; it can have any note as the tonic but is Dorian as long as it follows the outline above, and the equivalent applies for all the modes. For example, a song in the Dorian mode on E would be built from E, F♯, G, A, B, C♯, and D. The Mixolydian mode, obtained by beginning on G, has the outline tone–tone–semitone–tone–tone–semitone–tone——so that, for example, a song in the Mixolydian mode on C would be built from C, D, E, F, G, A, B♭. Incidentally, when a song is 'built from' certain tones, that song need not only use those tones but they provide its principal elements, with other tones used only in more circumscribed ways, for instance as occasional borrowings from related keys to add colour.

In many cases when I provide notation in this book, I have for ease of identification indicated with Roman chord symbols which chord is being played in a song at a given time. Roman symbols do not always perfectly match the popular music practice of constructing chords in a variety of ways, as bare perfect fifths for example, but nonetheless I use Roman symbols because they indicate the relations in which successive chords stand to one another (e.g. as tonic and dominant).

7. Thanks to Richard Leadbeater for help with these formulations. I disagree with Burns and Lafrance, for whom 'Paparazzi's' chorus features 'sound saturation, with every possible space in the arrangement filled with rich textural effects' (2014: 129). The chorus texture *is* fuller than the verse, but it remains sparse compared to that of 'Country Roads'.

8. Ditto many other news agencies, including Reuters and the Daily Mail (Macrae 2012; Wickham 2012). Occasionally other academic pieces on popular music receive wide media coverage——for example, Mauch et al. (2015), covered by the BBC, *Daily Mail*, *Time*, and so on. Mauch et al.'s finding that popular music's harmonic and timbral diversity has *not* lessened over time was not what the media trumpeted, though, instead focusing on their claim about three revolutions in popular-musical style. Journalists either mentioned the diversity issue only in passing——unlike coverage of Serrà——or highlighted Mauch et al.'s supposed *exception* to

this ongoing diversity, a temporary mid-1980s reduction in stylistic diversity (see, e.g., Morelle 2015). Whereas research purporting to document increased homogeneity was celebrated uncritically, counter-evidence was either ignored or selectively construed to preserve the belief in homogenisation.

9. Simon Frith, too, argues that evaluative distinctions are routinely drawn within popular music; thus, for him, popular music listeners are discerning, constantly drawing aesthetic distinctions. John Fisher makes a similar argument (2011: 413). I agree about listeners' discriminating practices. However, the *bases* of these discriminations can be problematic, hence new frameworks for evaluation are needed.

10. I say 'supposedly' because, although the relationships between indie and major labels have changed a good deal over time, no indie label can afford to disregard commercial considerations entirely. Indeed 'vast numbers of independent companies are making recordings ... due to their commitment to the system and their own financial success within it' (Negus 1996: 43; see also Lee 1995).

11. Actually, I don't totally reject the view that innovation is a source of value, but I object to the usual ways that innovation and its value are understood, through hierarchical contrasts with the formulaic and rule-bound where, by no coincidence (see Chap. 2), the latter are particularly associated with women.

12. Bernard Gendron's (2002) more positive view is that popular musicians' appropriation of avant-garde strategies has destabilised the high/low divide. Yet Gendron concludes: 'popular music's triumph over classical music ... has not required the end of cultural hierarchy and the art/pop difference. ... Indeed, the creation of new hierarchies and new art/pop dynamics were indispensable factors in the empowerment of popular music' (2002: 327). That is, as Gendron himself concedes, *some* popular music has gained status at the expense of other branches.

13. Andrew Chester, too, argues that aesthetic criteria for judging 'rock' should not be inappropriately drawn from the classical music paradigm. He endorses Langdon Winner's claim that 'rock is an art form in its own right with its own rules, traditions, and distinctive characteristics' (1970a: 86).

14. For Robert Walser, 'both "classical" and "popular" repertoires contain too much heterogeneity to be stable. What internal features

unite ... Stephen Foster, Little Richard, and Trent Reznor?' (2003: 25–26). If we discount Stephen Foster (who wrote many nineteenth-century American songs such as *Oh! Susannah*) as pre-rock-'n'-roll, arguably the remaining two musicians both make 'rock'. But if Walser is right that there is no unity even to rock, then there cannot be any unity to popular music overall either. For the related view that overlaps between popular, classical, and folk music preclude any firm differentiations between them see, for example, Partridge (2014: 21–24).

15. On the centrality of technology to popular music production and reception see, for example, Théberge (2001: 3). Technological mediation helps to distinguish post-rock-'n'-roll music from jazz and blues as forms centred on live, relatively immediate performance (Keil 1966; Small 1999: esp. 198ff, 296ff).

16. To clarify, the harmonic filler layer does not exhaust a song's harmonic content, to which *all* pitched elements——including melody, chords, and bass-line——contribute.

17. As Bradley puts it, in the rock-'n'-roll 'code', vocal lines 'were defined at least as much by their rhythmic character——with, yet not totally "on", the beats of the pulse——and their timbric roughness or smoothness, as by their melodic character' (1992: 59).

18. I base this list on Sweers (2005: ch. 2). Against Harker's (1985) critique of the whole category *folk*, Sweers argues that blanket rejection of *folk* makes it impossible to study how traditional forms have undergone transformation over time and become fused with rock and other genres. More generally, then, we can identify distinct musical forms without having to deny hybridity; rather, to understand hybridity we need to identify distinct forms that undergo hybridisation.

19. For example, Jerrold Levinson considers a set of features, including improvisatory playing, which is distinctive of jazz (2015: 133).

20. On cluster concepts, see Wittgenstein (e.g. 1958: 17–20), and Walton (1970) for the view that each genre of art has standard features that help us to place art-works in the genres to which they belong.

21. The concept informing 'Akihabara Majokko Princess' by Japanese pop artist Takeshi Murakami is that 'real art is centred in entertainment' (Schuker 2009). The 'work' was shown in the 2009–10 Tate Modern exhibition *Pop Life: Art in a Material World*.

22. By former British Symphony Orchestra conductor Sir Malcolm Sargent. Likewise, for the *Music Journal* in the 1950s, teenagers were 'influenced in their lawlessness by [rock-'n'-roll's] throwback to jungle rhythms' (for both, see Frith 1996: 129). And for Paul Johnson in 1964, teenagers at Beatles concerts were not listening to music but 'participating in a ritual, a collective grovelling to gods', while popular music reviewers were 'barely more literate or articulate than the moronic ranks facing them' (Johnson 1964).

23. The composer Sir Hubert Parry, for instance, said that 'the modern popular song' was made for urban dwellers who are 'always scrambling for subsistence' and 'think that the commonest rowdyism is the highest expression of human emotion' (see Frith 1981: 34).

24. On the 'grain of the voice' see Barthes (1977: 179–189).

CHAPTER 2

Tracking Popular Music History with an Aesthetic Map

1 Introduction

In this chapter I explore how hierarchies of value from the history of aesthetic thought have impacted on popular music. In Sect. 2, I introduce these hierarchies, which rank art above craft and entertainment and aesthetic pleasures above pleasures that are purely sensuous and bodily. These aesthetic hierarchies have entwined with social divisions of class, gender, and race. I then trace how aesthetic hierarchies have reappeared in popular music as its practitioners have sought to avoid confinement on the wrong side of the art/entertainment divide. In Sect. 3, I revisit rock's emergence out of rock-'n'-roll, with rock claiming greater aesthetic merit. In Sect. 4, I consider punk rock. Whilst partly setting itself up as politically driven and anti-aesthetic, punk also makes a partial claim to aesthetic merit. In this regard punk rock is torn between the value of innovation and that of raw, authentic expression. Here the modernist insistence on innovation and the Romantic insistence on expression both entwine and come apart.[1] In Sect. 5, I consider one version of the counter-claim that pop is aesthetically superior to rock, that made by the UK synth-pop band the Human League in the early 1980s.

Overall, a systematic pattern emerges for the art/pop hierarchy to reappear within popular music as the hierarchy of rock over pop. Rock has repeatedly claimed greater authenticity, autonomy, seriousness, and integrity than music at the 'pop' end of the spectrum. Similar divisions run right across the

© The Author(s) 2016
A. Stone, *The Value of Popular Music*,
DOI 10.1007/978-3-319-46544-9_2

popular music field: Stax *versus* Motown; funk *versus* disco; genuine rap *versus* pop-rap. But the terms in which these divisions are made—authenticity and innovation *versus* commerce and banality—find their defining statement in the rock/pop opposition. This chapter will therefore confirm—I hope—that aesthetic values have had a problematic impact on popular music. At the same time, I argue in Sect. 6 that their impact has been so pervasive that popular music must be defended in at least partly aesthetic terms. I then introduce my approach to aesthetic value in this book.

I am not alone in criticising the hierarchies that structure the popular music field—so do, amongst others, Bannister (2006), Blacking (1981), Dettmar and Richey (1999), Echols (2010: esp. xxiv–xxv and ch. 1), Frith (2001), Frith and McRobbie (2007), and Shuker (2001: ch. 7).[2] Some of these theorists have traced the role of aesthetics in shaping these hierarchies (Frith and Horne 1987; Gendron 2002; Leach 2001) —specifically including Romanticism, with its core value of expression, and modernism, with its core value of innovation (Knightley 2001: 135–7ff). What I hope to add is, first, more sense of how the aesthetic devaluation of the popular has been bound up with a devaluation of the body. In exploring this, I will be informed by feminist aestheticians such as Korsmeyer (2004) and critics of the art/craft opposition such as Shiner (2001). Second, I want to flesh out how aesthetic values imbue some actual stylistic features of particular genres and songs, as well as the stylistic conflicts between some genres. Third, I infer that we need a new framework under which to evaluate popular music aesthetically.

2   AESTHETICS AND ITS HIERARCHIES

In the history of aesthetic thought, fine art has been ranked above craft as well as the popular, everyday, and entertaining—where ultimately the category of craft incorporates that of popular entertainment, as we will see. Entwined with the art/entertainment contrast is a contrast between aesthetic experience and narrowly sensuous or bodily experience, so that aesthetic hierarchies are bound up with a devaluation of the body. These are very general claims, given that aesthetic thought is obviously vast and multi-faceted. But my aim is not to present a balanced picture of every current within aesthetics (were that even possible) but to identify the currents that have been dominant and had particular bearing on the making of popular music.

Aesthetics in its modern form emerged across Europe in the eighteenth century in tandem with the new concept of fine art. Previously, Larry Shiner and Paul Oskar Kristeller have argued, 'art' had the broad meaning of any kind of skilled human activity or making (Shiner 2001: 5; Kristeller 1951: 498–99).[3] Art was neither distinguished from craft nor divided from everyday enjoyment or popular entertainment as something elite, special, and elevated. The older usage endures at times, as in talk of 'recording artists', but it has largely been supplanted by the newer usage that arose in the eighteenth century, which defined 'a domain of Art with a capital "A"' (Buchenau 2013: 2). Art thereby became divided from (i) craft, the making of everyday objects for use and exchange, and (ii) popular entertainment, events and objects that bring people everyday pleasure. Unlike craft and entertainment, art was (under various conceptions): made for its own sake, not as a means to some other end such as financial gain; the product of inspiration or genius, expressing the artist's personal vision; to be enjoyed for its own sake, offering refined 'higher' pleasures—in John Stuart Mill's phrase, contrasting poetry's pleasures to the lower ones of the game push-pin (1859: 389). Overall, art was set apart as being made for aesthetic appreciation, not sensuous gratification or practical use. Thus aesthetics in its modern sense was integrally linked with the new concept of art as 'fine' art.[4]

In his 1820s lectures on aesthetics Hegel set out his influential version of this new view of art. Hegel is relevant because his thought will play an important role in my defence of popular music, its problems notwithstanding. For Hegel, aesthetics deals primarily with art, and art is the system of the fine or beautiful arts, *die schöne Künste*. Hegel thus excludes everyday life, crafts, and popular entertainment from the aesthetic domain (although not nature; see below). For him, art's true purpose is to present the 'absolute idea' in sensory form. Insofar as an art-work succeeds in doing so, it is beautiful or fine (*schön*). To achieve beauty in this way, an art-work must meet three demands. (1) It must have *serious* metaphysical and religious content, addressing the ultimate nature of reality, not mere trivia or ephemera. (2) The art-work must *present* (*darstellen*) this serious content concretely, in how its perceptible materials are organised, thereby making that content fully accessible to our senses rather than only alluding to or symbolising the content. (3) The art-work's sensory form must be *appropriate* to its content. For example, the ancient Greeks conceived of the divine as a pantheon of individual gods and goddesses, and the appropriate form for presenting that pantheon was stone carved into human-shaped statues (i.e. sculpture).

Demand (1) leads Hegel to exclude from aesthetics things that provide only fleeting pleasures and entertainment (*Unterhaltung*). For Hegel, only serious art-works that 'bring ... to our minds and express ... the *divine*, the deepest interests of humankind, and the most comprehensive truths of the spirit' belong to the aesthetic domain, for only they can give sensory presentation to 'the idea' (Hegel 1970: vol. 1, 70–71). For Hegel, art-works that present these truths have aesthetic value—that is, the value of presenting truth. This kind of value is particular to aesthetic phenomena because, although works of religion and philosophy also concern truth, they represent it (*vorstellen*) and conceptualise it (*begreifen*), respectively. For Hegel, some items other than art-works—specifically some natural things—can be aesthetic, and have aesthetic value, when they share in the property of presenting truth. Natural objects achieve this insofar as their shape—for example, that of crystals—goes some way to embodying the rationally organised structure of the idea, thereby approximating to the kind of presentation of truth that occurs in art-works (vol. 1, 116ff).

It is therefore *aesthetic* value that concerns Hegel, not exclusively artistic value. Nonetheless, he excludes the entertaining from the aesthetic domain because of demand (1). However, demand (1) leads to this exclusion only because Hegel takes it that the serious truths to be presented concern the idea as a rational structure. If the truths to be presented instead concerned the importance of materiality—as I'll argue later—then cultural items that entertain, arouse and please the body would be well placed to present those truths—doing so *by* being pleasurable.

Hegel takes it that we respond to art-works with both our senses and intellects. With our bodily senses we apprehend an art-work's perceptible shape; with our intellects we gain a tacit comprehension of its spiritual content. Because we access the content in and through the sensory form that presents it, our sensory apprehension becomes the vehicle or medium through which, implicitly, we grasp the idea animating the work. This is Hegel's version of a view held by many aestheticians—that our aesthetic responses are sensory and affective rather than narrowly rational, yet that the feelings involved are special, refined, and more spiritual or intellectual than ordinary affections. Ordinary pleasures arise when objects or events bring us bodily gratification through our senses, whereas aesthetic pleasures are higher and more elevated. In Hegel's version of this broader position, we have aesthetic experience when our sense-perceptions and the affective responses that they prompt become the medium of our comprehension of serious and important ideas. The sensory domain thus becomes 'over-grasped' or 'enveloped' (*übergriffen*) by the intellectual one.[5]

Kant's version of the idea that aesthetic experience is spiritually refined has exerted even more influence than Hegel's. In his *Critique of Judgement* of 1790, Kant distinguishes aesthetic pleasure from ordinary, sensuous pleasure on the grounds that the former is disinterested. In the background is Kant's distinction between judgements of taste (i.e. aesthetic judgements) and cognitive judgements. When making cognitive judgements, such as 'that shrub is blowing in the wind', we apply concepts to the materials of sensation, whereas judgements of taste are based on our feelings of pleasure in an object. Kant further distinguishes the latter judgements both from judgements of the 'good', that is, judgements that some object—a quilt, a chair, a pen—is an effective means to some end, and from judgements of the 'agreeable', which are based on an object's arousing pleasant sensations within me. In contrast, judgements of 'beauty' or taste are based on our pleasure just in the *form* of an object as it appears to us (Kant 1987: §3–4). This three-fold distinction between the good, agreeable, and beautiful parallels the three-fold distinction between crafts, entertainments, and the aesthetic, which Kant formulates as a contrast between the mechanical, agreeable, and fine arts (§44).

Aesthetic pleasure is disinterested, then, because when we have such pleasure we are enjoying the form of an object for its own sake, not because of any practical considerations (as when we enjoy a cake because it assuages our hunger) or pleasurable sensations that the object gives us (e.g. pleasant taste sensations). Instead pleasure in beauty arises when an object's form gives it a unified, harmonious appearance without my having to impose unity on the object by classifying it under concepts. In ordinary perception I do so classify objects: I intuit the materials of sensation, I unify them schematically (the work of imagination), and apply concepts to the results (the work of understanding). Normally, then, imagination serves understanding. In contrast a beautiful object has a unifying form, the presence of which sets my imagination free from serving the understanding. This liberates me to entertain various vague, fleeting imaginings regarding the object and to grope towards relevant concepts in an open-ended, indefinite way. This 'free play' of imagination and understanding is pleasurable, but the pleasure is not self-interested because it does not result from the satisfaction of my cognitive interest in classifying the object or from any gratifying sensory effects the object has on me. Rather the pleasure arises because I am temporarily *freed* from pursuing my cognitive and sensory interests. Hence my pleasure in beauty involves finer feelings, not appetites; it involves the free operation of my higher mental faculties of imagination and understanding, not my lower faculties of sensibility and desire.

Kant's concept of disinterestedness thus rests on a distinction between aesthetic and merely bodily pleasure, a distinction that Hegel also made. For Schopenhauer too—who builds on Kant and has greatly influenced artistic practice—when I have aesthetic experience my will is temporarily extinguished. I then attain relief from the incessant, restless pursuit of desire after desire which normally condemns me to perpetual dissatisfaction (Schopenhauer 1966: 1: 196–7). Aesthetic experience thus pleases me in a special way by *rescuing* me from the doomed pursuit of sensory gratification which fills everyday life. But—beyond Schopenhauer specifically—popular entertainment is generally taken to provide sensory gratification. Thus Schopenhauer's conceptual framework too implies that the aesthetic realm surpasses the popular realm, as transcendence leaves behind the doomed realm of bodily gratification.

Turning back to art's production, Kant's influence was again decisive when he conceived of genius as the mental power 'through which nature gives the rule to art' (Kant 1987: §46). With this formulation Kant helped to articulate the modern concept of the genius as an exceptional individual able to create original works of fine art by a vital, spontaneous process. The genius contrasts with those who laboriously manufacture things by mechanically following existing rules and formulae, as craftspeople do. Hence, in his 1799 novel *Lucinde*, written in Kant's wake, the German Romantic Friedrich Schlegel adversely compares Prometheus, who creates 'mechanically' by following artificially imposed rules, to Hercules, who creates by giving his natural impulses free rein. The genius does not lifelessly copy the rules established *by* others; rather, in creating he legislates *for* others (Schlegel 1971: 66–68).

Particularly through Romanticism, these notions of genius flowed together with the new importance that nineteenth-century intellectuals placed upon authentic self-expression. To fully realise and fulfil ourselves, it was increasingly thought, we must each express our inner natures, our unique individual sets of feelings. This is a creative process, for it is only in expressing our feelings that they first acquire determinate shape and articulation. The outcome of such creative expression is the art-work, which by mapping out the artist's feelings communicates his unique vision. But the importance of cultural expression was taken to extend beyond the individual artist. For the Romantics, beginning with Herder, the unique spirit of each national people or *Volk* expresses itself in its culture, and so 'folk cultures' have important expressive value (Taylor 1975: 3–50).

Over against the supposedly authentic and expressive realm of folk cultures stood the newly emerging popular culture of commercial, urban, industrialised modernity. It included music hall, minstrelsy, cabaret, and 'light' classical music for dancing. As these forms arose the meaning of 'popular' shifted, as Derek Scott has shown. From referring to any music that was widely known or liked—including Beethoven's symphonies, for instance—'popular' instead came to pick out certain forms and styles of music that were designed to provide entertainment. In turn their stylistic features—for example, the narrative verse/catchy chorus model of London music hall songs—became markers of music that was deemed facile, easy, and light. This popular sphere aroused considerable disdain. Allegedly it yielded frivolous pleasure, gave undue gratification to the body, mixed various musical and cultural forms irreverently, and committed all these sins in the vulgar pursuit of money (Scott 2008: 3–12, 87ff). This 'bastardised', 'contaminated' sphere was unfavourably contrasted with both high art and the purity of 'folk' cultures.[6]

As the nineteenth century shaded into the twentieth, popular culture went 'mass', coming to be manufactured by large-scale commercial bodies such as the sheet music publishing companies based in Tin Pan Alley. Amongst the many critics alarmed by this trend were Collingwood and Adorno. Collingwood's charge, we recall, is that making 'amusement art' is actually a form of craft: the craft of using pre-existing formulae to make objects that arouse stereotyped emotions. Collingwood makes clear, then, that craft and entertainment are not separate; rather, craft *includes* entertainment as one of its branches. Adorno, though, observes that the making of entertainment is no longer straightforwardly a matter of individual craft. Rather, individual craft activity has been incorporated into a full-scale industry churning out standardised products, albeit without fully using mass production techniques (Adorno 1991: 100–101). Moreover, these products are made to arouse emotions only for the further end of making profitable sales. Even so, for Adorno the culture industry remains aligned with craft—but craft as expanded and modernised into a profit-driven industry.

In sum, since the eighteenth century, a series of contrasts has predominated in aesthetic thought: art *versus* craft and entertainment; higher *versus* lower pleasures; original creation *versus* mechanical rule-following; authentic expression *versus* arousal of stereotypical emotions; artistic freedom *versus* commerce. These contrasts are scaffolded around further hierarchies between mind and body. There have of course been countercurrents, such as the Arts and Crafts Movement. But the dominant trend has been to draw hierarchical contrasts.

That said, a recurring theme has been that we respond to objects in a specifically aesthetic way just when we respond to them not cognitively but with our senses and by taking affective pleasure in what we sense. Surely this shows that aesthetic thought *values* the senses and *challenges* any ranking of intellect over body? Not straightforwardly so. Time and again, aesthetic theorists—Kant, Hegel, Schopenhauer being just a few leading examples—have divided the more spiritual and intellectual from the more immediately sensory and bodily kinds of response. Aligning aesthetic pleasure with the former, aestheticians have marked down the latter as *merely* sensory, interested, and appetitive. So: yes, the aesthetic includes the sensory and the bodily, *but* specifically as sublimated into something higher. Meanwhile, to enjoy popular culture is to indulge in exclusively bodily desires and pleasures.[7]

One reason why these hierarchies are problematic is that they are connected with social hierarchies of class, race, and gender, as many feminist and socially critical aestheticians have shown (see, e.g., Korsmeyer 1998). Very briefly: as the art/craft opposition took shape, the technical and manual labour of the working class and peasantry came to be denied art status. Likewise women's traditional activities—weaving, sewing, cooking, quilt-making—were consigned to craft status, as were the objects produced by members of 'primitive' societies, since these objects were neither made nor appreciated for their own sake but figured in religious, magical, and customary rituals and practices. Many aestheticians explicitly reserved for white men the powers of genius and authentic self-expression (see Battersby 1994). On this basis girls and women, such as Mozart's talented sister Nannerl, were denied support to pursue musical and other kinds of artistic careers. Class hierarchies were endemic to the institutions founded from the eighteenth century in the cause of fine art: galleries, museums, concert halls, and academies and societies of the arts. Their chief public was the aspiring middle class, whose members aspired to rise above the working class through their discerning tastes and refined behaviours, such as still, silent, totally attentive listening in the concert hall (a practice that, admittedly, took a long time to take root). The same convergence of aesthetic and social hierarchies occurs in popular music, we will see.

3   FROM ROCK-'N'-ROLL TO ROCK

From its inception rock-'n'-roll was on the wrong side of the art/enter-tainment divide. Rock-'n'-roll gave immediate enjoyment. Lyrically and musically, it celebrated fun and direct pleasure—even in name it was linked to sex and the body. With its insistent backbeat, rock-'n'-roll virtually compelled listeners to dance—it *aroused* people's bodies rather than lib-erating listeners *from* the immediate promptings of their bodies. This was music for dancing, not disinterested contemplation, as Chuck Berry said explicitly in 'Rock and Roll Music': 'It's got a backbeat, you can't lose it, any old time you use it … gotta be rock and roll music if you wanna dance with me'. The music was loud, with vocals often half-shouted (or shrieked, Little Richard-style), with the percussive side of the instrumentation brought to the fore, and with distortion, echo, and other effects adding 'noise' to the music, all making for an inescapably physical listening expe-rience. Rock-'n'-roll mixed aspects of black and white genres, middle- and working-class genres (respectively Tin Pan Alley pop and country), which had been separated before. Rock-'n'-rollers made no attempt to set them-selves above commerce: 'The early values of rock-'n'-roll were forged in the context of entertainment, whether in local dance halls or on national TV shows' (Frith 1981: 70).[8]

Formally, too, rock-'n'-roll songs tended not to innovate but to re-use the same forms—generally, either songs cycled through four repeti-tions of a twelve-bar blues chord progression or they used the AABA form popularised by Tin Pan Alley. Writing rock-'n'-roll songs, it seemed, was a craft: the craft of skilfully using tried-and-trusted elements with enough of a quotient of innovation—in the combination of elements or how they are used—to capture interest. Motown songwriters can be understood as craftspeople in these terms; so can the early Beatles, who put together such formulae as Little Richard's vocal style, chords played on the guitar in Chuck Berry style, and the hand-claps made popular in girl group music (Covach 2006: 165).[9] Beatlemania seemed to confirm that music crafted in this way appealed to the passions, not the intellect.

Against this background, musicians unsurprisingly sought greater artis-tic legitimacy over the course of the 1960s. One approach was to pursue instrumental virtuosity, especially in guitar playing (Eric Clapton, Jimi Hendrix). But central to the quest for artistic merit were the Beatles, above all when they released *Sgt. Pepper's Lonely Hearts Club Band* in 1967. Celebrated as 'an artistic statement in a music that was never regarded as art before' (Kaye, quoted in Garofalo 2010: 207), the album was heralded by *Time* as 'leading an evolution in which the best of current post-rock sounds are becoming something that pop music has never been before: an art form' (Wald 2009: 230).

The first trend that *Sgt. Pepper* crystallised was towards the emergence of the concept album. There is debate about what the concept behind *Sgt. Pepper* was, although plausibly McCartney's concept was to create alter-egos for the Beatles—that is, Sgt. Pepper's band—and so establish distance from the public and media spectacle that the Beatles had become (Northcutt 2006: 135–6). But whatever exactly was its concept, the album certainly seemed to be a whole greater than the sum of the songs included on it. Second, *Sgt. Pepper* did much to establish the distinction between singles—the domain of mere pop—and albums. The album now became a form in its own right, capable of having thematic unity and enabling musicians to explore serious themes in depth.[10] These developments marked a bid for art status: the album, especially if it was a concept album, was organised around ideas and the appropriate response to it was intellectual, a response of listening to and thinking about it. Third, *Sgt. Pepper* heralded the emergence of progressive rock, a 'logical development of the increasingly loft[y] ambitions that rock had adopted over the course of the 1960s' (Covach 2006: 323). Embodying these ambitions, the Beatles stopped performing from 1966 onwards to focus on making records conceived as 'studio audio art' (Turino 2008: 84–85).[11] Careful attention was lavished on every detail; there was extensive sonic experimentation, for instance with backwards taping; and instruments with classical associations were brought in, such as the string octet in 'Eleanor Rigby' and the half-orchestra in 'A Day in the Life'. In the case of *Sgt. Pepper*, the Beatles combined these features with serious lyrics, reproduced in full on the sleeve, and with a wide range of styles and borrowings from many musical traditions—which began when they included the sitar on 'Norwegian Wood' (on *Rubber Soul*) —all suggesting a breadth of ambition characteristic of art rather than entertainment. Fourth, in all these ways, *Sgt. Pepper* contributed to rock-'n'-roll's transformation into rock (so had Cream, The Who, and Hendrix; but *Sgt. Pepper* added weight and momentum to this current). For the National Observer in 1968, then, '"rock" [was] getting longer, more sophisticated, more ambitious, restless with chordal limitations and the three-minute format' (Oxford English Dictionary 2013). 'Rock' was born as something more complex, experimental, and serious-minded than its parent rock-'n'-roll.

Progressive rock distils the same developments. I cannot do it justice here (but see Atton 2001; Borthwick and Moy 2004: ch. 4; Macan 1997; Covach 1997), only sketch how progressive rock exemplifies the role of aesthetic values in rock's emergence from rock-'n'-roll. Progressive rock musicians, many of whom had been to art college and absorbed its values, wanted to make a kind of rock akin to art—that therefore was *not* pop. Accordingly they rejected the most identifiably 'pop' features of earlier popular music: the focus on singles and short songs, use of fixed formulae such as the twelve-bar blues chord progression, easy and fun subject-matter and musical material, and danceability. Instead, albums were to provide lasting artistic statements. Songs acquired more complex forms and were often long, taking whatever time was needed to develop their material without regard to standard conventions around song length. Accordingly songs might be divided into different sections, akin to the movements of a symphony, or distinct songs might blend into a suite; and songs incorporated extended instrumental sections and solos. Time signatures other than 4/4 became more common, as did changes of time signature between different sections. Virtuosity was celebrated, the range of instruments broadened (to take in, e.g., the Mellotron, flute, and cello), and influences from multiple genres, particularly jazz and classical music, were integrated. The point was not only to expand the scope of popular music but also to acquire some of the greater prestige of classical music (Walser 1993: 61–62) and, by then, of jazz. So, Robert Walser remarks:

> Rock critics' own preoccupation with art rock reflects their acceptance of the premises of the classical model. Performers who haven't composed their own material – 'girl groups', Motown, soul singers – have rarely won critical respect comparable to that granted artists who better fit the model of the auteur, the solitary composing genius. Sometimes performers stake their claims to classical prestige explicitly. Emerson, Lake, and Palmer's neoclassical extravaganzas, such as their rendering of Mussorgsky's *Pictures at an Exhibition* (1972), were intended as elevations of public taste and expressions of advanced musicianship. Keith Emerson's attraction to classical resources was unabashedly elitist; he considered ordinary popular music degraded and took on the mission of raising the artistic level of rock. (Walser 1993: 62–63)

One thing that progressive rock accepted from the 'classical model' was the importance of harmony and formal complexity. These aspects of the music tended to be the chief focus of progressive experimentation, elaboration, and virtuosity (see, for example, John Covach's reconstruction of the structure of Yes's 'Close to the Edge'; Covach 1997). More broadly, the aesthetic values central to progressive rock were those of experimentation and autonomy on the one hand, intellectual complexity and seriousness on the other. Both sets of values descend from modernism, whilst the mystical, psychedelic, and countercultural aspects of progressive rock align it with Romanticism with its stress on the imagination (Anderton 2010: 424). Still, progressive rock adheres most strongly to the modernist values of experimentation and self-conscious artistry, and this provides a starting-point for approaching punk's reaction against progressive rock.[12]

But let me first return to the body. Because traditional aesthetic hierarchies devalue the body, we would expect that devaluation to feed into popular music genres insofar as they reflect those hierarchies. This is so with progressive rock. It is 'head music', not body music; its principal values are cerebral ones (Garofalo 2010: 215). A concept, usually a serious theme or topic, organises the musical materials, which are derived to explore that concept, calling for thoughtful listening. The formal complexity of the music, too, calls for conscious attention and thought. Prog's use of unconventional time signatures, though, might seem to draw attention to rhythm and its organising role in the music. Yet these time signatures—such as the 7/4 of most of Pink Floyd's 'Money' (apart from the extended guitar solo in 4/4) —yield music that is ill-suited for dancing, which lessens the music's bodily appeal, calling for thought *about* rhythm rather than immediate participation in it. That said, prog regularly incorporates loud, heavy, assaultive passages—sometimes extensively so, as on King Crimson's *Red*—and this highlights the music's sensory effect. Again, though, the effect is to challenge our senses rather than provide sensuous pleasure; to that extent prog continues to express a level of distance from the sensory domain. In sum, 'if the early rock forms were major reorientations ... of the body and dancing into European popular music, the addition of "concepts" to the album ... displaced this emphasis once more' (Durant 1984: 218).

4   PUNK, AESTHETICS, AND '1 2 X U'

Punk opposed most of the musical trends of the 1970s, including progressive rock. Gary Numan—initially a punk, later a pioneer of synth-rock—summed up the punk attitude to prog when he inveighed against 'pompous supergroups ... [making] disgusting, self-indulgent solos that went on for half an hour' (Numan 1997: 48). Punks did not entirely repudiate the aesthetic domain, though—rather, punk's antagonism to many other popular genres had an aesthetic dimension. In rejecting progressive rock, punks were re-affirming expressive authenticity, against prog's supposed sterile excess of self-consciousness and undue preoccupation with artistry and complexity. Punks sought instead to return to core features of rock-'n'-roll as it had been before rock came along with its artistic pretensions—before 'the Beatles destroyed rock and roll' in Elijah Wald's polemical phrase (2009).

How is this agenda embodied in stylistic details of punk rock? Punk embraces simplicity, as regards both song forms and the components of each layer of sound. Single songs became the focus again, and were short, mostly using clearly defined verse/chorus form. Layers of sound were stripped back to the basics: vocals, chords on guitar(s), bass guitar, and drums. Other instruments were 'written off as … elitist accoutrements of a professionalist cult of technique' (Marcus 2011: 54). Most songs used just a few repeated chords—as in the famous instructional diagram from the punk fanzine *Sideburns*: 'This is one chord [A major]; this is another [E major]; this is another [G major]. NOW FORM A BAND!' (Moon 1977). Guitar solos were largely abandoned, or retained in so minimal a form as to amount to parody. Virtuosity and complexity, then, were rejected in favour of the immediate and visceral. Here, like much early rock-'n'-roll, punk rock is energetic and noisy. The energy comes from the fast tempos; the frequent use of highly percussive and abrasive styles of playing the guitar; and the typically even emphasis on eight beats to the measure by the bass guitar and sometimes the rhythm guitar too, creating urgent, driving rhythms (many Ramones songs are paradigmatic; see Fig. 2.1).

The noise comes from the prominence of the heavily distorted guitar, the level of distortion often half-submerging the harmonic content of the chords and blurring the distinctions between individual chords; and from the often non-melodic, shouted vocal style. Simplicity, energy, and noise were the watchwords.

However, punks did not simply return to expressive authenticity. Punk was also shaped by avant-garde values of experimentation, shock, transgression, and novelty (as many authors have documented: Marcus 2011; Garnett 1999; Hebdige 1979; Frith and Horne 1987: ch. 4; Laing 1985; Borthwick and Moy 2004: ch. 5; Knightley 2001: 137ff). What punk did was combine these values with a renewed emphasis on expression and authenticity.[13] We can trace how the combination got into the music by

Fig. 2.1 Ramones, 'Judy is a Punk', vocal melody, electric guitar, and bass guitar, timing ca. 00:14–00:25

focusing on '1 2 X U', the closing track on Wire's 1977 debut album *Pink Flag*. Although some critics such as Greil Marcus (1978) take *Pink Flag* to be anti-punk or already post-punk, I'll suggest that *Pink Flag* provides a window onto the unstable mix of aesthetic values at work in punk, and that to that extent that *Pink Flag* belongs within punk, even if it is already beginning to move beyond it.

Wire explicitly sought to make art—three of its four members had been to art college—and Wire are probably the leading representatives of punk's 'art-rock' side as distinct from its 'plebeian' or social-realist side (Borthwick and Moy's distinction 2004: 78). Guitarist Bruce Gilbert has even described Wire as an evolving art project that adopted rock in one of its phases, its products not being mere songs but rather 'art objects' (Neate 2009: 5). This concern for art status notwithstanding, *Pink Flag* has quintessential punk features. Inspired by the Ramones, Wire took brevity even further: the whole album lasts 35 minutes, and even the longest song extends only to 3.57 minutes. The instrumentation throughout is just guitar, bass, and drums (excepting flute on the longest song, 'Strange'). All the songs are in 4/4 and use a small number of chords formed in standard ways, often 'power chords' (see below). In these respects the music has an extreme simplicity (as can be seen from the description of '1 2 X U' below: see Table 2.1).[14] This simplicity partly reflects the band's lack of musical skill: 'with our musical abilities, what other options did we have? I certainly couldn't say I was a musician', admits drummer Robert Grey, then Gotobed (Neate 2009: 24). But in the punk context, that lack of musicianship was enabling, providing a way to avoid self-indulgent virtuosity.

'1 2 X U' is Wire's anthem as 'Anarchy in the UK' is for the Sex Pistols. Just 1.53 minutes long, '1 2 X U' has no introduction in the standard sense. Instead, after the spoken-word announcement of the song by vocalist Colin Newman, '1 2 X U' begins immediately with the same element that provides the chorus: a riff repeated four times (Fig. 2.2). The riff's components are power chords, that is, open perfect fifth intervals played on the guitar with distortion; they follow a bVII–IV–I pattern in the key of F♯ major.[15] In punk, power chords were used heavily, to embody aggression, noise, and simplicity—the first two because of the distortion, the last because of the emptiness of the open perfect fifth. The repetitions of the riff in '1 2 X U' have a roller-coaster quality as they drop from bVII to IV then rise to I, move on and off the tonic, and alternate between a straight eighth-note rhythm in each even measure and a slightly more varied rhythm in each odd one.

Because the repeated riff provides the chorus, with no vocal melody, the song defies our expectations about verse/chorus form. Conventionally a song's vocals become most prominent in the chorus, sometimes being double-tracked or with backing vocals being added. But in '1 2 X U' the vocals only appear in the verse. The guitar, however, conforms to the typical verse/chorus pattern: it becomes restrained in the verse, when Gilbert plays just one low-pitched flattened seventh chord repeatedly, with the

Table 2.1   Wire, '1 2 X U', song structure

Timing	Section	Measures	Description
00:01–00:08	Intro 1		Spoken-word introduction.
00:09–00:18	Intro 2/ chorus	8	No vocals. The central riff (Fig. 2.2) is repeated four times
			After an opening cymbal splash a standard rock beat comes in: the snare-drum sounds on beats two and four and the bass-drum on beats one and three, the latter barely audible beneath the bass guitar
			The bass guitar plays the root notes of each chord, to a rhythm mirroring that of the guitar
00:19–00:31	Verse 1	12	Again a cymbal splash opens the section, and the drums play the same pattern as before, while the guitar becomes more restrained. The bass guitar plays a pulsating, steady quarter-note rhythm on E_1 in contrast to the faster-moving eighth-note rhythm of the guitar, playing ♭VII an octave above the bass
			Newman's vocal comes in on measure 13, starting fairly quietly and crescendoing to a shout in the twentieth measure
			A double cymbal splash ends the section
00:32–00:40	Chorus	8	As Intro 2/chorus except for cymbal splashes throughout
00:41–00:54	Verse 2	12	As verse one with different lyrics
00:55–01:03	Chorus	8	As before
01:04–01:13	Middle-eight	8	After another opening cymbal splash, the snare-drum now sounds on each quarter-note beat, while the guitar plays a C♯ major chord—the dominant—again as a power chord, with the bass guitar playing the root note, both over a repeated eighth-note rhythmic pattern. The vocals return, sounding increasingly aggressive: 'I got you in a corner…'
01:14–01:43	Verse 3	26	Again a cymbal splash opens, then the section begins as verses one and two but with no vocals. But then an extra layer of guitar is overdubbed, playing ♭VII, first appearing on measure nine and thereafter recurring at the start of each odd measure. The initial guitar maintains its eighth-note rhythm while gradually rising to a crescendo, while the extra guitar moves over to play on quarter-notes in the final four measures. Newman re-announces '1 2 X U!' during the final measure
01:44–01:53	Outro/ chorus	8	The riff is repeated three times then the final, fourth repetition is cut short half-way through, ending abruptly on a single final I, marked by a cymbal splash

Fig. 2.2 Wire, '1 2 X U', riff (electric guitar), timing ca. 00:09–00:11

strings damped down, generating a sense of tension and controlled aggression; we find some release in the chorus when the guitar becomes loud and prominent. Anticipating that release, Newman's vocals crescendo to a harsh bark just at the end of each verse—but then, contrary to expectations, he falls silent in favour of the riff. Moreover, the release provided by the three-chord riff is strictly limited: because the upper notes of the first two power chords (i.e. B and F♯ respectively) become the roots of the chords following them, there is a sense of stasis, of being trapped (Pedler 2003: 248).

In sum, the song retains enough conventional verse/chorus form to arouse particular expectations, but then thwarts them. This defiance of expectations is central to the track and is reinforced by both the lyrics and the song's harmonic make-up. Half-shouted in brutal, faux-proletarian style, beginning, 'saw you in a mag, /kissing a man …', the words suggest stereotypical male desire for a female celebrity. This desire seems about to be consummated in the bridge section ('I got you in a corner…'), which is on the dominant, conveying energetic forward momentum. But the lyrical switch to 'I got you in a cottage' suggests an unexpected move into the terrain of gay sex. This isn't definite enough for us to decide one way or another, though; the meaning remains open. Reflecting this, the music moves back after the bridge to the restrained verse pattern, tensely repeating the flattened seventh, rather than advancing to the tonic: the apparently imminent consummation has never come. In these several ways the song promises fulfilment but refuses to deliver it—as it does, too, because Wire refuse to 'rock out', insistently returning to the restrained, chopping verse pattern instead. Thus the song is organised around an on-off pattern of expectations called up then thwarted, mirrored in the riff's see-saw, on-off rhythm. This reflects one of Wire's aims: to refuse to please listeners and instead offer them 'total bloody disappointment' (Gilbert, quoted in Neate 2009: 56).

These features of '1 2 X U' exemplify punk's aesthetic values. In its basic, meat-and-potatoes instrumentation, its use of just a few chords stripped down to open perfect fifth intervals, its brevity, and its emphasis on energetic dynamics rather than complicated harmonic developments, '1 2 X U' typifies punk's mission of recapturing the simplicity and energy of rock-'n'-roll. Indeed Newman described *Pink Flag*'s title track as paying homage to Chuck Berry, specifically to 'Johnny B. Goode'. Yet Newman opposed rock-'n'-roll's cheerful, fun ethos, which he took 'Johnny B. Goode' to epitomise, and he complains that early rock-'n'-roll was formulaic and lacked the melodic inventiveness that the Beatles introduced (Neate 2009: 18). Wire, then, rejected two of the most 'pop' features of rock-'n'-roll—easy enjoyment and formulaic structures. Instead Wire championed inventiveness and innovation—thus resituating rock-'n'-roll's positive aspects within music that defies rather than satisfies expectations and plays with rather than reproduces formulae. Those qualities of experimentation and innovation, though, had already been staked for rock *against* pop. Wire were returning to rock-'n'-roll *as rock*, not as pop—and the same is true of punk overall.

The texture of '1 2 X U' reflects Wire's adherence to rock. The guitar is the most prominent instrument; distortion and central repeated riffs are the currency of hard rock; and power chords are central to heavy metal. Against pop's easy enjoyment, '1 2 X U' conveys difficult emotions: Newman's vocals are angry and accusatory; the damped-down, highly percussive playing of the guitar in the verse embodies suppressed aggression; and when introducing the song Newman barks out its name militaristically: '1 2 X U!' Above all, an uncomfortable feeling is created as the song arouses then thwarts expectations. All this typifies one of punk's goals, namely to explore negative affects—aggression, alienation, rudeness, and hostility—often with vocals sneered, snarled, growled, or shouted. Relatedly, and again contrary to 'pop', punks often wanted to make serious and important points. *Pink Flag*'s lyrics tackle war and the media, discuss relationships outside the terms of conventional romance, and are couched in an abstract style unlike the vivid imagery that is typical of pop. To make the serious intent clear, Wire reproduced the lyrics in full on the album sleeve, as the Beatles had done with *Sgt. Pepper*: 'The lyrics were important ... They weren't just *I-love-you-baby* rock-'n'-roll', Newman attests (Neate 2009: 41).

The superiority to pop claimed by Wire and other punks was in part aesthetic. It was political too, as when punks opposed what they took to be commercial, unchallenging, and conformist genres such as disco. But that very opposition still had an aesthetic aspect, going back to the art/commerce divide. Moreover, the punk goal of expressing difficult emotions goes back to Romanticism, in which the full wealth of emotions merits expression. *Pink Flag* also embodies a modernist rejection of convention: its songs refuse to conform to norms regarding standard length or form. These two principles, expression and innovation, flow together: by defying musical conventions, punk songs can express their defiance of social norms, thereby expressing difficult emotions of alienation and resistance.

Yet Wire also professed to oppose rock: 'the whole idea was to be as *un-rock* as possible', says Bruce Gilbert (Neate 2009: 34). Again this had aesthetic motivations. In aspiring to be high art, and championing musicianship and formal complexity, rock had supposedly lost its direct emotional expressiveness. Here punk espoused values of vital spontaneity that descend from Romanticism. In Wire's case, the opposition to rock extended to punk rock itself insofar as it had become formulaic. Thus, *Pink Flag* asserted, songs could be shorter than three minutes; they need not have conventional verse/chorus forms but could be stripped down still further, say with the chorus reduced to a riff; songs could end abruptly at any point[16]; they could even use just one chord. By critiquing formulae that had come to define punk, Wire were nonetheless continuing the punk project, to which innovation was central. By the same token, Wire were continuing to make rock, insofar as rock has claimed the high ground of innovation in contrast to pop. If Wire were anti-punk in the name of punk, likewise they were anti-rock in the name of rock—not in the name of pop.

I've suggested that expression and autonomy flow together in punk. Consider Newman's spoken-word introduction of '1 2 X U': 'Here it is … again … [gasps, laughs] and it's called … [shouts] 1 2 X U!' On the one hand his words suggest that an actual performance by the band is being recorded, as per the value of authenticity. On the other hand the introduction demonstrates the artificiality of the process of making the record, which required numerous 'takes' of the song ('here it is … *again*') —contrary to any idea of the performance being an immediate emotional outpouring. This self-reflexive, self-critical moment reflects punk's modernist side. But, as this example begins to suggest, autonomy and expression are not always a stable mixture. Autonomy can turn against the idea of simple, direct authenticity—and this happened historically as punk rapidly unravelled into the manifold directions taken by post-punk, committed to avant-garde values in various ways.

What about punk's attitude towards the body? In some ways punk reaffirms the body by comparison with, say, progressive rock. The return to simple song forms effectively downplays the importance of the intellect, and the high degrees of noise and distortion re-emphasise the music's sensory force, its status as something to be felt, not thought about. Punk's return to authentic expression evinces a belief in the importance of affect. Besides being simple in form, punk songs also tend to be repetitive—as in the chorus of 'Judy is a Punk' (Fig. 2.1 above) – and this highlights the songs' rhythmic dynamism, as repeated rhythm patterns generate bodily momentum. Moreover, because punk vocals are often half-shouted, or are monotonous or imperfectly pitched, they tend to function rhythmically as much as melodically.

On the whole, though, punk's approach to rhythm downplays the body. '1 2 X U' is representative: the bass and guitar mainly play regular eighth- or quarter-notes with little variation in timing or emphasis, whilst the bass-drum is quite submerged. The tendency is towards equal emphasis on each subdivision of the beat, along with a level of noise that muffles the differences in emphasis that do exist. Hence '1 2 X U' deters dancing, as is true of much punk rock. One reason is that punk rock often confronts us with an unbroken wall of noise, rather than a plurality of distinguishable layers of sound each emphasising different beats and so creating a patterned set of forces pushing and pulling against one another. In that it repels dancing, punk again insists on being combative, rebarbative, and exploring negative affects more than pleasures. At the same time, in setting itself against dancing, punk diminishes the possibility of our moving with its sounds corporeally, and to this extent punk downplays the body. Notably, punk does this just at the points where it is rock *and not* pop— where punk sets itself against genres that are well-suited for dancing such as disco; where punk offers unbroken, distorted noise rather than spacing and rhythmic complexities; and where punk focuses on negative rather than pleasurable affects. Once again, it is when punk claims aesthetic superiority to pop that it moves away from the body.

5   The Rock/Pop Hierarchy and Its Reversals

I have only indicated some of the manifold ways in which rock has claimed superiority to pop—often by claiming authenticity, under various interpretations. Another family of ways in which rock has claimed authenticity is by blending with folk to constitute folk-rock (see Coyle and Dolan 1999). This folk-rock pathway again illustrates how claims on rock's behalf have drawn on the aesthetic legacy, in this case the art/folk/

entertainment triangle. Moreover, these claims for rock are only part of a still broader pattern for some popular music genres to claim greater authenticity, integrity, or innovative merit than others. Peter Guralnick, for example, excludes Motown from his history of soul music on the grounds that Motown was 'pop', 'industry-slanted', and inauthentic: out of a concern for 'cultural refinements' that would appeal to white audiences, he claims, Motown artists 'only occasionally ... reveal a flash of raw emotion' (1988: 1–2, 7–8). Judgements about sampling, remixing, and mashing-up are also revealing about the persistence of aesthetic hierarchies, for sample-based recordings are regularly condemned as unoriginal, lazy, or outright theft (Sinnreich 2011: 103). Yet, as Aram Sinnreich argues, sampling and related techniques actually stage a post-modern challenge to contrasts between copy and original, unique genius and mere follower, and producer and consumer (see, too, Goodwin 1990; Shusterman 2000: ch. 3). Nonetheless, interviewing numerous DJs and producers, Sinnreich found that they mostly accepted hierarchical contrasts between original and merely derivative work, using these contrasts to distinguish good from bad practitioners and recordings (Sinnreich 2011: 125–6). For these interviewees, originality remained bound up with the authenticity through which a DJ or producer (etc.) injects her personality or vision into sample-based material.

These manifold claims for the superiority of certain branches of popular music are problematic partly on social grounds. Because aesthetic and social hierarchies have been connected historically, they tend to go together in popular music too, with music made by privileged social groups being more readily classified as having aesthetic merit. Regarding gender divisions, for instance, women were long thought incapable of genius and suited only to follow rules and formulae. Such assumptions persist right into Erlewine's accusation that Katy Perry merely follows rules, therefore making formulaic pop (as we saw in Chap. 1). Likewise, Guralnick's complaint that Motown is mere white-oriented pop surely targets the Supremes above all—Motown's most successful act of the 1960s—reflecting the wider pattern for music by female vocalists or groups to be judged inauthentic. That perception itself goes back to the older assumption that women can only follow and copy but cannot innovate, so cannot express their own unique emotions artistically.

Race and the rock/pop division have also intersected, as rock's emergence out of rock-'n'-roll strengthened the division between 'black' and 'white' genres. That division already obtained in the rock-'n'-roll era—

when, roughly speaking, white musicians counted as making rock-'n'-roll while their black counterparts counted as making rhythm-and-blues. Yet there was extensive interchange between the two styles, with rock-'n'-roll largely deriving from rhythm-and-blues (an interchange that Chuck Berry highlights with his abundant lyrical references to 'rock and roll'). As rock emerged, though, the trajectories of 'black' and 'white' music diverged—into rock in the 'white' case, and from rhythm-and-blues into soul then funk and disco in the 'black' case, with rock pitted against the latter genres as mind music for thinking against body music for dancing. Notoriously, rock became explicitly opposed to disco, and that opposition largely continued in punk. Punks rejected disco mainly on the political grounds that it was commercial, manufactured, and fostered a narrow hedonism that was thought to entail social conformism (Dyer 1995: 518; defending disco, see Echols 2010). But given the interrelations between aesthetic values, the mind/body hierarchy, and the association of black people with bodily instinct and passion, it is no coincidence that a predominantly 'black' musical genre took on these connotations of being made for mere bodily pleasure and not active critical thought.

There was a racial dimension, too, to the punk agenda insofar as it was to return to rock-'n'-roll but *not* blues, as Johnny Ramone stated: 'Pure, white rock-'n'-roll, with no blues influence' (Fricke 1999: 26).[17] He may have meant that the Ramones avoided blues chord progressions, horn sections, and the virtuosity of some blues guitarists. But nonetheless Ramone is aligning punk with the history of 'white' rock, with rock-'n'-roll at its root. To be sure the racial politics of punk became complicated, at least in the UK, as punk hybridised with reggae and many punk groups took leading parts in the Rock Against Racism campaign. The broader point, though, is that the rock/pop division took on social and political dimensions as a continuation of the power relations that have been bound up with aesthetic thought.

The rock/pop hierarchy can also be challenged and reversed. Some 'pop' qualities are revalued within punk, despite its overall alignment with rock—singles were reasserted against albums, as were short songs with clearly defined forms; virtuosity was rejected; simplicity was championed. But there are many further 'pop' characteristics that can also be revalued: fun, pleasure, and enjoyment; undemanding subject-matter; danceability. The expressive authenticity that has often been claimed for rock can be rejected, perhaps in the name of artifice, or technology, or performance and masquerade. David Bowie's Ziggy Stardust persona is representative here—its context being the 1972 album *The Rise and Fall of Ziggy Stardust and the Spiders from Mars*, which Bowie intended to bridge the rock/pop divide by being at once a concept album and a collection of clearly structured and individuated songs (Laing 1985: 24). Bowie's deliberate adoption of the persona of Ziggy Stardust and his over-the-top, histrionic vocal expression make clear that the emotions conveyed in the music are something self-consciously staged and performed, not immediately felt.[18]

Further complications involved in reclaiming pop can be traced through the career of the Human League, who began by being experimental and artistic then moved into mainstream, commercial pop. More accurately, the Human League at first sought to combine experimentation with pop, an unstable combination characteristic of many New Wave bands. As the unstable mixture fell apart and its pop side came to the fore, the New Wave gave way to so-called New Pop in the early 1980s, the label under which such miscellaneous British acts as Duran Duran, Adam Ant, and Culture Club were grouped.

Initially called The Future, the Human League originated in the post-punk context of 1977, when they rejected punk as part-and-parcel of a rejection of rock. This rejection had aesthetic motivations: as the band's initial name shows, they subscribed to the modernist values of innovation and experimentation. This led them to oppose rock's privileging of the guitar as the key instrumental vehicle of authentic emotional expression. That expressivist value was jettisoned in favour of innovation, with the band adopting wholly electronic instrumentation. Conventions around the gig, too, were overhauled: the band tried playing tapes on stage instead of performing, coming on stage merely to switch on the tape-recorder, which was placed centre-stage (Reynolds 2005: 163–4). As part of the rejection of expressive authenticity, many of these early tracks were instrumental and espoused the connotations of coldness and lack of emotion that electronic equipment had at that time, while vocalist Phil Oakey's baritone voice projected a cold, detached, and indifferent singing style.

In these respects the early Human League might seem to belong with the avant-garde rather than pop. But they saw electronic experimentation as pop's natural partner on the grounds that pop, too, opposed rock with its focus on the guitar and expression. The link between electronic instrumentation and pop seemed to be confirmed by the disco collaborations between Giorgio Moroder and Donna Summer, which were a major influence on the Human League. Their combination of avant-gardism and

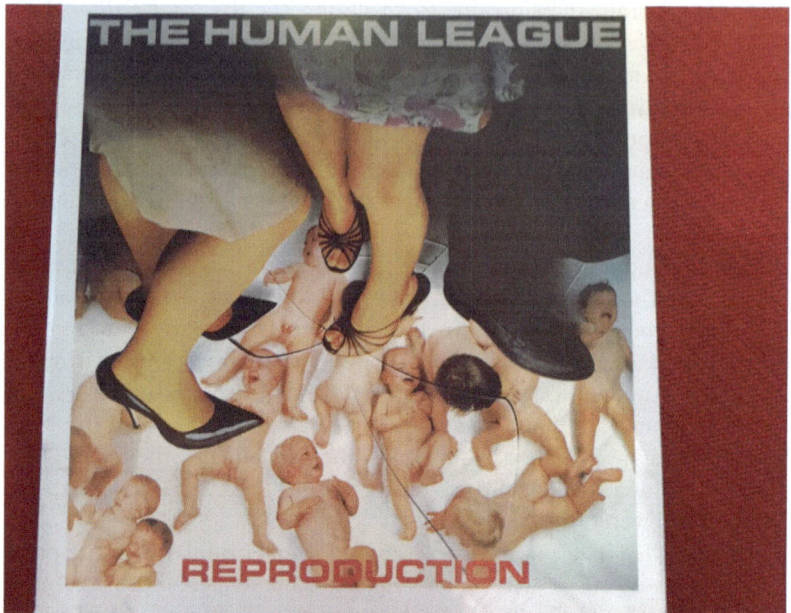

Fig. 2.3   The Human League, *Reproduction*, cover art

pop is distilled in the cover art, made to the band's specification, for their first album *Reproduction* (Fig. 2.3). According to (then) band-member Martyn Ware, the band instructed the Virgin Records art team that they 'wanted an image of a glass dance floor in a discotheque which people were dancing on and beneath this, a lit room full of babies … [to look like a] kind of dystopian vision of the future' (Ware, quoted in Stevens 2013). In Ware's view the art team misinterpreted this brief and produced an image that recommended the trampling of babies. I'm not sure that the image strays as far from the band's vision as Ware fears. It does, at least, distil their mixture of avant-gardism and pop. The dancers look fashionable and smartly dressed, suggesting pop, especially disco. Meanwhile the fact that babies (or rather pictures of babies) are under the dance floor suggests that natural reproduction has been pushed down into the past, replaced by technological reproduction—including that of the synthesised music of *Reproduction*. Thus the image (like the album title) bespeaks the band's self-consciousness about their use of new synthesiser technology,

Fig. 2.4   Heaven 17, *Penthouse and Pavement*, cover art

and this self-reflexivity in turn embodies an allegiance to modernism, as does the embracing of new technology itself.

Another way to re-embrace pop against rock was frankly to acknowledge the commercial context of popular music production, a route taken by two of the original members of the Human League, Martyn Ware and Ian Craig Marsh, who late in 1980 departed the band and formed Heaven 17. They housed Heaven 17 within a broader production company called the British Electric Foundation—inspired by the Chic Organisation—with a view to 'letting people know that the industry was just that, an industry, a business' (Ware, quoted in Lester 2008). In taking the disco band Chic as their model, Heaven 17 were clearly espousing pop. At the same time, in the self-consciousness with which Heaven 17 embraced commerce—shown by the cover of their 1981 album *Penthouse and Pavement* (Fig. 2.4) —they continued to uphold the modernist value of self-reflexivity.

Meanwhile, the reconfigured Human League went on to affirm pop less ambiguously than before. Many of the pop qualities that they now took up are heard on 'Don't You Want Me', the most successful single from their 1981 album *Dare!* —an album that was very much a collection of stand-alone songs. Vocals aside, the sound remained entirely electronic, but 'Don't You Want Me' added various new elements.

(1) It has a very clearly defined form: essentially a verse–pre-chorus–chorus cycle repeated twice. It incorporates a duet between male and female voices, a format popularised by Motown.

(2) The song is more expressive than previous Human League efforts (even though Oakey's singing still sounds somewhat detached, and the conflict between male and female interlocutors is obviously staged). The opening synthesiser riff powerfully affirms the tonic chord, expressing the confidence with which the male character expects his protégée to 'want' him. In the pre-chorus section his vocal lines are pitched lower than in the verse, expressing a mixture of disbelief and aggression—the melodic equivalent of a moment of drawing back in surprise. Oakey's vocals then rise by around an octave in the chorus, expressing the male character's increasing agitation and desperation. His final disappointment is conveyed by the drops of a (perfect) fourth—over 'ba-a-by', 'oh-oh-oh-oh'—that end each phrase of chorus melody. The same melodic gesture appeared in the pre-chorus, when the melody dropped by a fourth from 'want' to 'me' in 'Don't – don't you want me?' The male character is reduced to this repeated falling movement, having started out so confident and bombastic. For its part, the amateurish sound of Susan Sulley's vocal conveys her junior position vis-à-vis the male character but, equally, her determination to talk (sing) back to him.

(3) The sound is enriched and given warmth by many additional layers woven over the basic ones of vocals, synthesiser chords, synthetic bass, and programmed drums. The opening riff creates a sense of space, as the notes making up the tonic chord (in the key of A natural minor) are spread very widely, with the root note two octaves below the other notes. That space becomes filled out by numerous components: at different points there are synthetic horns, two concurrent tracks of chords panned to different sides of the stereo, percussive synthesiser parts sounding a sixteenth-note rhythm

under changing timbres, and an additional line of synthesiser melody in the chorus. Producer Martin Rushent added these layers—
'ear candy' in his words—to transform the song from being 'dark,
cold, and lonely', and presumably quite austere, into an 'upbeat
pop song' (Rushent, quoted in Buskin 2010).

(4) The lyrics are in pop's familiar territory: romance. Despite the male
protagonist's unpleasant sexual politics, the song can superficially
be heard as a love song—which was hardly true of such earlier
Human League lyrics as 'Listen to the voice of Buddha saying
"stop your sericulture"', which open their 1978 single 'Being
Boiled'.

(5) Finally, 'Don't You Want Me' has an immensely danceable rhythm,
established by the interplay between the percussion, bass-line, and
sixteenth-note synthesiser pulse. The bass-line echoes the central
synthesiser riff that introduced the track and, overall, pulls towards
the first half of each measure, while the sixteenth-note pulse skit-
ters energetically ahead of both percussion and bass. Overall these
components pull against one another in timing and emphasis without becoming too crowded or complicated to deter dancing: the
interacting layers contain plenty of breathing room into which
bodily movements can insert themselves (see Fig. 2.5).[19] Further
rhythmic forces, pushing and pulling, come from the other layers
of sound: many of the chords appear quickly and intermittently;
the synthetic horns function percussively; and the layers often pull
against one another in sonic space, the differences between their
rhythms being materialised spatially.

Fig. 2.5 The Human League, 'Don't You Want Me', drum-machine, percussive
synthesiser, and bass synthesiser, timing ca. 00:20–00:22

In sum, 'Don't You Want Me' is more plainly 'pop' than earlier Human League songs because it conforms more closely to several existing conventions.[20] These concern verse/chorus demarcation; the duet format; lyrical preoccupation with romance; the norm for vocal melodies to be expressive of emotions; norms about which emotions different melodic gestures express (a drop in pitch—incredulity; rising pitch—rising tension); the norm for music that is sonically full to sound warm and thus appealing. In addition, the track exemplifies the skill of crafting a song so that it fulfils enough conventions to please listeners while retaining enough originality or innovation to interest them—the original interest coming here from the wholly electronic timbres, the male character's unpleasantness, and the elements of austerity and harshness that these impart.

The early Human League, then, revalued pop by aligning it with artifice, technology, and modernity, against rock with its supposed expressive authenticity. Later, they instead restored pop to its normal meaning of familiarity and convention, re-connecting it with the emotional expressiveness that is conventionally expected from popular music. These two alternatives are indicative of two broader patterns. (1) Pop can be revalued by being re-aligned with valued qualities, such as avant-gardism, futurism, or self-reflexivity, which historically have been set against the popular. (2) Pop can be revalued while still being conceived in contrast to rock—as formulaic, a craft product, enjoyable, and so on; the merits of these qualities are simply reasserted. Those merits remain moot, though, whilst the rock/pop hierarchy remains in force.

6   Conclusion

That the aesthetic tradition has shaped popular music at least confirms that there is more to the popular field than mere commercial fodder. Yet aesthetic values have imparted a divided, hierarchical shape to this field. Likewise, when used by audiences as a basis by which to evaluate popular music, these values have consistently led audiences to value some popular music—its ostensibly more artistic branches—at the expense of others—the more ostensibly commercial or manufactured branches. These hierarchies tend to line up with gender and racial divisions. Yet although inherited aesthetic values provide problematic grounds for judging popular music, these values are also inescapable. Even those who evaluate popular music on socio-political grounds tend to draw on aesthetic criteria as well. Moreover, to abandon aesthetic evaluation—were that possible—and identify only social or political value in popular music would leave it vulnerable to the ongoing criticism that it has little aesthetic merit, however socially 'useful' it might be.

Since we cannot avoid assessing popular music aesthetically, then, we need frameworks for its aesthetic evaluation which do not enshrine hierarchical contrasts between art and entertainment. One possibility might be to turn to recent work in everyday aesthetics (e.g. Irvin 2008; Saito 2010), or to feminist aesthetics, since the latter criticises the concepts of genius and the canon as well as the downgrading of women's cultural activities as mere crafts. While I have much sympathy with everyday and feminist aesthetics, my approach is different. I propose instead to 'raid' the work of Hegel, Adorno, and Kristeva. This is despite the fact that they all downgrade entertainment, in comparison to fine art for Hegel and to autonomous and avant-garde art for Adorno and Kristeva. Nonetheless, I turn to these thinkers because they have important insights: into the domination of concepts over materiality in the modern world and our need to oppose that tendency (Adorno); into how aesthetic phenomena present us with truth (Hegel); and into the semiotic domain of bodily-based meaning which is the precondition of explicit, symbolic meaning (Kristeva). Together, these insights can illuminate how and why popular music has aesthetic value—as presenting truths about the importance of materiality, including as the root source of meaning.

It is therefore worth turning to these philosophers' work despite its problems. Because of those problems, though, their work cannot be directly applied or extended to popular music. For instance, it would not work to claim that popular song lyrics effect the revolutionary transformation of meaning which Kristeva finds, and praises, in modernist poetry and literature. Popular song lyrics generally don't do this, and we need to assess them on their *own* terms. Thus, we need to put post-Kantian aesthetic theories into an encounter with popular music, and allow the theories to undergo transformation in the process so that they yield grounds for valuing popular music *as* popular.

It might be objected that the resulting account of popular music's aesthetic value will not underpin people's everyday positive evaluations of popular music because those evaluations do not presuppose anything like my understanding of aesthetic value. But my point has been that we need to transform the frameworks that ordinarily inform people's aesthetic evaluations of popular music. If we stuck with those usual frameworks, we would retain prejudices against the popular realm and the body; to move beyond those prejudices, we need a new framework. That framework can still provide justification for people's judgements that popular music has positive value, albeit on new grounds. That said, I do intend my framework to link up with one set of grounds on which people normally value popular music—that is, its connections with materiality and the body. This is not normally seen as an aesthetic value, though—but I argue that that is what it is.

I begin with Adorno. His mission as a philosopher is to critique the dominance of materiality by concepts and to find places—above all in art—where materiality escapes that dominance. For Adorno, no such escape ever occurs within the products of the culture industry. Yet his concern for materiality means that his thought, despite itself, can help us to defend popular music.

NOTES

1. Keir Knightley has pointed this out regarding the Sex Pistols (2001: 139).
2. That said, rock/pop hierarchies are regularly deployed in popular music theorising. E.g. Walter Everett: 'The rock world has known albums of serious artistry by Yes and Pink Floyd, [and] of recreational value by Michael Jackson ... ' (1999: 89). Or Alexander Carpenter: 'Where Joy Division's angst, freneticism, and soul-searching were genuine, The Cure's music ... is an after-the-fact parody act ... pin-up cartoonishness' (2012: 45).
3. See also Williams (1983: 40–42). Philosophical reflection on the arts has existed since at least Plato and Aristotle, but arguably aesthetics did not exist in its current *sense* before modernity, because pre-modernity the arts were not conceived as *fine* arts. Even if, as Young argues (2015), pre-moderns already grouped together the later 'fine arts' as 'imitative arts', these were not necessarily already conceived as arts in the modern sense, i.e. essentially unlike craft; for imitation can be viewed as a craft resulting in pleasing products.
4. On the view that art is distinguished by its aesthetic qualities or effects, see Korsmeyer (2004: 27) and Kant (1987: §43–44).
5. At the same time, for Hegel, the aesthetic mode is still deficient relative to philosophy in that the comprehension is still implicit, embedded in the perception. We do not have to endorse this

Hegelian position in holding that popular music embodies truth, for since this truth concerns materiality we can best access it through our senses and bodily responses. Rather than the intellect 'over-grasping' this mode of access by translating this truth into conceptual form, the conceptual statement falls short of its sensory presentation, never quite doing it justice.

6. For examples of this condemnation, see Howes (1962) and Aretz, whose representative view is that folk music should be preserved against the modern 'commercial music ... that is generally of very poor quality'.

7. Terry Eagleton (1988) likewise holds that aesthetic theory has domesticated the body and its sensations (at a theoretical level). Frith agrees that aestheticians have tamed music's emotional and sensual power by taking it to offer 'the experience of *feelings under control*' (1996: 261).

8. Coyle and Dolan agree that 'at the origin of rock-'n'-roll ... we find no concern whatsoever with the genuine or authentic. Elvis ... expected the whole rock-'n'-roll thing to end at any moment; he was fully prepared shortly to be singing ballads like Perry Como ... The concern to distinguish authentic rock from industry pablum developed from sources antithetical to all that rock-'n'-roll represented to its early audiences' (1999: 26), specifically, they argue, from the 1950s folk scene and the wish to answer critics such as Adorno.

9. '... John Lennon told Jann Wenner that the Beatles did not set out to make art. They set out to make functional music. Like the blues, it was music with a purpose in ordinary daily life. ... [T]he purpose was to support dancing' (Gracyk 2013: 31–32).

10. This distinction has persisted ever since: in 1990 the British music industry insisted on the difference between pop as 'instant singles-based music aimed at teenagers' and rock as 'album-based music for adults' (Frith 2001: 95).

11. Lennon said: 'we could send out four waxwork dummies of ourselves and that would satisfy the crowds. Beatles concerts are nothing to do with music any more. They're just bloody tribal rites' (Northcutt 2006: 136). Rock-'n'-roll had long been seen in terms of 'tribal rites', mere instinctive bodies moving rhythmically in a frenzy; Lennon was aspiring to make something artistically superior (his life-long devotion to rock-'n'-roll notwithstanding).

12. It might be objected that I am recycling a now-orthodox narrative in which progressive rock is a degeneration of 1960s rock which punk mercifully put out of existence. This narrative is a simplification, Chris Anderton rightly points out (2010). It construes progressive rock narrowly in terms of its best-known British practitioners, especially those pursuing 'symphonic' prog, while neglecting other variants including European prog (Ahlkvist (2011) also objects to the neglect of 'neo-progressives' such as Marillion). Anderton nonetheless defines prog by its 'attempt to move beyond the standard structures and sounds of 1960s popular rock and pop music' (2010: 420). Certainly, there were many ways of moving beyond those standard elements: 'Krautrock' bands tended to do so by extending popular music's repetitiousness. Given National Socialist appropriations of classical music, it seemed to these German bands that the developmental paradigm was beyond repair, so that standard popular structures such as repetition must instead be radicalised (Stubbs 2014a). So there's more to prog than the standard narrative picks out. Still, I've stayed with that narrative because the dominant aspects of prog on which it focuses illustrate so perfectly how aesthetic values have impacted on popular music.

13. Dave Laing argues that direct, authentic expression was one of punk's two key principles, the other (partly opposed) principle being artifice, outrage, innovation, and challenge to norms (Laing 1985: 26–27).

14. In Table 2.1, as elsewhere, subscript numbers indicate the specific octave in which a given note falls. Middle C is denoted C_4. The lowest pitch is C_1 and the highest C_7 so that, e.g., the B just below middle C is B_3, not B_4.

15. Open perfect fifths are not strictly speaking chords, since the latter should contain at least three tones. Nonetheless I call them 'chords' because they are so treated in popular music.

16. 'We hadn't thought of the songs as being any length. That's how long they were, and when they stopped, another one started', says Lewis (Savage 1989).

17. On punk and race, see Duncombe and Tremblay (2011), Garofalo (2010: 270ff), Sabin (1999a).

18. Frith suggests something similar about Elton John's pop ballads and that this helps to qualify them as pop (2001: 93–94).

19. In Fig. 2.5 and throughout this book I follow Weinberg (1998) on drum notation. A note between the bottom lines of the stave denotes a bass-drum beat; a note above the middle line of the stave denotes a snare-drum beat; and a cross above or below the top line denotes a beat on the closed or open hi-hat. Hi-hat and snare are treated as a single 'voice'.

20. For Reynolds, the Human League now 'represented a new middle of the road'; their 'worldview and sentiments were positive, wholesome, in some ways just a notch away from conservative'; 'Don't You Want Me' was 'their most sonically conventional single yet' (2005: 333).

CHAPTER 3

Adorno and Popular Music

1   INTRODUCTION

In this chapter I start to build my case for the positive value of popular music on grounds drawn from Adorno. This approach might sound unpromising, given Adorno's denunciation of popular music——which extends to popular music post-rock-'n'-roll although he formulated it in the 1930s, I will argue. Nonetheless, I turn to Adorno for several reasons.

First, we can obtain important insights from his analysis of the structure of popular songs. His account of these songs' 'standardised' forms, while not fully accurate as he states it, does illuminate how popular songs are constructed——*repetitively*. He also claims that individual parts are slotted in and out of songs' standardised forms interchangeably: for instance, a song might have a I–V–vi–IV chord sequence, or one might re-order the chords into I–vi–IV–V, or amend them——say, to I–ii–IV–V. In principle any substitutions or combinations are possible, and which elements are swapped in or out affects neither the whole form nor the rest of the elements. Adorno's interchangeability claim is overstated, but does illuminate how the elements of which popular songs are built are brought together——*contingently*. In conceiving of repetition as standardisation and contingency as interchangeability Adorno characterises popular music in unduly pejorative terms. Even so, it is worth extracting the insights that his pejorative formulations contain, since they advance our understanding of popular music as a cultural form.

© The Author(s) 2016   69
A. Stone, *The Value of Popular Music*,
DOI 10.1007/978-3-319-46544-9_3

Second, I turn to Adorno because he makes a powerful critique of the overall trajectory of Western societies, a critique within which his position on music takes shape. This trajectory, Adorno shows us, is towards the ever-increasing domination of material things by conceptual understanding, as we classify, categorise, and analyse these things in order to manipulate and control them, particularly in modern mathematical science and its applications in technology and industry. Based on this critique, Adorno values those 'autonomous' works of art and music that he takes to be organised by the necessary development of their individual materials——for example motives——into all their implications and thereby into whole works. He values these works on the grounds that their form arises *from* their materials, not *vice versa*. As such these works embody an alternative to the modern tendency for form to dominate and regulate materials (in the guise of concepts and intellectual judgements, which Adorno understands to be unifying forms of a sort). However, Adorno sees popular music as tying in with that tendency for forms and concepts to dominate materials, by embodying a dominance of standardised form over interchangeable materials.

I'll argue, however, that when we instead recognise (thanks to Adorno himself) that popular songs are structured by repetitions of contingently assembled materials, we see that these songs are actually so structured that their materials generate their forms. Adorno's work then gives us grounds to value popular music positively, as embodying an alternative to the concept's dominance. Furthermore, when he valorises 'autonomous' music, Adorno connects its value to its presentation of the truth that the domination of concept over materiality is harmful. Here too Adorno's work indirectly provides us with grounds to appraise popular music positively, as presenting the truth that it is good for materials and material bodies to realise themselves.

In sum, I turn to Adorno because, despite himself and contrary to his own intentions, his work offers us both insight into the typical structure of popular music and a basis on which to value popular music positively. Before we can extract these insights from Adorno, though, we need some initial understanding of his thought. In Sect. 2, I reconstruct his views on modernity, music aesthetics, and——in Sect. 3——popular music. In Sect. 4, I explain how his criticisms of the latter apply to post-rock-'n'-roll music, but that what he describes as standardised form is better understood as repetitive construction.[1] In Sect. 5, I argue that what Adorno sees as part-interchangeability is better understood in terms of elements being assembled contingently. In Sect. 6, I illustrate these points about repetition and contingency by discussing Gary Numan's 'Are "Friends" Electric?' My broader line of argument continues in Chap. 4, in which I explain how repetition and contingency give popular songs a kind of structure in which form emerges from materials, and explore how this kind of structure has aesthetic value.

2   Adorno on Modernity, Music, and Aesthetics

In *Dialectic of Enlightenment*, Adorno objects to the domination that we exert over the unique individuality of material beings, living and non-living, using conceptual understanding and reason. This domination has advanced over the course of world history to the point where now 'the enlightened earth radiates disaster triumphant' (Adorno and Horkheimer 1997: 3). This is partly a matter of the intellectual dominance over material things which is achieved in modern mathematical science. Science has also enabled us to exercise increased practical control over material things. That control counts as domination to the extent that these things' own impulses are suppressed——for example, when hens undergo life-long confinement in cages or barns. By extension, non-living things too are dominated when their inherent tendencies are curtailed or thwarted. In craft production an artisan works with the material grain of, say, the wood that he is carving into a chair. But in mass production materials are chopped up into featureless components at the start of the process, or may even be synthetically produced; these materials offer no grain and are simply slotted into their places in whatever end-products are being made.

Human beings too increasingly get slotted into roles in large corporations and institutions, roles specified from above by bureaucratic reason. The unique materiality of human individuals is pushed into line or suppressed. Thus, the domination that we exert over non-human nature recoils back upon our own nature. Having been suppressed, though, our impulses become liable to burst back out in periodic orgies of brute irrationality——emblematically, for Adorno, in National Socialism, when ruthless industrialisation went hand-in-hand with irrational hatred of Jews and other non-Aryans. For Adorno, it is the *extension* of human domination over nature which leads to these recurrent outbursts of suppressed natural forces and impulses. His proposed solution is that we should acknowledge that our rational and conceptual faculties emerge from and depend on our bodies and somatic impulses. It is our bodily impulses that motivate us to categorise and reason in the first place——to control nature so as to advance our own well-being (by building houses, channelling electricity, etc.). Yet our impulses, and the materiality of our bodies and nature, always outstrip the rational powers that they generate. No concepts or theories, however sophisticated, can ever completely comprehend the full richness and sheer existential presence of the material realm. Object always outreaches subject (Adorno 1982; and see Cook 2014).

It is against this backdrop that Adorno values those works of art and music that he takes to display *autonomy* (Zuidervaart 1990). For Adorno, an art-work is autonomous inasmuch as it is organised by a law (*nomos*) that it gives to itself (*auto*) from within. Thus, an autonomous work embodies a course of *necessary*——law-governed——development out of itself. This might sound strange; after all, art-works are not conscious agents or legislators. But the idea is that an autonomously formed art-work begins with some materials specific to a certain medium, with the work becoming formed as the artist draws out the 'law' immanent in those materials. The resulting art-work may be said to display autonomy at least as much as the artist does, for he only creates autonomously insofar as he draws out the implications of his materials, which therefore count as the primary generative agency. In art-works of this type, the materials thus generate the form of the whole.

For Adorno, such works have value because they present an alternative to the domination of concepts over materials that obtains elsewhere. Adorno connects concepts and reason with form, on the grounds that concepts and judgements are functions through which the intellect imposes unifying form on what it experiences. (This view of concepts and judgements comes from Kant. For example, in categorising certain perceptible materials under the concept 'puppy' I unify them; in judging 'the puppy is cute' I unite the subject, *puppy*, with a predicate, *cuteness*.) In evolving their forms from their material parts, then, autonomously organised art-works pit themselves against not only the dominance of form over matter but also, simultaneously, the domination of concept over matter.

Now, the idea of autonomous art- and musical works may seem suspect on various grounds. For one thing, Adorno castigates much classical music, as well as popular and non-Western music, for falling short of this standard.[2] Nonetheless, the idea of autonomy does have *some* application to *some* classical music, as we can see by tracing how this idea applies in Beethoven's Symphony No. 5 in C Minor.[3] It is worth elucidating the idea of autonomy as it applies in this instance because it is in contrast to this model of the autonomous musical work that we can understand popular songs to be assembled repetitively and contingently. Adorno's ideal of autonomy can thus serve a useful heuristic purpose, and we can use it that way without endorsing it as the true standard for the assessment of all music.

The famous motive that opens the first movement of Beethoven's fifth symphony connotes 'fate knocking on the door', if we trust Anton Schindler, Beethoven's biographer (Schindler 1996: 147). Heavily emphasised, the three-note motive on G drops to the minor third (E♭) and is held with a dramatic pause (see Fig. 3.1; taken from Beethoven 2001: 3). To follow out the 'law' immanent in this motive or musical idea is to work out the wealth of musical relations that it implicitly contains, by subjecting this idea to successive variations through which those relations are elaborated and made explicit. Above all, the relations at issue are those in which the notes composing the motive stand to the other notes in the key——C minor in this case——and the further relations of these interrelated tones to parallel sets of interrelated tones in other keys more or less close to C minor.

The opening motive also has a distinctive rhythm——short-short-short-long following a pause. This rhythm draws out the relations in which the motive's component notes stand to the tonic C——they are constantly directed towards it as their goal, and until that point is reached the music is not at rest. This is drawn out by the three short notes on G——the dominant——making a repeated and powerful movement downwards to E♭——the minor third   thus gravitating towards the tonic but then stopping, embodied in the tension of the dramatic pause. Arguably, then, tonal relations generate the motive's rhythm, and also imply the possibility of various other rhythmic patterns that the work will explore. These tonal and rhythmic implications begin to be drawn out straight away as the motive, after one repetition, is presented in successive overlapping variations by different instruments, at different pitches, in first descending then ascending forms.

Fig. 3.1 Beethoven, Symphony No. 5 in C Minor, First Movement, measures 1–2, first violins

Fig. 3.2   Beethoven, Symphony No. 5 in C Minor, First Movement, measures 57–66, first violins

We can see more of how the (first) motive's implications become unfolded by considering how the second motive is generated out of it. The second motive first appears at measure 63 (Fig. 3.2). It is then presented under successive variations while the first motive gradually reasserts itself, making explicit the fact that the first motive is more fundamental (as the source from which the second motive arose).

This second motive contrasts markedly with the first one. The second sounds lighter: rather than descending ominously it has a gentle, lilting, symmetrical contour; and thus it is also smoother rhythmically, offering repose and equilibrium rather than the dramatic tension of the first motive. Even so, the second motive emerges out of the first in several ways. The second motive is built in the new key of E♭ major to which the music has modulated; E♭ major is the relative major of the original tonic of C minor, and the new tonic, E♭, is the point to which the first motive descended.[4] The modulation occurred through a pivot B♭ chord (in measure 58, partially visible in Fig. 3.2)——VII in C minor but, crucially, also the dominant chord in the new key of E♭ major.[5] The shift of tonal centre is immediately reinforced by a horn fanfare descending from B♭ to E♭, i.e. from dominant to tonic in the new key. The second motive then begins by reprising (but in ascending form) the movement from B♭ to E♭, acknowledging the modulation that has occurred. Moreover, these opening, rising notes of the second motive reverse the direction in which the first motive descended *from* the dominant; this clarifies that the new motive is the counterpart and reversal of the first. Thus just in being opposed to the first motive, the second motive still arises in the exploration of the relations implied in that first motive, including contrastive relations. This goes too for the second motive's smoother rhythm and contour, which arise to elaborate further its contrast with the first motive.

This illustrates how the whole work develops necessarily out of the initial motive according to a 'logic' through which the 'fully adequate ... listener understands what he perceives as necessary, although the necessity is never ... causal' but rather logical (Adorno 1976: 5).[6] To begin with, the opening motive is explored in its initial shape under many permutations in pitch, direction, and instrumental timbre. Then, further development requires the work to move beyond its limits so far——those set by the key of C minor. So the music modulates (to the relative major, one of the keys most closely related to C minor).[7] Now the first thing to explore is the difference that the modulation has made. A new motive is needed to embody this difference by contrasting with the first motive. Ultimately, every element of the sonata unfolds along similar lines.

We might contest this notion of logically necessary development and doubt that any musical work ever really develops with the logical necessity that Adorno claims. He admits that not *all* art music does so, but he values mostly highly those works that best conform to this model (unlike, say, Stravinsky's work, which Adorno condemns for employing past styles and forms and folk-musical elements that are not evolved necessarily).[8] Still, the necessity with which musical parts evolve out of one another depends on a set of rules and norms——a musical grammar——existing as a system of conventions tacitly embodied in musical practice at a given time. For instance, in Beethoven's fifth symphony the modulation from C minor to E♭ major obeys the norm that the relative major key is one of those to which minor-key music most often modulates. Thus, background rules tacitly regulate the art-work's formation. This might make us question whether such an art-work is 'autonomous' after all, for the 'laws' that it follows seem after all to exist externally and not internally to that work.

Has Adorno simply assumed that the rules of the Austro-German tradition are logical necessities? No; he agrees that these rules qualify the work's autonomy.[9] Even the most autonomous musical work only exhibits autonomy partially, because the self-determination of its parts depends upon their conformity to musical-grammatical constraints. But there is still a significant degree of autonomy here, first, because the constraints enable the parts to generate one another productively and assume an overall form. Second, the constraints are not simply external: they are built internally into the materials of which the work is made. For instance, Beethoven's short-short-short-*long* motive is built in C minor so that the connections of this key with others, and the internal relations among the steps of the C minor scale, are embodied in the motive at the outset, rather than bearing upon it from the exterior. In these respects, in acting from musical-grammatical laws, the materials are still developing from within themselves.

We still might think that this whole picture overstates the work's logical structure and neglects the contingent choices that artists make about how to take forward the developments of the musical materials they have chosen to use. For Adorno, though, the artist's role is to use his or her creativity to identify and choose the most logical option out of those available. That said, the developmental agenda also makes it important for artists to innovate: the logical development of the materials may require a bold departure from the conventions of the time. A particular musical event might strike us as being the outcome of a free decision——as perhaps with Beethoven's horn fanfare that announces the recession of the first motive and the arrival of the second. But there are logical reasons for this fanfare. It makes explicit the modulation and change of motives. It descends from B♭ to E♭, i.e. from dominant to tonic in the new key, while being set to the short-short-short-long rhythm, thus straddling the outgoing first motive and the incoming second motive. Beethoven's creativity led him to find an element that 'fits' logically at this point, contributing to the music's inexorable development. Or so Adorno would have it.

We may think, nonetheless, that Adorno has over-extended the model of autonomous development: it may apply to some classical music to a degree, but shouldn't be used to judge all music. I agree. However, for my purposes a merit of Adorno's model is to highlight by contrast the typical structure of popular music, which is not organised by necessary development. Another merit of Adorno's model, for my purposes, arises from his account of how autonomous musical works have positive value, so let me now explain this.

Adorno's account of the value of autonomous musical works is multi-faceted, but one strand concerns the connection between art and truth. Adorno's belief in this connection sets him apart from formalists such as Eduard Hanslick. For Hanslick, a piece of music is elaborated out of an opening motive according to laws that result in necessary developments, following one another with inexorable logic. Adorno was certainly influenced by Hanslick (see Paddison 2004: esp. 207–10). Yet Adorno turns formalism against itself, for he holds that *just when* musical works are formed autonomously——and are free from social and political interference——they remind us of important truths.

The first of these truths is that human individuals too can exercise autonomy, albeit of a different kind to art-works——conscious self-determination. Intra-artistic autonomy thus has direct social and ethical import. To the extent that autonomy structures the art-work, that work reminds us that autonomy is needed for a flourishing human life, implicitly criticising societies that stifle human autonomy. When art-works do this they have 'truth-content' (*Wahrheitsgehalt*)——not just 'truth'. The expression 'truth-content' highlights the fact that, unlike formalists who emphasise form *against* content, or anti-formalists who emphasise 'truth', Adorno thinks that it is *by* exhibiting autonomy that art-works acquire true content.[10]

However, for Adorno, it is not the autonomous work as a whole that parallels the autonomous human individual, but the *motive* as it freely unfolds (Witkin 1998: 14). In turn the whole work is analogous to a *society* that permits all agents the autonomy to organise their relationships into a whole. The autonomous work thus exemplifies an ideal type of social whole that permits freedom to all its members. Adorno's view, then, is that certain musical works are structurally isomorphic with certain forms of social organisation, in terms of their respective part-whole relations. Say that the parts——i.e. motives——freely generate and shape their relations with one another through their own qualities, as in Beethoven's Fifth. Then the ensemble of relations among the parts has the same kind of structure as a society that allows individuals to relate freely rather than forcing them into prescribed roles.

This brings us to the second truth-content of autonomous musical works: that particular material individuals also need to develop freely in order to flourish. Indeed, human individuals are material——we are embodied beings each with unique sets of impulses and needs——so that part of our need for autonomy is for our material impulses and powers to find expression and fulfilment. But the point extends to non-human living beings, which suffer when they are constricted and dominated, prevented from living according to their own inclinations; and by further extension to non-living material things, which are dominated when their inherent tendencies or characters are thwarted or overridden (Stone 2006: 233–34). Autonomous works show us that material particulars in music——motives——can develop autonomously and that it is good for them to do so; and by implication that the same goes for these several kinds of material individuals. Such works suggest that a good society would allow material particulars to develop freely.

Adorno takes it, then, that autonomous musical works present us with truths. He is influenced by Hegel, who holds that art-works can embody metaphysical truths about the absolute idea. For Hegel, art-works that do this do not state the truth explicitly but *show* it in how their sensory materials are configured. Likewise, for Adorno, the sonata movement of Beethoven's Fifth symphony does not overtly state the social-political theses 'social relations should permit individuals freely to organise their interactions' or 'society should allow material particulars to develop freely'. Instead the work *shows* this truth in how its parts and whole are configured. This is another reason for Adorno's using the expression 'truth-content' (shown) rather than 'truth' (stated).

Adorno does not simply follow Hegel on art and truth, however. Hegel holds that we ultimately need to access the truth in representations and concepts and not only presentations: thus, art must become superseded by religion and philosophy, which deal respectively in representations and concepts, whereas art deals in presentations (Hegel 1970: vol. 1, 10–11). Hegel does not mean this historically, as he has sometimes been misunderstood to do——i.e. to hold that art in the modern era is destined to wither away. Art persists and remains important, he recognises. But as moderns, heirs of the Enlightenment, we cannot remain satisfied with an exclusively aesthetic mode of access to truth. Art is thus ultimately subordinated to philosophy, in Hegel's scheme. Adorno rejects this, in the following way.

Whereas for Hegel (i) art-works concern *the idea*, for Adorno, autonomous art- and musical works concerns *material individuals*. The truth that these works express does not pertain to the organising rational structure that subtends the particulars, as in Hegel. Rather, the truth that these works present is the reverse: that material particulars take priority over the organising whole. (ii) For Hegel, presentation must be superseded by concepts because only concepts can fully grasp the idea, which is a rational organising structure. In contrast, for Adorno, the truth about materiality can only be fully accessed *when presented*, given what this truth is about, i.e. the priority of material particulars to concepts and understanding, where the former always outstrip the latter. To be sure, we can state that this priority obtains, as I am doing now. But this statement will inevitably fall short of the fact that materiality has priority to and exceeds the understanding. We cannot attain a fully adequate conceptual understanding of the understanding's limits. The truth that materiality exceeds understanding is best conveyed, then, by being presented——embodied in a work's part-whole relations. In this way, Adorno extricates Hegel's connection of art and truth from his thesis that art must be superseded by philosophy. The resulting position on art and truth can do much to illuminate popular music's value, once we allow that it is not only autonomous art- and musical works that can present the truth that materiality is the precondition and source of conceptual understanding. But to get to that point, we next need to turn to Adorno's account of popular music.

3 ADORNO'S CRITIQUE OF POPULAR MUSIC

In most of this section I reconstruct Adorno's complaints against popular music with little critical assessment, turning to a few criticisms at the end. This reconstruction may seem unnecessary, but because of Adorno's opacity, I want to clarify what I take to be his central claims, especially since I will subsequently argue that his real insights need to be extracted from the distortions present within his analyses.

Adorno put forward these analyses in his 1930s essays on popular music, especially 'The Fetish-Character of Music and the Regression of Listening' of 1938, 'On Popular Music' of 1941, and 'On Jazz' of 1936. His target was mainstream hit songs, the swing jazz of the big bands, light classical music, and film music. Their fundamental characteristic, for Adorno, is standardisation. Popular songs conform to a narrow range of standard forms: 'mother songs, home songs, nonsense or "novelty" songs, … laments for a lost girl' (2002: 437–8). Adorno also has in mind the fact that the Tin Pan Alley songs then played on mainstream network radio generally had 32-bar AABA form. That is, they had an 8-measure (A-) verse repeated twice, one contrasting 8-measure (B-) verse, possibly in a different key related to that of the A-section, then a final repeated 8-measure (A-) verse, all possibly followed by further repetitions. John Covach sums up that 'what holds [this repertory] together musically is a fairly uniform approach to musical form' (2006: 25). Hence Adorno's claim that popular songs are written by taking a standard form and slotting individual details or elements into it.

Adorno explains this standardisation in terms of the music industry's drive to maximise profit, which for him shapes and explains all the central features of its products (songs)——features that are there to help these products to sell, be the unit of sale sheet music or recordings. Songs must not be unfamiliar but be fundamentally the same as other pre-existing, already popular songs, so that listeners will not be deterred or puzzled but will like the new song if they liked its predecessors. But if it's patently obvious that one song is more-or-less identical to another then the new song still won't sell, since people will see no need to buy it (1976: 31). Eversameness must be disguised by 'pseudo-individuating' details that make each song seem unique but are merely superficial. Which musical features count as pseudo-individuating details? Middleton lists five features noted by Adorno: blue notes, dirty timbres, syncopations, improvised breaks, and harmonic embellishments (Middleton 1990: 50). Richard Leppert adds the 'hook' (2002: 339), i.e. 'a musical or lyrical phrase that stands out and is easily remembered' (Burns 1987: 1). Riffs are another candidate; and Adorno mentions 'haphazard dissonances' used as mere splotches of colour (1976: 25). In the end, for Adorno, many properties can pseudo-individualise if they add distinctiveness to a song that nevertheless has a standard form.

For Adorno, subjection to songs that have this structure——standard form plus pseudo-individual veneer——damages people's listening capacities. They aren't prompted to engage in 'structural hearing'——grasping individual musical elements under progressively enlarged wholes as the music unfolds (Adorno 1976: 5; and see Subotnik 1995: ch. 3). Instead, listeners only react to pseudo-individual details, as atoms, without attending to the whole course of their evolution——for there is no such course to attend to. We react at a purely sensory level, with like or dislike depending on whether the details please us. Our listening degenerates to the level of immediate somatic reaction——a primitive, childlike, thoughtless level (Adorno 2002: 291).

Adorno reasons that popular songs are models of heteronomy. First, they are entirely shaped by economic dictates that act on them from outside. Second, these songs' internal structure exhibits heteronomy, for their forms dominate their parts. The form is fixed, the parts fitted into this pre-set form like sardines into a can. Slotted in and out of this rigid scaffold, the parts are rendered powerless to generate form by relating productively to one another. Far from offering a glimpse of autonomy in a heteronomous world, then, popular songs participate in and confirm the heteronomy that is everywhere in abundance.

For Adorno, there is a structural isomorphism between how part-whole relations are configured in popular songs and in capitalist modernity. In the songs, the form dominates the parts, preventing the parts from developing and reducing them to mere atoms. In capitalist society, large-scale institutions dominate individuals, reducing them to cogs in the machine; and conceptual understanding dominates materiality. But the isomorphism is not such that popular songs alert listeners to the wrongs of modernity. Popular songs do not offer knowledge about this social formation but merely replicate it and help to hold it in place.

Countless criticisms have been made of Adorno's account of popular music as of his broader portrayal of the culture industry. There are two criticisms that I want to endorse:

(1) Adorno misconceives the music industry as pursuing economic goals only, not artistic ones as well. He accepts that musicians may have artistic motivations, but insists that economic constraints are imposed on them by the industry. This neglects the complicated negotiations between artistic and economic goals that obtain at every level of the production process (Frith 1981; Negus 1996: 36). The industry pursues profit; but that pursuit does not single-handedly dictate what the resulting music is like. The dynamics and power relations involved are more complicated and multi-faceted than that (Shuker 2001: ch. 2).

(2) Surely listeners aren't 'passive dupes', but actively impose their own interpretations on cultural products, rather than those products forcing listeners into thoughtlessness. If Adorno replies that the music industry *makes* people into dupes, the counter-reply is that the industry *cannot* have that effect, given that human responses to cultural products are necessarily active and interpretive. However, Adorno thinks that our capacity for active interpretation is short-circuited because popular music arouses our bodies and not our minds. But if our bodily responses already involve thoughtful, sense-making activity (as I'll argue in Chap. 5), then we retain ample scope for active engagement.

Problem (1) pertains to Adorno's economic explanation for the top-down structure of popular music, (2) to his account of the harmful psychological effects of listening to popular music. How much truth, then, is there in the remaining strand of his account of popular music——his analysis of its top-down form-matter structure? Here I shall argue that there *are* important insights to be extracted from that analysis, despite its undue negativity.

A prior question, though, is how far that analysis really applies to popular music since rock-'n'-roll.[11] We might think: not far. The pre-war music that Adorno criticised comprised mainstream radio, Tin Pan Alley, dance bands, and Hollywood film music. This was a mainstream from which country and rhythm-and-blues were excluded, so that these traditions, rock-'n'-roll's two key tributaries, fell outside his critique. Yet Adorno never retracted or modified his views when those traditions broke into the mainstream through rock-'n'-roll. On the contrary, he restated those views in his 1962 *Introduction to the Sociology of Music*. He must therefore have thought that his critique continued to apply to post-war popular music. After all, mainstream pre-war pop is a third stream that fed into rock-'n'-roll, while the swing jazz that Adorno criticised incorporated elements from early jazz——improvised passages, rhythmic syncopation——and, in turn, early jazz was one stream out of which rhythm-and-blues developed. Arguably, though, the jazz elements incorporated by the big dance bands underwent 'superficial adaptation ... into an aesthetic framework defined by the European tradition'——an aesthetic of sophistication, aspiration, and polish aimed at a middle-class white audience (Garofalo 2010: 6; see also Small 1999: 277–79).[12] In contrast, and for all the problems surrounding the white appropriation of black styles, rock-'n'-roll was fundamentally based on rhythm-and-blues, itself the result of generations of hybridisation between the musical practices of various racial and ethnic groups, with those of black Americans at the centre.[13] So was Adorno wrong to think that his analysis continued to apply? On the contrary, I will argue, his analysis of form-matter structure *does* have application to, and shed light on, post-rock-'n'-roll popular music.

4   From Standardisation to Repetition

For Adorno, standardisation is one core feature of popular music, along with part-interchangeability. Although every genre from the sonnet to the fugue to the western has its standard features at a given time, in an autonomous work received forms are modified to permit the evolution of the specific materials at hand. But popular-musical forms, unlike those of a sonata or sonnet, 'use the types as empty cans into which the material is pressed without interacting with the forms' (Adorno 1991: 26). Popular songs are thus '"custom-built", a predicate usually reserved for automobiles' (25). What light does this allusive comparison with Fordist mass manufacture shed, beyond the fact that many professional song-writers have worked on virtual assembly lines, as in the Brill Building, or that Berry Gordy envisioned Motown on the model of the Detroit motor industry?

Bernard Gendron (1986) argues that Adorno's comparison between Fordist manufacture and popular song construction goes deeper, referring to the 1950s rhythm-and-blues genre of doo-wop. This genre of vocal group singing, a hybrid of mainstream pop and rhythm-and-blues, originated in black groups singing on street corners. Often overlooked today, doo-wop was central in the rise of rock-'n'-roll——Gribin and Schiff have called doo-wop the 'forgotten third of rock-'n'-roll' alongside rockabilly and blues (1992: 8). Following Gendron's lead, although not the details of his analysis, let's consider the 1954 song 'Sh-boom (Life could be a dream)' by The Chords. The first doo-wop song to succeed in the mainstream pop as well as rhythm-and-blues charts in the USA, 'Sh-boom' is one of several contenders for the title of first rock-'n'-roll hit.[14]

As is typical of doo-wop, in 'Sh-boom' the lead vocalist sings the main melody and lyrics while the others provide backing vocals, intoning nonsense or fragmented words or syllables——'ooh', 'sh-boom', 'dream'. This practice of using nonsense syllables gave doo-wop its name. 'Sh-boom' follows 32-bar AABA form——again typically of doo-wop, and an inheritance from Tin Pan Alley. Each verse of 'Sh-boom' thus lasts eight measures, although the song is more than doubled in length by the introduction, outro, and interpolated passages of vocal improvisation—— extensive improvisation again being typical of doo-wop. The instrumentation consists of guitar, bass, and drums (but doo-wop instrumentation could be minimal: sometimes a vocalist hummed the bass-line, or handclaps replaced drums). The chords are presented on the guitar, with the A-verses running through a I–vi–ii–V^7 sequence in the key of F major. This is a common variation on the I–vi–IV–V progression that is present in around 70 % of all doo-wop songs according to Runowicz (2010: 51)—— heard, for instance, in Frankie Lymon and the Teenagers' 'Why Do Fools Fall in Love?'.[15] In 'Sh-boom' the chords succeed one another very rapidly, with each chord maintained for just half a measure so that the whole chord cycle recurs four times in each A-section (the first iteration is shown in Fig. 3.3).

Fig. 3.3 The Chords, 'Sh-boom', vocal melody and electric guitar, timing ca. 00:06–00:11

Seemingly, then, there is a standard form for doo-wop songs, analogous to the standard design of a given model of car in Fordism. (1) A lead vocalist provides the melody and main lyrics, with other vocalists harmonising with nonsense syllables. (2) The chords and ensemble singing are foregrounded in the texture, with other instruments playing accompanying roles (the bass is quite muted in 'Sh-boom', for instance). (3) 32-bar AABA form is standard, with the B-section presenting a different but related chord sequence to that of the A-section (in 'Sh-boom' the B-section modulates to D major and cycles through V–I–IV–iv–♭VII). (4) As in popular music overall, the usual metre is 4/4 with emphasis on the backbeat. (5) I–vi–ii–V or I–vi–IV–V chord sequences are typical (of doo-wop), with each verse revolving through the sequence a given number of times.

This standard format permitted great variety among doo-wop songs. For one thing, different doo-wop songs convey very different meanings. The chords and vocals in 'Sh-boom' move along swiftly which, together with the major key, conveys optimism——'Life could be a dream'. Yet the chords succeed one another so rapidly that they suggest a level of nervous anxiety——a subtext 'life *could* be a dream … but only if we act quickly'. This is reinforced by the uneven rhythm of the chords and vocals.[16] Thus the rhythmic qualities of the chords and vocals give the song unique connotations, despite its I–vi–ii–V pattern being shared by many other doo-wop songs.

Yet perhaps these are mere pseudo-individual details that leave the underlying standardisation untouched. That underlying standardisation turns above all on (feature 3) the AABA form together with (5) the fixed chord sequences that that form regulates. The key may be E♭ major as in 'Sincerely' by the Moonglows or G major in 'Earth Angel' by the Penguins, but the template remains identical. And those songs may use I–vi–IV–V instead of I–vi–ii–V, but this difference is superficial: ii has been replaced by its close relative IV. Thus ultimately all doo-wop songs follow the same harmonic template. Variations may exist in rhythm, tempo, or vocal improvisations, but these are only superficial additions that do not follow *from* the chord sequence. That is, unlike how variations function in music that exhibits necessary development, in 'Sh-boom' and other doo-wop songs the variations do not elaborate on the harmonic content or unfold its implications, but merely overlay it. The variations do not lead to any transformation in the harmonic content over time, but rather disguise the fact that this content is repeated unchanged for most of the song and is identical to the content of very many other doo-wop songs.

That said, doo-wop is unusual among popular music genres in having a standard form. Other genres have standard features——as we've seen, punk rock songs typically have simple forms and fast tempos, feature heavily distorted guitar, have bass-lines consisting of the root notes of each chord, and frequently use eighth-note rhythms. But it is relatively unusual for a popular music genre to involve adherence to a single form, such as AABA, or to one or two set chord sequences. Usually songs of a single genre can use all sorts of forms——verse/chorus, AABA, simple verse, or compounds——and all manner of chord sequences. That doo-wop is standardised, then, doesn't suffice to convict popular music *overall* of standardisation.

On the other hand, doo-wop's I–vi–IV–V and I–vi–ii–V sequences descend from the I–IV–V sequence that is basic to 12-bar blues and in turn rock-'n'-roll. And whereas particular chord sequences are not usually specific to genres, some chord sequences are very common across songs of many genres: I–V–vi–IV for instance. More broadly still, the *pattern* of repeating a short sequence of chords a given number of times to make up the harmonic layer of a song or song section is standard across popular music since rock-'n'-roll. 'Sh-boom' exemplifies this pattern, with the guitar repeating the four-chord sequence four times in each verse.

For comparison, take Chuck Berry's 1958 hit 'Sweet Little Sixteen'. In its original recorded form on *One Dozen Berrys*, the song is in C♯ major and most of the verses run through the same chord sequence, V–I–V–I–IV–I–V–I——a version of a 16-bar blues progression (which in turn is an expansion of 12-bar blues). In 'Sweet Little Sixteen' each chord in the sequence is maintained for two measures, presented on the guitar in 'boogie' style, i.e. comprising the root note combined alternately with the fifth and sixth scale degrees, set to an eighth-note rhythm (on the boogie, see Everett 2008: 61; Moore 2012a: 22, 25–26). As this applies to, e.g., the last two lines of the first verse, see Fig. 3.4. The pattern displayed here——for each chord in turn to be presented over a particular duration to a given rhythm——has become paradigmatic for popular music since rock-'n'-roll.

Given a chord sequence in which each component chord is presented over a given duration (perhaps one measure, half a measure, or two measures, etc.), phrases of melody can then be aligned temporally with these chords. A common approach is for each phrase of melody to coincide with a revolution through the chord sequence. Take the verse of U2's 'Sunday Bloody Sunday', on *War* (the first and last lines are shown in Fig. 3.5).

Fig. 3.4 Chuck Berry, 'Sweet Little Sixteen', vocal melody and electric guitar, timing ca. 00:13–00:24

Each revolution through the three-chord cycle (B♭ minor–D♭ major–G♭ major, i.e. i–III–VI in the key of B♭ minor) takes two measures, as does each phrase of melody. Four phrases of melody coincide with four repetitions of the chord cycle, yielding an eight-measure verse. In this case, though, there is significant variation in how the chords are presented. The first time around, in measures 22–23, the chords are played as open perfect fifths in a highly aggressive, percussive, and militaristic style, evoking the war and violence against which the song rails. Subsequently——as in, e.g., measures 28–29——the chords are instead arpeggiated, the III chord is inverted, and the VI chord is formed unconventionally (containing the root, a perfect fifth, and a sixth). Consequently the chords now sound softer and have an arching, hopeful shape, embodying optimism that war and violence may be left behind——as per Bono's lyric that he 'won't heed the battle call'.[17]

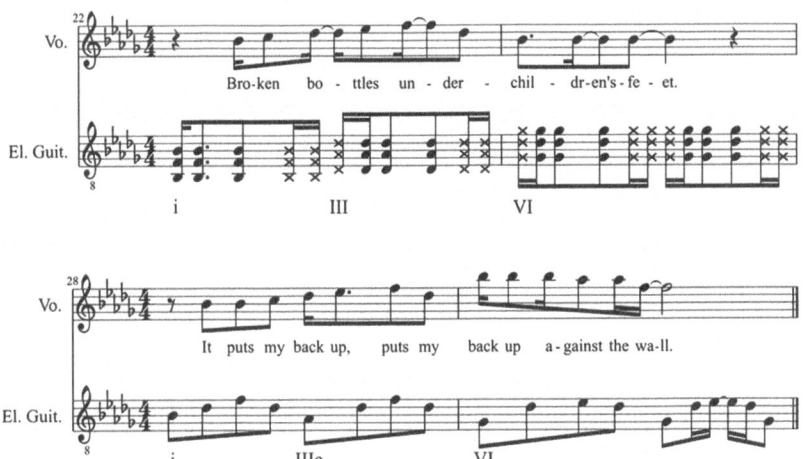

Fig. 3.5 U2, 'Sunday Bloody Sunday', vocal melody and electric guitar, timing ca. 00:51–55 and 01:05–01:10

Going back to 'Sh-boom', though, melody and chords are not aligned so straightforwardly, as most of the two-measure phrases of melody begin in time with the third chord, ii, in the I–vi–ii–V⁷ sequence (see Fig. 3.3), so that the melody and chords are aligned by overlapping in regular ways, rather than coinciding. Even within this pattern of overlapping alignment 'Sh-boom' contains further variations too: the very short opening phrase——'Life could be a dream'——is one instance; while the fourth phrase is elongated so that the verse melody lasts the full length of the chord cycle. Often melody and chords are aligned under permutations of this sort. Going back to 'Sweet Little Sixteen' (Fig. 3.4), each four-measure phrase of melody is aligned with the chords not under a IV–IV–I–I then V–V–I–I pattern, as we might expect, but instead under a I–IV–IV–I then I–V–V–I pattern. Thus, the first verse ends not after two measures of I but in the middle of two such measures, the second of which begins the second verse. Thus, as in 'Sh-boom', the chords and lines of melody are aligned by overlapping rather than coinciding. So there are many variations on the common approach to constructing songs by aligning the cycles of their parts.

It is also standard for chord cycles and phrases of melody to be aligned temporally with repetitions of the bass-line and of the rhythmic pattern presented by the percussion. A common pattern is for both the bass-line and the percussion pattern to last for one measure and to be repeated four times for each four-measure melody line and each cycle through the chords. Take the 1996 single 'Firestarter' by the British electronic dance band The Prodigy (on *The Fat of the Land*) (Fig. 3.6). Each pair of short vocal phrases——half-chanted, half-shouted, rather than sung, a style indebted to both rap and punk——is followed by a two-measure pause. This vocal style is rooted in call-and-response, in which the vocalist falls silent after each phrase to let the other instrumentation or backing singers respond. The resulting four-measure vocal part is aligned with two

Fig. 3.6 The Prodigy, 'Firestarter', vocals, electric guitar, bass synthesiser, and drums, timing ca. 00:51–00:58

repetitions of the two-measure programmed breakbeat, four repetitions of a pulsing two-note pattern on the synthetic bass, and four repetitions of a leaping octave pattern on what sounds like electric guitar.[18]

Post-rock-'n'-roll music normally has four layers: vocals, harmonic filler, bass, and percussion. 'Firestarter' retains those layers despite having no chords as such. Its harmonic filler instead comes from the high-pitched octaves, which create an incessant, whining sound; from a synthesised skidding sound, on A, that is heard in the non-vocal measures; and from the siren-like, hideously distorted riff that opens and is interspersed through the song (based on a sample from 'S.O.S.' on *Last Splash* by the Breeders). These elements generate a potent cocktail of energy and malevolence.

I began this section by asking how far Adorno's critique of standardisation in popular music applies to post-rock-'n'-roll music. I considered how doo-wop has a standard form. Doo-wop is unusual in using AABA and fixed chord sequences, though. But I've identified broader ways in which post-rock-'n'-roll music more broadly does have a standard form. That standard form is to contain small-scale elements at each of the four usual layers of texture——vocal, harmonic content, bass, percussion—— which are repeated a given number of times per song or song section or subsection, with these repetitions aligned temporally with one another. It transpires, then, that Adorno's notion of standardised form applies to post-rock-'n'-roll music insofar as popular songs are typically organised *repetitively*. It is repetition that is, or should have been, the ultimate target of Adorno's complaints.

Let me set out the nature of this repetitive mode of construction. Looking back at 'Firestarter' (Fig. 3.6), it clearly illustrates how layers of sound are assembled by repetition. Indeed the verse is more repetitive than, say, that of 'Sh-boom', since in 'Firestarter' the octave leaps and bass pulses recur unchanged in each measure. The chorus contains slightly more variation, but the overall construction remains highly repetitive. Specifically, songs are constructed as the elements or musemes present at each layer are repeated (Middleton calls this 'musematic' repetition) and as these repetitions are aligned with one another temporally to make up sections of song. In turn, whole songs are made up from repetitions of these sections ('discursive' repetition; Middleton 1990: 269). There are various templates for how to distribute and combine sections: verse/chorus, AABA, simple verse, and so on (Covach 2005). But sections may also be combined and repeated under particular schemata that do not fit any of these standard templates (as with 'Are "Friends" Electric?'; see Sect. 6).

Popular music, then, does not have a standard 'form' in the sense of using a single standard template to regulate the discursive repetitions of sections of material, be it AABA, verse/chorus, or otherwise. But it *is* standard for popular songs to be structured by discursive repetitions, i.e. repetitions or near-repetitions of entire blocks or sections of musical material. This is part of popular music's broader mode of repetitive construction, which also includes musematic repetition. Repetitive construction, as popular music's standard form or principle of organisation, thus includes the various 'forms'——verse/chorus, and so on——that we might think of if asked to identify a song's formal design.

At its highest level of generality, as repetitive construction, the formal design of a popular song is as in Table 3.1.

However, we might think that repetitive construction is too broad and open-ended a principle to qualify as a form at all. And far from being standardised, this 'form'——repetitive construction——seems so broad and open-ended as to accommodate infinitely many musical materials. What might nonetheless make repetitive construction problematic emerges in contrast to the developmental paradigm. In popular music elements are *repeated* under variations, whereas in the developmental paradigm motives are repeated under *variations*. That is, in the latter case, out of these variations new musical elements (motives) are generated and the original elements are transformed. And these variations arise as logical developments from the preceding motives. The musical elements, as motives, are thus mutually generating. In contrast, in popular music the variations are not generative: either they don't unfold the implications of other elements

Table 3.1 A model of repetitive construction

Song form (e.g. AABA, verse/chorus)
|
Section form (e.g. A-section + B-section; verse + chorus)
|
Length: in measures——each measure marked out by
1. (one/two/a half, etc.) repetition(s) of the percussion rhythm, which is aligned with
2. (one/two/a half, etc.) repetition(s) of the bass-line,
3. (one/a half/a quarter, etc., of a) phrase of melody,
4. and (one/two/a half-, etc.) repetition(s) of the chord sequence,
|
(e.g. I–vi–ii–V),
|
each chord repeated a given number of times per measure to a particular rhythm

or, if they do, that unfolding does not lead to further developments in turn. Instead, the preceding elements are simply repeated. 'Sh-boom', say, does not begin by presenting the I–vi–ii–V sequence and then evolve successive modifications that elaborate its implicit harmonic relations. Repetitive construction precludes that kind of dynamic evolution of parts out of one another.[19]

It is the fact that the parts of the song are not generated out of one another that is a potential problem. For it appears that the parts are reduced to atomic components: at each layer of sound, a simple pattern or sequence is repeated unchanged (or nearly so). This can be seen particularly within the harmonic layer, where each chord seems to be treated as an atomic unit and the set of atoms stacked together to comprise a sequence. As Allan Moore puts it: 'Most popular musicians conceive of harmonies as *a priori* vertical concatenations of pitches (i.e. as chords) rather than as the resultants of horizontal movements of separate contrapuntal voices' (2012a: 71). And 'the harmonic practices of rock encourage the identification of harmonies as discrete entities not subject to voice-leading processes. … Inner parts rarely have a linear role, merely existing to fill out the chord' (Moore 1995: 190). To paraphrase and simplify: in the contrary, common-practice approach to harmony, each note within each chord follows in rule-governed ways from a given note in the preceding chord and leads on to another note in the next chord. Thus, harmony has not only a vertical organisation but also a horizontal one, composed of a developing set of interweaving melodic lines. In contrast, in popular music, chords tend to be treated as self-contained blocks of musical material.

It seems, then, that form may dominate materials in this repetitive paradigm in that the materials are reduced to atoms, made powerless to enter into productive relations with one another. To that extent repetitive construction *can* potentially be considered to be a kind of form that is imposed on materials like a Procrustean bed. But whether repetitive construction really is this kind of top-down grid depends on whether the parts (or materials or elements) of a repetitively constructed song really are slotted into its form like inert atoms. Adorno alleges so: 'The schemata are so separated from the concrete course of the music that everything can be replaced by something else' (1976: 29). On his view more or less any parts can be slotted into any popular song, because the parts do not produce one another or the entire form, but are inert.[20] But is this true? How far *does* part-interchangeability obtain in popular music?

5   FROM INTERCHANGEABILITY TO CONTINGENCY

What might part-interchangeability involve? If a song's doo-wop form stipulates, say, three repetitions of the A-section and eight repetitions of a I–vi–ii–V chord sequence per A-section, then *those* components, at least, cannot be exchanged for any others because the form mandates their inclusion. However, one could take out the bass-line of 'Sh-boom' and replace it with another one, or interpolate a new vocal melody based around different phrases. And while the I–vi–ii–V sequence stipulates which (relative) chords are to be used, one can build that sequence in any key one likes and accompany the sequence with whichever other elements one pleases——or replace that sequence with another standard doo-wop variation.

This picture of interchangeability might seem overstated. Surely, one might think, there *are* constraints on what chord substitutions are possible: ii and IV can substitute for one another because they share two tones, for instance. Bass, vocal, and other melodic lines must surely make principal use of notes that are either contained in the concurrent chords or that harmonise with them (albeit at different pitches and octaves), with non-harmony notes being used in more circumscribed and temporary ways. And shouldn't melodies move in directions that cohere with a song's key? For example, a phrase of melody might well end on the fifth scale degree——as if posing a question to help propel the song onwards——or end on the tonic to impart closure at the end of a verse. 'Sweet Little Sixteen' does this: the first three phrases of melody in the first verse end on the dominant (G♯), while the fourth and final phrase 'answers' these questions with a conclusive C♯ (the tonic). Arguably, then, norms of musical grammar limit how far interchangeability obtains.

Or do they? How far *does* popular music abide by norms of musical grammar? This is debated. For one thing, popular music uses not only major and minor keys but also minor-pentatonic scales that descend from the blues (see Everett 2009: 167), as well as modes——the Dorian, Mixolydian, and so on (see, e.g., Pedler 2003: ch. 8). We find this mixture reflected, for example, in the harmonic ambiguity of 'Sweet Little Sixteen' (Fig. 3.4). In Berry's vocal melody there is a strong presence of B-natural, not B♯ as we would expect if the song were in the key of C♯ major (as I represented it to be). Yet when the piano fleshes out the chords it plays B♯, as per the conventional major scale. We might therefore take the melody to be in the Mixolydian mode. Or we might take the melody to be in C♯ major but with the seventh scale degree flattened (to B natural), reflecting a blues influence. Similar mixtures are found elsewhere: the B-section of The Beatles' 'A Day in the Life' (on *Sgt. Pepper*), which is in E major, features chords I, V, and ♭VII. Thus VII is flattened (to D major); but when V (B major) is played it includes D♯. Thus popular songs draw on a mixture of tonal systems and are often harmonic hybrids.

Norms inherited from common-practice music form part of this mixture. These norms are reflected, for instance, when Lady Gaga's 'Paparazzi' modulates from C minor in the verse to the closely related key of A♭ major in the chorus: in common-practice music, modulation is normally to a key closely related to the original one. Yet sometimes popular music departs from common-practice norms——as in 'Paparazzi' again, since the modulation takes place abruptly without cementing the new key by reaching it through a V–I cadence. David Temperley (2007) identifies another popular-musical departure from common-practice norms: especially in the verse, melodies sometimes use notes that are not contained in the concurrent chords not merely in passing but as stable elements. Indeed, it is not that unusual for melodies and chord sequences to be built on different scales, most often with minor-pentatonic melodies over major-scale chords (Everett 2009: 168).[21] In sum, melody in popular music 'is not as strongly constrained in rock as it is in common-practice music' (Temperley and De Clercq 2013: 203).

Ken Stephenson identifies a host of further departures from common-practice norms. One departure is in where resolutions from dominant to tonic typically occur: not at the end of one section but the start of the next one (Stephenson 2002: ch. 3). Take 'Sh-boom' (Fig. 3.3): I follows V at the *beginning*, not the end, of each chord cycle, hence at the beginning and not the end of each verse. Moreover, Stephenson suggests——as a pragmatic rule-of-thumb——that because of this tendency the best way to ascertain a song's key is to identify the first tone or chord sounded in the song, which may be presumed to be the tonic unless subsequent developments suggest otherwise (35).

Another departure is in which chords normally follow one another. At first Stephenson suggests that rock practice reverses the normal order in which chords and their component notes succeed one another in common-practice music (102-3) but as he later says, in fact

rock's harmonic practice is not easily or usefully summarized in a chart of typical successions. ... First, the common practice is not entirely rejected

... ; many songs follow the earlier standard in some passages and the new standard in other passages ... and many other songs make no distinction ... [So] any chart displaying all the successions frequently used would be complicated beyond usefulness. (108)

In essence, chords in popular music can follow one another in a plurality of ways. This is bound up with the way that chords are approached vertically rather than horizontally, as noted above. As Alf Björnberg puts it, 'harmony in rock music is less strictly governed by the rules of traditional functional harmony than is the case in [classical or jazz] music' (Björnberg 1984: 1; those rules being those that specify which notes and chords lead into which others). Indeed, noting that chords IV, V, and bVII (in that order of frequency) appear equally often both before and after I, De Clercq and Temperley conclude that 'rock is not governed by rules of "progression" at all; rather, there is simply an overall hierarchy of preference for certain harmonies over others, regardless of context ... [as per] Moore's ... comments about the "non-functional" nature of rock harmony' (2011: 61). They note slight preferences for, *inter alia*, using V before rather than after I, but broadly their findings confirm Stephenson's.

Thus, melodies may or may not use non-chord tones as stable elements. And melodies and chords may be built on major, minor, or pentatonic scales, or in modes, or may mix these systems. Phrases of melody and chord cycles may end on tonic, dominant, or elsewhere: for instance, the chord cycle in 'Sunday Bloody Sunday' concludes each time on VI; and in the song's verse melody, the antecedent phrases end on the tonic and the consequent ones end on the dominant, a reversal of the more standard pattern. Rather than asking questions that are then answered, U2's reversal instead contrasts grim existing reality ('answer') to hopeful possibility ('question').

This is not to say that popular music is chaotic; rather, it is pluralistic and eclectic. It draws on various tonal systems with their attendant norms, especially those of common-practice music, folk (which often uses modes), and blues (already a hybrid system). In amalgamating these systems popular music has forged additional norms of its own. One such norm is for the tonic to sound at the very start of a song. Another is for the seventh scale degree to be flattened when it occurs as the root of a chord. Another statistical norm is for the IV chord——not V——to be the most commonly used chord after I (Stephenson 2002: 113; Temperley and de Clercq 2011).

So it is not the case that *any* element of a popular song can be replaced by *any* other. Nonetheless, because of popular music's pluralism, there *is* a good deal of latitude in which elements can potentially be replaced by others. In any given case, there will generally be a range of possible substitutions that all make equal sense. In contrast, in some classical music the options at a given point in a piece of music's development are fairly tightly circumscribed by the musical-grammatical conventions of the time.[22] One might still think that classical and popular musicians alike make creative decisions about which elements to combine; the latter just have more options. But the difference is more fundamental than that, in that popular music is not guided by an ideal of necessary development as some classical music is. Having used a i–III–VI chord sequence in the verse of 'Sunday Bloody Sunday', U2 did not then evolve melody, bass-line, and percussion rhythm out of these chords with a view to deriving their implications. Because of the lack of a developmental imperative, popular musicians have more scope at any point to include a whole range of materials. The relaxation of rules in popular music is thus bound up with its repetitive mode of construction.

Why, then, do musicians choose in specific instances to combine particular elements and not others? One factor is the meanings that a set of combined elements conveys, including emotional meanings. Consider the 1985 song 'Primitive Painters' by the British indie band Felt (on *Ignite the Seven Cannons*). Lasting for six minutes, the song is unusually long in popular music terms, and for most of it a single chord sequence is presented again and again by both the Hammond organ and guitar (the only exceptions are in parts of the long introduction and in the bridge). The sequence is I–IVb–♭VII–I in E major. In keeping with the song's leisurely pace, each chord is repeated for two measures, strummed on the guitar to a gentle rhythm while also being sustained on the organ. The latter transitions between the chords so smoothly that the changes are barely perceptible. The song's rhythmic qualities are further submerged by the song's very lush texture——saturated in reverb and with additional layers of guitar in the background playing melodic fragments throughout.

In 'Primitive Painters', then, a single chord sequence is reiterated for nearly the whole song. Why *this* sequence? The explanation seems to be its emotional quality: the chords rise then return 'home'. Repeating this many times over creates an uplifting and elevating quality, as of someone who keeps reaching for and attaining higher and higher levels of fulfilment. Felt's singer Lawrence confirms that emotion plays this role when he advises would-be song-writer Will Hodgkinson to 'mark the end of each verse with a definite major chord, or perhaps a suspended chord … to suggest a sense of mystery' (Hodgkinson 2007: 119). On this song-writing model different chords should be tried out and retained or discarded depending on whether they express a desired emotional quality: happiness, mystery, and so on. Song-writers might not be aware beforehand that they want to convey a given emotional quality, but after some trial-and-error certain musical elements may still be selected because they feel 'right'――this because they express a given emotion, which the song-writer may recognise, after the fact, that she wished to express.

Likewise, the particular way that the chords in 'Primitive Painters' are formed conveys certain affective qualities. The IVb chord within the I–IVb–$\flat$VII–I sequence is an unusual form of the A major triad. Usually A major on guitar contains the notes A_2, E_3, A_3, $C\sharp_4$, and E_4. But in 'Primitive Painters' the A major chord is inverted, with C# in lowest position; this being the guitar, this inversion carries with it a modification of all the components of the chord, so that it contains $C\sharp_3$, A_3, E_4, and A_4. This changes the chord's affective quality. We can ascertain this using Tagg's substitution method (1982), whereby we confirm what connotations are embodied in a particular museme by substituting another museme for it and noting the difference. If we play 'Primitive Painters' on guitar with an A major chord in root position, it has a sturdy, powerful quality, sounding more straightforwardly 'rock-'n'-roll'. Compared to this solidly grounded root position chord, the first inversion used by Felt sounds very different: because the chord is pitched higher and contains one fewer note than the root position chord, the effect is a thinner sound that seems fragile, vulnerable, and less stable. This is because there is one fewer occurrence of the tonic note (E) and because the sixth scale degree ($C\sharp$), which connotes 'pleasurable longing', is foregrounded (Cooke 1959: 90). This version of the chord thus conveys more aspiration upwards but also less power to get there, more vulnerability to failure. This impacts on the whole chord sequence, for when it moves on to $\flat$VII and then to the tonic, the resolution feels more triumphant for having come past a moment of doubt.

Musical elements may be chosen for other kinds of meaning besides their emotional qualities. For example, the fragility of the inverted chord in 'Primitive Painters' helps to locate the song within the genre of 1980s British indie, which cultivated a naive, unworldly character, reflecting its goal of avoiding the commercial mainstream (Borthwick and Moy 2004: 189–190). In keeping with this unworldliness, Felt's IVb chord lacks the classic rock-'n'-roll connotations of aggressive, muscular confidence. A whole range of meanings is thus conveyed through this chord, not only emotional ones. Elements may also be used on other grounds——for example for their rhythmic profiles, which may add to a song's rhythmic tension or dynamism and thus its danceability. Or an element with a particular timbre may be chosen for its unique sound, not quite like any sound heard before. Still, meaning in its broadest sense is consistently *among* these factors, for timbral and rhythmic qualities convey meanings too, such as meanings of being innovative or embracing dance.

Are elements interchangeable, then? Yes and no. Felt *could* have used the usual A major chord; no preceding course of musical development specified that a specific chord-formation *must* follow at this point. In this sense, the fragile formation of A major could have been replaced by other formations, or other chords altogether had Felt wanted to convey something different. There *are* some constraints on what materials Felt could have used, though. Had 'Primitive Painters' used the same relative chord sequence but been built in, say, the Lydian mode on E——the fourth degree of which is A♯——then Felt would have had to use an A♯ and not an A chord at this point. Still, the song in fact being in E major, various chords can still be used at this point in the sequence, all making more-or-less equal logical sense but communicating distinct meanings.

However, this reveals a sense in which, after all, the chord-formation used is *not* interchangeable with any number of others. Had Felt had used the standard A major chord, the whole song's affective quality and genre location (as indie music) would have changed. On the one hand, then, the inverted A major chord is potentially replaceable because its presence and formation are not necessitated by any logical unfolding. On the other hand, whereas that chord under this formation *need* not have been used——it is there contingently, not necessarily——once it *is* used it shapes the whole song's meanings. Substituting (say) a standard A major chord might not significantly affect the other parts of 'Primitive Painters' in the sense that they could all remain in place. Yet in another sense that substitution *would* significantly affect all those other parts by changing the meanings that they carry as a whole.

The elements of popular songs, then, are better understood not as being interchangeable but rather as being combined contingently. In any one case, many other elements and combinations were possible, given that popular songs are constructed not developmentally but repetitively, and would have made roughly equal logical sense, given popular music's eclecticism. If interchangeability obtained, though, this would be problematic because it would involve top-down domination of materials by form——their reduction to impotent, inert atoms. But that problem does not arise with contingency, as I'll explore in what follows.

To sum up so far, an element that is present in a song contingently rather than necessarily could have been absent from that song, or could have been taken out, and need not have been combined with given others into this song. Yet certain elements are in fact included because of the connotations they bring to songs——emotional, genre-related, rhythm-related, or timbre-related connotations, or connotations of other kinds. Different elements might have been used instead, given the lack of a programme of developing all elements out of one another logically. But in that case the whole song would have had different connotations. Thus, every particular element used makes an integral contribution to the song's meaning. In this sense, it is not true that replacing any one element with any other would not significantly affect the whole song; rather, while logically possible, any such change would significantly alter the song's meaning. It follows that contingently assembled materials are not dominated by form but rather *generate* form. To begin to explore this, let's look at a song that is assembled in this contingent way: 'Are "Friends" Electric?' by Gary Numan and Tubeway Army.

6   'ARE "FRIENDS" ELECTRIC?'

The synth-rock song 'Are "Friends" Electric?', a UK number one hit in 1979, is on a concept album, *Replicas*, in which Numan evoked a dystopian future, drawing on science fiction stories that he had written. Machines are gradually and secretly eliminating human beings in the interests of social order, and machines with cloned human skin make up the police force and work as 'friends' providing various services, from sex to playing chess.

Numan describes how he composed the song:
   I wrote it on an old pub piano [that] ... was out of tune. It was initially two different songs, which is why it's over five minutes long. I had a verse from one, the chorus from the other, and was struggling to mix them together [and] ... one day I played them one after another and suddenly they sounded right. So the song is a combination ... The main melody is one note sharp, since I hit a wrong note on the old piano, and it sounded better. (Simpson 2014; see also Numan 1997: 63)

Keyboard Synthesizer

Fig. 3.7 Tubeway Army, 'Are "Friends" Electric?', A-section riff (synthesiser)

Numan's remarks highlight two ways that the song's component elements are present in it contingently. The first pertains to the notes of the keyboard melody. By chance Numan came to include a wrong note into the melody, thus apparently approaching that melody not as a progressive unfolding but as composed of atomic elements——single notes that can be swapped in and out until a result is achieved that 'sounds better'.[23]

Numan also describes the 'harsh note' as the 'crucial note' that 'transformed [the song] from almost a ballad into something quite unusual' (Maconie 2013: 211). The note——B♭——which doesn't belong in the C major scale in which the song is built, appears frequently in the short passage of keyboard melody that is central to the A-sections of the song (Fig. 3.7). Unexpected and out of place, the repeated B♭ suggests something amiss and uncomfortable, especially in its third occurrence when the melody jumps up very sharply by over two octaves——a sudden, disconcerting leap. That said, given the frequency of the flattened seventh in popular music, we might simply hear the melody as being in C Mixolydian and not C major (as Theo Cateforis does; 2011: 172), or not hear the B♭ as out of place even if we take the key to be C major. However, the Bs that occur elsewhere in 'Are "Friends" Electric?' (in the C- and D-section melodies, for instance——see Table 3.2) are B-natural, and overall the song sticks to the notes of the C major scale with almost leaden simplicity. Against this background, the false note stands out.

The passage in Fig. 3.7 subdivides into four segments, each lasting half a measure. The first three segments comprise arpeggiated open fifth intervals (that is, each contains just a root note——respectively C and B♭—— and the note a fifth above it——respectively G and F, both doubled at the octave). Thus the passage begins I–♭VII–I, before seeming to begin another ♭VII——but instead another interval breaks in, again falling from B♭, but by not a fifth but an augmented fourth, to the final E. Now, the augmented fourth is one form of the tritone——an interval of or equal to three whole tones——which, in medieval times, was seen as the 'devil in music' to be avoided, but which later composers such as Wagner used to signify evil and danger, trading on the interval's acquired connotations.[24] In the Numan case, the tritone's presence conveys that something wrong,

Table 3.2 Tubeway Army, 'Are "Friends" Electric?', song structure

Timing	Section	Description	Repetitions
00:00–00:31	A	The keyboard melody as in Fig. 3.7 comes straight in, accompanied by (non-synthetic) bass guitar and drums. Vocals enter after four measures	6
00:31–00:41	B	This time the central repeated element is another short passage of keyboard melody which incorporates a rising line:	2

The accompaniment is flanged, distorted guitar, plus bass guitar and drums as before. There are no vocals

00:41–01:12	A	As before, save for accompanying keyboard portamento in the first four measures	6
01:12–01:22	B	As before	2
01:22–01:53	C	This time the repeated element is a series of keyboard arpeggios:	6

These are arpeggiated seventh chords formed unconventionally, containing no thirds; their ambiguous quality contributes to the song's discomfiting feel
Spoken vocals enter after the first four measures

01:53–02:11	D	Another sequence of keyboard arpeggios takes centre-stage, again seventh chords without thirds in the first three cases and a bare seventh (no third or fifth) in the final case:	3.5

There are no vocals, but a distorted guitar presents a repeated melodic fragment that descends from dominant to tonic

02:11–02:41	A	As before, but again with opening portamento	6
02:41–02:51	B	As before	2
02:51–03:22	A	As before	6
03:22–03:32	B	As before	2
03:32–03:37	A	Just one repetition: no portamento, no vocal	1
03:37–03:48	B	As before	2
03:48–04:18	C	As before	6
04:18–04:36	D	As before	3.5
04:36–05:25	A	As before, but with opening portamento and no vocals	8 to fade

bad, and ominous is impending. The dissonance is not resolved but left in place at the end, after which the passage is repeated numerous times. The sense that something wrong is coming recurs with each repetition, making the 'false' note crucial to the song's dark, threatening atmosphere——its evocation of the dystopian future in which machines are eliminating human beings.

The wrong note, then, contributes decisively to the song's evocative connotations. The note is present contingently: had Numan's piano not been out of tune he would not have included it. In that case the song's evocative connotations would be different. Perhaps it would sound more straightforwardly melancholy. Still, because Numan *did* include this wrong note the song came to evoke a disturbing, unpleasant future, whereas a B natural, while entirely possible, would not have imparted the same evocative quality.

The second locus of contingency indicated by Numan relates to the song's sectional organisation. The song consists of four rotating sections (Table 3.2). Seemingly, then, the sections——each comprised of a given number of repetitions of its component materials——are self-contained blocks of material that can be assembled in varying combinations. Or a section might be taken out of the assemblage and inserted into a different song elsewhere, as per Numan's comment that the sections initially belonged in two different compositions (I take him to mean the A- and B-sections on the one hand and the C- and D-sections on the other).

However, the particular combination of sections that *is* used contributes to the song's meaning. By popular music standards 'Are "Friends" Electric?' is unusually long and its form is unconventional, for it is not clear which sections count as verses or choruses. The song simply rotates its four sections, each based on a different synthesiser melody and with each melody equally prominent. The vocals do not resolve the uncertainty, for the B- and D-sections are instrumental, in the C-section the vocals are spoken and not sung, and in the A-section Numan's singing is cold and unemotional. Moreover, the vocals are always secondary to the synthesiser. This unconventional form, with no obvious centre, adds to the sense that we are in an unfamiliar and uncomfortable place——a dystopian future——without secure landmarks.

In this light, let me qualify my earlier comments about the flat note's role in the A-melody. The flat note *tends* to make the A-melody sound ominous, but ultimately the note generates that quality through its co-operation with other parts of the song. If the wrong note occurred in a verse that was followed by a brighter chorus, then the sense of danger and foreboding would be reduced. The song's form would convey that the danger has been averted. Instead, the disconcerting form of 'Are "Friends" Electric?' co-operates with the A-melody so that they come to convey uneasiness together. Both tend to do so in their own right, but those tendencies could be taken in alternative directions given a different combination of elements.

The uneasy connotations of both form and A-melody are reinforced rather than mitigated by the texture. The Mini-Moog synthesiser predominates and its electronic sounds carry their late-1970s connotation of being artificial, inhuman, and cold. 'Real' bass guitar and drums are also used, not their synthetic counterparts. As a result, the texture embodies a dominance of synthetic over natural instruments, paralleling the dominance of machines over humans in Numan's imagined future society. So the texture again confirms the bleak message, the more so because it is so sparse: the instrumentation is minimal and much of the track contains no vocals. In consequence the synthesised melodies stand out and sound stark and austere, which they do, too, because of their simplicity, composed as they are of short passages repeated many times over.[25]

In sum, the sections of 'Are "Friends" Electric?' are present contingently: they needn't have been combined, initially belonging to different compositions as they did; Numan did not evolve them as integral parts of a whole. Yet, having been combined, the sections give the song its specific form without a conventional verse/chorus division, which feeds into the song's evocative significance. A different set of sections, combined according to a conventional verse/chorus template, would have yielded a song with different evocative connotations, perhaps more wholesome or optimistic ones. And that would have impacted on the evocative significance of the song's other components: its melodies, instrumentation and texture, and so on.

What has begun to emerge is that popular songs' elements contribute to songs' overall meanings not as atoms or monads but through their *co-operation* and interaction with one another. These elements function as members of a whole. For example, the flat note in the A-melody of 'Are "Friends" Electric?' contributes to the song's ominous quality not in isolation, but through the way that the other materials with which this melody is combined reinforce its potential ominous quality. Moreover, as we've begun to see, it is not only the harmonic and formal-organisational aspects of popular music that interact in this way to give rise to specific meanings. Texture, timbre, and vocal style are among the other factors that also contribute to a song's meaning. I shall discuss this in Chap. 4.

Once combined into a particular set, then, each element contributes connotations that qualify those of all the others.[26] As a result each element comes to have, in its specific context in a given song, a particular significance that it would not have to the same degree, and perhaps not at all, outside of this whole. Thus, a popular song typically has a structure in which the parts qualify one another, at the level of their meanings, to constitute a whole to which each makes an integral contribution. This is so although the parts are present within that whole contingently rather than flowing inexorably out of one another.

On this basis, I shall argue in Chap. 4 that popular songs as meaningful wholes emerge out of a process of coalescence and reciprocal interaction of the specific materials that are their parts. In this sense, the whole forms of popular songs arise out of and depend on their material constituents, and not *vice versa*.[27] Before I go on to explain this, let me recapitulate the steps that have led us to this point.

7   Concluding Summary

Adorno criticises popular songs for having standardised forms and interchangeable parts. It has transpired that popular songs do have a standardised form in that they are constructed repetitively. But arguably this mode of construction dominates songs' individual materials by reducing them to inert, interchangeable atoms. However, I then argued that interchangeability is better understood as contingency, in two senses.

First, post-rock-'n'-roll music is a hybrid cultural form that draws on a plurality of musical traditions and sets of harmonic norms, adding further norms of its own. All musical traditions hybridise with others, but this is particularly so of popular music, which only emerged at all from the bringing together of diverse traditions——blues, jazz, gospel, country, folk, mainstream pop——which were relatively self-contained in the prewar period. Consequently, although there are some constraints on which musical elements can be combined within popular songs, there is considerable flexibility in what combinations are possible. Generally a song can be constructed from various possible sets of elements. It is therefore a matter of contingency which elements are used in a given case. Second, these elements are present contingently in the sense that popular music does not adhere to an ideal of developmental necessity. There is no expectation that a song's components should be evolved out of one another to realise an unfolding series of implications. The result, again, is to leave musicians with considerable freedom as to which elements they can combine on a given occasion.

To be sure, all musicians make creative decisions. But in a significant part of the art-music tradition the options are more heavily constrained by grammatical norms and the ideal regulating creative practice is to produce a work with a maximal degree of developmental necessity. In the absence of that ideal in popular music, musicians follow a different principle in deciding which elements to use and combine. That principle is to seek coalescence at the level of *meaning*, which is of various kinds: evocative, emotional, rhythm-related, and so on.

However, my point is not that considerations of meaning rather than form and structure are important in popular music. Nor is it that considerations of expression rather than form predominate, as Baugh argues (1993). Rather, my argument will be that popular music typically has a particular *kind* of organisation in which the whole song, as a meaningful unit, emerges out of the specific set of individual materials that coalesce together into it. The point concerns not form *versus* meaning (or *versus* content or *versus* expression), but *how matter-form relations* are configured in popular music, such that materials generate form——'form' in the sense of the song as a whole that is unified in terms of its meaning.

Thus, once we think in terms of contingency and not interchangeability it turns out that contingently assembled materials are not dominated by form but generate it. But although Adorno was wrong in conceiving contingency and repetition negatively——as part-interchangeability and standardisation——his conception of those latter has still enabled us to grasp the nature of contingency and repetition in popular music. Moreover, Adorno's view that concepts depend on materiality, and should be acknowledged to do so, will underpin my argument in Chap. 4 that the typical bottom-up, matter-form structure of popular music gives it positive aesthetic value. This value arises because bottom-up, matter-form structure embodies and presents the truth that conceptual understanding depends on material forces and processes. So I will argue in the next chapter.

Notes

1. I am informed by scholarship on Adorno's views on materialism (Cook 2014), the culture industry (e.g. Cook 1996; Witkin 2003), music (e.g. DeNora 2003; Paddison 1993; Subotnik 1991, 1995; Witkin 1998), and aesthetics (e.g. Huhn and Zuidervaart 1997).

2. Also, Adorno is insufficiently critical of the hierarchies of composer over performer, conductor over orchestra, and of this whole musical apparatus——the canon of great musical works, the concert hall and its rituals, the elite performing ensemble——over the listeners (see Small 1998). Adorno is not unaware of these power relations (see, e.g., Adorno 1976: ch. 7), but he does not sufficiently integrate this awareness into his account of this musical tradition.

3. I choose Beethoven deliberately. Although Adorno criticises the Beethoven mystique, he still esteems Beethoven for making 'the most completely organized ... music that can be achieved ... one hears the first bar of a Beethoven symphonic movement only at the very moment when one hears the last bar' (Adorno 2002: 255).

4. A key's relative major or minor has all the same notes as that key but a different tonal centre——for example, A minor is C major's relative minor, as neither key contains any flats or sharps; E♭ major and C minor are relatives because both contain the same three flats.

5. Modulation commonly occurs via a pivot chord: a chord common to both origin and destination keys and that leads smoothly into a transition from dominant to tonic (V–I) in the destination key, cementing the new tonal centre.

6. The '"play" of music [in Beethoven] is a play with logical forms as such: those of statement, identity, similarity, contradiction, the whole and the parts; and the concreteness of music is essentially the force with which these forms imprint themselves on the material, the musical sounds' (Adorno 1998: 11).

7. Music can modulate to more distant keys, but it usually modulates to keys closely related to the origin key: those of the dominant and subdominant, and the relative minors or majors of the tonic, dominant, and subdominant. Thus, C minor's most closely related keys are G minor, F minor, E♭ major, B♭ major, and A♭ major.

8. Adorno's hostility to Stravinsky is bound up with his view that in the twentieth century the art music tradition should move beyond tonality, as with early Schoenberg (Adorno 2006). Dissonances should no longer be resolved away but let endure as stable entities in their own right, highlighted at prominent points in the musical development. This does not mark any fundamental change in Adorno's music aesthetics, for dissonances are still to be reached

and explored in the elaboration of the implications of motives. To explore those implications fully, artists need to break from the convention of resolving or minimising dissonances——in order more fully to unfold the implications of their materials.

9. The 'motive power driving the detail beyond itself is always tonality's need for what comes next in order to fulfil itself. ... [So] tonality and its representation circumscribe the social content of Beethoven's music. It is the music's bourgeois bedrock. The whole work can only come into being through tonality' (Adorno 1998: 49; and see Witkin 1998: 45).

10. 'Insofar as a social function can be predicated of art-works, it is their functionlessness' (Adorno 1997: 8, 227). Some might think that art-works' autonomy is too different from individual human autonomy to bear on the latter, but the two kinds of autonomy need not match exactly: there need only be enough similarity for the former to suggest implications regarding the latter.

11. Some are highly critical of Adorno (e.g. Baugh 1990) while others give him more credence. That said, it's widely agreed that Adorno's critique of 'jazz' really applies to big band swing, which he misleadingly equated with jazz *per se*. On the broader application of his criticisms to mainstream pre-war pop, see, e.g., Middleton (1990: 45–48). Regarding rock-'n'-roll, some think it so different from Tin Pan Alley pop that Adorno's critique doesn't carry over (e.g. Paddison 1982). Others such as Gendron argue that the critique does carry over.

12. See also Bradley (1992: 57). Wald appraises the big bands more favourably, exploring racial hybridisation in their make-up and sound (2009).

13. On the hybridity of rhythm-and-blues, see Small, who nonetheless rightly insists on the overall centrality of black American styles (1999).

14. See Shaw (1978: xxii). Notoriously, 'Sh-boom' had less success than the cover version that the white, major-label Crew Cuts released hot on its heels. The Crew Cuts version was number one for weeks; the Chords' original only reached number nine.

15. '[B]ecause ii and IV share two tones——scale degrees 4 and 6—— these two chords are functionally interchangeable although they have different colors' (Everett 2008: 219; see also Moore 2012a: 279).

16. The rhythm of the guitar and vocals in 'Sh-boom' is 'dotted'. Contrasting the feel of the dotted rhythm to that of the 'shuffle' rhythm, Everett says that the former is 'Much less informal and lazy sounding'; as in 'Sh-boom', it conveys urgency and a lack of ease (Everett 2009: 306–7).

17. On 'Sunday Bloody Sunday' see also Fast (2000: esp. 38).

18. Due to the complexity of this beat, I have not treated hi-hat and snare as one 'voice' as I've done elsewhere. The breakbeat presupposes a 16-note subdivision of the beat which, however, no single part of the percussion ensemble explicitly sounds out.

19. Andrew Chester contrasts 'classical' and 'rock' paradigms (1970a, b), calling the former 'extensional'. Here complex pieces of music are built up from simple atoms (motives) added together——*but* this addition occurs through a developmental logic, I'd add. 'Rock', Chester says, is 'intensional': built by endlessly varied inflections, nuances, and expressive adaptations of rhythm, timbre, and melody——but where these are variations on elements that are *repeated*, I'd add.

20. Likewise Scruton: 'There is all the difference between harmony formed through voice-leading, and harmony formed by hitting strings without regard to the relations among the inner parts' (1997: 502).

21. Temperley and de Clercq, studying 194 songs from a *Rolling Stone* list of 500 'greatest songs', found that 50 songs combined major chords and minor melodies (2013: 201–3).

22. I say 'some' classical music partly because much twentieth-century art music goes down the path described by Robert Grossberg: 'There are, for all practical purposes, no musical limits on what can or cannot be [music]. ... There is nothing that cannot become a ... song or, perhaps more accurately, there is no sound that cannot become a part of [music]. Its musical limits are defined [only] ... by the alliances constructed between selected sounds, images, practices and fans' (1992: 131). Grossberg says this of rock, but his claim applies better to art music.

23. Contrast Scruton's view that an essential feature of melody is 'the internal constraint exerted by every note on every other. A melody is a sequence in which no note can be altered without changing the character of the whole. ... The "wrong note" phenomenon causes

us to cry out in protest at every departure from the known musical line. ... A non-melodic sequence of tones can be chopped and changed without eliciting protests' (2011: 29).

24. Tritones feature heavily in the blues; this was a factor in the description of the blues as 'the devil's music' and perhaps the legend of Robert Johnson's pact with the devil. See Rudinow (2010: esp. ch. 4).

25. Numan wrested synthesisers away from their progressive rock usage in the service of virtuosity and formal complexity (see Numan 1997: 48). Hence the stark simplicity of the keyboard melodies in 'Are "Friends" Electric?'. Essentially, Numan transferred the punk rejection of virtuosity from guitar to synthesiser (Cateforis 2011: ch. 6). In this way Numan also turned the Mini-Moog's limited capacities into an asset.

26. In Chap. 6, I'll argue that elements have their connotations through networks of relations, relations that are not entirely conventional——the relations include real resemblances between musical elements and extra-musical phenomena, for example.

27. When I asked whether form dominates matter at the start of this section, though, I equated 'form' with repetitive construction, whereas in arguing that 'form' emerges from materials I use 'form' to refer to the song as a meaningful whole. One might then object that even if meaningful wholes emerge from materials, repetitive construction does not, and in that latter sense the materials might still be dominated by the form. My answer in Chap. 4 will be that repetitive construction is a flexible principle that permits materials to be brought together and qualify one another to form wholes. Thus repetition *enables* materials to exercise a kind of generative 'agency'. I will clarify this in part by examining and distinguishing the several senses of 'form' in play so far.

CHAPTER 4

Matter and Form in Popular Music

1   INTRODUCTION

In this chapter I explore how the elements of popular songs are brought together contingently but, in being combined, qualify one another to produce integral wholes. I shall argue that ultimately this process happens at the level of meaning: elements have certain potential connotations and in being put together these connotations can either transform or reinforce one another——or fail to speak to one another, in which case work is needed to adapt them so that they cohere.[1] Typically as a result, a song emerges as a meaningful whole to which all its elements make integral contributions. In this sense, material elements give rise to form in popular music.

In Sect. 2, I examine this process with regard to the Beatles' 'A Day in the Life'. Arguably the pinnacle of rock-as-art, the song nonetheless illuminates how popular songs are typically constructed out of materials that coalesce or are adjusted to do so. In Sect. 3 , guided by that examination, I explain what factors are involved in materials coalescing or failing to coalesce. In Sect. 4, I argue that in principle all the musical parameters at work in popular songs contribute to this process——not only their harmonic content but also their timbres, rhythms, textures, dynamics, and more. Of course, individual elements or musemes often function under several parameters at once. For example, the A-melody in 'Are "Friends" Electric?' has not only harmonic content but also a rhythm and a specific timbre, that of the Mini-Moog synthesiser. There has been a tradition

© The Author(s) 2016   109
A. Stone, *The Value of Popular Music*,
DOI 10.1007/978-3-319-46544-9_4

in musical thought and practice, however, to regard form and harmonic and metric structure as fundamental while other parameters such as timbre and texture are deemed secondary, with rhythm sometimes included in the latter camp. But numerous popular music theorists have argued that this distinction between fundamental and superficial parameters fits popular music badly, and I agree. In Sect. 5, I substantiate further my argument that no parameters have a priori privilege in popular music by considering how timbre, texture, melody, and harmony interact within R.E.M.'s 'Losing My Religion'. In Sect. 6, I clarify how my view of popular songs as meaningful wholes relates to the ontology of recorded popular music. In Sect. 7, I argue that the constitution of whole songs out of material parts gives popular songs aesthetic value in that their materials generate their form, not vice versa.

2   'A DAY IN THE LIFE'

'Are "Friends" Electric?' was put together from separate sections of musical material, initially located in two different songs. This invites comparison with another song that originated in two separate sections of material: 'A Day in the Life' on the Beatles' *Sgt. Pepper*. The A-sections were contributed by John Lennon, prompted by various events reported in the news including the death of an acquaintance of the band, Tara Browne. The B-section, placed in the middle of the song, narrates a busy early-morning routine and was contributed by Paul McCartney in response to Lennon's verses. By considering 'A Day in the Life' in some detail, we can add weight to the claim that popular songs are typically constructed repetitively and from sets of elements that are brought together contingently rather than being evolved necessarily out of one another. We will also see that 'A Day in the Life' is constructed repetitively and contingently despite its 'art rock' status.

Unlike the two sections that seamlessly fitted into 'Are "Friends" Electric?', Lennon's and McCartney's sections differ greatly. Lennon's verses begin in the key of G major, but the chord sounded most frequently is E minor (vi in G major), towards which the tonal centre increasingly gravitates (Moore 1997: 53). This helps to give the verse its sad, sombre feeling, reinforced by the lyric 'and though the news was rather sad'. The pace is slow; Lennon's vocal moves along world-wearily, dispassionately; he sounds bored by the merry-go-round of media events that he recites. His vocal is artificially double-tracked, which gives it an unreal quality, adding to the sense of his detachment from the media spectacle (see Northcutt 2006). In contrast, when McCartney's voice comes in in the B-section, his words are brisk and cheerful——'Woke up, fell out of bed'. He seems at home in the bustle of everyday reality——'Dragged a comb across my head'——unlike Lennon's estrangement. The B-section moves at twice the pace of the A-section, with the bass and drum parts becoming more urgent. All this helps to give this section its more upbeat sound, as does its being in the key of E major.

The song might seem typical of popular music in being composed of two sections that do not intrinsically belong together and were written separately. However, perhaps the B-section *does* evolve out of the A-section. Each A-section gravitates from the key of G major to its relative minor, E minor; then the song modulates to E major for the B-section; afterwards the music returns to E minor-cum-G major for the last A-section; and then the music returns to E major for the 'outro', that is, the dramatic super-extended tonic chord played on four grand pianos, left to resonate and gradually fade away (unless we take the 'outro' to be the jumbled, garbled message that follows and closes the entire album; the boundaries between whole album and song are left ambiguous). There is a logic to these transitions between sections. Yet in other respects the song reflects the popular music norm of repetitive construction. For instance, the B-section chords rotate between I–bVII and I–V, essentially oscillating between rest and movement, archetypical of rock-'n'-roll. In this regard the B-section does not, after all, develop the ramifications of material presented in the A-section. On the contrary, we can see the song's structure as repetitive overall, applying to it the model of repetitive construction from Chap. 3 (see Table 4.1, which is informed by the full score in McCartney et al. 1993: 166–175).

'A Day in the Life', though, is less repetitive than most popular songs. Sections A and B are at different tempos and include internal temporal variations; for one, throughout the A-sections the notes played by the bass guitar vary in duration as well as pitch. The A-section chords follow an ABACC pattern that is more complicated than the shorter, more repetitive kinds of pattern common in popular music such as I–V, I–IV–V, and so on. The second A-verse is foreshortened by a measure, while the third is extended to lead into the bridge section that follows it. In addition, and unusually for popular music, the drums present varying rhythmic patterns throughout the A-section. Most of these patterns mark beat one of eight on the bass-drum and include an emphasis on beat three of eight on the

Table 4.1   The Beatles, 'A Day in the Life', song structure

Song form: ABA comprising intro, A X 3, bridge, B, bridge, A, bridge, outro

A-section	B-section
Initially 10 measures, explicitly measured out by the percussion instruments:	20 measures, explicitly measured out by the drums, with the tempo double that of section A,[2]
1. In the first iteration there are no drums, but instead maracas sound every eighth-note subdivision of the beat. Afterwards the drums play a succession of changing patterns, each a measure long. These usually feature the bass-drum on beat one and the snare-drum on beat three (of eight), but beyond that there is ever-changing variety in the placement of additional drum-beats	1. Where the snare-drum and hi-hat sound on every eighth-note division of the beat; towards the end of the section the particular drum pattern with which the A-section had ended returns
This is aligned with:	This is aligned with:
2. Five phrases of melody each two measures long (5 X 2),	2. four phrases of melody, each made up to five measures in length through vocal pauses (4 X 5),[3]
3. The whole chord sequence, with each chord maintained for half a measure:	3. the chords, each maintained for a measure:
I–iii–vi–vi⁷	
I–iii–vi–vi^7	I–I–I–I–♭VII
IV–vi–ii–IV^7	♭VII–I–V–I–V
I–iii–vi–vi^7	V–I–I–I–♭VII
IV–♭VII–vi–vi	♭VII–I–V–I–V,
IV–♭VII–vi–IV,	4. and the bass guitar, which mostly plays to an eighth-note rhythm and makes successive descents from tonic (E) to dominant (B)
4. and the bass guitar, which mainly plays the root notes of each chord in turn but periodically varies the rhythms and durations of the notes	

snare-drum. But the other drum-beats are variously placed and timed in different measures, leading the listener through a near-continual succession of slight variations.

The song, then, explores the possibilities for variation and permutation contained in its materials. Even so, this move is made *within* the repetitive paradigm. After all, although the drums present successive rhythmic patterns, each one lasts for a measure, with the bass-drum on beat one marking its start. And before the drums come in, the maracas have established the eighth-note subdivision of the beat to which the measures of the A-sections are set, and the maracas continue in this role throughout these verses. Ultimately, then, the percussion part *is* measured out according to

a repetitive principle, and it is against that background that rhythmic variations are explored both by the drums and the other instruments.

Moreover, as to whether the B-section constitutes a logical development
out of the A-section, the recording process suggests otherwise. When the
Beatles began recording they were unsure how to join the A- and B- sections and so they simply left two gaps between them. Thus, on the version
on *Anthology 2*, which is a composite of several takes in the recording
process, the song runs as follows. We begin with three A-section verses,
then the first gap is introduced by the additional, wistful line 'I'd love to
turn you on' (often taken to be a drug reference, alluding to Timothy
Leary's mantra 'tune in, turn on, drop out'). The gap's length in measures
is explicitly counted out by road manager Mal Evans (to the tempo of the
B-section), closing with the abrupt sound of an alarm clock ringing——an
intrusive return to reality. After the B-section's final words 'I went into a
dream' the next gap begins, lasting for ten measures, and filled out with
percussion, bass, and chords played on the piano. The final A-verse then
comes in, its last line 'I'd love to turn you on' leading into a last orchestral
section and then the closing chord with which the song ends. Thus, the
Beatles purposely highlighted the distance between the A- and B-sections
through such devices as the alarm clock and Evans's counting, the artificiality of which is highlighted further by his voice being heavily treated with
echo. The A- and B-sections were thus treated as being *separate*, not logically interconnected, and needing artificial means to join them.

Ian Macdonald describes the eventual means that the band used to
make them join:

> McCartney ... decided that the twenty-four bar bridges would be filled by
> a symphony orchestra going from its lowest to its highest note in an unsyn-
> chronised glide: a 'freak-out' or aural 'happening'. ... George Martin halved
> the number of players and ... each player was asked to finish on whichever
> note in the E major triad was nearest the highest on his instrument. ...
> [Each] *glissando* was recorded in mono four times before being mixed back
> to the master as a single monstrous noise. (2005: 231)

During the first bridge the orchestra slides up in pitch and volume to
a resounding E major chord. The second bridge is filled by the orchestra backing up the vocal melody, again gradually increasing in volume.
In the final bridge, another orchestral slide leads up to the song's super-
extended closing chord (for which the orchestra is abandoned, with the

chord played on pianos only). These several passages were intended to integrate the A- and B-sections. But the sections could have been joined in alternative ways, as is indicated by the gaps left between them in earlier takes. Nonetheless, once added, the orchestral and piano passages reflect and reinforce the song's already disparate character by providing yet more disparate material.

The track illustrates that not any set of musical parts or song sections automatically 'works' by coalescing into a meaningful whole. Sometimes parts need work to adapt them into a unity, possibly long work. In 'A Day in the Life' the end result of that work is that the A- and B- sections qualify one another so that neither remains as it would have been in isolation. The cheer and bustle of the B-section, and McCartney's bright, upbeat vocals, highlight by contrast the sadness and estrangement of the A-section, Lennon's leaden delivery, and his longing to escape from the alienated world into an alternative, happier realm ('I'd love to turn you on'). For its part the A-section shines a negative light on the B-section, casting its bustle and activity as ultimately banal and meaningless. The suggestion is that the unreality of the meandering, free-floating A-verses may ultimately come closer to 'true' reality than the mundane, workaday B-section——and thus that what counts as 'reality' is debateable, and reality an ambiguous phenomenon. Thus the meanings conveyed in both sections become ambiguous by being set in contrast to one another, and gain an additional higher-level set of meanings around ambiguity itself.

In this way the track's disparate sections come to form an integral unity, in which each has the meaning it does only in relation to the other. It is not a harmonious unity but one to which the difference between the sections is essential, yielding an overall quality of ambiguity. The orchestral and piano parts add to the song's already disparate character, but in doing so, ironically, they help to unify the song by reinforcing its unifying qualities of disparateness and ambiguity. Thus, these passages add to the song's coherence by consolidating its meaning.

If all popular songs contain diverse components, 'A Day in the Life' is unusual in being so self-reflexive about that diversity. This self-reflexivity in turn is part of the 'art' character that helps to unify the track. And this is another way that the orchestral and piano passages unify the song——by contributing to marking it as art. This is partly because they establish a link with pre-twentieth-century classical music. But they also contribute to the song's 'art' character because they are present contingently, connecting with contemporary art music and its use of aleatory elements——

McCartney had been listening to John Cage and other avant-garde musicians. Finally, too, the diversity of the elements included in the track is intended to testify to the breadth of its artistic ambition, so that the connotations of art and diversity tie together.

In saying this I do not endorse the idea that popular music is better the more it rises to the status of art. The fact remains, though, that many popular musicians, including the later Beatles, have sought to make art or import some of art's supposed valuable qualities into pop. In 'A Day in the Life', these artistic connotations then contribute to the song's unified meaning as a whole. 'A Day in the Life' succeeds in having a rich and interesting set of unified meanings, though, not because it has attained the status of high art, but because it exemplifies the process by which connotations typically coalesce within popular music, connotations that may or may not include ones around 'art'. So we can now draw some provisional conclusions about these processes of coalescence.

3   Coalescence and Its Conditions

'A Day in the Life' illuminates not only that popular songs are put together from diverse parts but also that those parts may need adaptation and modification, possibly quite substantial, before they cohere. In turn, this illuminates what is required for materials to coalesce. First, as we saw in Chap. 3, certain harmonic and rhythmic constraints must be met before a set of elements can viably be put together——although these constraints are very broad and flexible in popular music. All, or at least most, of the materials in a given song section should be in the same key ('most' because of the substantial minority of songs whose melody and chords are in different keys). All the materials in a section should usually be in the same metre, usually 4/4 (but one exception is Led Zeppelin's 'Kashmir', on *Physical Graffiti*: the vocals and drums are in 2/4, the guitar and strings in 3/4, but their strong beats converge after every 12 beats).

These minimal constraints met, the next thing is that, harmonically, a set of materials——vocals, harmonic filler, bass-line——need to present combinations of pitches that 'work' in sound and meaning. The pitches need not always be consonant: dissonances can work, as in 'Are "Friends" Electric?', where the flat note contributes to the song's meaning. Also, to coalesce rhythmically, different materials need to sound out and emphasise different beats in the measure, often moving at different tempos and to different subdivisions of the beat (e.g. with drums sounding on four beats in each measure and faster-moving guitar on eight). These emphases need to interlock by weaving in and out of one another, pulling with and against one another, to form a dynamic combination. This too is a matter of meaning. A dynamic rhythmic combination is one that invites the listener to find sense in it at a bodily level, by moving in time with it.

Materials may meet minimal harmonic and rhythmic constraints but fail to coalesce at this level of meaning. Thus, more is required for coalescence than conformity to norms of musical grammar, not least given the flexibility and plurality of popular-musical norms. Ultimately, the 'more' that is required is that the connotations embodied in a song's elements should speak to or shed light on one another, whether spontaneously or after mutual adjustment. That is, when elements with different connotations are brought together, those connotations may reinforce one another or take one another's potential connotations in a particular direction, in either case yielding a higher-level combined meaning. Or elements may fail to do this and instead cancel one another's connotations out so that the whole means less than its parts potentially did.

To bear productively upon one another musical elements need not point all in the same direction. The A- and B-sections of 'A Day in the Life' have opposed connotations, but through this very opposition they reflect upon one another to give the song its higher-level ambiguous quality. A similar case is Radiohead's 'Paranoid Android' (on *OK Computer*), which has three sections that differ in tempo, key, and rhythmic and dynamic qualities. Much as with 'A Day in the Life', the disparate sections of 'Paranoid Android' help to give the song a unified overall character——that of being ambitious, experimental, and wide-ranging.[4]

More generally, it is typical for songs' higher-level meanings to be multi-faceted and exhibit a level of complexity. Taking 'Are "Friends" Electric?', its elements' connotations coalesce together to evoke a dystopian, machine-dominated future, but this evocative quality is itself multi-faceted, where its facets are contributed by the multiple elements that work together to produce it. We can, then, think of a song equally as having a unified meaning that emerges, at a higher level, from the connotations of its manifold components, or as having a unified structure of meaning——a unity-in-diversity.

But not all popular songs contain materials that coalesce; not all songs 'work'. Discussing 'Relax' by Frankie Goes to Hollywood, Stuart Maconie comments that it 'has a weird, lumpy middle section that seems to have been badly spot-welded on from another song' (2013: 263). Coalescence of parts, ultimately at the level of meaning, may be a regulative ideal for popular music, but not all songs fulfil this ideal or do so perfectly. That it is a regulative ideal, though, is suggested by cases such as that of 'A Day in the Life': having decided to combine a given set of materials, musicians work to unify them as best they can.

But why pursue coherence in single songs and not whole albums? Clearly some albums, concept albums especially, are intended to be coherent wholes; others are just collections of songs, and perhaps those songs are interchangeable parts. Many albums, though, fall between these two poles, comprising collections of songs that still share a fairly unified sound. For instance, Blur's 1997 album *Blur* sounds audibly unlike their previous four albums. The guitar figures more centrally; the recording is deliberately unprofessional at times, featuring a considerable amount of extraneous noise (as on 'You're So Great'); contrary to the pointed Englishness of their earlier albums, Blur now embrace the influence of American alternative rock bands such as Pavement; and vocalist Damon Albarn is 'much more prepared to write in the first person', in contrast to his earlier detached, ironic, third-person style (Street et al. 2009). *Blur* illustrates a broader pattern for all or most songs on an album to distil a band's sound at a given time. Alternatively, some albums present different elements of that overall sound distributed across different songs, as the songs on Chuck Berry's *One Dozen Berrys* range across the several styles that he fused into rock-'n'-roll.

Rather than thinking about unity in albums I have focused on individual songs, and will continue to do so, on the assumption that coherence within albums is secondary. For albums normally consist of individual songs in some sense (even though some concept albums blur songs' boundaries, say by combining them into suites). Insofar as albums normally comprise a plurality of songs, the question of the unity of individual songs has priority.

4   FUNDAMENTAL FORM VERSUS SUPERFICIAL SOUND

It is not only under their rhythmic and harmonic parameters that musical materials may or may not coalesce with one another. Their texture, timbre, and dynamics also contribute to that coalescence or non-coalescence. Going back yet again to 'Are "Friends" Electric?', the Mini-Moog's timbre, and the song's texture in which synthesised timbres predominate over 'natural' ones, contribute to the song's meaning, working with the

ominous connotation supplied by the A-melody. Moreover, the texture——in which Numan's vocals are absent, semi-spoken, or secondary
to the synthesiser——contributes to the lack of a clear verse/chorus division, reinforcing the song's quality of lacking a centre (because ordinarily
vocals become more prominent during a song's chorus). Other factors too
can affect how far a set of materials coalesces——for instance, the way that
the sounds are distributed in sonic space.

A question arises, then. In popular music, do timbres, textures, dynamics, and so on in principle affect the meanings of harmonic contents and
formal designs just as much as the latter affect the meanings of the former? Or do harmony and form have priority in the mix? Certainly music
theorists have often distinguished between more fundamental musical
parameters——harmony and form——and more superficial ones. Cooke
(1959) and Lerdahl and Jackendoff (1983), for instance, express versions of this view. Cooke calls timbre and texture 'characterizing agents';
what they characterise is pitch and rhythm (1959: 37–38). For Lerdahl
and Jackendoff, pitch and metre are structurally central to music, timbre
and dynamics secondary (see, e.g., 1983: 9). And for London (2015),
rhythm and pitch are primary and essential as timbre and dynamics aren't.
On these views, rhythm is one of the fundamental factors——but to the
extent that it is formalised as metre. Non-metric aspects of rhythm——
notably patterns of syncopation——are superficial (hence, in this vein,
Adorno's claim that the complicated rhythms of jazz are mere surface
embellishments).

These divisions of fundamental from superficial factors can motivate
criticism of popular music. Remember 'Four Chords' by Axis of Awesome,
regularly taken to expose the homogenous and formulaic nature of popular music. Listening to three songs excerpted by Axis of Awesome——
Denver's 'Country Roads', Gaga's 'Paparazzi', and U2's 'With or
Without You'——we saw that despite their harmonic overlap these songs
differ greatly in texture, timbre, vocal style, rhythmic qualities (but not
metre——all are in 4/4), and genre. But if harmony, form, and metre are
fundamental then these differences are merely superficial and disguise the
songs' underlying sameness.

Not surprisingly, some popular music theorists, such as Bruce Baugh,
have argued that the distinction between fundamental and surface features
fits popular music badly. For Baugh, we cannot appreciate the aesthetic
qualities or value of 'rock' music——meaning popular music overall——if
we judge rock by traditional aesthetic standards which are derived from

concert-hall music. (In fairness, those standards may fit other forms of music badly too, including some concert-hall music. But that is beyond my scope here.)[5] The standards in question are formalist, Baugh maintains, and they go back to Kant. Admittedly Kant ranked music the lowest art, but Hanslick adapted Kant's aesthetics to produce a formalist approach to music. For Hanslick, no agreement on the emotional qualities of a musical work is possible, because differently constituted people will respond differently to the same piece of music. In contrast, form exists objectively within the music and takes shape according to necessary laws that can be studied scientifically. Thus it is by its formal structure that a piece of music must be evaluated and that objective judgements about the merits of different pieces can be reached. And a work's formal structure emerges out of the development of the harmonic implications of the music's motives, so that form and harmony are mutually constitutive.

Baugh concedes that rock songs generally *do* have simple, standard forms. By formalist standards we will judge these songs simple, boring, and lacking in aesthetic value. To appreciate where the merits of these songs lie we need new aesthetic standards, Baugh argues. These are to be generated by reversing the traditional formalist ones, thus evaluating rock by its *material* qualities and how they materially *affect* us. From this general principle Baugh derives more specific evaluative standards: first, the 'materiality of tone' (1993: 23). We are to judge rock songs on the individual sounds that make them up, as those sounds materially, concretely present themselves to us, depending on the particular way that a musician sings or plays them, given her individual approach to timing and inflection and how she invests the sounds with expressive significance. Second, we are to judge rock songs based on how their material sounds affect us emotionally and how powerfully and effectively they do so. We feel these effects in our bodies: thus rock should be assessed by its power to affect us bodily: 'an aesthetics of rock requires an emancipation of the body, an emancipation of heteronomy' (28). Third, Baugh argues that rock songs should be judged by their rhythmic qualities, because these are central to how the sounds sound, to musicians' performance styles, and to how sounds affect us viscerally. Fourth, loudness can be important to the music's power to affect us viscerally and can therefore be a virtue in rock.

Baugh is right to challenge the traditional view that form and harmony alone are fundamental to musical value, but his positive standards have problems. To see this, let's concentrate on material sound. Against Baugh, Stephen Davies (1999) argues that how a piece of music materially sounds

necessarily depends upon its formal properties. Rock, like all music, is patterned sound; its formal patterns are the source of how it sounds materially
and what it expresses emotionally. To illustrate, the I–IVb–♭VII–I chord
sequence in 'Primitive Painters' sounds elevating because of the formal
relations between these chords, their arrangement in a series that rises
then returns to the tonic. We may feel as if we respond immediately and
viscerally to rock music, Davies says, but really our responses depend upon
our musical enculturation since childhood, which has made our grasp on
music's formal patterns second nature to us.[6]

What does Davies mean by 'formal'? He mentions not only melodic
contours and harmonic progressions but also higher-level arrangements of
sections——that is song forms——as well as metric structures and rhythmic patterns (Davies 1999: 195). In part, then, Davies is claiming that
some of the musical properties that Baugh takes to be material——notably
rhythm——are actually formal (possibly because Davies is understanding
rhythm in terms of metric structure whereas Baugh may be understanding
it in terms of non-metric patterns of syncopation). Partly, too, Davies is
claiming that qualities that Baugh regards as simply material——notably
how tones sound——have formal underpinnings. Finally, Davies is claiming that Baugh underestimates how far any rock song's sound, expressiveness, and effect depends on the song's 'melodic and harmonic shape, its
words, [and] its overall structure' and not only on the variables that Baugh
emphasises: timbre, rhythm, and loudness (1999: 197).

The substantive issue that divides Baugh and Davies is *which* musical
elements and parameters are most important in rock. For Baugh, traditional music aesthetics has concentrated on melody, harmony, and large-
scale form to the neglect of other parameters that are more important in
rock, including rhythm, performance style, timbre, volume dynamics, and
expressiveness. The latter variables have been treated as merely superficial
or secondary when in popular music they have paramount importance.
Richard Middleton agrees that within popular music

> formulaic processes operate within parameters relatively highly valued by
> traditional musicology: harmony, melodic shape, basic rhythm pattern.
> Variant processes, on the other hand, often take place in parameters little
> valued by traditional musicology (and much harder to notate): slight pitch
> inflection or rhythmic variation, timbre and timbre changes, accent, and
> attack. (Middleton, quoted in Holt 2006–11)[7]

Parameters that other scholars have added to this list are texture; recording and production techniques and effects; and 'noise'——distortion, feedback, echo, fuzz, reverb, and so on (Waksman 1999, 2003). The overall claim is that variables besides melody, harmony, and large-scale form are relatively important in popular music and are the focus of its innovation, creativity, and experimentation.

That these parameters are indeed important is illustrated by the way that 1980s rock music typically sounds very different from rock music of the 1960s and 1970s. This is so even though many of the same sequences of chords are in use throughout, with I, IV, and ♭VII most frequently used overall. And as far as I am aware there are no systematic differences between the kinds of melodic contours or large-scale forms used in rock between these two periods. Yet 1980s rock sounds distinctive, as Campbell and Brody describe:

> Rock got a 'beatlift' around 1980. The new sound was lean, clean, vibrant, and colored with an array of synthesiser timbres and effects. It harnessed the energy of punk ... [and] it distilled a purer form of rock rhythm, typically spread throughout the texture, from bass and kick drum to high-pitched percussion and synth parts. Its leanness and cleanness came in large part from an open-sounding mid range: crisp single-note lines and sustained chords replaced thick guitar chords and riffs. (1999: 345)

To elaborate: Compared to earlier rock, 1980s drum-sounds are bigger because of the combined use of reverb and noise gating (i.e. cutting the sound off suddenly), which highlights the drum sound further against the subsequent silence——as on Bruce Springsteen's 'Born in the U.S.A.', for instance, released in 1984. Many layers of sound in 1980s rock have quite a marked percussive quality——for instance the stabbing synthesiser sounds on Duran Duran's 1985 hit 'A View to a Kill'. Synthesisers are used more often and more prominently than in pre-1980s rock, and chords played on the guitar are more often sustained and left to ring out rather than being strummed repeatedly, which leaves the texture more open. Influenced by punk, the bass part is often simplified to play the root notes of each chord to a rapid eighth-note rhythm. The overall sound, then, is more percussive and gives more sense of expanding to fill a big space. This is largely due to innovations in timbre——how drum-sounds are recorded, the presence of synthesisers——and texture——the expanded role of drums and synthesisers, the bass guitar's simplified role, and the greater openness created by the rhythm guitar.

Moreover, approaches to timbre and texture are important in demarcating genres, which rarely diverge systematically in which chords or chord sequences they use, which melodic shapes they favour, or what large-scale forms they use. More often timbre, texture, rhythm, and production are decisive. Consider the emergence of alternative rock in the 1980s in contrast to the then-dominant rock sound as just described. R.E.M., who were central to the formation of alternative rock, eschewed much of that dominant sound, perhaps most clearly on their first album, *Murmur*, of 1983. Harmony was not the issue here——R.E.M.'s first single, 'Radio Free Europe', uses rock-'n'-roll's familiar I–IV–V sequence (in A major). Instead timbre and texture were at issue: R.E.M. insisted 'on clean, natural sounds and acoustic, organic-sounding instruments' (Niimi 2005: 20). They avoided synthesisers, using acoustic and electric guitar plus the traditional bass, drums, and vocals, with little or no treatment. When R.E.M. used other instruments these were ones with 'natural' timbres such as the piano. Stipe's vocals, often difficult to decipher, are fairly low in the mix. Reverb was used sparingly so that when 'an obviously reverb-enhanced effect is heard on the album (like the giant snare drum reports in "Perfect Circle" …), it plays against the context of an essentially naturalistic sonic landscape' (Niimi 2005: 77). In sum, the emergence of the dominant 1980s approach to rock timbre and texture enabled R.E.M. and other alternative rock bands to stand out by rejecting much of that approach.

Timbre, texture, and so on are thus very important in popular music, especially in demarcating genres and constituting a focus for innovation and change over time. But are they of *paramount* importance, as harmonic factors are not? Perhaps popular music theorists have emphasised timbre, texture, rhythm, dynamics, and so on, too one-sidedly against melody, harmony, and large-scale form. So Walter Everett argues:

> Purely musical effects——nearly always connected in some way to matters of pitch relationships——contribute to any … listener's appreciation. … If the masses believe they are attracted only to rhythm or loud volume and 'can't hear' the pitch or have no conscious understanding of functional tonal relations, I say they are merely unaware of why, for instance, they become … excited to expanded dominant-seventh retransitions enhanced by added uncontrolled dissonance. (Everett 2000: 270)

Everett then provides interpretations of a range of songs to support his conclusion that 'pitch relationships often have strong expressive implica-

tions for what are often thought to be extra-pitch subjects' (271–72)——
so that pitch relations remain crucial to popular music.

However, we can reconcile Everett's re-emphasis upon pitch with the
contrary emphasis on non-pitch parameters. We need not say that the latter are important as pitch is not, but rather that non-pitch parameters tend
to affect how pitched elements function in popular music and what meanings they convey. Reciprocally, though, pitched elements affect what is
conveyed by non-pitched elements. Thus, these various elements reciprocally affect one another. In practice some elements may have the greatest
effects within particular songs and genres: in rap or jungle, say, rhythmic
connotations may qualify pitched ones more than the other way around.
But this is one possible variation on an overall norm of all-round reciprocity in which elements under different parameters affect one another
without any having a priori privilege. Let me use a further example to
substantiate this claim about all-round reciprocity: R.E.M.'s 'Losing My
Religion'.

5   'LOSING MY RELIGION'

'Losing My Religion', from R.E.M.'s 1991 album *Out of Time*, deserves
consideration partly because it suffers a highly negative assessment from
Roger Scruton in his *Aesthetics of Music*. Lamenting the decline of the
West's musical culture, Scruton unfavourably compares 'Losing My
Religion' with Cole Porter's 'I've Got You Under my Skin' and the Beatles'
'She Loves You' (Scruton 1997: 502). This is ironic since the latter's 'Yeah
yeah yeah' refrain was the *bête noire* of 1960s opponents of rock-'n'-roll.
Still, Scruton's criticisms of 'Losing My Religion' raise important issues.

First, Scruton complains about the 'shapeless cries of the singer',
Michael Stipe. For the most part the song's vocal melody does have an

Fig. 4.1 R.E.M., 'Losing My Religion', vocal melody, timing ca. 00:17–00:26
and 01:14–01:30

unusually flat contour, staying very near the tonic (see Fig. 4.1)——but not entirely. In measure 12, for example, the vocal melodic line leaps up by a major sixth, a melodic gesture that recurs elsewhere in the vocal. However, most of the vocal phrases descend by a minor third from C through B to A, as does for instance the phrase that spans measures 13–14——'you are not me' (which ends half-way through the measure, this being a song in which the vocal phrases and chords are aligned by overlapping rather than coinciding; the vocal phrases rarely start exactly in time with chord changes). Overall, then, the melody advances through a series of short descending movements.

Second, Scruton complains that the chords are uninteresting: 'no triad is ever inverted, and nothing ever moves between the chords, so that all is absorbed in rhythm' (1997: 502). Rather than being derived through voice-leading, he objects, the chords simply follow one another as self-contained blocks with their components arranged in standard ways. That is, the chords do not follow one logically through the notes in each chord deriving from those in the preceding chords.[8] Without that kind of logical succession, in which harmony acts as a rhythmic force, the only force left to power the movement from one chord to the next is rhythm on its own. But, Scruton continues, rhythm acting on its own independent of harmonic progression is actually mere beat, not genuine rhythm at all. 'Beat is not rhythm, but the last sad skeleton of rhythm, stripped bare of human life'. For Scruton, music has genuine rhythm when its temporal organisation flows out of its harmonic organisation, so that beats 'bring each other into being' and do not merely follow one another (35). Absent that derivation and what remains is a mere succession of isolated units of musical material set to measurable intervals of time.

Given the preoccupations of traditional music aesthetics, it is unsurprising that Scruton's complaints about 'Losing My Religion' concern the subordination of its melody and harmony to rhythm-as-beat. Scruton does not mention timbre or texture. But this is where the song is most obviously unconventional——enough so that Warner were reluctant to release the song as the first single from *Out of Time* (Rosen 1997: 108)–for the mandolin is the lead instrument, occupying the role that rock more often assigns to the electric guitar. The mandolin is used rarely in popular music, most often in folk-rock. Scruton, however, refers only to the chords as played on the acoustic guitar, that is, to accompany the mandolin. Yet it was the latter on which the song's series of chord sequences was initially written by R.E.M.'s guitarist Peter Buck. The mandolin's role and timbre do much to shape the song's overall sound and connotations. Because it is acoustic rather than electrified and has associations with folk-rock, the mandolin carries connotations of the natural and authentic, as does the acoustic guitar. The mandolin's presence thus feeds into the song's atmosphere of emotional honesty and sincerity, along with such lyrics as 'I'm choosing my confessions'.

Now, in saying that 'Losing My Religion' has qualities of authenticity——as indeed did R.E.M.'s earlier sound, for example on *Murmur*—I do not mean that to say that this song 'really is' authentic in the sense of giving direct, honest expression to the band members' emotions in a way that other music that is more 'pop' and commercial does not. Rather, R.E.M. use stylistic elements——the acoustic guitar; the mandolin; the lyrics; the vocal style, which is direct and communicative——which instantiate qualities of authenticity in various ways. This may be by directly speaking about sincerity ('confessions'), for instance, or in the received connotations of the mandolin and acoustic guitar——their association with folk, and the fact that by not being electrified they have a connotation of being 'natural'. We can analyse ways in which elements of popular music convey connotations of authenticity without having to endorse either the idea that some of this music really is authentic as other parts of it is not or that connotations of authenticity add value.

Going back to Scruton's criticisms, one might object that this difference made by putting the mandolin in lead position is only superficial and that the underlying chord sequences remain entirely familiar. To assess this charge let's see how the song is made up. It is opened by a nine-measure introduction featuring mandolin, acoustic guitar, bass guitar, and drums; in this, the mandolin and acoustic guitar present an initial sequence of chords: see Fig. 4.2 (in which, is as standard, the guitar is shown an octave higher than it sounds). Thereafter the vocals enter and there are two iterations of a 16-measure verse; in this verse the guitar and mandolin move through a i–v–i–v–i–v–iv–VII chord sequence in the key of A natural minor, with each chord maintained for two measures. Violins are added during the second verse. An eight-measure chorus follows, marked out by a distinct chord sequence on mandolin and acoustic guitar——VI–VI–i–i–VI–VI–i–VII (each maintained for one measure), plus handclaps and backing vocals. The whole cycle of two verses then chorus is repeated once, then there is an eight-measure bridge, instrumental in its first half, which runs through a series of brighter major chords: i–VII–VI–VII–III–IV–III–IV (with the IV 'borrowed' from the parallel major key,

A major). A final verse and chorus follow, then the song closes with an eight-measure instrumental 'outro' on the tonic chord.

As Fig. 4.2 illustrates, the interplay between the chords on mandolin and acoustic guitar is important. The two instruments don't entirely coincide: the mandolin regularly plays additional melodic runs and, during the introduction, a simpler chord sequence (VI–i–VI–i–VII) than the guitar. Even when the two instruments are playing the same chords, the mandolin is pitched an octave higher than the guitar and its sound is 'thinner', in that chords on the mandolin typically contain one or two fewer notes than the same chords on guitar. Thus the particular sets of pitches under which

Fig. 4.2 R.E.M., 'Losing My Religion', mandolin and acoustic guitar, timing ca. 00:01–00:17

the two instruments present the chords differ. There is also a difference in the duration of the notes on the two instruments——not captured in the notation——because notes decay more rapidly on the higher-pitched mandolin than on the guitar. Furthermore, in 'Losing my Religion' many of the chords on the mandolin are inverted——i is in first inversion, VI in second inversion, and v in second inversion when it appears in the verses——contrary to Scruton.

The combined result is that the mandolin and guitar lines come close together without ever quite uniting. This makes the mandolin sound somewhat lonely, as if its notes are cut off from and can never quite reach down to the thicker guitar field around them. The inversion and relative 'thinness' of (many of) the chords on mandolin enhances their fragile quality and the sense of their distance from the guitar——drawing close together, but never quite uniting. In sum, the relation between mandolin and acoustic guitar, and between their versions of the chords, fundamentally shapes the connotations that these chords convey.

Consequently, we need not concede that the song innovates only in timbre and texture while being formulaic harmonically.[9] The unusual combination of timbres affects what the chords convey, so that they function and signify here in ways that are specific to this song rather than formulaic. Because all the song's parameters interrelate and affect one another, distinctiveness under one parameter feeds through to the others.

Let's reconsider the chord sequences in this light. The verse is unequivocally minor, fluctuating between i and v before concluding by moving through iv to VII. The chorus, though, oscillates between i (A minor) and VI (F major), creating ambiguity: because the key of F major contains A minor (as its iii chord), we wonder whether the chorus has shifted to the major key. Compared to the verse the chorus therefore suggests uncertainty and hope: perhaps we are not in a minor key after all; maybe there is some hope of happiness. The bridge section, too, suggests optimism to an extent that sets it apart from the rest of the song, because apart from the initial minor tonic the chords are all major and bright, including a D major chord borrowed from the key of A major. The return to the verse in A minor, though, confirms that there is no hope after all.

The lyrics reinforce that conclusion: 'fantasies come crashing down', 'that was just a dream'. These lyrics have sometimes been taken to concern religion, but Stipe explains that he was using a southern US expression, 'losing my religion', meaning being at one's wit's end (Fletcher 2002: 188). The cause of this despair is unrequited love——hence the recurring line 'Oh no, I've said too much': the narrator is scared of having revealed his feelings to the person he secretly loves. In this light, there is some hope of achieving happiness and of love being requited during the chorus——'I think I thought I saw you try'——but that hope is dispelled in the verse.

The melody draws out the same connotations. As we saw earlier, it mostly has a very flat contour, spanning a narrow pitch range. These features sometimes convey lack of emotion, sometimes feelings held in check (Machin 2010: 102–104). The former does not apply in 'Losing My Religion', because connotations of emotional honesty and expressivity are embedded in the song by its 'natural' instrumentation. In this case the flatness of the vocal melody conveys feelings held in check: the narrator does not lack emotion, but is reluctant to show it since he does not envisage it being reciprocated. That hopelessness is reinforced by the phrases repeatedly falling to the tonic by a minor third. The vocal line is largely flat, then, not because Stipe lacks the power to shape it but because that flatness serves an expressive purpose. Hence the occasional melodic gesture of rising by a major sixth: intermittent surges of hope within an overall lack of hope, which coheres with the emotional quality of the chord sequences.

As a whole, the elements of 'Losing My Religion' under its several parameters affect one another, strengthening and sometimes amending one another's connotations and so interlocking into a whole. The chords and instrumental timbres affect the quality of the vocal melody so that it sounds not restrained but downcast. The form of the song, with its distinction between despondent verse and hopeful chorus, dovetails with the formation of the chords on mandolin and guitar. The mandolin with its dual courses of strings tuned in unison has a 'chorus' effect, suggesting a possible unity (the two who could be lovers); but the guitar and mandolin versions of the chords never quite coincide (nor do the two people).

In this light we can return to the argument made by Baugh and others that variables besides harmony, melody and organising form are central to popular music. Certainly timbre, texture, rhythm, and so on *are* important. But we should not concede that these are the sole focus of innovation and that popular music is formulaic in form, harmony, and melody. Taking 'Losing My Religion', which might be considered formulaic in its chords and form and uninteresting in its melody (and is so considered by Scruton), I've suggested that matters are more complicated. The song's timbres and texture *interact* with its harmonic and melodic aspects and its form, and give them unique meanings not found in other songs, even ones that share some identical harmonic components.

6 COHERENCE AND RECORDING

I have claimed that coalescence of meanings is a regulative ideal in popular music, an ideal of which particular songs may fall short. But one might think that popular songs' elements *necessarily* cohere, in a sense so strong that every popular song is equally coherent. This thought arises from the role of recording in popular music. So we need briefly to reconsider debates about the ontology of popular music. These were prompted by Gracyk (1996) when he argued that, in 'rock', recording does not merely document an already existing work that is the performance.[10] Rather, in 'rock', the recording *is* the work——where I take 'rock' to encompass the whole post-rock-'n'-roll field (admittedly contrary to some of Gracyk's statements).[11]

Historically, recording has often been assumed to be a means of capturing a prior performance faithfully and accurately, but the practice of recording popular music belies such assumptions. Very rarely do 'rock' songs fully exist before they are assembled in the studio through many partial performances, in a process in which 'composition, performance, and recording technology all blur into one another' (Brown 2000: 364). Even when a song definitely pre-exists this intra-studio process, say by existing as a 'demo' recording, that demo has issued from a prior round of recording. If the song took definite shape before that in a repeated practice of jamming or performing, that activity was already regulated by the goal of laying down a recording. Recording orientates performance practice. In turn the sound of the music *as* recorded——for instance as incorporating the echo generated by a particular studio——and its technological manipulation *in* being recorded and produced——for instance, how far tracks of sound are separated or allowed to bleed into one another——are integral to the final recording.

Gracyk argues that, being recorded, 'rock' works do not present the same ontological puzzles as classical works. When a composer writes a score by which performances are to be guided, ontological puzzles arise because neither the score nor any individual performance is identical to the musical 'work'. Thus one wonders whether that 'work' is an abstract object that the score either describes or creates (see, e.g., Levinson 1980). However we answer these puzzles——and even if we follow Lydia

Goehr (1992) in regarding musical 'works' as discursive constructs rather than really existing entities——no such perplexities arise regarding rock recordings. 'Losing My Religion', for instance, exists in concrete shape as a recording, initially a master recording of which reproductions can be made. No abstract musical object needs to be postulated to explain this relation of master to copies. Copies of 'Losing My Religion' are that just as long as they are derived from the master using appropriate reproduction processes that make the copies exactly identical, sonically, to the master (with possible allowance for some decay in sound quality). The 'original', the master, has no special ontological status; it is just the first of indefinitely many copies.

A related view of rock's ontological status, suggested by Stephen Davies (1999), is that, being recorded, works of rock are very thick particulars, unlike classical or jazz works. According to Davies, works of jazz (in the sense of 'heads') are very thin: the same work can be realised in many ways, leaving scope for extensive improvisation. Classical works are thicker: the score specifies relatively strictly what can count as a performance of this work. Rock is thicker still: the original recording realises all the features of the work and another instance of the same work must possess all those features——it must exactly reproduce the master copy——to count as an instance of that work. We might wonder whether Davies has overstated the difference between jazz and rock, for at least sometimes with jazz it is records, for example *Kind of Blue*, that are seen as the 'works'. Nonetheless, Davies's point is still helpful with respect to the ontology of rock.

However, Gracyk distinguishes rock *songs* from *recordings* of these songs. In everyday parlance a single song can be recorded under different versions: the several versions of, say, 'All Along the Watchtower' are all versions of the same song. What makes them so? The usual assumption is that a 'song' consists of a melody, lyrics, and accompanying chords, organised into a certain form. Musicians can produce different versions of a song by realising the melody under different nuances of pitch, timing, emphasis, and so on; by presenting the chords to a new rhythm or using different instruments; or by changing the attendant bass-line or percussion. Musicians might also alter the words, chords, or notes of melody slightly, but only slightly. This assumption dovetails with the idea that harmony and form are fundamental while timbre, texture, rhythm, and so on, are superficial.

But rather than capturing an ontological status that popular songs really have, this assumption may merely reflect social and legal convention. Copyright law generally assigns the writer of a musical 'work' certain rights over that work, rights that may be assigned to others, including the right to record the work. As Paul Théberge comments: 'The origins of copyright law are rooted in a ... notion of the musical work (defined as *a combination of melody and harmony*) and its fixation in graphic form (the musical score)' (2004: 141; my emphasis; see also Sinnreich 2011: 64–65, 68). This notion of the work privileges harmony, melody, and form. And the 'song' in that sense is presumed to exist primarily as something specified by a score and only subsequently recorded. The poor fit between these assumptions and the practice of popular music-making has surfaced in court cases and out-of-court settlements around the use of samples. The law permits a degree of reproduction of copyrighted works as long as this constitutes 'fair use'——which might seem to permit sampling. Yet legal argument has focused on whether those who have sampled recordings of earlier 'works' have taken a 'substantial part' of them (Green field and Osborn 2004: 90–91). What counts as a 'substantial part' or 'substantial amount' is open to interpretation, but sampled bass-lines and drum parts *have* regularly been judged 'substantial'. It seems, then, that the substance of a popular song *is* more than melody plus chords plus form after all.

That said, when Orange Juice in 'Rip It Up' (on their album of the same name) reproduce the minimal, two-note guitar solo from 'Boredom' by Buzzcocks (on their *Spiral Scratch* EP), we wouldn't normally see 'Rip It Up' as another version of 'Boredom', as we do see Jimi Hendrix's 'All Along the Watchtower' as another version of the Bob Dylan song. But had Orange Juice reproduced the entire melody and chord structure of 'Boredom' we likely would think that they had recorded their own version of that song. Such intuitions, though, may merely reflect the power of the melody-plus-accompaniment paradigm. That paradigm is unsuited to the nature of popular songs as coalescent wholes to which *each* element is integral, at least in principle. I prefer, then, not to distinguish 'song' (as fundamental) from 'recording' (as particular realisation) but to treat popular songs as songs-*as*-recorded. Songs-as-recorded can share more or less of their component elements with other songs, and in legal practice it is normally when melody, chords, and words are shared that one recorded song is identified as a new version of another existing one.

If the primary 'works' in popular music are songs-as-recorded, then those works are ontologically very thick. All of the features of their sound as recorded help to constitute what these works are. Take Joy Division's 1979 album *Unknown Pleasures*: its different layers of sound were sharply demarcated in the recording process, creating an eerie spatiality that is central to the album's sound and is one of the properties that constitutes it as the album it is. Individual sonic details and nuances may likewise be constitutive properties of a work insofar as it is recorded, as with the sound of smashing glass that occurs in Kraftwerk's 'Showroom Dummies' when the dummies, voiced by Ralf Hütter, announce that 'we start to move, /and we break the glass' (on *Trans-Europe Express*). Perhaps recorded works are so thick ontologically that every single one of their details is constitutive of them——these works being 'replete' (Brown 2000: 363; see also Zak 2001: 22). But then whichever musical elements are assembled on a given recording, they are all, in all their nuances, essential to that work——which would have been equally true of any other set of elements. If so, then all recorded works are equally coherent: their parts cohere just by virtue of co-existing on record.

However, when Maconie criticised Frankie's 'Relax' for its middle section being 'badly spot-welded' onto it, he criticised the *recording* of 'Relax'. So if every feature of a song-as-recorded is essential to it, then this extends to the *in*coherence of Frankie's recording of 'Relax', as of many other recorded songs whose parts have not coalesced.[12] Others might re-record 'Relax' and generate something more coherent. But if recorded songs can lack coherence, and if that incoherence can actually be among the constitutive features of a given recorded song, then something more must be required for coherence than the mere juxtaposition on record of certain elements. Elements can co-exist and collectively constitute a particular song-as-recorded without that song-as-recorded thereby achieving coherence in the sense of its parts coalescing. This is because coalescence, as I have argued, ultimately obtains at the level of songs' meanings, not merely by virtue of these songs being recorded.

7   WHOLES, FORMS, AND MATERIALS

I have argued that, typically, popular songs are constructed repetitively. Elements are presented at four layers of sound——melody/vocal, harmonic filler, bass, and percussion——with each element repeated a given number of times per section and with these various cyclical repetitions aligned temporally with one another. As to which elements or materials are brought together in a given song, popular music's eclecticism leaves musicians considerable leeway. Ordinarily, various combinations of elements will all make equal logical sense and satisfy minimal constraints of harmony and rhythm. Beyond that, elements need to cohere in respect of their meanings. These elements should carry connotations that reinforce one another, or that contrast in ways that generate unified meanings at a higher level (e.g. that of ambiguity or artistic breadth), or otherwise enter into productive combinations that generate higher levels of meaning. Harmony, form and melody have no a priori priority over other parameters within these processes.

I shall now argue (1) that insofar as the goal for popular songs is that their parts should coalesce into meaningful wholes, popular songs are to be so constructed that their materials generate their forms. I'll then argue (2) that this matter-form configuration gives popular music aesthetic value, on grounds drawn from Adorno and Hegel. Not all popular songs have equivalent aesthetic value; they realise the popular music form in different ways and exhibit varying degrees of coalescence. But to the extent that their parts do coalesce, they have value *as* popular music, not despite being it.

I first need to clarify the concept of form, which I have been using in a range of senses. In Chap. 3, I asked whether popular songs have a standardised form, taking 'form' to mean an organising template such as verse/chorus, AABA, and suchlike (see Covach 2005). Call this 'form' in sense 1. These 'templates' proved to belong within a higher-level principle of formal organisation——'form' in sense 2——that is typical of popular music overall, namely repetitive construction. Repetitive construction operates at the level of individual musemes (musematic repetition) *and* song sections (discursive repetition), and, in respect of the latter, verse/chorus and similar templates are particular ways of organising repetitions of sections.

We encountered further senses of 'form' in the debate between Baugh and Davies. Here 'form' sometimes referred to musical works' overall formal organisation, as in sense 2 above. But sometimes 'form' referred instead to harmony, melody, and metre——'form' in sense 3——as distinct from timbre, texture, dynamics, inflection, 'surface' rhythm patterns and other purported 'surface' factors, which counted as material insofar as they were superficial. Partly too, Davies used 'form' to refer to *interrelations* between individual elements such as notes, chords, sections, beats, timbres, layers of texture, and so on——'form' in sense 4, as interrelations among lower-level components. Andy Hamilton likewise notes that 'form' can be used in that latter way in aesthetics, contrary to an alternative use of 'form' to mean something's phenomenal, perceptible surface appearance (2007: 87)——'form' in sense 5, of which form in sense 3 is an application to music. But if 'form' means 'interrelation between elements' then timbre, texture, dynamics, and so on, are no more 'material' than chords or melodies, for songs contain interrelations between elements under all these parameters (e.g. the interweaving between layers of texture; the relations between different instrumental timbres). Thus senses (4) and (3 and 5) of 'form' are in tension, and both differ from 'form' in sense (2) of 'overall structuring organisation', as in repetitive construction (which incorporates such templates as verse/chorus, i.e. form in sense (1)).

Now, the sense in which popular songs' forms emerge from their materials is different yet again. What emerges when materials interact and their connotations affect one another is an overall web of meaning. The emergence of such a web of meaning across a set of musical materials binds them into a whole, at a more substantial level than that of simply being combined on record. It is the form of a song as a *meaningful whole*—— form in sense 6——that emerges out of its materials when they coalesce. A 'meaningful whole' counts as a form (i) insofar it brings (deeper-level) *unity* to a song——recalling that a form, such as a concept or judgement, is a principle conferring unity on materials; (ii) insofar as it exists where a song's elements *interrelate* in respect of their meanings (connecting with form in sense 4).

How does this relate to repetitive construction——form in sense 2? Repetitive construction is the general principle on the basis of which elements are brought together in popular music. Elements at each layer of sound are repeated cyclically, with or without variations, with these repetitions aligned with one another temporally. This mode of bringing elements together makes it possible for them to 'communicate' in terms of their connotations and to coalesce together to form a structure of meaning. Repetitive construction, then, does not itself emerge from a song's materials but provides the initial framework within which these materials are put together. Yet repetitive construction does not dominate materials but *enables* them to come together so that their connotations can qualify one another, or to be adjusted to do so. Insofar as repetition is form, it does not curtail materials or crush their inherent tendencies but *enables* these tendencies——the elements' potential meanings——to qualify one another and so exercise a kind of agency. Here form operates on behalf of materials to enable them to realise themselves.

But in what sense do the elements of popular songs count as 'materials'? My claim is not that these elements are material in virtue of being exclusively physical, although certainly they have a physical base in overtones, frequencies, sound-waves and their spatial and temporal properties, and so on. But musical elements do not reduce to their material base. This non-reducibility can be conveyed by describing these elements as 'musemes' (informed by Tagg, although not in his particular sense of this term). By analogy with 'phonemes', a museme is a meaningful unit, where its meaning depends on a physical base. Or, better, a museme is a potentially meaningful unit——it potentially contributes certain meanings to a song, but how and whether this potential gets realised depends on the interaction of other musemes. Further, a museme is any component of a popular song that is an identifiable unit; and in addition musemes are *repeated*: they are the materials on which repetitive organisation works. A museme could be a riff, a phrase of melody, a bass-line, or percussion rhythm; or an individual sound, such as the skidding synthesiser sound on A in 'Firestarter'; or a one-measure rhythmic pattern under which successive chords are presented on the guitar, as in 'Sweet Little Sixteen'. Thus as Middleton says, the nature and size of the museme must be regarded flexibly (1990: 189).

The senses in which musemes are 'material' can now be identified, (1) in contrast to the senses in which repetitive construction is 'formal': musemes are the individual constituents that repetitive construction brings together and organises. In further senses, musemes are 'material' in contrast to the song as a meaningful whole that is also 'formal': (2) vis-à-vis the song as a meaningful *whole*, its musemes are its *parts*, the individual constituents that generate this whole in being brought together and coming to interlock. Also, (3) in contrast to the song as a meaningful whole that is *unified*, a song's component musemes are *multiple*. Hence they can be taken apart again and re-used in other songs, as sampling makes explicit. And whereas unity is the hallmark of form, it is the hallmark of matter to comprise a manifold of elements that undergo unification. Finally, (4) a song's musemes all embody potential meanings that affect one another, so that these elements interact on the basis of the various particular qualities and connotations that they each have——that is, on the basis of their material *particularity*. On the other hand the whole form, as a unity, is allied with universality, as a structure of meaning that pervades all the parts.

To clarify, then, popular music does not privilege materiality in the way that Baugh maintained. For Baugh, 'rock' prioritises material sound rather than harmonic structure and large-scale form. Contrary to Baugh, harmony and form still matter in popular music. The way that popular music prioritises materiality is rather that the materials of popular songs——under *all* their parameters——come together contingently and coalesce into wholes.

Materials generate form in popular songs, then, insofar as they qualify one another to produce meaningful wholes. Here materials do not generate form in the same way as in music that conforms to the developmental paradigm, that is by elaborating the implications of motives and thereby generating a logically interconnected system. In popular songs the materials instead generate structures of meaning to which each material makes an integral contribution. But this is still a way in which materials interact productively to generate form.

Now, as we saw in Chap. 3, Adorno believes that music that is organised developmentally——that is autonomously——has truth-content. To the extent that musical works realise this ideal type, they present a truth about the importance of autonomy for human individuals and other living beings. These works show that there is value in material things of all kinds being able to develop in accordance with their inherent tendencies. Autonomous works do not state these truths in so many words but *present* them, because of how their matter-form relations are configured, such that their materials generate the form of the whole work. This configuration embodies the truth that materials can and do generate form, and that form depends upon the materials generating it. This point can be extended to popular music, for it too has a typical configuration in which materials generate form, albeit not in the same way as in developmentally organised music. But in that their materials do generate their forms, popular songs also present truths about the dependency of form and conceptual thought on the body and about the creative powers of matter out of which forms and concepts arise.

In Adorno's view, because autonomous musical works have truth-content they also have aesthetic value, in a broadly Hegelian sense of aesthetic value. In Hegel's sense, art and to some degree nature have aesthetic value in that they present the truth in sensory form. Hegel takes it to be good for truth to be accessible at a sensory as well as an intellectual level: purely intellectual access to truth is not sufficient for us, as the sensing, embodied beings that we are. A truth that is only available to the intellect is not one that we could ever fully endorse. Adorno follows Hegel on these assumptions, as I do.[13]

But there are also differences. For Hegel, (i) the truth that art-works present is that the *idea* organises and gives overarching rational structure to the material world and all its particulars. In contrast, for Adorno, the truth that autonomous musical works present is that *material individuals* can and should develop freely, that form depends on materials, and that form should permit materials to develop freely. I've argued that the same truth is presented in popular music. For Hegel, (ii) only serious, fine art presents truth, which after all concerns the idea and is therefore only presentable by appropriately serious art that subordinates material pleasures to rational concerns. But because the truth presented in popular music concerns the primacy *of* materiality, music of this form is perfectly capable of presenting this truth while being popular. Music that entertains, that gives sensory and bodily pleasure, is well equipped to express truths about the need for the body to realise itself. And for Hegel, (iii) the artistic presentation of the truth must ultimately be superseded by the comprehension of that truth in concepts, given, again, that this truth concerns the idea as rational structure. In contrast, the popular-musical truth about materiality can only be fully conveyed when it is presented, given what this truth is about, that is the priority of materiality to conceptual understanding. This truth has to be shown and not stated, otherwise the music would be presupposing the very primacy of conceptual form over sensory experience which is being denied.

It may seem to be a leap to say that, because popular music has a typical structure in which materials generate form, it affirms the central importance of the materiality *of the body*. For the kind of 'materials' that generate form in popular music are quite abstract. These materials, as musemes, are not necessarily immediately perceptible in their distinctness from the whole mass of a song's interwoven sound-layers; it may require analytical listening to disinter these materials in their distinctness. Also, these materials do not reduce to their physical basis in sound-waves and their processes. For these two reasons, they do not obviously pertain to the body. I have taken it, though, that the emergence of meaningful wholes from interacting materials is analogous to the emergence of intellectual thought——concepts, judgements, and reason——from the body, analogous because that latter emergence takes place as the body's material elements——forces, impulses, energies——interact. I will strengthen the analogy in subsequent chapters, in particular when I consider the semiotic processes by which, in infancy first and foremost, our bodily forces crystallise into meanings that are embodied in the guise of affects. Moreover, popular music's treatment of rhythm, as well as of meaning and words, also establishes a connection with bodily materiality in the sense of concrete, moving, human bodies. So when popular music's matter-form configuration is situated among these other aspects of popular music, the 'matter' in that configuration does have definite connections with the human body. Let's proceed to these further dimensions of popular music, beginning with rhythm.

NOTES

1. These potential meanings are embodied in musical elements on a partly but not entirely conventional basis, I'll argue in Chap. 6.
2. The change of tempo makes it hard to describe the lengths of the song's components consistently. My solution is to take each measure in the B-section to last for half the time of a measure in the A-section. Elsewhere, as in *The Beatles Complete Scores*, occasional measures of the B-section are instead notated as being in 2/4.
3. As Moore observes, the A- and B-sections cohere at the level of 'hypermetre' (higher-order groupings of measures) because multiples of five organise both sections (1997: 53).
4. Compositions containing disparate parts are found in many musical traditions. I mention the disparate parts of popular songs, though, to explain how such songs are not counter-examples to my thesis about the coalescence of parts.
5. The standards that Baugh criticises overlap heavily with those of the developmental model endorsed by Adorno. These standards may not do justice even to classical music: James Young, for one, argues that classical music gives importance in their own right to parameters other than harmony and formal organisation——to timbre, rhythm, texture, dynamics, and so on (see Young 1995).
6. Robert Walser (2003) makes related criticisms of Robert Grossberg's view that popular music affects listeners in an immediate way that bypasses meaning and the intellect. Walser replies that musicians produce these effects by manipulating codes that are so familiar that the music's effect *appears* immediate (Walser 2003: 21–22; see also Tagg 2012: 111).
7. For Moore too, these factors that challenge notation 'most nearly capture the music's particular strengths' (1997: x); ditto Chester (1970b) and Tagg (1982: 42).

8. Popular musicians rarely approach chords as Scruton recommends——as Moore notes, in popular music chords tend to be treated as discrete entities (1995: 190).

9. That concession is regularly made in writing on popular music. For example, Starr and Waterman say that Madonna's 'Like a Virgin' has a 'straightforward' form and that 'As in much popular music, the timbre, texture, and rhythmic momentum of "Like a Virgin" are more important to the listener's experience than the song structure' (2006: 260). John Andrew Fisher refers to the 'rudimentary and predictable nature of rock's tonal structures', maintaining like Baugh that nonetheless there is much interest in the 'music as heard' (1998: 109).

10. Against Gracyk, Davies (2001: esp. 30–36) argues that performance remains important in rock, specifically performance *in the studio*. Kania (2006) defends a position closer to Gracyk's. See also Brown (2000), Fisher (1998).

11. Gracyk distinguishes rock-'n'-roll from its descendant rock, but he also holds that rock should be identified not as a genre but by the ontological status of its 'works' as recordings (as exemplified by *Sgt. Pepper*). But, Gracyk shows, recording was already essential to Elvis's Sun Studio recordings. So if 'rock' is an ontological category then it encompasses rock-'n'-roll——and shouldn't be called 'rock' at all, since the ontological category is rather that of popular music, and rock is one of its metagenres.

12. However, arguing that 'Relax' *is* aesthetically coherent, see Warner (2003: ch. 6).

13. The value here is *aesthetic*, not artistic, because it is not only artworks that can realise this value. Hegel allows that natural things can present truth to a degree.

CHAPTER 5

Rhythm, Energy, and the Body

1   INTRODUCTION

Much popular music has a strong rhythmic dimension, as many listeners, musicians, and theorists agree. Because popular music is highly rhythmic, it arouses our bodies. It solicits us to dance and move in many ways, and it affects us corporeally in other ways too: songs can energise, elate, enrage, depress our spirits, or wind us down. These affective reactions have somatic roots, being bound up with changes in levels of bodily energy. To be sure, other kinds of music, including art music, often have somatic effects too. But popular music is particularly noted in this regard, and is my concern here.

Theorists have mostly celebrated popular music's rhythmic dimension and bodily appeal.[1] Here is Lawrence Grossberg:

> As many a rock and roll fan has commented, the power of the music lies not in what it says but in what it does, in how it makes one move and feel. … Rock and roll is corporeal and 'invasive' … [and] without the mediation of meaning, the sheer volume and repetitive rhythms of rock and roll produce a real material pleasure for its fans. (1990: 113)

For Grossberg, then, rock's effects 'do not necessarily involve the transmission, production, structuration, or even deconstruction of meaning'. Likewise for Jeremy Gilbert and Ewan Pearson (1999), some popular music——electronic dance music——acts directly on our bodies by prompting us to dance, bypassing the intellect in a radical subversion of

© The Author(s) 2016   141
A. Stone, *The Value of Popular Music*,
DOI 10.1007/978-3-319-46544-9_5

the mind/body hierarchy. I agree that popular music subverts that hierarchy, and does so in part through its rhythmic dimension, but I do not think that this takes place in the ways claimed by Grossberg or Gilbert and Pearson. My alternative account will be developed in this chapter.

I develop this account by responding to an objection to the rhythmic force of popular music which comes out of Adorno's work. He identifies the rhythmic and corporeal force of popular music but finds it problematic. He claims that popular music has an unvarying 'basic beat' with which it dominates listeners. Hence this form of music does not empower our bodies or afford us possibilities for bodily self-realisation but rather compels us to move and undergo certain affective and energetic reactions, while short-circuiting our intellects so that we cannot reflect critically on these processes (see, e.g., Adorno 1976: 29).[2]

Adorno alerts us to a real area of concern here. But the problem, I'll argue in Sect. 2, is actually as follows. In being organised repetitively, popular music is regulated by 'measured time' (Abel 2014). This is abstract, mathematical time, made up of discrete, homogeneous intervals or units that can be multiplied or divided indefinitely many times to measure out and co-ordinate repetitions of a song's elements. This kind of time is part of clock-time, which Adorno identifies——plausibly, I believe—— as a construct of modern mathematical science and an integral factor in industrial society. Clock-time has been key to the division of labour and the factory system, enabling productive tasks to be broken down into their components and those components timed, apportioned to different individuals, then co-ordinated. Clock-time has also enabled the scientific measurement and control of natural processes. Thus, popular music's repetitive organisation makes it potentially complicit with capitalism and the domination that capitalism exerts over the materiality of both nature and individual human bodies. Perhaps in this way, despite what I have argued so far in this book, popular music's repetitive organisation *is*, after all, connected with the modern dominance of form over matter, in the sense of the dominance of clock-time as an abstract intellectual construct over material bodies and nature.

I'll argue, though, that ultimately popular music uses measured time in a way that challenges that dominance. Measured time enables repetitions of songs' material elements to be mapped onto one another, where each of these elements has its own rhythm. Through measured time, then, these different rhythms become co-ordinated so that some pull with and others against one another. Crucially here, popular music typically has a layer of explicit percussive rhythm, discussed in Sect. 3. The rhythms of the other layers of sound either reinforce or pull against the percussion rhythm and so come to form a force-field of partly conflicting, partly intertwining energies, as Sects. 4 and 5 explore. It is in virtue of these complex rhythmic pulls-and-pushes that popular songs solicit us to move our bodies in time with them, I argue in Sect. 6. But songs do not exert compulsive causal force upon our bodies (as Adorno feared). Rather, we *make sense* of songs' conflicting energies at a bodily level: in moving to music we are effectively thinking through its rhythms with the tacit, practical intelligence of our bodies, by modelling movements of our body parts on shifts of emphasis and timing in the music.[3]

The measured time that enables this rhythmic dimension to crystallise within popular music, and to elicit the intelligent activity of our bodies, is a formal, abstract construct. Yet this formal, conceptual construct *enables* the music to take on an energetic character and *enables* our bodily and material powers to come to self-realisation in our responses to the music. In this way popular music is so configured that form serves matter, and the truth is presented that it is good for formal principles and intellectual forms to facilitate, not suppress, the development of material bodies and their forces. So I argue in Sect. 7.

Having said this, while it is standard that popular music has this rhythmic and bodily character, it is not universal, and different songs and genres realise this character in different ways and to different degrees. For instance, in much 1980s indie rock the bass-lines are indistinct and the different emphases presented by different instruments are half-buried under a thick layer of fuzz or noise, yielding music with little perceptible rhythmic dynamism, to which it is difficult to dance. In what follows, then, I am concerned with rhythmic qualities that popular music has generally, not universally.

2   BEAT, MEASURE, DOMINATION

Post-rock-'n'-roll popular music typically has a layer of explicit beat. This is provided by percussion instruments and is usually made up of rhythmic cells that are repeated, throughout each song or song section, under varying degrees of modification. It is rare for improvisations to disguise or complicate matters, except in genres that hybridise with jazz——jazz-funk, jazz-rock, and so on. Normally, though, each song has a constant percussion pattern that is maintained throughout.

One function of the explicit beat layer is to spell out and make explicit songs' metric organisation. An example is the drums in Michael Jackson's 'Billie Jean' (the 1983 single version, also included on *Thriller*, and subsequently included on *Number Ones*, see Fig. 5.1). The drum pattern here is the one most standard in popular music. The snare-drum sounds on the even divisions of the 4/4 beat (two and four), the bass-drum on the odd divisions (one and three). Between them the drums thus spell out the 4/4 metre to which 'Billie Jean', like the vast majority of popular songs, is set, with each measure evenly divided into four quarter-length intervals of time. By counting to the recurring drum pattern listeners can identify where each measure begins and ends and so how the music is organised (Covach 1997: 11). The hi-hat makes it explicit that each quarter-length interval can be halved again, but the bass- and snare-drums are fundamental in making explicit the song's temporal organisation. In 'Billie Jean's' long introduction we clearly hear the percussion play this role. The drums are present from the very start, and the bass guitar, bass synthesiser, and cabasa (a Latin percussion instrument) come in on measure three. Staccato chords, played on another synthesiser, enter on the 11th measure. Thus, the drums immediately establish the metric framework with which the other instruments in turn fall in.

If explicit beat spells out metre, reciprocally metre regulates the repetitions of the elements presented at each layer of sound. Metric constraints

Fig. 5.1 Michael Jackson, 'Billie Jean', cabasa, drums, bass guitar, and synthesiser, timing ca. 00:20–00:24

govern the length of each element (e.g. the length of the bass-line in 'Billie Jean') and the points in time when each element begins and ends, thereby ensuring that the elements at each layer of sound are co-ordinated with one another. Higher-level groupings of measures determine the length of each song section and the points at which instrumental patterns change between sections. Let's refer back to my earlier model of repetitive construction (Table 3.1). The chorus section of a hypothetical song might be constructed out of (1) four repetitions of a four-chord sequence within which each chord is presented for one measure, these aligned with (2) four phrases of melody each four measures long, (3) eight repetitions of a two-measure bass-line, and (4) sixteen repetitions of a one-measure percussion pattern. These repetitions can be co-ordinated due to the background presupposition of a uniform metrical grid against which the timings and durations of all the iterated units are measured out.

Previously, I argued that repetition enables musical materials to exercise a kind of agency in contributing to the generation of songs' meanings. But perhaps in another way repetitive organisation *does* dominate the musical materials, by providing a quasi-mathematical 'grid' into which they must be fitted before their connotations can interweave. Further, the measured time that's put to work in this 'grid' is a scientific and mathematical construct: it is abstracted from the uneven, qualitatively varying lived time of human experience and from the uneven temporal processes that we experience in nature. This is not to say that mathematical time does not really exist, only that it is different from time as we experience it in our own lives and in nature as we inhabit it. For purposes of controlling natural processes, time is reduced to successive units of identical duration——'nows'——each infinitely divisible; we can reckon and calculate with these so as to intervene effectively in natural processes. The musical result is metre, where a measure is the basic temporal unit, each of these units can be divided (e.g. into four quarters), and those divisions can be subdivided again ad infinitum. In the other direction, measures can be added endlessly to build up compositions of any length——extending, in the final analysis, to 'the pitiless eternity of the clockwork' (Adorno 2002: 279). Either way the presupposition is homogeneous time: time cut up into atomic components, all identical.

So much for the problem that repetitive organisation seems to be connected with measured time and so, potentially, industrial capitalism and its domination over the materiality of nature and of human bodies. I will now argue that in its typical approach to metre and rhythm popular music actually offers a solution to this problem.

3   Explicit Beat and the Backbeat

We should look more closely at explicit beat or explicit rhythm, one of the typical layers of sound in popular music (Moore 2012a: 20–21; Gracyk 1996).[4] It is 'explicit' in several respects:

(1) The drums that are standardly used in popular music (snare-drum, bass-drum, toms, hi-hat, and cymbals) are 'unpitched', as are most of the other percussive media in common use in popular music—hand-claps, floor-stomps, tambourines, maracas, and so on.[5] Being unpitched, these instruments provide *only* rhythm without also contributing to melody and harmony.

(2) Typically the percussion layer does not appear in popular music merely episodically but is a constant presence throughout a song. Some rhythmic patterns presented by percussion instruments may be only episodic: cymbal splashes or drum 'fills' marking transitions between sections, for instance, or drum 'breaks' (i.e. solo passages). But generally those episodes are just part of the whole percussion layer, which remains present throughout a song. Popular songs with no such layer of unpitched percussion, such as the Beatles' 'Eleanor Rigby', are rare. Somewhat more common are songs that feature percussion only for some sections—for example, the first verse and pre-chorus of David Bowie's 'Life on Mars?' (on *Hunky Dory*) contain no drums. Most often, though, percussion is there throughout.

(3) The percussion normally presents a short rhythmic pattern or cell that is repeated either for the whole song or a whole section (e.g. when different rhythmic patterns are presented in the verse and the chorus). Usually these basic patterns are repeated under variations or with additional episodes such as drum fills. As in 'Billie Jean', it is common for a percussion pattern to last for one measure and so be repeated once per measure. Multiple repetitions of these patterns are then assembled to make up the entire percussion layer of a track.

Many permutations exist, though. A song's basic rhythmic cell may last for more than one measure, as with the instantly recognisable synthetic bass-drum rhythm that opens New Order's 1983 track 'Blue Monday' (later included on the compilation *Substance*) (Fig. 5.2). Longer multi-measure percussion patterns are less common but do occur; one instance

Fig. 5.2 New Order, 'Blue Monday', drums, timing ca. 00:00–00:03

Fig. 5.3 U2, 'I Will Follow', drums, timing ca. 00:15–00:21

is in U2's 'I Will Follow' (on *Boy*; Fig. 5.3). As in this case, longer, multi-measure rhythmic patterns tend to consist of varying iterations of a shorter pattern. In 'I Will Follow' the odd measures iterate a basic snare-and-bass-drum combination, while measure two presents it in altered form and measure four presents a variation on the altered pattern in measure two——an ABAC design.

> (4) In the context of this overall approach to explicit rhythm, popular music tends to emphasise the backbeat—that is beats two and four in each measure in 4/4 time.[6] The standard way that this is done is by the snare-drum sounding on beats two and four and the bass-drum on one and three. Because the snare-drum is smaller than the bass-drum its sounds have higher frequencies (although no precise pitch) and therefore stand out more, so that the snare's whip-crack sound cuts through the texture more audibly than the duller thud of the bass-drum. The prominence of the snare-drum can be increased further by other means, such as its being struck more forcibly, mixed louder, treated electronically, recorded with echo, or a combination of these. For example, Bruce Springsteen's 'Born in the USA' emphasises the snare-drum beats so heavily that they sound like explosions.

This bass-and-snare-drum combination is pervasive in popular music, but only under countless variations. Measures of 4/4 time can be subdivided into eight parts with additional drum sounds then placed on some of these subdivisions——generating, for example, a double backbeat (Fig. 5.4). Or additional bass-drum beats can be inserted, yielding, for instance, the Motorik beat (Fig. 5.5), much used in 'Krautrock' and intended to evoke

Fig. 5.4   The double backbeat

Fig. 5.5   The Motorik beat

Fig. 5.6   The Winstons, 'Amen, Brother', drums, timing ca. 01:26–01:28

the mindless automatism of motorway driving (see Stubbs 2014b). By sub-dividing the 4/4 beat further, additional possibilities for variation can be produced. Each quarter-note beat can be divided into three parts (so that the metre is effectively 12/8) or the beat can be subdivided into 16 parts, generating the very busy and complicated rhythms heard in funk (Brody and Campbell 1999: 129), often sampled and looped to make up the percussion layer in rap. One of the songs most often so sampled is the Winstons' 'Amen, Brother' (the B-side of their 1969 single 'Color Him Father'), specifically the first one or two measures of the 'Amen break', the song's four-measure-long drum solo, source of the archetypal 'breakbeat'. The hi-hat presents eighth-notes, but the distribution of bass- and snare-drum sounds presupposes a sixteenth-note subdivision of the beat (see Fig. 5.6). Changing which percussion instruments or parts of the drum-set are used, for instance by using only tom-toms, yields further variations on the standard popular music beat, as does the use of time signatures other than 4/4——most often 3/4 and 6/8——although 4/4 remains overwhelmingly common. And, albeit rarely, songs can include changes in metre, or measures can be unexpectedly dropped or added.

We can identify further sources of variation from Charles Keil's picture of 'groove' (Keil and Feld 1994). Although groove is variously defined, theorists agree on the basic phenomenon: variations over time on a repeated rhythmic pattern (see Abel 2014: 18–24; Butler 2006: 5; Middleton 2006: 145–6; Roholt 2014: 10–11. Sometimes, under these variations, the basic pattern itself gradually evolves over time, as in James Brown's 'Funky Drummer'). For Keil, music more specifically has groove when:

(a) It includes some instruments that sound out a steady beat—say, four beats to the measure on the bass-drum—while other instruments sound slightly ahead of or behind that same beat—say, the snare-drum sounds slightly before or behind beat two in each measure—thus 'leaning' forwards or backwards (Keil and Feld 1994: 61–62; and see Roholt 2014). The 'timing discrepancies' that interest Keil are minute—as when a forward-leaning snare-drum regularly sounds on, say, what is effectively point 1.9 in the measure or even 1.85. It's unlikely, though, that a human drummer would exactly maintain a steady beat on 1.85. Micro-variations are bound to occur, and for Keil these micro-variations give songs lived vitality and rescue them from monotony;

(b) Music includes timing discrepancies or nuances whose 'feel' is irreducible to the measurable temporal alterations at work (Keil and Feld 1994: 54). Yet Keil acknowledges that measurable alterations *are* at work (154–6), and I find it helpful to approach timing nuances in such terms. Suppose that in a 4/4 song the snare-drum repeatedly sounds not on but before beat two. If we subdivide the measure further, into eight parts, we might now find that the snare sound occurs on beat two of eight—or, if it now falls between beats two and three, we could subdivide the measure again, into sixteenth-notes. This might now locate the sound on either beat three or four of 16—or if it still falls between beats, we could subdivide the measure into 32 parts. And so on. With the minute discrepancies that interest Keil, many levels of subdivision of the beat are necessary to capture precisely where sounds are placed. But even when we find the right subdivision, our original song spelt out a 4/4 beat, so the snare-drum sound (in my hypothetical example) remains discrepant with respect to that beat. Timing nuances arise, then, when one instrument presupposes a finer-grained subdivision of the measure to the others.

In sum, Keil's work allows us to adduce several further ways in which popular music's standard beat can be varied: through timing nuances, consistently maintained or not; through small variations adding up to longer-term shifts in a rhythmic pattern; and through different instruments presupposing finer- and coarser-grained divisions of the beat.

Popular music's standard beat, then, is usually present under variations——so much so that even a song that presents that standard beat unadorned and without variations counts as just one more variation on the normal pattern *of* variation. Why do these variations matter? We can extract an answer from Dick Bradley's account of rock-'n'-roll. Rightly treating it as fundamentally derivative of rhythm-and-blues, he says of rhythm-and-blues that:

> The setting up of a regular, more or less homogeneous rhythmic 'background' and a partly or wholly improvised foreground of one or more instruments and/or voices, set against the background, offers ... an *image* ... of 'individual' actions in the context of the shared experience of externalized, alienating time. By 'externalized time' I refer to ... the mediation of the clock ... [as] a precondition for the economic system of capitalism. (1992: 48)

That is: for Bradley, the standard beat upheld by the rhythm section of a rhythm-and-blues band enacts measured time, a concomitant of capitalism. Yet:

> Against a stretched-out, unyielding temporal background——the beat—— the singer, guitarist, horn-player or whoever, uses ... anticipations of the beat, delays, accelerations ..., melodic improvisation ... and ... freely varied timbre/sound production, to detach his or her ... sound from the beat, cutting across or against the beat. (49)

That strategy continues in rock-'n'-roll, for Bradley, so that the beat ceases to be alienating and is made into a resource against which individuals can realise themselves freely and creatively (50). In the contributions of vocalists, lead guitarists, and so on, a musical symbol is created of individual freedom from oppressive clock-time (51; for a similar view, see also Tagg 1997).

For Bradley, that freedom is symbolised by the rhythmic, melodic, and other variations that vocalists or 'lead' instrumentalists effect against the constant beat. But we can also apply Bradley's argument to the beat itself.

Yes, we might say, the snare- and bass-drums (or other percussion instruments) present a standard beat and it does presuppose clock-time, but that standard beat is only realised under countless variations. The variations on what each percussion instrument is doing, and how and when it does it, embody the freedom of individuals to modify and inflect the standard beat.

Moreover, there is another stronger sense in which popular music's standard beat establishes an alternative to clock-time——not only in the endless variations on the standard 4/4 bass-and-snare beat but *in* the standard 4/4 bass-and-snare beat. To see this, let's turn to Gracyk's account of explicit rhythm. Following jazz historian Gunter Schuller (1986: 8), Gracyk describes the popular music backbeat, which descends from early jazz, as a 'democratised beat'. By stressing the beats that are 'weak' or 'back' within Western metre, jazz and popular music side with the underdog, with the beats that have been assigned subordinate places in the metric hierarchy. To explain this I need to clarify the notions of rhythm, metre and beat.

The definition of rhythm (in and beyond music) is contested, but I take it that a musical rhythm arises when there is a series of connected sounds in which some stand out over others——some are 'strong' and others 'weak' in some way. Several factors, not just volume levels, make for strength or weakness.[7] A rhythm, then, is a pattern of stressed and unstressed sounds. Metre, for its part, is 'bonded rhythm' (Sachs, quoted in Hamilton 2007: 136): a system for organising and imposing regularity on rhythmic patterns so that the strong and weak points regularly fall in certain places relative to one another. Not all music is metric (much song that follows the varying emphases of speech is non-metric) and different metric systems exist in different cultures, but my concern is with metre in its Western form as it has crystallised from 1600 onwards, since this kind of metre is what popular music generally presupposes. In this system, points (or 'pulses') in the flow of time to which the music unfolds are measured out evenly and used to demarcate the music into measures each containing a given number of pulses. The first pulse——or beat——in each measure is strongest.[8] This is because it marks the boundary between measures, the start of each measure and each multi-measure section, and the point from which to count out the time to which the music is set. While the first beat in each measure is thus accented, musicians may or may not physically stress it (subtly or conspicuously).

Beats, then, are on the one hand the points or pulses in time that mark out the divisions of the measure to which a song is set. In this sense, beats need not be explicitly sounded out; concomitantly, music can be metric and have a definite pulse without having any explicit beat layer. On the other hand, in popular music, there normally is a layer of explicit percussive rhythm——what I've called the 'explicit beat' layer——and so it is normal that at least some of those pulses are overtly sounded out. Standardly, when the metre is 4/4, the bass- and snare-drums distribute between them the task of sounding out the four pulses that divide up each measure. Thus, implicit pulse becomes explicit beat and the standard shape of the explicit beat in popular music is the bass-and-snare 4/4 combination.

Metre, then, establishes a hierarchy between the beats in each 4/4 measure, with beat one on top, and behind it beat three, then two, then four.[9] Because it stresses the backbeat, popular music's standard beat embodies a rejection of that metric hierarchy, re-emphasising the beats that are marked metrically as weak.[10] Implicitly, then, popular music's typical stress on the backbeat subverts the hierarchy bound up with metre and by extension rejects the broader power relations, of industry over people and science over nature, which are effected through measured time.

One question arising here concerns genres that re-emphasise the downbeat——'the one', in James Brown's words——notably funk, and some rap. The analysis so far would suggest that such music restores hierarchy and metric form, but if anything funk and genres influenced by it are even more rhythm- and body-focused than other popular music genres. We'll be in a position to explain this in the next section, so I postpone this issue to Sect. 4.

However, Gracyk's phrase 'democratised beat' is potentially confusing, as Mark Abel points out (2014: 49–50). Aren't the formerly weak beats simply raised to dominant position, rather than all the beats being equalised, as 'democratisation' suggests? The answer depends on whether popular music, despite stressing the backbeat, still also presupposes that there is an accent on the downbeat, that is beat one. In that case beats one (and three) would be privileged metrically while beats two (and four) are privileged in actual practice——resulting in rough overall equality. But *does* popular music presuppose that the downbeat is accented? Joel Rudinow argues otherwise, stressing popular music's African rhythmic influences:

> Western musicology has been given to theorizing the back beat as a 'displacement' of accent from presumed normal expectations ... and thus as an instance of 'syncopation', which is in turn understood to be basically

a matter of upsetting rhythmic expectations ... however, the presumption as to which expectations are 'normal' is objectionable from the point of view of ethnomusicology ... unlike European and European-derived musical traditions, African-derived rhythmic organization does not always *accent* the reference beat (the one) ... [which] need not even be enunciated ... it would be a misleading and objectionable presumption to theorize the back beat as essentially or necessarily a '*displacement* of accent' or a '*departure* from normal rhythmic expectations'. (2010: 121–2)

In short, perhaps post-rock-'n'-roll music simply operates with a new norm on which beats two (and four) rather than one (and three) are accented. John Mowitt likewise suggests that 'standardization has effectively effaced the backbeat's status as a syncopation', which he calls the 'becoming-"normal" of the backbeat' (2002: 32). That is, the emphasised backbeat is the new norm.

I disagree. Contrary to Rudinow, popular music inherits and works with Western metre as well as African-derived rhythmic practices. And Mowitt himself says that the backbeat remains 'strictly speaking' a syncopation (32), presumably in that the beats it stresses are not metrically accented. I believe, then, that popular music *does* accent the downbeat, even as it also institutes a new norm to stress the backbeat. As a result the two forces——metric and rhythmic, structural and practical——become pitted against one another to generate conflicting energies. To see this I need to show how metric accent is presupposed in popular music, which entails looking beyond explicit beat to the rhythmic aspects of other layers of sound.

4   Sources of Rhythmic Tension

The percussion layer of popular music may be explicitly rhythmic, but all its other layers of sound are rhythmic too——necessarily so, for rhythm is fundamental to all music. Rhythm can exist without melody or harmony but not the other way around: any melody unfolds a pattern of notes where, even if none are physically stressed more than the others, some still stand out due to their longer duration, raised pitch, harmonic function, and so on. More specifically, in popular music, each layer of sound is typically made up of repetitions of small elements, each with a rhythm that is reiterated——unchanged or varied——each time that the element recurs. These rhythmic qualities tend to be pronounced in popular music, partly because instruments are played in quite percussive ways, and partly because of the role of repetition, which means that rhythmic patterns recur and recur again and so build up momentum.

Also, most importantly, the rhythmic qualities of popular song elements are enhanced by their relations with the songs' explicit beat layer, because these elements come either to pull rhythmically *against* the emphases presented by the percussion or *with* those emphases. Given the norm that the snare-drum beats are stressed, reciprocally at least some other elements tend to pull against the snare-drum and with the bass-drum. Because the bass-drum typically sounds on beat one of each measure, the instruments that reinforce the bass-drum are pulling the emphasis towards the beats that are metrically accented.

Going back to measures 11–12 of 'Billie Jean' (Fig. 5.1), the snare-drum heavily and prominently stresses the backbeat. But every other instrument that features in these measures pulls against the snare-drum and pulls, to at least some degree, with the bass-drum. First, the bass guitar: although each note of the bass-line is stressed fairly evenly, a slightly greater stress falls on the notes occurring on beats one and five, in time with the bass-drum beats. The bass-line thus exemplifies the norm for 'the bass player [to] center his part around the rhythmic pattern played in the bass drum, making sure to stress those notes rhythmically while filling in other notes in order to create an interesting bass line' (Covach 2006: 217–8). In 'Billie Jean' the first bass note in each measure, on beat one, stands out further by being on the tonic pitch F♯ and being reinforced by the first stabbing synthesiser chord in each measure. The backbeat remains most emphasised overall, but the bass guitar and synthesiser create a significant counter-pull towards beat one, helping to prevent the backbeat from becoming mechanical or militaristic.

Moreover, the bass guitar and synthesiser parts indicate that metric accent *is* presupposed, for each cycle through their repeated elements begins on beat one of the measure. The synthesiser signals this with eighth-note tonic chords on the first beat of each measure, at once cementing the tonic and confirming the metric accent. Likewise, each iteration of the bass-line begins on beat one of the measure; this is signalled by the bass-line starting out from the tonic at this point. Moreover, the bass-line divides into two halves: the first rises by an octave; the second descends by a (major) perfect fourth then rises back to close on the dominant, marking the end ('question'). This division of the bass-line confirms the metric accent, since beats one and three are accented as marking the start of each half.

This illuminates a broader way that popular music presupposes metric accent. Chord cycles generally begin on beat one of a measure and chord changes generally occur at that point too. The norm for chords to change on beat one is observed in many of the examples considered earlier, such as 'Sweet Little Sixteen' (Fig. 3.4) and 'Sunday Bloody Sunday' (Fig. 3.5). Of course there are variations: in 'Sh-Boom' (Fig. 3.3) each new chord begins slightly behind beats one and three in the measure. But overall beat one is central to the movements in the layer of harmonic filler and so to songs' harmonic organisation. We might wonder whether the timing of vocal phrases likewise reflects metric accent. Broadly it does, but less plainly than that of chords, for vocal lines more often anticipate or hold back relative to beat one. In the earlier examples, Berry's and Bono's phrases consistently start after each corresponding chord.

'Billie Jean' illustrates something else too. The synthesiser and bass guitar lines don't only reinforce the bass-drum; they also stress the second 'half' of each second beat in 4/4 time, a point in time not enunciated by either the bass- or snare-drums. The bass-line puts a slight emphasis at this point in that it returns to the tonic pitch here, while the second synthesiser chord likewise sounds here, whereas we might have expected it to sound later, on beat three. Now, we might think that here the bass-line and synthesiser chords 'lean' slightly ahead of the bass-drum with which they remain broadly aligned. Indeed the unstable, hurried chord creates a sense of tension and contributes to the song's qualities of anxiety, nervousness and agitation (as do the scratchy, uncomfortable sound of the cabasa and the pacing quality of the bass-line as it restlessly 'walks' up and down).[11] Overall, then, the track has a 'forward-leaning' groove with connotations the reverse of the relaxed, laid-back qualities of 'backward'-leaning grooves.

Moreover, the syncopated chords in question (on ii) can be seen as occurring on beat four of an eight-beat division spelt out by the hi-hat, cabasa, and bass guitar. This is not the sort of minute timing discrepancy considered earlier, yet something interesting is going on. To represent matters in binary terms:

(a) Bass-/ snare-drums:	1 0 **1** 0 1 0 **1** 0
(b) Keybd:	1 0 0 **1** 0 0 0 0
(c) Bass guitar:	1 0 0 **1 1** 0 0 0

Returning to the idea that the popular music beat is 'democratised', the unexpected placements of sounds in (b) and (c) introduce a further type of democratisation. Any 4/4 measure can be subdivided indefinitely many times, but initially into eight equal parts. Thus

> 1   2   3   4
> becomes
> 1 and 2 and 3 and 4 and

Each eighth-note pair (1-and) adds up to a quarter-note beat (1) at the higher level, where each quarter-note beat begins on the *first* of each eighth-note pair, giving it priority. This norm filters down from the higher-level prioritisation of beat one. Here, then, is another hierarchy implied in metre, which can be subverted by beginning a sound on the *second* half of any quarter-note beat (whether or not the sound runs on into the next beat). The same kind of subversion or syncopation (call it 'timing displacement') can be accomplished at any subdivision of the beat: the finer-grained the subdivision, the more possibilities for subversion.[12]

These kinds of syncopation presuppose measured time and metric hierarchy just as the stressed backbeat does: the norm must be presupposed to be subverted. Thus, popular music presupposes metric hierarchy in a particular way: it *uses* that hierarchy, playing it off against the stress on the backbeat and against timing displacements to create a dynamic pull of energies between different beats——those that are metrically accented and those that are rhythmically stressed or sound in unexpected places. Metric accent is mobilised into a resource for producing dynamic pulls and counter-pulls of energy within a song.

We are now in a position to answer my earlier question regarding genres that re-emphasise the downbeat, that is, beat one. This re-emphasis can be clearly heard, for instance, in James Brown's 'Make It Funky (Part 1)'. The bass-drum sound on beat one is stressed more heavily than usual, and, because the iterations of both the horn riff and the scratchy guitar riff also begin on beat one, the combined effect is to emphasise beat one above beat two, the latter nonetheless being sounded by the snare-drum. Thus, 'Make It Funky' does not abandon the standard 4/4 bass-and-snare combination altogether: the snare-drum still sounds on beats two and four, while the bass-drum sounds on beat one and after beat three (leaning backwards). But the bass-drum is struck more forcefully than normal, and the weight of the other instrumental parts is piled towards the first bass-drum beat to a degree that overturns the usual predominance of the snare-drum beats. The energy is pulled heavily off beats two and four, but the snare-drum's sound——its way of cutting through the texture—— pulls the energy back to a significant degree towards the even beats. Thus, we have here an intensified version of the normal popular music practice of playing off overt rhythm and metric accent against one another, exemplifying the norm to *use* metric accent to produce rhythmic dynamism. This helps to explain why funk, and other genres and tracks that stress the downbeat, do not thereby cease to be rhythm- and body-based. On the contrary, they take even further than other popular music genres the strategy of mobilising metric accent to produce rhythmic dynamism.

5 'BLUE MONDAY'

In this section, I want to substantiate my overall claims regarding the dynamic tension between metre and rhythm in popular music by using a second extended example: New Order's 'Blue Monday'. Vocalist Bernard Sumner says of 'Blue Monday' that 'I don't really regard it as a song [but] a machine to make people dance' (Sumner, in Bewarp and Crona 2013). More prosaically, 'Blue Monday' is an early piece of electronic dance music with a machine-like, unemotional character. It deserves consideration here partly because it is often assumed that rhythm properly speaking——perhaps contrary to mere beat or lifeless succession——arises only where there is organic flow (see, e.g., Scruton 2007). For instance, Joel Rudinow holds that music cannot fully possess rhythmic energy unless it embodies nuances imparted by performers in their unique individuality (see Rudinow 2010: 115). Similarly, Mark Abel states that music made on computers can only ever have a poor groove, if it achieves any groove at all (2014: 255). This is surprising, since computers permit ever-increasing levels of timing nuance to be factored into music (see Gilbert and Pearson 1999: 124). But even in the absence of any such nuances, electronic music *can* still have rhythmic dynamism. 'Blue Monday', made when computer-based music technologies were less sophisticated and timing was relatively rigid, shows that this need not rule out rhythmic dynamism. Indeed the track responds to these constraints by foregrounding its own synthetic and mechanical character, yet in a way that creates a propulsive rhythm.

For manageability's sake, let's concentrate on the first of the song's three sections, which lasts just over two minutes (see Table 5.1; the whole song lasts seven and a half minutes).[13] Allan Moore describes

Table 5.1   New Order, 'Blue Monday', first section, structure

Subsection	Measures	Instrumentation
1 (Opening)	8	The distinctive two-measure synthetic bass-drum pattern (Fig. 5.2 above) is repeated four times before any other instrumentation enters. This sets the scene for other instruments to become situated in relation to this beat
2	8	Four further repetitions of the bass-drum pattern occur while a two-measure, very flat keyboard pattern with a squelchy, percussive sound and added echo fades in, establishing that the song is in the Dorian mode on D, and running through a set of pitches that anticipates the synth-bass line
3	16	A synthetic snare-drum now enters, playing on beats two and four of each measure, plus hi-hat, playing even sixteenth-notes The keyboard reaches full volume, maintaining the same melodic pattern as before, with some slight rhythmic variations A two-measure-long synthetic bass pattern enters, alternating between an F–C–D sequence——as shown below——then a G–C–D series

Keyboard Synthesizer

According to the band, this bass-line re-uses the one from Sylvester's 1978 disco single 'You Make Me Feel (Mighty Real)'. But it is common in disco more broadly for bass-lines to present alternate octaves to an eighth-note rhythm——the very pattern into which the synth-bass settles in the next subsection of 'Blue Monday'. Versions of this 'high-energy' leaping octave pattern are also widely used in electronic dance music, in 'Firestarter' and 'Paparazzi' among others, for example

Break	2	Unaccompanied drum break
4	8	The synth-bass and drums (but not the keyboards) resume, with the synth-bass now cycling through the same series of pitches but set to a simplified eighth-note rhythm. The bass-drum now sounds on just beats one and three of each 4/4 measure while the hi-hat sounds on the even halves of each of these quarter-note beats. Thus by now the beat is relatively close to the standard popular music beat, but for the placement of the hi-hat

Drs.

(*continued*)

Table 5.1   (continued)

Subsection	Measures	Instrumentation
5	8	The bass guitar is now added, playing two very simple phrases that return relentlessly to the tonic:

		From this point onwards the tom-toms appear intermittently, playing fragments that echo all or part of the rapid, sixteenth-note phase of the earlier bass-drum pattern
Break	2	Another drum break occurs while the synth-bass cycle continues
6	18	The drum pattern resumes (but not the bass guitar). Added to this and to the ongoing synth-bass are choir-like harmonies, derived from a sample of Kraftwerk's 'Uranium' (on *Radio-Activity*). From measure three a sustained, descending keyboard melody comes in, onto which (from measure 11) is superimposed a second higher-pitched keyboard melody, again descending but for a sharp final rise. Immediately that this subsection ends, the song's middle, vocal section begins

'Blue Monday' as having 'arch' form: its middle, vocal section lies between its two outer sections (2012a: 175). The first section's form is 'accumulative', according to Mark Spicer (2004: 39–42): its subsections are demarcated by the additions and disappearances of various instruments which gradually build up overall.

Despite the complex process by which the instrumentation accumulates, many of the constituent musemes are minimal and simple. This reflects New Order's debt to punk——out of which they emerged, initially as Joy Division——while rhythmically and formally the track owes much to disco——in which long, highly repetitive tracks were common——and, in its frank embrace of the machine, to Kraftwerk.[14]

The track's opening subsections enable us to see how some of the song's component layers of sound interweave rhythmically. Let's focus on measures 27–28 (Fig. 5.7). By this point the drums are presenting an identifiable variation on the standard popular music beat, although the snare-drum is less prominent than normal and the bass-drum is relatively loud and conspicuous. The bass-drum beats are very evenly stressed, as are the synth-bass and keyboard synthesiser notes; this reflects the band's stated intention to create a robotic, machine-like track. There being no

Fig. 5.7 New Order, 'Blue Monday', drums, synthesiser, and bass synthesiser, timing ca. 00:47–00:49

significant differences in stress, by default the backbeat is emphasised——by the snare-drum on beats two and four of each measure——but so are the sounds that fall on the first beat of each measure, by virtue of being accented metrically. The metric organisation and, with it, accent is clearly identifiable because the sounds are so evenly stressed that they become quite metronomic. Without this effect of the song's metric organisation the emphasis on the snare-drum beats might become rather static and militaristic, having no counter-force pulling against it.

Thus 'Blue Monday' achieves a compulsive rhythm——already at this point in the track, as throughout——*despite* stressing each division of the beat very evenly. In punk rock, the same flattening-out of stresses tended to yield music that contained little rhythmic differentiation and too unbroken a wall of noise to be danceable. In 'Blue Monday' the evening out of stresses works very differently, leaving a single central tension between metric accent and backbeat. 'Blue Monday' ingeniously strips the popular music approach to rhythmic tension down to its essence: rhythmic emphasis versus metric accent.

'Blue Monday' makes little use of timing discrepancies——although one significant discrepancy occurs later in the track, which arose by accident, but which the band retained.[15] But on the whole, reflecting the song's machine-like quality, its elements occur squarely 'on' the beat. Yet there is one important timing displacement to note. From the fourth subsection onwards the hi-hat sounds on the second half, not the expected first half, of each quarter-note beat. The hi-hat thus sounds 'after' the beat from the perspective of the metric division spelt out by the bass- and snare-drums, adding an aspect of syncopation.

A different kind of syncopation is created by the interplay between the synth-bass and the bass-drum. Because of the unusual bass-drum pattern, which effectively means that this part speeds up and slows down alternately, some but not of all the synth-bass notes coincide with the bass-drum beats. When the bass-drum is slower-moving, the shorter synth-bass notes fall between the drum sounds; but when the bass-drum speeds up, some of its beats fall between the synth-bass notes. Here sounds are not placed unexpectedly relative to the metre but rather weave between the sounds presented at another layer of the texture. But this is a still a kind of syncopation, and (I think) is what blogger Aaron Lariviere means when he says of 'Blue Monday' that the 'synthetic bass line almost imperceptibly pulls against the beat, making a mostly static rhythm feel propulsive' (Lariviere 2013). Specifically, while the synth-bass and bass-drum are broadly aligned at the metric level, nonetheless the synth-bass pulls against the bass-drum by alternately speeding 'ahead' of the bass-drum then slowing down 'behind' it. Again, 'Blue Monday' achieves this propulsive result by juxtaposing two instrumental layers both containing solely components that occur 'on' the beat (i.e. occur or start on the first half of each beat).[16]

In sum, popular music typically creates rhythmic tension (1) by mobilising the tension between emphasised rhythm and metric accent, (2) by timing some sounds and silences in unexpected places relative to the metric division of the beat, and/or (3) by so timing sounds and silences at different layers of the texture that they weave in and out of one another. The goal of creating tension is the important thing; the means by which tension is created are miscellaneous. Those means can be electronic and artificial; organic flow and spontaneity are not necessary for rhythmic energy.

Admittedly, 'Billie Jean' and 'Blue Monday' alike are highly danceable, and we might wonder how far their features generalise to popular music overall. It is because they are highly danceable, though, that they bring the rhythmic character of popular music into relief. Many other songs and genres realise this character less fully than 'Billie Jean' and 'Blue Monday', but that is compatible with it being typical of popular music as a *form* to contain rhythmic dynamism. Central here is the presence of an explicit beat layer to which every layer of sound becomes related, so that songs become fields of energies pulling and pushing with and against one another. We apprehend the music in this way insofar as we come to enact its rhythmic tensions with our bodies and their energies and so experience the music as sharing in the character of the bodily movements and energies that it incites. Or so I argue next.

6   BODY MUSIC

Critics and defenders of popular music agree that it acts on our bodies and does so due to its rhythmic dimension. But what is the nature of this action? A common assumption is that the action is causal, so that popular music's rhythms affect our bodies much as one rolling billiard ball knocks into motion another with which it collides. However, this cannot possibly be how popular music's rhythms affect our bodies, because our bodies are not mere causal mechanisms. We are agents, and bodily agents. As Simone de Beauvoir puts it, the body is 'our grasp on the world and the outline of our projects' (1988: 66).[17] Beauvoir means that I don't use my body as an external vehicle for executing my plans, much as I use a car or bicycle for getting to work. Rather I, as body, decide what projects to pursue just in deciding how to do something physically by forming a bodily sketch or outline of the action, which I then execute. But if my body is thus a location of agency and not a mechanism, then efficient causation cannot be the route along which musical rhythms affect us somatically. How then do these effects occur?

For Beauvoir and like-minded phenomenologists of embodiment such as Merleau-Ponty (2002), I undertake my projects as inherently bodily projects that involve me-as-body navigating and negotiating the world and its physical constituents. To do this, I-as-body must first make sense of the spatial dimensions of the surrounding world from the perspective of my possibilities of movement. I do this sense-making tacitly, not primarily by making explicit calculations but by practically attempting actions, correcting and adjusting my movements, and eventually forming habits, such as the postures by which I keep a bicycle balanced upright. There is, though, a secondary perspective that we can each take on our bodies——regarding them as if from the outside, as objects. For Merleau-Ponty, I adopt this perspective when breakdowns occur in my habitual routines: if something malfunctions, say if I become ill, I turn and look at the body that from the primary first-person perspective I am (2002: 157). In turn the secondary perspective makes possible a tertiary perspective in which, having objectified my body and its processes, I approach their properties in increasingly abstract and scientific terms, thereby producing scientific biological knowledge of the body as a physical system.

Now, my bodily agency can be variously interpreted. For the early Sartre, I freely envisage possible actions and in their light I confer meaning on the world around me (Sartre 1993: 628). If I choose to take an uphill walk, a nearby hill becomes an opportunity or challenge, not an obstacle or indifferent natural feature. Plausibly, though, the relation between environment and activities is more reciprocal than this. Environments, situations, and objects are not formless until we frame possibilities; rather, any environment presents determinate possibilities to begin with. A steep hill does not offer the possibility of a casual, effortless stroll. Objects and situations *afford* us definite possibilities of action.[18]

From this perspective music affords various possibilities of action, and the possible actions afforded by popular music in particular include singing or singing-along; imitating performers' gestures and behaviours; playing along, if one has the skills; moving in time; dancing; exercising; and regulating one's emotions (by listening to certain songs to cultivate a given mood). Bodily movement is central to all these activities. Playing, performing, and singing-along involve repeated bodily movements, and uses of popular music in exercise depend on its propensity to energise us. Emotional regulation, too, has a bodily component, being bound up with music raising or decreasing our levels of energy.

The movements that popular music encourages us to make do not reduce to dancing. There is an immense variety of ways of moving to popular music, with dance practices themselves ranging from the anarchic to highly structured and rule-governed dance routines (e.g. the Macarena), from individual to collective behaviours, and from the restrained and decorous to the ecstatic and euphoric. Other ways of moving to (popular) music fall short of dancing proper: bobbing one's head, tapping one's fingers or feet, jiggling slightly while performing tasks around the house, or making gestures such as punching the air or leaping. And some popular music genres affect people energetically in ways that do not obviously constitute dance: for example, punk rock is highly energising, but that energy is most readily discharged in pogo-ing, jumping around, or in aggressive gestures, rather than dancing in a structured sense. Head-banging to heavy metal is similar.

Focusing on bodily movement rather than dance more narrowly, then, how specifically does popular music afford possibilities for movement? A clue comes from a remark of Bill Haley's about rock-'n'-roll:

> I felt that if I could take, say, a Dixieland tune and drop the first and third beats, and accentuate the second and fourth, and add a beat the listeners could clap to as well as dance this would be what they were after. (Gillett 1983: 24)

Haley's remark relates to the norm for different layers of sound to empha-sise different beats, and put sounds and silences in unexpected places. This invites listeners to align movements and gestures of their different body parts with these differences of emphasis or timing in the music, for example by clapping hands on beats two and four (with the snare-drum) while sepa-rating the hands on beats one and three (with the bass-drum). Someone might do this while, say, first centring their pelvis on beats one and two then thrusting out their hip on beat three and four. Schematically, we align different body movements with different divisions of the beat and make each movement when the emphasis falls in a given place. As we move, we exert energy. We feel the energy in our bodies shift from one place to another, as different body parts are tensed and relaxed in moving them.

For the most part we do not consciously plan these gestures, although that can happen. But generally moving to music is exemplary of activ-ity carried out at a directly bodily level without deliberate mental con-trol. Moreover, there is no set way in which particular rhythmic patterns must become mapped by bodily movements. Here the intelligence of the body gets freely to work, devising endless ways to map rhythmic shifts corporeally (and usually incorporating social and cultural mediations so that particular dance styles carry social connotations). Crucially, through the music offering us possibilities of movement, we gain a possibility of bodily self-realisation and empowerment instead of merely suffering the effects of compulsive force. Our bodies are enabled to exercise agency by generating meaningful patterns of movement. In addition, our bodies are enabled to exercise their latent intelligence in making sense of music's rhythms by generating these patterns. By virtue of its pronounced rhyth-mic qualities, then, popular music appeals to our bodies as perceptive agencies, an appeal to which we respond intelligently——by making sense of the music's rhythms in our bodily movements——and creatively——by finding individual and endlessly variable patterns of movement that map those rhythms. This is a positive value of popular music. But, contrary to Grossberg, the value is not that popular music exerts brute effects on our bodies and bypasses our intelligence outright. Rather, popular music invites us to participate in its rhythms, and to move with them, exercising the intelligence latent in our bodies.

Earlier, I've argued that popular music has value in presenting us with truths about the importance of materiality. Here, though, it seems that popular music instead invites us to use our bodily intelligence, rather than presenting the truth that that intelligence exists and is the root of the explicit intellect. In the last section, I want to clarify how it is that, by being so configured that it typically makes this invitation, popular music does present a truth that form can and should facilitate the self-realisation and creativity of the body.

7 FORM, RHYTHM, AND MATERIALITY

To return to our earlier problem, the rhythms of popular songs presuppose measured time: popular songs are constructed repetitively with homogeneous time serving to measure out and co-ordinate the repetitions of their elements. But the repeated elements have their own rhythms and take on rhythmic functions vis-à-vis the explicit beat——supporting it, pulling against it, or alternating between the two. Thus, measured time *enables* the rhythms of each layer of sound to come into dynamic interrelation. The pull of stressed backbeat against metric accent presupposes metre; the tensions produced by unexpected placements of sounds or silences rely on the metric subdivision of the beat. Thus, measured time is used in popular music to intensify its rhythmic quality and consequently the invitation to movement that the music makes to our bodies. As such, too, measured time is used to further the realisation of the intelligence and creativity of our bodies in moving in response to the music. This way of employing measured time subverts the power relations that are embedded in clock-time insofar as it organises scientific inquiry and industrial social life. Whereas ordinarily clock time is an instrument by which material nature is analysed, controlled, and dominated, in popular music measured time becomes a resource for creating force-fields of energy that empower and restore agency to human bodies.[19]

Here popular music is typically configured in a way that favours materiality. This is because its form——here in the sense of the measured time that regulates songs' repetitive organisation——does not dominate songs' materials. Instead, this form enables the materials——the elements repeated at each layer, each with its own rhythmic quality——to interlock rhythmically. Specifically, form as measured time enables the materials' differing rhythms to pull variously with and against each other, generating energetic dynamism. In this respect the music solicits our participation——indeed, often compels that participation, not by having brute causal effects on us but by offering us an opportunity to exercise our bodily intelligence. In sum, popular music form enables our bodies to achieve a level of self-realisation.

These claims interweave with those of Chaps. 3 and 4. There I argued that matter-form relations are so configured in popular music that form, in the sense of repetitive organisation, enables songs' materials to come together and interact to generate forms in the further sense of songs as meaningful wholes. In that way popular songs typically present the truth that form depends on and arises from materials and, indirectly, that meaning and thought depend on and arise from bodily forces. In this chapter I have, in part, provided more sense of how repetitive organisation plays this enabling role. Repetitive organisation is measured and presupposes metre and metric hierarchy, but it also enables elements to interrelate rhythmically, which is part of how they coalesce (when they coalesce): their different emphases need to interlock so that they form higher-level rhythmic patterns. This process involves meaning.

Take 'Billie Jean'. The standard bass-and-snare combination, along with the hi-hat sounding eighth-notes, creates a sense of normality and mainstream life. This is the more so since an eighth-note subdivision of the beat is common in rock, in contrast to the finer-grained subdivisions common in funk and genres influenced by it. However, the uneven, hurried rhythm of the staccato synthesiser chords, with each second chord sounding ahead of its expected placement, suggests nervous anxiety, like someone worrying, anticipating the future in advance, or unable to suppress a nervous tic or gesture. This reinforces the already restless quality of the bass-line, which resembles someone pacing. The result is that the percussion contrasts in quality with the bass-line and chords. The cabasa mediates between the two, presenting eighth-notes with a scratchy, uncomfortable sound. The overall connotation is that ordinary, mainstream life is being disrupted by a problem, that the protagonist is being pulled off track.

Alternatively, consider 'Blue Monday'. As we've seen, the track uses sounds that are almost always 'on' the beat and largely operates with a single tension between rhythmic emphasis and metric accent. It thus generates rhythmic dynamism on a highly machine-like and regular basis. In this way, its overall meaning is to explore the rhythmic power of machinery, including its power to compel us into movement. This is cast positively, as a way that machines can liberate us from our minds, offering escape. The celebration of the machine is encapsulated in the title, which comes from the phrase 'Goodbye Blue Monday' in Kurt Vonnegut's novel *Breakfast of Champions*, 'a reference to the invention of the washing machine, which improved housewives' lives', according to New Order's keyboardist Gillian Gilbert (Simpson 2013). The lyrics describe coldness and distance, an absence of emotion, again suggesting that machinery can release us *from* emotions and introspection into the realm of bodily movement. But we can also hear the positive value accorded to the machinic in the song's rhythmic character, as highly machine-like and artificial rhythms are used to generate much dynamic energy.

In this chapter I've also dealt with a second way that popular music affirms materiality, in addition to the fact that popular songs as meaningful wholes emerge out of their material components. Popular music also affirms materiality in that it uses measured time to intensify songs' rhythmic qualities and energetic character, in turn affording us opportunities for creative, intelligent bodily movement. It may be objected that nothing is 'affirmed' here at all. Certainly it is not typical of popular music as a whole to set forth explicit statements about rhythm, energy, or the body (although some songs carry complicated sets of connotations about these matters, as with 'Blue Monday'). Nonetheless, implicitly an affirmation of the importance of materiality is made just in how popular music is configured.

Here, let's recall again Hegel's view that art-works can present the truth in how their materials are organised into whole forms. For Hegel, when form effortlessly orchestrates materials into a balanced whole——as in ancient Greek sculptures of the gods——then the truth is presented that form does organise matter, and that the idea gives rational structure to the world's materials. By analogy: when measured time as a formal scaffold becomes a factor in generating rhythmic intensity, energy, and appeal to the moving body, then the truth is presented that form can facilitate the agency of our material bodies and that it is good that form do so. By implication, form need not suppress or restrict our bodies and it is undesirable for it to do so. This truth is presented in that popular music offers us instances, or examples, of cultural creations in which form is employed to promote the intelligent movement and thus self-realisation of our bodies.

Finally, I hope that this chapter has clarified how popular music's matter-form configuration pertains to the concrete materiality of the human body and does not only involve materials in the more abstract sense of small-scale repeated elements of songs. However, fully to see the connections between these senses of materiality in popular music, we need to think about the nature of the processes by which material components generate meaning, including the affective character of that meaning and how song words contribute to it. These are the subjects of Chaps. 6 and 7.

NOTES

1. However, Tagg criticises pro-body views (e.g. Tagg 1994, 2012: 101ff). Among those taking pro-body views are Baugh (1993), Echols (2010), Hesmondhalgh (2013), and Middleton (1990).
2. '[O]ne gets into a "jam", into rhythmic problems, which can be instantly disentangled by the triumph of the basic beat', Adorno complains of jazz (1991: 105). This 'basic beat' permeates and is rigorously maintained in swing jazz, he holds, being merely disguised by the improvised passages, but not really challenged (e.g. 2002: 470). This is unfair to swing jazz, but the issue about 'beat' is broader and others object to this 'beat' as well. Scruton calls beat the 'last sad skeleton' of rhythm, rhythm denuded of life and reduced to bare temporal succession (1997: 502), while for Bloom the rock beat has the crudity of sexual intercourse (1987: 73). Jacques Attali, too, complains that pop's rhythms——of 'exceptional banality ... not all that different from military rhythms' (1985: 109)——enshrine the power of social order.
3. Roholt makes a related argument concerning groove, which he identifies as the feel of timing nuances occurring over time with respect to a repeated rhythmic pattern (2014: 38). For Roholt (i) how a groove feels is crucial, and timing nuances are made so as to create a certain feel; (ii) we understand grooves through bodily activities——finger-snapping, foot-tapping, and so on; (iii) the groove's feel therefore has a bodily character, because 'the feel of a groove is the affective dimension of the motor-intentional movements' of listeners (105). Hamilton's related argument is that musical rhythms are already apprehended as moving: bodily and musical rhythm are constitutively connected (2007: ch. 5).
4. '[R]hythm ... emerges as a distinct "layer" in jazz and rhythm and blues, notably through the use of identifiable (repeated, musematic) syntactic units by drummers' (Middleton 1990: 281). This continues into rock-'n'-roll.
5. Percussion in popular music is usually 'unpitched' in the following sense. When struck, a drum (say) vibrates in several different ways simultaneously, at frequencies that do not stand in mathematically simple relations to one another, as do the frequencies that are produced when one plays pitched instruments, where each of these 'harmonics' is a whole-note multiple of the 'fundamental' frequency

that defines the pitch——for example, C_1, C_4, and A_3. When frequencies stand in mathematically awkward relations to one another we do not hear them as having any definite pitch.

6. Rudinow and Mowitt trace the rock-'n'-roll backbeat to Earl Palmer, who drummed with Little Richard among others (Mowitt 2002: 26, 81; Rudinow 2010: 120). Abel explains the backbeat differently (2014: 52).

7. 'Rhythm may be defined as the way in which one or more unaccented beats are grouped in relation to an accented one [and] ... such factors as duration, intensity, melodic contour, regularity, ... play a part in creating an impression of accent' (Cooper and Meyer 1960: 6–7). Lerdahl and Jackendoff (1983) distinguish phenomenal accent (stress), metric accent, and structural accent (where a sound is highlighted by its place in pitch relations).

8. 'Meter is the measurement of the number of pulses between more or less regularly recurring accents. Therefore, ... for meter to exist, some of the pulses in a series must be accented——marked for consciousness——relative to others. When pulses are thus counted within a metric context, they are referred to as *beats*. Beats which are accented are called "strong"; those which are unaccented are called "weak"' (Cooper and Meyer 1960: 4).

9. 'Fundamental to ... meter is ... periodic alternation of strong and weak beats ... For beats to be strong or weak there must exist a *metrical hierarchy*——two or more levels of beats' (Lerdahl and Jackendoff 1983: 19). For them, if we ascend a level——that is, in 4/4, from quarter-notes to minims——the 'strong' beats at 4/4 level (one and three) are the ones that remain present at the minim level; hence their strength. Robert Jourdain has a different explanation of the accent on beats one and (less so) three: because three is a prime number we grasp 3/4 metre whole——*one*–two–three, *one*–two–three, but because four is divisible by two we hear 4/4 as 'two groups of beats, with lighter accentuation at the start of the second pair: ONE–two–Three–four ... [etc.]' (1997: 127).

10. In addition, the standard popular music beat 'democratises' in that it combines European metre with an emphasis on the backbeat that arguably has African provenance, thus bringing together European- and African-derived traditions.

11. Richard Leadbeater has pointed out that each pair of synthesiser chords falls into a antecedent and consequent pattern: the

antecedent is on both the downbeat and the tonic; the consequent——the 'question'——is both syncopated and on a similarly unstable, querulous ii. In the song's paranoid lyrics, the protagonist is anxious to deny 'Billie Jean's' claim that he is the father of her child——but, it seems, no denial ('answer') is firm enough to quell his anxiety lest, after all, he is the parent (the 'question').

12. If metre is triple rather than duple——where each beat is counted out 'one-and-a', 'two-and-a', and so on——then subversion can be achieved by beginning or placing sounds on the 'and' or the 'a' of a beat.

13. As noted in Table 5.1, 'Blue Monday' is in the Dorian mode. This mode is made up of the pattern of tones and semitones obtained by playing all the white-key notes from D to the D an octave up (thus, TSTTTST). But while the outline of the mode is obtained in relation to the note D, songs in the Dorian mode can take any note as the tonic as long as they maintain the TSTTTST pattern. So a song built on, say, the Dorian scale on E takes E as the tonic and derives the rest of the notes in the key by following the Dorian outline.

14. These debts are acknowledged in that the track not only re-uses 'Mighty Real's' bass-line but also samples Kraftwerk and re-creates the bass-drum beat that features in much of Donna Summer's 'Our Love' (on *Bad Girls*). The bass guitar line is derived more loosely from a riff in Ennio Morricone's theme music to *For a Few Dollars More*.

15. A programming accident led to a discrepancy between the percussion and the rhythmic keyboard line (which begins shortly after the vocals), so that the latter sounds behind the beat. The discrepancy can be heard from 02:15 to 03:19, 03:33 to 05:24, then very briefly afterwards. Sumner discusses it in Bewarp and Crona (2013).

16. In using highly regular means to create rhythmic complexities, 'Blue Monday' anticipates much subsequent electronic dance music, in which 'producers have been able to utilize a few basic units to generate complex dissonances within the seemingly restrictive context of pure-duple meter' (Butler 2006: 166).

17. I've corrected Parshley's misleading rendition 'the instrument of our grasp on the world, [and] a limiting factor for our projects'.

18. My understanding of affordance comes from Beauvoir and Merleau-Ponty. DeNora also uses the concept in music theory (2003: 45), saying that one possibility that music affords us is to 'entrain our bodily movements to its properties'——not only in dance, which 'is simply one of the more formalised activities where this entrainment occurs'.

19. For Abel, too, 'groove music' critiques measured time (2014: 175, 255; by groove music he means popular music of the twentieth century as a whole). This music elevates metre to its dominating principle, but 'the very rigidity and regularity of the modern time experience is turned against itself through ... syncopation to generate flexibility and unpredictability' (175).

CHAPTER 6

Meaning and Affect in Popular Music

1   INTRODUCTION

In this chapter I look at how meaning is expressed in popular music. I've claimed that many particular songs convey specific meanings, for instance that R.E.M.'s 'Losing My Religion' traces how the protagonist's romantic hopes rise then are dashed. I have also claimed that the overall meanings of popular songs typically arise as the connotations of their multiple elements coalesce into higher-level structures of meaning. In this chapter I want to substantiate and explore this claim further.

One kind of meaning in music is often seen as central: emotional meaning.[1] Of all the arts, music is plausibly the one most intimately connected with our emotional lives. Unsurprisingly, then, public discussion of popular music often focuses on its emotional qualities, which tend to be understood in terms of songs giving authentic expression to the felt emotions of musicians. I argue against this widely held view in Sect. 2, suggesting that musicians can only express their emotions by drawing on musical materials that already convey desired emotional connotations.[2] Therefore, in Sect. 3, I situate emotional meaning among other kinds of meaning in popular music, noting how these shade into one another so that emotional qualities are important to popular music, but *as* they entwine with songs' other connotations. I then examine some of these entwined connotations in Joy Division's 'Transmission' (Sect. 4) and the Sugarhill

© The Author(s) 2016
A. Stone, *The Value of Popular Music,*
DOI 10.1007/978-3-319-46544-9_6

Gang's 'Rapper's Delight', especially its re-use of elements from Chic's 'Good Times' (Sect. 5). This illuminates the importance of processes of re-use and re-contextualisation in popular music.

In Sect. 6, I re-assess how far popular songs' meanings are conventional. Many popular music theorists emphasise convention, focusing on audience responses and interpretations. In contrast philosophers of music tend to reject conventionalism, albeit usually with more-or-less explicit reference to classical music. I defend a middle position that, regarding popular songs at least, their meanings are partly but not entirely conventional, with conventional and non-conventional factors carrying different weights in different songs.

In Sect. 7, I argue that popular-musical meaning is *semiotic*, in senses taken from Kristeva's 1974 work *Revolution in Poetic Language*. The semiotic realm, for Kristeva, is one that we inhabit in infancy but that remains ever-present throughout our lives, albeit alongside the 'symbolic'——the sphere of explicit linguistic meaning——once we enter the latter. Within the semiotic realm, meaning (i) is tacit and (ii) emerges from the play of similarity, difference, and other relations between small-scale elements——such as bodily expressions, movements, and gestures—— including those that other people make when speaking to us. These relations are not all conventional. Further, (iii) rhythmic and pitched qualities contribute centrally to these relations, and (iv) the meaning that emerges is embodied in the shape of affects. In sum, the semiotic realm is one where bodily processes generate a kind of significance that is crystallised in emotional patterns. The processes by which meaning emerges in popular music likewise exhibit features (i) to (iv), and are thus continuous with the semiotic realm and qualify as semiotic in their own right. Since the semiotic is a bodily realm, popular music too has the significance of a bodily realm, one continuous with the earliest, bodily-based phase in our lives. In this way, popular music once more affirms the importance of materiality.

We might wonder how far my claims about meaning, emotion, convention, and the semiotic generalise to other musical forms beyond post-rock-'n'-roll music. This question lies beyond the scope of this book, but I don't rule out the possibility that my claims have more general application. Rather, by focusing on meaning in popular music, I hope to provide a solid footing on which comparisons with other musical forms may be explored.

2 EMOTION, EXPRESSION, AND AUTHENTICITY

In public discussion the prevailing common-sense is that popular songs give expression to the felt emotions of musicians, or ought to do so. Musicians are thought to pour out their emotions into their instrumental or vocal contributions, at least to the extent that they are good musicians.[3] For example, Béatrice Han-Pile speaks of

> the rage communicated by Edge's guitar in 'Bullet the Blue Sky', the angry frustration of Larry's drum line in 'Sunday Bloody Sunday', or the intense desire expressed by Adam's sensuous bass line in 'If You Wear that Velvet Dress'. Bono's tender performance of 'Sometimes You Can't Make It on Your Own' builds an intensely nostalgic climate. (Han-Pile 2006: 159)

Actually Han's reference to all U2's members is unusual. More often writers on music concentrate on vocalists near-exclusively, especially if they also write the lyrics. Frequently the implied speaker of the lyrics——the implied referent of the 'I' in, say, 'she's just a girl who says that I am the one' in Michael Jackson's 'Billie Jean'——is identified with the biographical individual who sang or wrote these words, so that for Bob Stanley 'Billie Jean' expresses Jackson's personal fear of 'gold diggers' (2013: 551–5). Along the same lines Stanley refers the development of Jackson's vocal style over time to his personal difficulties. Even when vocalists deliberately assume personae, as when Eminem acts the part of the brutal character Slim Shady, these personae tend to be taken as outlets for otherwise unexpressed sides of musicians' real personalities.

Tying in with this tendency to treat music as expressing musicians' emotions is a tendency to prize authentic self-expression. Many revered popular musicians, Kurt Cobain for one, are taken to be committed to authentic self-expression even to the point of dying for it. Here music that is deemed authentic is ranked above music that is deemed merely formulaic, where 'authentic' means 'giving genuine expression to the artist's feelings'. Ideals of authenticity and sincerity are thus closely connected. But this is just one of a range of interconnected ways in which authenticity is understood and prized in the reception of popular music. 'Authentic' can also mean 'made with artistic integrity'——that is the musician followed artistic impulses and not commercial constraints. By extension, too, a musician who innovates and breaks from musical precedent can be deemed 'authentic'—— staying true to their vision at the expense of established norms.

Further evidence that authentic expression is widely valued in popular music culture (as in much reception of music of all forms) comes from the great efforts made to assure audiences that music is 'authentic', through videos, dress codes, promotional materials, and so on. Diane Railton and Paul Watson note that the videos for early singles by the Arctic Monkeys 'became a crucial means of both confirming and consolidating their claims to authenticity' (2011: 63). Their video for 'I Bet You Look Good on the Dancefloor' (on *Whatever People Say I Am, That's What I'm Not*) uses a pseudo-documentary style, 'seemingly shot during the recording of a performance of the song', so as to 'produce an image of Arctic Monkeys as an authentic live act who have no need for lip-synching, make-up and other artificial devices'. In like vein Simon Frith (2005) picks out some of the devices that establish Bruce Springsteen's supposed authenticity: his wearing the clothes of a manual worker, writing songs about the lives of ordinary people, interspersing his concerts with autobiographical anecdotes, and his active, energetic, and often very long-drawn-out performances that bear witness to the effort and commitment he is putting in. Clearly these senses of 'authenticity' are various, but there are also identifiable connections among them.

These intersecting ways of valuing 'authentic expression' are problematic. This is partly for socio-political reasons. The musicians whose work can most readily be received as authentic are those most able to retain control over its making, recording, and marketing. Given the power relations that pervade the music industry, this has historically tended to be men, often white men (see Negus 1992). So when we celebrate authentic music, we may end up buying into hierarchies of gender and race.[4] The emphasis on authenticity can also lead to conservatism, as 'real' instruments——guitar, bass, drums——are treated as being more authentic than synthetic ones——drum-machines, synthesisers, samplers.[5]

Philosophically, too, there are problems with these ideals of authenticity. Generally a popular song is not first written, then performed, then recorded, but rather the three functions coincide, as 'songs are "written" by trying out ideas, or jamming, often in the studio … [and] recording constitutes the moment of fixation or completion of the work' (Toynbee 2004: 127). Recording is a process; it may be quick, or may extend over months, even years. Does the musician feel the relevant emotions throughout this process? Does he or she feel the same emotions each time the song is subsequently performed? Even if we answer 'yes', that still means that the musician has to get him- or herself into that emotional state on each occasion——which entails a work of performing, practicing, and staging these emotions rather than their being simply given and poured out. Paul McCartney's imploring, passionate vocal on 'Oh! Darling' sounds like a spontaneous outpouring of desperate love. But actually he had to spend several mornings practicing at using this screaming, Little Richard-inspired style that he had not used for some time (Macdonald 2005: 350).[6] His outpouring of passion was staged, just as stage actors rehearse how to perform the display of an emotion as if they genuinely and directly felt it.

In any case, *how* does a musician translate their emotions into musical shape? Let's consider the first transition from verse to chorus in the melody of Madonna's 'Like a Virgin' (on the 1984 album of that name). The verse lyrics tell us how the narrator has emerged from a wilderness of hurt and failed relationships. In the last clause, 'yeah, you made me feel shiny and new' the melody rises away from the tonic (F♯) to pause on a long-drawn-out 'new' (Fig. 6.1).

Madonna prolongs this syllable for more than a measure, creating tension, while lowering her voice in pitch from A♯ to G♯, so that we anticipate that the fall will continue down to the tonic. The lyrics, too, suggest that the difficulties chronicled in the verse will be followed by the happiness of the new relationship, which we expect to be embodied in the chorus. This happens as Madonna sings the central words 'Like a virgin', dropping to the dominant (C♯) on 'Like' and rising back up to reach the tonic on 'vir-', the move from dominant to tonic decisively establishing the arrival 'home'.

Moreover, the fact that the return to the tonic coincides with the start of the word 'virgin' cements our sense of a new start and that the comfort, warmth, and reassurance of a loving relationship have finally arrived.[7] These connotations are reinforced by Madonna's unexpected minim pause after 'new' and the also surprising rise (of a perfect fourth) from G♯ to the C♯ ('Hey') an octave above the C♯ on 'like'——confounding our expectation that the prolonged G♯ will lead directly into the tonic. Instead these elements accentuate the gap between the verse and the chorus, reinforcing

Fig. 6.1   Madonna, 'Like a Virgin', vocal melody, timing ca. 00:38–00:46

our sense of a new beginning and that the new relationship is quite unlike its failed predecessors. This melody line also exemplifies the norm in popular music to return from dominant to tonic not at the end of a section but the start of a new one. The tonic is reached on the first beat of measure 23, the first measure of a new section——the chorus——*not* at the end of the verse. By conforming to this popular-musical norm the melody line again conveys the novelty of the new relationship (new section——chorus) compared to the old ones (verse).

Billy Steinberg, one of the song's co-writers, says that it distilled his experience of leaving behind a series of bad relationships at the start of a new, successful one (Madonnatribe 2014). But neither Steinberg nor Madonna could have translated that experience into melodic shape using any musical materials whatever. Steinberg used existing musical formulae: a rising melody line with a prolonged final syllable, expressing tension and anticipation; a subsequent ascent from the dominant ($C\sharp$) to the tonic, expressive of reassurance and satisfaction; and the placement of that return to the tonic at the start of a new section, accentuating the sense of a new start. Steinberg did not necessarily deploy these formulae deliberately, but he certainly drew on his familiarity with norms of musical practice. The resulting melody line is expressive of a transition to happiness because it reflects these norms, some inherited from common-practice music——regarding dominant-tonic transitions——and others specific to post-rock-'n'-roll music——regarding sectional organisation and the placement of the tonic. It is primarily the contour of the melody, as it obeys these norms, that carries the expressive connotations, not the efforts of Steinberg or Madonna to pour out their personal feelings (unlikely in Madonna's case: she eschews authenticity in favour of ironic, knowing manipulation of codes).

It is not only norms about melody that musicians deploy to expressive effect. When singers half-speak or half-shout their lines they mobilise shared understandings about the expressive significance of shouting (anger, frustration) or speaking quietly (restraint, intimacy). When singers use certain accents, dialects, or regional turns of phrase they again rely on public understandings about their significance; Chuck Berry did this quite deliberately, enunciating his words clearly to sound more white and enhance his appeal to white audiences (2005: 85). Generally, then, musicians' expres*sion* of their emotions in music remains dependent on the express*iveness* of the musical, aural, and cultural norms and materials that are drawn on. To be sure, musicians often do want to express their feelings musically, but this requires work with materials that already have suitable meanings.

Moreover, authenticity is itself a quality——perhaps an emotional quality, at least in part——that musicians may want their music and personae
to embody. To express authenticity, musicians need to draw on musical
and other materials——clothes, dance styles, and so on——that connote
authenticity, such as Springsteen's manual worker's garb. Some stylistic
features have this connotation: melismatic singing, for instance, in which
several notes are sung to a single syllable, suggests an outpouring of feeling so uninhibited that it flows across metric divisions and stretches syl-
labic ones freely, thus connoting authenticity in the sense of sincerity.[8]

Conversely, other musical elements connote *in*authenticity, in a range of
senses: as artifice, drama and exaggeration; knowing irony (à la Madonna); or
lack of emotion——coldness, distance, and detachment. For example, going
back to 'Blue Monday', its almost totally synthetic palette, machinic rhythms,
and harshly enunciated vocals convey a lack of emotion. 'Blue Monday' did
not acquire those qualities by being left emotionally empty by New Order
refusing to pour out their emotions into the song. Rather, 'Blue Monday'
uses elements that carry connotations of the unemotional, machine-like and
rigid. For one thing, New Order re-created the bass-line used in Sylvester's
'Mighty Real', but stripped it of the various embellishments under which it
was originally presented and of its original alternation between descending
form in the verse and ascending form in the chorus. Those features helped to
make the bass-line sound emotional and dramatic in its initial setting, reinforced by Sylvester's impassioned, excited singing. By simplifying the bass-
line, New Order take out that dramatic, impassioned quality, emphasising by
default the bass-line's rhythmic function, but thereby also giving the bass-line
an *un*emotional quality because of its new machine-like minimalism.

In sum, when popular music is expressive of emotions this is not simply
because musicians pour out their feelings into the music, as common-sense
has it, but because the musical materials that are used already embody
emotional connotations of which musicians avail themselves. However,
emotional quality is just one of several kinds of meaning that popular
songs can carry. Let me sketch some of these kinds and how emotional
quality entwines with them.

3   KINDS OF MEANING IN POPULAR MUSIC

As well as embodying expressive connotations, musical elements can
embody (1) *social identities*. For example, Afrika Bambaataa used an accel-
erated sample of the main melody of Kraftwerk's 'Trans-Europe Express'

in his 'Planet Rock', a track that helped to propel rap in an electronic direction. In doing this Bambaataa 'disengaged black manhood from its association with primitivism and allied it instead to a different masculine trait: the calculated, rational control of advanced technology' (Duffett 2010: 202). Thus Bambaataa gave a new articulation to black masculinity, allying it with technology rather than nature. As this example suggests, musical features do not simply reflect pre-given identities. Identities are dynamic rather than static, constantly being re-imagined, and so the translation of identities into musical shape inevitably re-articulates those identities at the same time.

(2) Popular music is often evocative, too, of *places, locations and atmospheres*. Take M.I.A.'s abrupt juxtapositions of materials from very different global contexts——'Bamboo Banga', the opening track on her 2007 album *Kala*, quotes Jonathan Richman's 'Roadrunner' and samples a song from the Tamil film *Dalapathi*. The effect is to evoke a modern multicultural city in which different communities exist side by side in potentially creative, but not always easily harmonious, ways. Or consider the guitar part in the introduction to U2's 'Where the Streets Have No Name' (on *The Joshua Tree*). The guitar comes in after an extended keyboard section, and for nearly half a minute more a single track of guitar repeatedly plays an arpeggiated version of the tonic chord (D major). This is played using digital delay so that each note is repeated, and the repetitions overlap with the following notes, to produce a very busy sound, full of swift movement. This continues once the guitar moves over to strum, extremely rapidly, two alternate variations of the tonic chord. Amidst all this busy movement the guitar makes very little *harmonic* movement, fundamentally remaining on the tonic throughout. (What harmonic movement there is comes from the bass and keyboards, although the former only appears in the 26th measure.) The result is to create a sense of a fixed, still background against which smaller elements move rapidly in the foreground. It is as if someone small is running across a much larger space, a space also evoked by the echo on the guitar. This distinction between still background and moving foreground is reinforced by the way the guitar gradually rises in volume, again conveying change against a static (harmonic) background.[9] The opening words confirm these connotations: 'I want to run, I want to hide', and to 'tear down the walls'. The middle clause suggests that the narrator is currently *not* hidden but exposed, in a large, empty space, across which he is running. Crucially, though, the guitar has already established these connotations before Bono's vocal comes in.

Evocation of atmosphere and expression of emotion often entwine. When the guitar in 'Where the Streets Have No Name' evokes wide open space and rapid movement, it suggests restless travelling, and in turn emotional qualities of agitation and striving. This indicates how the various kinds of meaning in popular songs typically interrelate. In 'Where the Streets Have No Name' the interrelation extends to (3) the *aesthetic values* that are being conveyed. One of these values is authenticity: the central expressive role played by the guitar is in line with the rock tradition of making the electric guitar the key vehicle of emotional expression (as by Jimi Hendrix, notably). But The Edge's style of playing the guitar is also innovative: he eschews virtuosity and finds other ways to generate expressive qualities, in this case by combining busy surface movement with underlying stasis. This embodies another aesthetic commitment, to the value of autonomy: not merely following rules and traditions but breaking with and re-making them.[10]

So these are several kinds of meaning: (1) articulation of social identity; (2) evocation of place; (3) embodiment of aesthetic commitments; and (4) expression of emotion. These kinds of meaning can link up and reinforce one another within a song or pull in opposing directions. Let's take an example of the latter.

Songs can articulate a privileged social identity, as in the aggressive masculinity and heterosexuality of the Rolling Stones' 1965 single '(I Can't Get No) Satisfaction'. It is above all 'Satisfaction's' central guitar riff that conveys aggression, in the guise of frustration: built in the key of E major, the riff rises from the dominant (B) to the subtonic (D), holds the latter as if trying to reach up from it to the tonic, but then, rather than doing so, falls back down (Fig. 6.2). Thus, the guitar starts by moving purposefully up towards the tonic E but, instead of reaching it, falls short without achieving satisfaction. On the one hand, the song construes this feeling of frustration in terms of masculine anger and aggression——in part through the lyrics, when Jagger complains that he 'can't get no girl reaction' and that a man on a television advert 'can't be a man' because he 'don't smoke the same cigarettes as me'. On the other

Fig. 6.2 The Rolling Stones, '(I Can't Get No) Satisfaction', riff (electric guitar), timing ca. 00:00–00:03

hand, the frustration is that the protagonist *cannot* achieve the satisfaction of being a man. By implication masculinity is failing——falling back down, like the riff——rather than winning out. 'Satisfaction's' expressive quality of frustration at once connotes self-assertive masculinity——insofar as frustration embodies anger——*and* conveys that masculinity is failing and cannot be attained——insofar as frustration reflects impotence and failure. Thus the expressive quality through which the song embodies its identity-related connotation of assertive masculinity at the same time undermines that latter meaning and imparts another, conflicting one. The expressive quality exceeds the identity-related meaning and is in tension with it.[11]

This does not prevent 'Satisfaction's' meanings from interacting productively to coalesce into a whole. For these meanings do not cancel one another out and leave a flat plane of meaninglessness, but have enough purchase on one another to conflict. The result is a whole containing connotations that are in tension——and that tension, a higher-level meaning of the whole song, ties in with its root affect of frustration. Tension—— including tension between component meanings——becomes one global connotation that binds the song together. This reminds us that coalescence of meanings does not equate to a song's having one single monadic meaning. Lower-level meanings coalesce to form structures of interwoven meaning that unify songs——more-or-less complex structures that can contain manifold aspects. These manifold aspects can sometimes be in tension with one another, and can even be highly disparate, if this is still consistent with their belonging to a unified structure.

Anyway, my aim in this section has been to sketch some kinds of meaning in popular music and to indicate that emotional expression is one of these kinds. While songs have connotations of manifold kinds, emotional qualities are generally among them, entwined with other connotations to make them emotionally laden. These connections between emotional and other meanings suggest that we should study emotional expression in popular music under the broader rubric of meaning. So I now want to focus on meaning in its own right in two particular cases, to provide a basis for drawing some conclusions about the nature of meaning in popular music.

4   'Transmission'

First I turn to 'Transmission', recorded in 1979, one of Joy Division's best-known songs.[12] Why this song? One initial consideration is that we have already looked at 'Blue Monday' by New Order, who were Joy

Division before they re-grouped and added keyboardist Gillian Gilbert after the suicide of their singer and lyricist Ian Curtis. Consequently we would expect 'Transmission' to show continuities with 'Blue Monday'. One point of continuity is that the central instruments in 'Transmission' are the bass guitar and drums, which between them give the track a rhythm no less propulsive than that of 'Blue Monday'.

The backbone of the song is the melodic sequence played on the bass guitar, which remains unaltered over virtually the whole song.[13] There are only two exceptions (see Table 6.1): the first is the occasions when a rising, more optimistic-sounding bass-line marks the transitions between sections. The second alteration occurs in the two 'chorus' sections (taking the verses and choruses to be demarcated by changes in the vocals, in the absence of any changes to the chord sequence). At these points Peter Hook moves over to playing rough-hewn chords by deliberately hitting the 'wrong' as well as the 'right' strings. Otherwise the bass-line remains unchanged——which fits in with its almost-flat contour, its minimal harmonic movement, and its being played with almost machine-like regularity, with no rests or difference in emphasis between the notes, which are nearly all of uniform length. The bass-line is indebted to punk (inspired by seeing the Sex Pistols play, Joy Division had originated as a punk band), including its typically fast tempos: that of 'Transmission' is 156 beats per minute. The bass-line's urgency combines with its machinic, almost monotonous regularity to generate a sense of relentlessness.[14]

Another feature of the bass-line that deserves comment is its very simplicity, another punk inheritance. If we think that art or music must be complex to have aesthetic worth, then this bass-line will fare poorly. But that judgement would be too hasty, because this bass-line is illustrative of how a very simple musical element can have interesting connotations—— and does so because of, not despite, its simplicity. After all, the bass-line would not connote relentlessness if it changed over the course of the song, was played with less regularity, or had a more varied contour.

Finally, the bass-line establishes the mode in which song is built: the Dorian mode on D——the same mode in which 'Blue Monday' is built. Conventionally, the Dorian mode is considered to be sombre and serious rather than sad as the natural minor scale is.[15] 'Transmission' reflects this. The first phrase of the bass-line is on the tonic (D) and the second phrase descends to the subtonic (C) before the next phrase reverts to D again. By simply alternating between staying on the tonic and departing from it, implying a I–VII oscillation, the bass-line generates considerable

Table 6.1   Joy Division, 'Transmission', song structure

Timing	Section	Measures	Instrumentation
00:00–00:02	Intro (part 1)	1	Keyboards play a very quiet form of the tonic (D) chord; it sounds rather spectral, as if it comes from a distance.
00:02–00:14	Intro (part 2)	8	While the keyboards continue, the bass guitar enters, playing the following very restricted melodic line, again with a quiet, remote sound.

Timing	Section	Measures	Instrumentation
00:14–00:39	Guitar solo 1	16	The lead guitar comes in, slightly overdriven and fairly low-pitched, playing short phrases, mostly centred on the sixth scale degree (B), jumping up an octave at one point then back down. The low pitch and overdrive give the guitar an industrial sound There are also drums, which actually entered in the song's ninth measure; bass guitar, which is louder now; and keyboards, which remain quiet. The section ends with the momentary appearance of a rising bass-line that announces the first verse:

Timing	Section	Measures	Instrumentation
00:39–00:51	Verse 1	8	Ian Curtis's vocal melody begins, accompanied by bass (resuming its basic sequence), keyboards, and drums——these last three continue from now on
00:51–01:04	Guitar solo 2	8	Another lead guitar lead line plays, largely repeating part of the previous solo
01:04–01:29	Verse 2	16	The vocal melody returns. On the ninth measure a second track of guitar enters, playing power chords with intermittent feedback: the song is beginning to rise to a crescendo. The vocals stop on measure 11, and the rising bass melody marks the end of the section
01:29–01:42	Verse 3	8	The vocal melody and other instruments continue, the keyboards louder from here on, making a pulsating, twinkling sound

(*continued*)

Table 6.1 (continued)

Timing	Section	Measures	Instrumentation
01:42–02:07	Guitar solo 3	16	Another lead guitar part comes in, beginning on a bent note, and falling into two halves, slower- then faster-moving, both centred on the tonic. The power chords had dropped out but they return after the ninth measure, emphasising the second half of the guitar solo. The other instruments continue to rise in volume
02:07–02:32	Chorus 1	16	The vocals return; the bass is played more abrasively now as Peter Hook hits some of the 'wrong' strings and lets them ring out, effectively forming chords, building towards the crescendo, as does the keyboard, becoming louder. Again the rising bass-line closes the section
02:32–02:50	Verse 4	12	'Well, I could call out': the vocals have leapt up by an octave, allowing Curtis to unleash the power of his voice; the crescendo is reached (although the bass drops back to single notes)
02:50–03:15	Chorus 2	16	The bass again plays abrasive chords, but the instruments are already dropping off in volume; the crescendo is past. Again the rising bass-line marks the end
03:15–03:36	Outro	10	A guitar power chord and a final bass note (D) fade out. As the pulse gradually slows, the drums continue for six-and-a-half more measures then stop, leaving a keyboard chord, which then stops too, whereupon the song ends

energy——but its near-stasis, in this Dorian context, suggests lack of hope, a feeling of being trapped and unable to escape (after all, the bass alternates between D and C——not C#). The dominant (A) propels the transition in both directions, adding to the energy. Energetic vigour is thus combined with a dark mood, feeding into the relentless quality.

We can now add the drums into the picture. They present——with machine-like precision and rapidity——a two-measure rhythmic cell (Fig. 6.3) that, like the bass sequence, is repeated almost unchanged for the whole song (the only variations occur when the drums first enter and when additional tom-tom beats appear intermittently). This pattern is recognisably a complicated variation on rock's standard bass-and-snare-drum combination. Each two iterations of the whole pattern map onto each

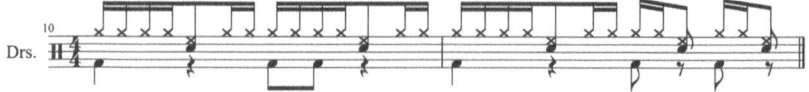

Fig. 6.3   Joy Division, 'Transmission', drums, timing ca. 00:14–00:16

repetition of the four-measure sequence on the bass guitar, so that their component sounds interweave to create a compulsive rhythm.

The treatment of the drums with echo generates a sense of space, as does, more subtly, the very quiet, distant-sounding synthesiser chord that opens the song and remains present in the background for some time. The sense of space is reinforced when the passages of guitar melody come in and out, leaving regular silences when they are absent. More broadly, space is evoked by the layers of sound being clearly demarcated from one another (a deliberate effect of the recording process). Yet the space sounds uncomfortable and empty, not relaxed or as if it offers freedom. These negative connotations are a combined effect of various elements: the sombre Dorian mode; the extreme restrictedness of the bass guitar melody; the drums having been performed and recorded with almost clinical precision; and the audible discreteness of the sound layers (as if they resemble people standing stiffly apart, at mutual remove).[16] Yet in contrast to this sense of space, both the bass guitar and drum parts are full of energetic movement at the rhythmic level: in this regard they contain very little space and instead sound unremitting and insistent, with the hi-hat filling up almost all of the sixteenth-note subdivisions of the beat. It is as if we can, while 'inside' the rhythm section of the music, escape from an uncomfortable emptiness that subsists 'outside' it. The music, especially in its rhythmic aspect, offers an activity and energy that 'fill in' the emptiness that we otherwise face.

Now we can factor in the guitar, which is present in two layers. The first plays the role of lead guitar, moving in and out of the texture and initially centring on the sixth scale degree. This sounds an optimistic note——since it is B, not B♭, and 'the Dorian sixth, in its greater distance from the fifth, at least carries the illusory possibility of escape' (Moore 1995: 188). The lead guitar endeavours to bring a degree of hope, then——but this is crushed by the bass guitar, drums, and Curtis's dark, low-pitched vocals, which create an encompassing mesh from which no escape is possible after all.

The second guitar layer appears during the second verse and plays power chords, alternating between the tonic and the subtonic in harmony with the bass-line. Each power chord is sustained over two measures, creating a tremendous sense of mounting energy and powering the song's crescendo. As I've mentioned earlier, a power chord is an open perfect fifth interval that is subjected to distortion and that can be sustained at length because the distortion compresses the sound, which causes it to decay relatively slowly. Such chords signify power, as Robert Walser explains, because the distortion embodies the excessive effort needed to produce the sound, and because the sustained nature of the sound suggests an 'unflagging capacity for emission' (Walser 1993: 42).

Power chords are a staple of heavy metal, although they are extensively used in punk rock too. But in heavy metal, unlike punk, the chief use of power chords is to showcase the guitarist's mastery over the powerful energetic and sonic resources that he releases and dominates. This meshes with the way that heavy metal reproduces the background soundscape of industrial modernity——the low, thick, rumbling guitar sounds produced by Tommy Iommi in Black Sabbath, for example——over which the singer then prevails and from which the guitar too breaks free during solo passages (Tagg 1994: 218).

In 'Transmission', the power-chord guitar part avoids these connotations of mastery because it is so minimal——alternating between just two chords with unvarying regularity, in step with the drums and bass. The guitar melodies, too, are so devoid of virtuosity, display, or flourish that any sense of domination over the sonic landscape is eschewed. The connotation is the reverse: that the power is in the machinery (of the electric guitar) and the energetic forces that the technology unleashes and communicates to us. The machine-like regularity of the rhythm section strengthens this connotation. We are in industrial modernity, a place where machinery exercises vast power——but we're subjected to this realm, trapped in it, *not* able to prevail over it.

This has not been an exhaustive analysis of 'Transmission', but it should be enough that we can draw conclusions about the track's overall meaning. Emptiness surrounds us, but we can escape from that emptiness, temporarily, into music and the activity that it embodies and arouses in us through its rhythms. But in this respect music is of ambiguous value: part of the apparatus of modern industry, it unleashes energies and activities in us while yet subjecting us to industrial regularities and rhythms. Both music and industrial machinery allow us to escape from bleakness into frantic activity. But the escape is not exactly happy——more desperate, as we throw ourselves into something that offers only temporary and ambiguous respite. Thus the energy levels rise as the song advances, expressive of this mounting desperation.

It is interesting that these connotations prefigure those of 'Blue Monday', yet with notable differences. 'Blue Monday' explores the way that rhythm can offer us a release from introspection and from emotions and the pain that they can involve——an escape into an emotionally blank realm of bodily movement. While 'Blue Monday' does not cast this bodily realm as wholly positive——on the negative side it involves numbness and blankness——the overall sense is that this realm is positive and liberating. In contrast, in 'Transmission', the same qualities, while cast as having a liberating aspect, are on the whole portrayed negatively. Thus 'Transmission' is a much darker track than 'Blue Monday'.

I have deliberately bracketed the contribution of the vocal melody and lyrics to 'Transmission's' connotations. Yet the melody and lyrics do play a part, although they do so in conjunction with the rest of the music, not in isolation. Initially low-pitched and restrained, the vocals gradually rise in pitch and volume across the whole song, conveying increasing desperation. And the lyrics articulate some of the meanings of which the music is expressive: beginning with 'Radio, /Live transmission', the words directly hint at the link between modernity, industry, music, and domination—— a domination in which energies are transmitted to us and compel us to 'Dance, dance, dance to the radio' and to 'synchronise love /To the beat of the show'. The radio is not portrayed positively but as subjecting us to the rhythms of modernity, which indeed dominate us inescapably on all fronts. The lyrics, though, do not single-handedly impose this bleak meaning on the song. Rather, Ian Curtis's lyrics only draw out meanings already generated by the other layers of sound.

Shortly, I will extrapolate to some of the mechanisms by which the song's component musemes carry the connotations that they do, including the contribution made by musical grammar and the way that musemes, such as power chords, can be re-contextualised and thereby acquire new connotations. But first re-contextualisation is the focus of my next discussion, of 'Rapper's Delight'.

5   From 'Good Times' to 'Rapper's Delight'

I argued earlier that typically the parts of popular songs come together contingently rather than generating one another through a necessary development. Just as elements need not go together, reciprocally elements that have been combined in a given song can be taken apart again: part of one song can be re-used in another. Sampling makes this explicit: through this technique, any element of a song——a fragment, a brief sound, or something more extensive——can be extracted for re-use elsewhere. Indeed new songs can be composed wholly by combining multiple elements of pre-existing songs, as with M.A.R.S.S.'s 1987 release 'Pump Up the Volume', which included more than 30 samples (Manuel 1995: 233).

However, sampling only brings out a feature that popular music has always had, for often parts of songs are composed by copying parts of pre-existing songs. As I mentioned earlier, 'Rip It Up' contains a guitar solo that re-creates the one in 'Boredom'. Most often, musicians copy and re-create pre-existing parts under modifications. Sampling enables such modifications to be made electronically by shifting a sampled element in pitch, tempo, emphasis, timbre, or along other parameters. Another variation is for a musician to try to re-create a pre-existing instrumental part but end up generating something substantially new. The bass-line of U2's 'New Year's Day' arose when Adam Clayton tried to re-create the bass-line of Visage's 'Fade to Grey'——which Clayton's bass-line ultimately resembles very little (McCormick 2005: 166).

When parts of one song are re-used in another, those parts carry over connotations they had in their earlier location. This is not because a given part brings some fixed quality to its original location and the new one alike. Rather, any element brings a potential quality to its original location, and that quality gets developed and taken in a certain direction by the other elements of that song. The result is that the element has an actual rather than merely potential meaning within that song——think, again, of the ominousness of the flat note in the A-melody of 'Are "Friends" Electric?'. When it is re-used elsewhere, then——at least if the new audience knows of its earlier location or if that location is overtly acknowledged in the new context——an element may bring with it the actual quality that it had acquired within its previous location. But now this quality becomes a potential again, for the other elements of the new whole will affect how this quality is taken forward. That is, the new whole affects and modifies the connotations of the re-used part; but what is modified are the connotations that the part brings forward from its previous location. The process is repeated if the part is re-used anew in a third location, and a fourth, and so on.

Take, for example, the re-use of the bass-line and percussion of Chic's 'Good Times' in 'Rapper's Delight' by the Sugarhill Gang, which was, famously, the first rap record to become a major hit in the USA. 'Rapper's Delight' relies very heavily on 'Good Times' (on Chic's album *Risqué*). Apart from its introduction (and a brief recurrence of the introductory material at 04:40–04:55), 'Rapper's Delight' principally consists just of the four-measure-long bass-line from 'Good Times' along with the accompanying percussion, that is hi-hat, bass-drum, and synthetic hand-claps on the backbeat. These elements are repeated continuously to constitute the rhythm layer of 'Rapper's Delight', along with a regularly occurring slicing violin sound, again excerpted from 'Good Times'. All this is overlaid with the Sugarhill Gang's rap. Additional passages of guitar and piano come in and out of the track for its first third, after which guitar and chimes play the same role, and in the final three minutes just guitar. These several additional elements also appear in 'Good Times'. There is debate as to whether the rhythm track is sampled (from the lengthy breakdown section in the twelve-inch version of 'Good Times') or was re-created in the studio (see Daly 2005). I take the latter to be the case but this does not matter here, for either way much of 'Good Times' is being re-used.

Being re-used, the rhythm track (bass and percussion) brings with it the celebratory, party ambience of its original setting in 'Good Times'. Having acquired that connotation within 'Good Times', the bass-line now imparts it to 'Rapper's Delight'. Indeed, the re-used rhythm track carries this connotation through so powerfully that some find it 'incontrovertible that "Rapper's Delight" … resembles more a disco recording than anything from the first wave of recorded hip hop' (Ealham 2015: 141). But situating 'Rapper's Delight' wholly within disco neglects the way that the connotations carried over by the Chic bass-line become modified in their new setting. This happens despite the new song's minimal texture—— or rather because of it, for that minimalism contrasts with the lush, rich texture of 'Good Times', in which the rhythm layers are filled out by energetic guitar, piano, violins, and multiple vocals. Together with the vocals in 'Rapper's Delight' being rapped, not sung as in 'Good Times', the bare texture of the former tilts the balance of musical parameters strongly towards rhythm and away from melody and harmony. Indeed, for around half the time, the only harmonic and melodic content of 'Rapper's Delight' comes from the bass-line. The stripping-away of (much of the) guitar, violins, and piano from 'Good Times' removes the connotations of sophistication, escapism, and luxury that are conveyed by the many-layered texture of 'Good Times'; Chic, after all, sought to be the disco version of Roxy Music——the epitome of glamour.

By drastically thinning out the texture, 'Rapper's Delight' conveys, in contrast to 'Good Times', that its terrain is everyday urban reality as it is, shorn of idealisation and aspiration. Yet those connotations depend on the contrast with 'Good Times', a contrast that arises because 'Rapper's Delight' re-uses much of 'Good Times' and so establishes its intertextual relation with the latter. Re-situated in this overall setting the bass-line gains a new connotation of the presence and weight of everyday urban reality, by virtue of its central role in a texture that has shifted the musical axis away from luxury and sophistication towards what is direct and plain; away from higher-pitched registers towards the bass, what is low down and real rather than highfalutin; and away from harmony towards rhythm, with its bodily connotations, again suggesting material reality.

Thus when elements from one song are re-used in another song, their earlier connotations may well carry over——here the celebratory mood, the invitation to dancing and enjoyment and to the body, and the link with disco. This happens here because 'Rapper's Delight' explicitly re-uses parts of 'Good Times', so that the earlier location is acknowledged. But the re-used elements also take on new connotations in the new wholes into which they are inserted——here, for one, the already highly rhythmic function of the bass-line is highlighted still further by its being transplanted into a whole that privileges rhythm over harmony. These new connotations depend on the earlier ones, although by transforming them——here the bass-line is stripped of its quality of 'chic', of sophistication, but its new connotation of direct urban reality arises by contrast with its up-market quality in its earlier setting.

It is no surprise that I've used a rap song to illustrate re-contextualisation, for intertextuality is crucial to rap (see, e.g., Williams 2013). Indeed, arguably intertextuality is crucial to black cultural practices more broadly. For Henry Louis Gates (1988), black culture makes central use of the practice of Signifying, in which black artists explicitly re-use existing black cultural resources, thereby acknowledging their dependence on their predecessors *and* the importance of those predecessors' contributions. To be sure, all culture is more-or-less intertextual. But this may or may not be openly embraced, and in rap it *is* embraced. Rap's intertextuality does not set it apart from the rest of popular music, though. Rather, rap self-reflexively embraces a principle of re-use that is at work in popular song construction generally, a principle on which rap therefore sheds light.

Rap also highlights, once again, the contingency with which song elements are typically combined in popular music. It is this contingency that makes it possible for popular-musical elements to be extracted and re-used elsewhere, without this representing any sort of violation, destruction, or bowdlerisation of these elements. In contrast, bowdlerisation *is* liable to occur when musical materials that belong intrinsically within necessarily interlinked wholes, such as the motives in Beethoven's symphonies, get extracted and reproduced in isolation from those wholes.[17]

6   Meaning and Convention

I now want to draw out some conclusions about how popular music conveys meaning, by way of engaging with the extensive debate about the role of social context in establishing these meanings. As I noted earlier, popular music theorists often maintain that popular music's meaning is socially constructed. Tia DeNora argues this with respect to music more broadly, maintaining that by itself a piece of music is 'anything, everything, nothing' (2000: 31). She explains that

> the ways in which music partakes of patterns and conventions at the moment of production (even assuming such a matter can be specified) by no means guarantees the ways in which it is appropriated and so comes to be meaningful in particular social circumstances. (29)

For DeNora, to get at the latter we need to look, empirically, at the appropriations that people make.

DeNora's remarks show that there are in fact two levels on which social construction potentially works: that of audience response to and take-up of music, and that of the music's 'production'. Lucy Green distinguishes these levels by calling them 'inherent' and 'delineated' meanings in music, the latter conferred on details of musical style through the social processes of their reception, the former inhering in those details prior to their reception. It is these 'inherent' meanings that have been and will remain my concern throughout this book——although, for Green, 'inherent' meaning is already shaped by social processes (Green 2008: xvi).

DeNora is more doubtful that we can identify any 'inherent' meanings at all, social or otherwise. Although her project is to do justice to music's affective force, its power to move and affect us, she describes that force as being 'constructed' by listeners who 'refer or attend to' music's properties (2000: 30; also 2003: 1–3). By implication, the force or power ultimately resides in these listeners and interpreters, not in the music's stylistic details.

On the other hand, on DeNora's own account, listeners 'construct' the music's force by attending and referring to its properties——which entails that these properties *do* exist and figure into the music's interpretations. We may conclude, then, that songs' stylistic details do affect how these songs become interpreted, because these details already have connotations of which interpreters take account (albeit often unconsciously, through tacit familiarity with norms of musical practice).

We can take this position without having to hold that stylistic details have given connotations just due to their physical make-up——for example the properties of their component sound-waves——independently of social or cultural factors. Rather, some element such as melisma might carry a specific connotation——say, being expressive of intense passion——because of the history of melismatic singing, through gospel into soul, as that history has become sedimented into subsequent uses of melisma *and* into listeners' enculturated ways of perceiving melismatic singing. The question remains, though, how far these embedded meanings are conventional.

Philosophers of music are often inclined to reject conventionalism, using the following type of argument. Say that the snare-drum has a military connotation because it has a history of use in the army——that is, because of this convention around its use. But why has *this* convention arisen? Why is the snare-drum used in the army rather than, say, the tambourine (which after all would be easier to carry), and why is the snare-drum widely used in the army rather than, say, in toddlers' playgroups? The *sound* of the snare-drum must be the explanatory factor (see, e.g., Kania 2014: 3.1), perhaps due to the violence connoted by its whip-crack sound as it cuts through other surrounding layers of sound. That is, there must be a basis in musical sounds for the particular conventional meanings that they acquire.

Thus far runs the usual anti-conventionalist argument. With this in mind, let's reconsider 'Transmission'. Its bass-line, taken in abstraction from the rest of the song, already has a quality of relentlessness. This can be attributed to its Dorian tonality, nearly-flat contour, urgent rhythm, and almost total lack of change over time. The drums reinforce this relentless quality rhythmically, by virtue of their machinic character and lack of variation. *Why*, then, do these features of the bass and drums mean that they sound relentless? One factor is (1) *resemblance*.[18] The rhythmic patterns played on the drums and bass with unvarying regularity resemble industrial machinery as it operates with unvarying regularity, never-endingly repeating the same motions. The resemblance also gives these patterns a machine-like quality, so that they evoke an industrial setting. Resemblance is at work, too, in giving the track's overdriven guitar its connotations——its contribution to the song's rise to a crescendo and the attendant sense of mounting desperation. Overdriven and distorted guitar are expressive of strain and exertion because the volume of sound exceeds or overwhelms the equipment's capacities, which resembles a person breaking down or being pushed to their limits by strong feelings (Walser 1993: 42).

These are just two instances of a broader pattern whereby musical features acquire particular connotations because they resemble non-musical phenomena, including human expressive behaviours. Likewise, a vocal melody that spans a narrow pitch range resembles the speech of a person who is exerting self-restraint, holding their emotions in check. A melody spanning a wide range sounds more uninhibited, open, and passionate (Machin 2010: 102–6; Thompson and Balkwill 2010: 777). Sometimes popular musicians create these resemblances deliberately, engaging in a kind of 'tone-painting'——as with the machine-like, repetitive drum pattern with which Kraftwerk evoke a travelling train rolling over tracks in 'Trans-Europe Express'.

A second factor apparent from 'Transmission' is that sounds can *embody* the causal forces that make them be as they are. The power chords on the guitar embody the electrical power needed to sustain them, and the lack of virtuosity of the guitar melodies conveys the self-restraint involved in producing them, the refusal to indulge in virtuosic display. Together these suggest the power of electrical machinery rather than power on the part of the individual musician who triumphs over the machinery. Again, a broader pattern is made manifest here for musical features to (2) *embody the causal factors that have given rise to them*. Those forces might be technological sources, or the expressive behaviours responsible for musical features——as when an angular guitar riff is expressive of aggression or anger because of the force and abruptness with which the strings need to be struck to produce this kind of sound.

Now, resemblances (between musical elements and other phenomena) and causal relations (between musical elements and their causal origins) are not necessarily conventional, at least not entirely. Producing an angular guitar riff really might require the strings to be struck with some force; and forceful striking (e.g. of strings) is a behaviour that is commonly expressive of aggression or anger in everyday human life—— where aggression causes this behaviour by expressing itself in it. Likewise, distorted guitar really does resemble someone being pushed beyond their limits, and highly regular rhythms really do resemble industrial machinery more than the uneven rhythms of nature. This is not to say that conventions play no part in meaning, but that non-conventional factors bear on what conventions get established.

Besides resemblance and causal dependence, (3) *norms of musical grammar* are another factor in meaning. In 'Transmission', again, one such is the norm for the Dorian mode to sound sombre rather than melancholy. This sombre quality can be referred back to the combination of notes and intervals in the Dorian mode——its containing C and not C♯, B and not B♭. But why does that combination have a sombre connotation? Although written some time ago, Deryck Cooke's explanation remains worth considering, namely that each step of the twelve-tone scale has a certain meaningful function:

> *Tonic.* Emotionally neutral; context of finality. ... *Minor Third*: Concord, but a "depression" of natural third: stoic acceptance, tragedy. *Major Third:* Concord, natural third: joy. ... *Dominant*: emotionally neutral; context of flux, intermediacy. ... *Minor seventh*: ... 'lost' note, mournfulness. (Cooke 1959: 89–90)

Cooke explains these qualities based on the harmonic series, thus ultimately on physical grounds (1959: 41). But he does not deny that conventional factors can also play a role. Notably, thirds used to be seen as dissonant, and Cooke explains this by saying that the Church was hostile to the pleasure of natural harmony in the case of major thirds, while minor thirds were found dissonant because of their sad quality (51–64).

How far scale steps have intrinsic meanings remains contested. But I find it reasonable to think that some intrinsic dimension may well be involved. In 'Transmission', which is built in the Dorian mode, the guitar melodies sound optimistic because they centre around B, not B♭ as they would if the song were in D minor——so that, as we noted earlier, 'the Dorian sixth ... at least carries the illusory possibility of escape' (Moore 1995: 188). Meanwhile the bass-line sounds gloomy and relentless partly because, being in the Dorian, it alternates between D and C——not C#, as it would if the song were in D major. To adapt Moore's formulation, the Dorian seventh, in its greater distance from the tonic, conveys less possibility of resolution and rest.

Still, any attempt to resolve here whether musical-grammatical meanings are intrinsic, conventional, or——as I suspect——both, would be vain and is anyway unnecessary. For either way, since a mixture of conventional and non-conventional factors is involved in popular music's meaning in other respects——that is factors (1) and (2) (and as we'll see below, factor (4), that of re-contextualisation), that meaning will retain mixed sources whichever side its harmonic aspect may fall on. Admittedly, though, this is to assume that harmony is just one contributor to popular-musical meaning, with no special privilege. However, it has often been thought that harmony is the *fundamental* parameter in giving rise to songs' meanings or, at least, their expressive qualities.

For example, Geoffrey Madell claims that 'in the main the expressive character of music is conveyed ... by the harmonic character of the music' and that 'the expressive power of Western music is, to a very large extent, a matter of tonal and harmonic tensions and their resolution' (2002: 11, 14–15). Peter Kivy has come to take a related view, although, for Kivy, harmonic tensions and their resolutions make the music expressive of desire, tension, peace, and so on (Kivy 2002: chs. 5–6), whereas for Madell those tensions and resolutions stimulate, frustrate, and satisfy *our* expectations and thus arouse these emotions in us (a position that is closer to Leonard Meyer's; see Meyer 1956). Both Madell and Kivy have classical music in mind, but do their claims also apply to popular music?

Not necessarily. Chord sequences and other harmonic elements in popular music are typically short and repetitive rather than long and progressive. One might conclude that popular songs are still expressive on a primarily harmonic basis but that these songs cannot be so powerfully expressive of emotions as long, progressively developing pieces in which resolution is repeatedly deferred or reached only after lengthy journeys though many modulations and variations. Leonard Meyer suggests as much: 'The greater the buildup of suspense, of tension, the greater the emotional release upon resolution' (1956: 28). Perhaps equivalent journeys are made over entire popular music albums? But album-length journeys do not seem to be a prerequisite for popular songs having emotional significance, which they can do, powerfully, despite being brief. Indeed, brevity can heighten emotional impact: a song's expressiveness can be the more powerful for being achieved in a very short space of time with highly economical means. And what is lost in length of journey can be made up through, say, distortion and aggression, shock, abruptness, directness, and so on.

This suggests, though, that other factors besides harmony are crucial to popular music's expressiveness (and its meanings more broadly). *If* that expressiveness relied exclusively on harmony then long journeys might be necessary, but they are not because other parameters are also crucial. This does not mean that harmony plays no role.[19] My comments on, say, 'Like a Virgin' and 'Satisfaction' suggest that harmonic considerations are important: the norm for a return to the tonic to convey satisfaction and conversely for movement that reaches towards but does not attain the tonic to convey frustration. Less straightforwardly, harmonic considerations also shape the evocative connotations of the opening of 'Where the Streets Have No Name'. For the guitar never leaves the tonic but presents successive forms of the tonic chord, arpeggiated and with digital delay, to present busy surface movement against a still background. Yet these harmonic factors contribute to songs' meanings together with other factors and with elements functioning under other parameters. 'Where the Streets Have No Name' illustrates this: the harmonic aspect of the opening guitar part connotes movement across space *together* with the style in which the guitar is played, how it is recorded and produced (with digital delay), its role in the texture, and its dynamics (increasing in volume over time). In sum: harmony is just one variable in popular-musical meaning.[20]

Finally, another variable is (4) *re-contextualisation*. This arises because the overall meanings of popular songs do not result merely from the summing of monadic components each adding in their own connotations. As musemes qualify one another in being combined, their potential connotations are taken in particular directions and thus reinforced or altered. 'Transmission's' bass-line already connotes relentlessness to a considerable degree, but only *fully* assumes that connotation by being reinforced by the machine-like rhythm of the drums, being set off by contrast with the more optimistic solo guitar passages, and through its Dorian tonality being confirmed by the power chords. Had the bass-line been put in a different combination its incipient connotation could have been taken somewhere else. Recall how McCartney's cheerful and bustling B-section of 'A Day in the Life' acquired a different quality of ambiguity——is all this bustle really empty and meaningless?——through its combination and contrast with Lennon's melancholy A-section.

In consequence, similar or identical musical features can take on different meanings in different wholes. And when features are taken out of their original contexts and re-created, re-used, inserted elsewhere, they do not only bring with them the sedimented meanings they acquired in those prior contexts, as with the bass-line of 'Good Times' and its connotations of partying and sophistication. Also, those sedimented meanings get turned in new directions by being combined with a different set of surrounding elements; the meanings of elements in their new location are thus changed——in the case of this bass-line, coming to connote direct urban reality. Consequently, the connotations that are 'sedimented' in particular musical elements——that is, the connotations that are generally recognised within a given society, tacitly, as attaching to those elements——become reshaped continually as those elements undergo re-contextualisation.

It still does not follow that meanings are entirely conventional, even insofar as they result from processes of re-contextualisation. Take the widespread use in punk and post-punk rock of power chords, previously the preserve of heavy metal.[21] In punk and post-punk——including 'Transmission'——power chords came to embody simplicity rather than virtuosity, artlessness rather than mastery, directness rather than domination. Yet this connotation was always potentially present in power chords because they lack a third——however, the use of power chords in heavy metal had taken their meaning in a different direction. By altering accompanying features of musical style——for example using simple rather than complex melodic lines——punks and post-punks drew on and activated a potential connotation that power chords had always contained by virtue of their harmonic make-up but that had not been realised in heavy metal. In turn that potential connotation existed because of the resemblance between power chords' simplicity——their stripped-down, minimal formation——and simplicity and directness in human behaviour—— for example speech that is devoid of circumlocution and gets straight to the point. So non-conventional factors were involved in the re-contextualisation process.

Overall, we may take a middle position between conventionalism and anti-conventionalism. Real, non-conventional factors of resemblance and causal dependence bear on musical elements' connotations, as do norms of musical grammar which are not obviously entirely conventional. Non-conventional factors can even be at work in re-contextualisation processes. At the same time, none of this shows that convention plays no part. Most plausibly, a mixture of conventional and non-conventional factors is in play, where these different factors can have different weights in different cases.

However, a further issue arises here regarding objectivity. I seem to have taken it that we can identify the meanings of popular songs because they have an initial layer of meaning objectively present in them, awaiting discovery and decoding. But DeNora raises doubts about this.

She praises Roland Barthes for recognising that his responses to Vivaldi are his own——'visceral, proximate, and bound up with the temporal weft of his being' (22). To take the contrary view that one's responses track features in the music is to make an 'objectivist' error, DeNora claims, and to assume 'that music's meanings are immanent, inherent in musical forms as opposed to being brought to life in and through the interplay of forms and interpretations'.[22] In making this error and claiming that songs just 'have' certain meanings, actually we only project onto these songs our merely personal responses to them. Having said that, DeNora goes on to endorse Richard Middleton's view that social meanings can become sedimented into stylistic properties. But she nonetheless maintains that ascertaining *which* meanings are sedimented in which properties requires looking empirically at listeners' actual responses to the music. Otherwise the theorist is liable simply to assume that the meanings she finds in a song are just those that are objectively sedimented in it (DeNora 2003: 32).

I am more optimistic that we can attain objectivity despite, and sometimes through, our personal responses. We should not just project our own felt responses onto a song——but to avoid doing so we should acknowledge our responses, for then we can consider how far those responses reflect on the one hand adventitious circumstances ('they're playing our song') and on the other hand our perception of the connotations of the music. This divide need not be sharp. If I feel nostalgic to hear a song because I first encountered it at school, that memory can potentially alert me to actual features of the song: its era and context and its ways of reflecting or diverging from these. But while the divide between adventitious and music-dependent responses isn't sharp, there *is* a distinction. If I feel melancholy listening to The Smiths' 'Heaven Knows I'm Miserable Now', this is a more music-dependent response than if I feel happy because I first heard the song in the now-fondly-remembered company of an old friend.

This is not to say that our more music-dependent responses happen in a cultural vacuum in which we somehow escape surrounding influences. Cultural knowledge and categories may be necessary for me even to perceive the properties to which I respond: I might need an awareness of popular music genres, of critical reactions to a band's style, of the communities that have embraced this band, and so on (on this role of cultural knowledge, see Gracyk 2007). Cultural 'baggage' can also impede perception of musical features——if I know, say, that a song is by an artist who is disfavoured critically and this hinders me noticing the positive qualities of her latest release. However, to distinguish between cultural categories and emotional responses that are more and less illuminating of musical properties, we need additional ways——*beyond* these responses and repertoires of cultural categories——to identify the music's perceptible properties. On that basis we can assess which cultural judgements and responses are more or less illuminating. A vast body of music-theoretical work can help us to identify these properties (including empirical studies of which emotional qualities listeners regularly attribute to different musical elements; see, e.g., Zentner and Eerola 2010).

To illustrate what I mean about objectivity, let's consider Bruce Springsteen's 'Born in the U.S.A.' Springsteen adopts the voice of a working-class man, born without prospects in a 'dead man's town'. He joins or is conscripted into the US army, is sent to 'kill the yellow man' in Vietnam, loses a 'brother' (probably meaning a friend) in the war, and then returns home to a hopeless, seemingly unemployed existence: 'Nowhere to run ... nowhere to go'. Despite this dismal narrative the song has been widely received as a patriotic anthem. It was famously claimed by Ronald Reagan, who praised Springsteen's 'message of hope' when he was campaigning for re-election as president. Does this show that in itself the song has neither dismal nor anthemic connotations but can be taken however respondents please?

I think not. 'Born in the U.S.A.' does have musical features that support the patriotic interpretation, in particular its bombastic and belligerent chorus. Roy Shuker describes it as militaristic (Shuker 2001: 145–6). This quality derives partly from Springsteen's bellowing vocal and partly from the affirmative sound of the keyboard riff out of which the chorus melody develops. The riff consists of a short series of versions of the tonic chord, B major (Fig. 6.4). Beginning and ending with sustained open perfect fifths, the riff connotes power——indeed a determined, cyclical return to power——a connotation that descends partly from that of the power chord in its heavy-metal usage and suggests a message 'we can triumph'. Adding to the militaristic flavour of the chorus are the snare-drum beats, which are so heavily emphasised that they sound explosive and so evoke war and violence. The overall result is that the anthemic chorus overwhelms the chronicle of defeat in the verse.

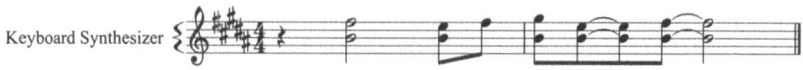

Fig. 6.4 Bruce Springsteen, 'Born in the U.S.A.', riff (synthesiser), timing ca. 00:01–00:05

This very contrast between verse and chorus can be interpreted differently, though. For Jefferson Cowie and Lauren Boehm, that contrast is the means by which Springsteen criticises American nationalism, for the song's verse/chorus form enacts the way that nationalism side-tracks working-class energies into the futility of war. Corrie and Boehm say, 'the economic foundations of the industrial working class were disappearing ... What remained was a deafening but hollow national pride ... [along with] an atomized and confused sense of self lost in the endlessly reverberating chorus of a nation' (2006: 356). The song's verse/chorus form dramatises how nationalism drowns out an underlying confusion and isolation, and the song thus brings this damaging cycle to our attention. On this account the song does have musical features that support a meaning of demoralisation and social criticism.

In conclusion, the song's meaning is not exhausted under either patriotic or anti-patriotic interpretations, but this is because both have a basis in stylistic details of the song. More than that, both have a basis in the *same* details of the song——its apparently bombastic chorus in contrast to its verse, where the former may be heard as being really bombastic or as being hollow and empty precisely in its bombast. 'Born in the U.S.A.' admits of at least two opposed interpretations——but *not* any interpretation whatsoever. If interpretations are not to be mere arbitrary projections, they need to have some basis in stylistic features of a song, in this case the contrasting verse/chorus form or the power of the riff combined with the explosive snare-drum beats. Other possible interpretations, say that 'Born in the U.S.A.' is expressive of serene calm and peace, would be downright implausible.

7   MATERIALITY AND THE SEMIOTIC

I now want to argue that popular-musical meaning typically arises in a particular way: *semiotically*.[23] In her book *Revolution in Poetic Language*, originally published in 1974, Kristeva introduces the concept of the semiotic in regard to language, which, for her, always has symbolic and semiotic aspects. The symbolic encompasses semantics and the syntactical rules that enable us to construct meaningful sentences and thereby communicate with one another and represent things. Meaning is thus bound up with judgement and the 'thetic function', in which speakers tacitly assume positions as subjects speaking about objects to other subjects (Kristeva 1984: 43). On the other hand, the semiotic encompasses the sensory qualities of words and sentences, including their pitched, timbral, and rhythmic qualities. The semiotic and symbolic are not opposites; it is not that the latter is meaningful and the former not. At the semiotic level, words and sentences *already* possess meaning, as when a rapid flurry of high-pitched syllables conveys excitement or agitation, whatever words the speaker uses in whichever language.

Semiotic meaning nonetheless differs from symbolic meaning. The source of this difference, for Kristeva, is that the semiotic has its roots in the infant's direct, body-to-body relationships with the people who care for him or her. Kristeva understands these relationships in a broadly psychoanalytic way. The infant is initially awash with its drives and energies: its needs and wishes to drink milk, suckle the breast, excrete, sleep, move its limbs, and so on. Soon these energetic flows take on regular patterns——routines of sleeping by night and waking by day, napping and feeding at regular times, kicking, cradling the breast in a certain way while feeding. These patterns stem partly from the guiding influence of care-givers and partly from the infant's endogenous development. As the infant's impulses become more regular they sediment into affects, longer-lasting and relatively stable patterns of feeling. Gradually, too, the infant's initial expressions of its sensations and wishes in raw cries and totally inarticulate sounds become patterned. The infant gradually discerns patterns in other people's speech, maps these patterns onto the affects that these people are simultaneously communicating in their verbal and non-verbal behaviours, and learns to correlate all this with his or her own feelings and behaviours. Parents' widespread use of 'motherese'——infant-directed speech——helps the infant to detect these patterns. In motherese *how* mothers (or fathers) speak rather than *what* they say is central, for which purpose the musical aspects of their speech——its pitched and rhythmic qualities——are accentuated (Trehub et al. 2010). The semiotic thus pre-exists the symbolic temporally in the life of any individual. Participation in the semiotic is also a causal precondition of entering the symbolic, which children do by coming to grasp explicitly what was already at work in the semiotic. Were children not already embedded in that field, they could never rise to articulate its contents verbally and thereby access the symbolic realm. But the semiotic persists throughout our lives: it is not discarded once we access the symbolic but remains an ongoing causal precondition of the latter.

In addition, the semiotic remains operative throughout our lives in that meanings of a semiotic kind circulate around us all the time. Barthes highlights this broader public operation of semiotic processes. In his 1957 text *Mythologies* he elucidates the distinction between semiotic and explicit meaning using the example of a picture in the magazine *Paris Match* showing a black soldier saluting the French flag. The picture does not primarily refer to the soldier as such, that is denote him. Rather, by depicting this soldier, the picture *signifies* certain ideas that it does not directly represent: namely that the French nation is rightly powerful and commands wide support from its imperial subjects, contrary to anti-colonialist claims (Barthes 1972: 115). This message is connoted rather than denoted, communicated *in*directly rather than directly. For Barthes, then, the picture has a pro-imperialist significance rather than a pro-imperialist meaning. Nonetheless, I prefer for grammatical reasons to talk about 'meanings', on the understanding that these can be semiotic and implicit as well as symbolic and explicit.

The semiotic, then, has four features.

(i) It is a realm of *implicit* rather than explicit meaning. But its implicit meanings are produced in a specific way:

(ii) They arise through *patterns of relations* between small-scale elements. These can be relations of resemblance and similarity, contrast and difference, such as the difference between a mother's low-pitched expression of disappointment and a high-pitched expression of excitement. Or the relations can be ones in which certain elements are connected or disconnected causally, including when one element is expressive of another that has caused it to be as it is. A salute is an expression of obedience; a low-pitched phrase, 'I'm disappointed in you', is expressive of displeasure. The relations can also involve metaphor and synecdoche, as when the French flag stands to the French nation as part to whole. Conventional associations can be involved in these relations.

(iii) Musical qualities, particularly those of *pitch and rhythm*, are central in the semiotic. They are vital in enabling the infant to come to identify explicit meaning in the utterances made to and around it by other people, especially its main care-givers. The infant learns to do this because pitched and rhythmic qualities already convey connotations, through mechanisms noted under (ii). For example, the interval of a minor third is widely used in everyday speech to convey sadness (Curtis and Bharucha 2010). Or a low-pitched utterance ('I'm very disappointed') might go together consistently with gestures of withdrawal and disapproval on the mother's part, cementing its negative connotation.

(iv) Finally, the semiotic is a *bodily-based realm*. It is the realm in which the infant is first awash with its impulses and energies and undergoes a gradual process in which these become patterned and stabilised into affects. Affects are already patterns of meaning, but not explicit ones. An affect of depression embodies a global sense of sadness about the world and its emptiness, perhaps because of an infant's perception that it must inevitably separate from the caregivers (or so Kristeva suggests). This sense is embedded in how a set of impulses is patterned——for example into a slowing-down and turning-inward of energy.

The way that meaning emerges in popular music closely parallels the semiotic in all four respects. (i) The connotations of individual musical components and the overall meanings that they generate within whole songs are *implicit*, not stated (aside from the words——more on their role in Chap. 7). (ii) These implicit connotations arise in a particular way, through the *relations* among musical elements and their relations to other extra-musical phenomena. These include relations of resemblance——for example between metronomic drumming and industrial machinery——relations of causation and causal expression——for example between a jagged riff and an aggressive gesture——relations of re-contextualisation——for example the contrast between the place of the bass-line in 'Good Times' and its changed place in 'Rapper's Delight'—— and the relations involved in musical grammar——for example the distances between different scale steps. The relations in question also unfold between musical elements within a given song as they qualify one another, either reinforcing or opposing one another or taking one another's connotations in specific directions. (iii) *Rhythm and pitch* are crucial to these processes. (iv) The whole meanings that result in songs generally have an *affective* dimension. As we saw earlier, although emotional quality is only one of several kinds of popular-musical meaning, it interweaves with songs' other meanings so that they are affectively laden. Even when a song is *un*emotional, as with 'Blue Monday', this is still an emotional quality. That affect is always involved parallels the fourth feature of the semiotic, that is that the meanings that first arise for the infant exist in the shape of affective patterns.

The way that meaning unfolds in popular music, then, has continuities with the semiotic realm of our infancy. But that realm is a material one, in that our bodies and their processes are at its centre. To the extent that popular music is continuous with the semiotic, then, it too has the significance for us of a material domain. We experience popular music as material insofar as it shares in much of the character of the bodily-based realm of our infancy.[24] This is another way that popular music affirms the importance of materiality and presents us, indirectly, with a truth about how meaning arises——namely within the semiotic realm first and foremost, a realm that is and remains the precondition of explicit, symbolic, verbal meaning. Popular music, as a whole, presents this truth by being so organised as to foreground semiotic meanings——whatever specific meanings are embodied by particular songs or genres. Whatever these specific meanings are, they typically arise in a certain way——semiotically——so that the primacy of the semiotic realm is thereby presented.

In Chaps. 3 and 4, I argued that popular music affirms materiality in that songs' forms as meaningful wholes typically arise out of lower-level interactions among their material parts. Materials precede forms; parts precede wholes. In Chap. 5, I argued that popular music affirms materiality in that it is typically so organised as to be highly rhythmic and energetic, and to appeal to our bodies. In this chapter I have brought in a third kind of affirmation of materiality which ties the previous two together. The material components of songs, which generate their forms as meaningful wholes, do this in semiotic ways. So although these components are 'material' in a fairly abstract sense——as small-scale components——the way that they co-operate productively is 'material' in a somewhat more concrete sense. Namely, it is continuous with the bodily and affective processes by which meaning emerges for the human infant. In addition, rhythm figures importantly in these processes and in how musical elements interlock, while also giving popular songs their highly rhythmic and energetic character such that they appeal to human bodies.[25]

It might seem that I have missed a way that popular music affirms materiality, for I have not discussed its *arousal* of emotions in us. I have instead focused on emotional qualities as perceptible qualities of popular songs. This is because I take it that when (popular) music arouses emotions in us, this happens because we respond empathetically to the emotions we apprehend in the music. I have taken it that 'arousalist' positions on which music expresses emotions *just in* arousing them in us are false, on the grounds that there must be perceptible emotional qualities in the music to arouse our emotional responses in the first place.[26] But this is not to deny that arousal happens or that it is an important value of music generally that it can arouse our emotions. Even so, I have not looked at the processes or mechanisms by which our emotions become aroused by popular music, even though our bodies and their energies and movements are surely central to these processes (see Davies 2011: ch. 4). For example, on the account of emotion proposed by William James, the physical arousal of our bodies——in rapid heart-beats, blushing, trembling, and so on——is primary and our experience of these bodily changes as emotions is secondary (James 1890: ch. 25). However, because I believe that qualities in the music precede and enable our responses, I judged that the first intellectual task was to deal with those qualities and so, in turn, with other kinds of popular-musical meaning. Although this provides a basis on which one could examine our responses and consider their somatic roots, I don't have space to undertake that examination because, given my account of meaning, another issue arises more immediately: the role of lyrics.

This issue arises straightaway because popular songs mostly have lyrics, which seems to suggest that——contrary to the picture I've presented——meanings actually get into popular songs from the 'top down', being explicitly stated in their lyrics. Perhaps the lyrics spell out the idea in light of which the musicians amass a song's materials; or perhaps the materials take on meaning only in light of the lyrics; or perhaps the lyrics come first and shape the rest of the music. Thus, it looks as if the symbolic may regulate and control the semiotic in popular music and as if the music may actually affirm the dominance of explicit over implicit meaning, and of conceptual understanding over bodily and affective processes. In the next chapter I shall argue that this is not the case, because popular songs give musical sounds and their implicit connotations priority over lyrics and their explicit statements. Let's proceed to this.

NOTES

1. Philosophers sometimes distinguish emotions from moods, taking it that emotions combine feelings with beliefs or judgements (e.g. I feel sad *that* I have to leave my daughter to go to a conference) whereas moods involve more global experiences of the world in a certain light (everything seems depressing to me wherever I look). Juslin and Sloboda define an *emotion* as a relatively brief, intense, and object-directed affective episode; a *mood* as a longer-lasting,

less intense, and not clearly object-directed affective state; *feeling* as the subjectively experienced quality of emotions or moods; and *affect* as the broadest category, covering all these phenomena (2010: 10). I speak of both emotions and affects, fairly interchangeably. This is because I take it that songs' emotional qualities are 'object-directed' in being bound up with their other connotations——as the ominousness of 'Are "Friends" Electric?' is bound up with its evocation of a dystopian, machine-dominated future. But these connotations remain tacit and 'semiotic' (as I'll explain) so that the attendant emotional qualities are nonetheless vague—— somewhere between the precision of emotions and the diffuseness of affects for Juslin and Sloboda.

2. Many other popular music theorists have also criticised this widely held public picture of emotional expression. Further, theorists have criticised ways in which ideas of authenticity validate some parts of popular music rather than others. And theorists have exposed the complex processes by which appearances of authenticity are constructed. Among many others, see Bannister (2006); Dettmar and Richey (1999); Dibben (2009); Echols (2010); Frith (2005); Grossberg (1992: esp. ch. 8); Moore (1998, 2012a: 259–71).

3. Public common-sense about popular music is my target in this section, not expression theories of art——some of which are sophisticated, such as Robinson (2005).

4. That said, the blues is often seen as giving authentic expression to black people's sufferings and resilience. Along similar lines, rap is sometimes valued for being authentically expressive of black urban life (or for being an authentic derivation from the oral tradition of the dozens; see, e.g., Wald 2012). Others deem rap *in*authentic because of its use of samples and because rapped vocals, being non-melodic, are judged emotionally unexpressive. Other black styles have also been dismissed for being inauthentic and mere entertainment——disco and Motown soul, to mention two.

5. Thanks to Brian Garvey, who pointed this out to me.

6. As Middleton says: 'Performance acts; portrayal; mimicry [here, of Little Richard]; these terms point towards a further obvious factor——singers *perform*' (2006: 94).

7. Again, I thank Richard Leadbeater for help with these formulations.

8. When I discussed 'Losing My Religion' and its sincerity in Chap. 4, then, I didn't mean that Stipe is really being sincere when he sings about unrequited love. Rather, the song gives the impression of or 'performs' sincerity, through its confessional-sounding lyrics and by other means. One is the clarity and prominence of the vocals, which suggest that Stipe really wishes to communicate—— unlike his earlier, often indecipherable vocal style. Stipe's seemingly anguished self-display in the video contributes to the performance of sincerity too. But again the video confirms that that sincerity *is* performed: Stipe modelled his performance on that of David Byrne in the video for 'Once In a Lifetime' (by Talking Heads), which Byrne in turn 'based on that of a preacher' (Buckley 2002: 217). We have successive imitations rather than any direct outpouring of emotion.

9. For Moore, The Edge's guitar creates 'the illusion of space by a divergence between fast, intricate surface movement and slow, underlying harmonic change' (1998: 21).

10. Asked about his influences, The Edge mentions Tom Verlaine, but says that he took from Verlaine 'the fact that he did something no one else had done' (Editors of *Rolling Stone* 1994: 125).

11. Others have asked how the music of the Rolling Stones can have merit and appeal to women despite its aggressive masculinity (e.g. Gracyk 2001: chs. 10–12). Part of Gracyk's answer is that the music-as-sound and its meaning can diverge. I would add that the music's several meanings diverge too.

12. The song was first written in March/April 1978, presented on a 1979 Peel session, recorded in demo form in March 1979, and recorded in single version in July/August 1979. My discussion is of the single as included on the 1988 *Substance* compilation.

13. This use of the bass guitar in the central melodic role is unusual in popular music. Hook evolved it, often playing high-pitched bass-lines, because as he puts it: 'If you played higher up the guitar, it was easier to hear yourself, 'cos your equipment was so crap' (Ott 2004: 53). This blurring of the usual popular-musical distinction between melodic and bass layers became central to Joy Division's sound. Having said this, the bass-line in 'Transmission' is not especially high-pitched; 'She's Lost Control' is more representative.

14. Hook says of the bass-line that 'it's a very, very simple riff. ... You can sit back on the verse, you can pound it on the chorus, but the

riff never really changes. The riff is the solid backbone of the song' (Hook, quoted in Marcus 2014: 46–47).

15. The Dorian scale on D contains a B rather than a B♭, so that songs built on this scale sound brighter than songs in D minor. But because the D Dorian scale lacks F♯ and C♯, songs built on it sound less bright than songs in D major.

16. Producer Martin Hannett 'demanded totally clean and clear "sound separation" not just for individual instruments, but for each element of the drum kit'; in addition, Hannett 'applied a micro-second delay to the drums that was barely audible but which created a sense of enclosed space' (Reynolds 2005: 184. See also Ott 2004: 62–63).

17. 'Rapper's Delight' is controversial (i) because of its affinity with disco, (ii) due to the opportunistic, commercial circumstances of its production (producer Sylvia Robinson hastily cobbled the band together seeing that rap was poised for chart success), and (iii) due to rapper Big Bank Hank's theft of lyrics written by Grandmaster Caz (see Katz 2012: 75–78). For these reasons Jeff Chang deems 'Rapper's Delight' to mark the first death of hip hop (2006: 129)——its first fall from spontaneity and authenticity into commerce. For Brendon Griffin, 'the single presented hip-hop in a neutered, second-hand fashion, tailoring it to the disco market' (Griffin 2002). These comments illustrate how the ideal of authenticity pervades discourse around rap as other genres. Since I am sceptical about authenticity, I think it worth approaching 'Rapper's Delight' at a critical distance from that ideal.

18. On resemblance in music generally, see Davies (e.g. 2011), Kivy (2002: ch. 3), Turino (2008: 6–7).

19. Everett (2000) reminds us that pitch structures and harmonic systems remain important in popular music. And besides chords, melodies, melodic fragments, and bass-lines all function harmonically.

20. It might be argued that the same is true of other musical forms, including classical music, which may not be ideally served by the theoretical focus on harmony. But this is beyond my scope here.

21. On power chords in heavy metal see Walser (1993: 2 and 42–43).

22. Others take views similar to DeNora's. For instance, Leonard Navarez questions the 'myth' that Joy Division distil the sound of late 1970s Manchester, concluding: 'A musical act from a city does not immediately connote the "urban". . . . Any "urban" interpretation

must first be asserted in collective arenas, to frame diverse meanings and to prevail upon other, nonurban discourses from which listeners might interpret music' (2013: 73). By implication, prior to these assertions Joy Division's music connoted the rural just as much as the urban——that is, it had no definite connotations of place at all.

23. Other music theorists take semiotic approaches, including Tagg (e.g. 1982) and Machin (2010). However, they do not use the concept of the semiotic in its Kristevan sense, as pertaining to the bodily-based realm of human infancy. That said, Hebdige (1979) takes from Kristeva the idea that visual, material, aural, and fashion artefacts are composed of elements organised by contrasts and combinations so that they embody meaning. Yet on the whole Hebdige's semiotic approach relates only loosely to Kristeva's. In contrast, in *Voicing the Popular* (2006) Middleton develops a framework that is more closely informed by psychoanalysis——but above all that of Lacan rather than Kristeva, who comes in only in passing.

24. By analysing the words and syncopations in Buddy Holly's 'Peggy Sue', Brady and Torode (2000) propose that rock's rhythms re-stage the rhythms of children's relations to their mothers, but Brady and Torode make no reference to Kristeva's account of the semiotic.

25. There is a potential tension within my set of claims here. As overall structures of meaning that unify songs' parts and that arise from the interlocking of those parts, songs' meanings are aligned with *form* and therefore, by extension, with conceptual understanding as distinct from material existence. Yet insofar as these meanings are semiotic, they are aligned with *materiality* and not form. But this is because songs' overall meanings have at least two aspects: as *structures* of meaning they align with form; as structures of *meaning*, where this is semiotic meaning, they align with materiality. The combined effect of both alignments is to present materials as generative of form, including by being generative of meaning at a semiotic level that is the precondition of explicit, conceptual meaning——a semiotic level that is more 'formal' than its material components but less 'formal' than the symbolic, paving the way for the latter.

26. Some of our emotional reactions to songs arise by chance from personal associations ('they're playing our song'). To avoid attributing all these chance emotions to a song we must specify that the emotions it expresses are just those that it tends to arouse in us in response to *it*——to the music 'itself'. But to respond to the music 'itself' we already need to apprehend the music as expressive of certain emotions. Arguably, then, arousalism presupposes that music is expressive independently of how it affects us. See Kania (2014: 3.1).

CHAPTER 7

Meaning in Sounds and Words

1   INTRODUCTION

In the previous chapter I argued that meaning in popular songs emerges in a way that is continuous with the bodily-based realm of the semiotic. Bodily-based, affective, implicit meaning is thereby affirmed to be more fundamental than the explicit meanings that concern the intellect. However, it might seem that popular songs actually acquire their meanings from the top down, with explicit verbal meanings in a regulating role. One version of this 'top-down' view is that songs' meanings originate in ideas held by their writers——as when Bruce Springsteen's distress at the fate of Vietnam veterans inspired him to write what became 'Born in the U.S.A.' Equally a song's meaning may be taken to be stated in its lyrics. The two positions can be combined. Perhaps the lyrics tell us what idea a song-writer had in mind, and perhaps that organising idea finds direct statement in the lyrics. But whether ideas, words, or both are the focus, the assumption is that songs acquire their meanings from something intelligible——an idea, or verbal statements that are comprehensible by the understanding. On this view, these explicit meanings shape how songs' stylistic elements are combined and adapted, so that explicit meaning regulates semiotic meaning and the material processes of its production. Popular music would then embody and affirm a dominance of the understanding over the body after all. I will argue against this top-down picture, mostly by giving an alternative account of lyrics in Sects. 3, 4, and 5.

© The Author(s) 2016   213
A. Stone, *The Value of Popular Music,*
DOI 10.1007/978-3-319-46544-9_7

But first, in Sect. 2, I argue against the view that songs' meanings derive from ideas on the part of their writers.[1]

2   The Idea of Meaning

Usually the person taken to originate a song's guiding 'idea' is the lyricist, melody-writer, and vocalist, commonly a single individual in popular music. He or she is taken to have an idea of a song's meaning, by which all the musical materials are shaped. That idea may be communicated through the lyrics or disclosed in interviews, or both. Take public discussion of Joy Division. Their oeuvre is often treated as getting its meaning from the 'top down'——as being determined almost single-handedly by vocalist and lyricist Ian Curtis, the gloom of the music supposedly reflecting Curtis's deteriorating and increasingly depressed state of mind leading up to his suicide.[2]

This notion has taken firm hold even though Curtis's actual role in the band was different. Curtis served as a kind of choreographer: he picked out the strongest bass-lines, riffs, rhythmic cells, and so on, which the band then developed. Curtis often chose the bass-lines to be the melodic centre of songs, modelling his vocal melodies on them. He either wrote lyrics to fit in with these melodies or drew on lyrics that he had already drafted, from which he selected and adapted lines that he could fit to phrases of guitar melody, or to bass-lines, and so on (see Hook 2012: 75, 140–2, 148). Thus, the lyrics were woven into the music afterwards rather than driving its composition at the outset.

Nonetheless, the popularity of the idea that Curtis was the unique source of the meanings of Joy Division's music reflects a widespread assumption, namely that the lyricist-cum-vocalist in a band establishes the meanings of their songs and so counts as the 'song-writer'. He or she is assumed to have a regulating idea of a song's meaning in line with which all the musical materials are shaped. The words of the song specify this idea and so guide listeners as to what a song means. Even when the actual words are laid down late in the recording process, the idea that those words specify is taken to have been present in a regulating role all along. The basic position, then, is that songs accord with an 'idea' of their meaning on the song-writers' part: an idea, say, of what emotion a song is to express or what theme it is to explore. And that idea is made explicit by the lyrics.

Admittedly, there are cases in which the roles of vocalist and lyricist diverge, especially at the 'pop' end of the spectrum in which professional song-writers rather than vocalists often write the melodies and lyrics. But these roles can diverge in rock too: In The Who, Pete Townshend wrote the lyrics and Roger Daltrey only sang them; in Oasis, Liam Gallagher only sang the lyrics that Noel Gallagher wrote; and dedicated lyricists without any other musical role wrote the lyrics on earlier King Crimson albums. The common-sense response to such cases is that the lyricist and not the vocalist determines the meaning, which preserves the assumption that lyrics state the meaning of songs.[3]

It might seem improbable that a song-writer should have a fully formed idea of what a song is about before writing it. As Negus and Pickering point out, 'we do not have a fully formed, reflexively comprehended experience which we then reproduce in verbal or sonic form. ... The expression not only forms the experience but also transforms it' (2002: 184). Indeed, plausibly a song-writer can never fully know in advance what their idea of a song's meaning is, because any such idea can only take on definite content in being given expression in words or music. But this remains compatible with the song-writer having some such idea and with that idea shaping the musical materials. That idea can be initially implicit yet govern a song's materials in that they are produced, refined, and modified to yield a result that realises and makes explicit the idea. Even without being explicitly known at the outset, the idea can nonetheless provide the effective criterion by which successive musical parts are tried out and discarded or retained. We can know after the fact that the idea has performed this organising role because we can see how it animates and accounts for the materials once they have been produced.

However, the lyricist-cum-vocalist-cum-songwriter rarely supplies all of a song's instrumental parts single-handed. This is not unknown: Prince played almost all the instruments on some of his albums such as *1999*, and Beck played most of the parts on his earlier albums. Even so, it does not necessarily follow that all those parts were shaped in line with the lyrics-cum-vocals. In any case, although technological developments have made it easier for a single individual to perform multiple functions in this way, in practice it remains relatively uncommon for songs to issue from just one individual. Musicians continue to benefit from collaborating with others and drawing on their skills.

Thus it has been and remains common for popular music to be made in fairly democratic and collaborative ways——as when a band composes by jamming together——or with the fundamental element in a song being supplied by an instrumentalist and not the vocalist-cum-lyricist.[4]

For example, Mick Jagger wrote the vocal part and lyrics for 'Satisfaction' prompted by the riff (and the line 'I can't get no satisfaction') that Keith Richards produced. Jagger only spelt out the quality of which the riff was already expressive: frustration (Leahey 2012). Again, guitarist Peter Buck wrote the harmonic structure of 'Losing My Religion' on the mandolin, to which other instrumentation was then added, with the melody and lyrics contributed only late in the process (Rosen 1997: 108). The song was not written to realise the theme of unrequited love supplied by vocalist Stipe. Rather, Stipe's melody and lyrics were created in response to the music.[5]

Nevertheless, the assumption remains widespread that it is lyricists whose ideas shape songs' meanings. After all, pragmatically, it can be difficult to know what idea a song might be expressing until that idea receives some verbal statement. Thus the lyrics provide the royal road to the idea presiding over a song——and even when lyrics are oblique or allusive they remain more explicit than instrumentation. Moreover, some popular songs *do* appear to realise an idea on the lyricist's part. In these instances the lyricist furnishes initial melodies and basic chord sequences, sometimes in the guise of a demo recording, in light of which other band members craft their respective parts. Even so, musicians do not work out bass-lines, percussion rhythms, or the precise details of the harmonic layer (under what rhythm to present the chords, in what style to play them) by simply deriving these details from the melody. Rather it is normal for each instrumental part to be created in its own right and the parts then to be adapted together in the recording process (see Zak 2001: 53).

Let's consider for example U2's 'With or Without You', relevant here because the song might seem to realise an idea held by lyricist and vocalist Bono. The song originated as a vocal melody written by Bono, who supplied the attendant chord progression, I–V–vi–IV (i.e. D major–A major–B minor–G major in the key of D major). For Bono, the song is about his anguish at the conflict between his commitments to the band and to his family:

> The lyric is pure torment. One of the things that was happening at that time was the collision in my own mind between being faithful to your art or being faithful to your lover. ... I thought these tensions were going to destroy me but actually, in truth, it is me. ... So that song is about torment, sexual but also psychological, about how repressing desires makes them stronger. (Bono in McCormick 2005: 173–4)

By implication the song originated in Bono's anguished feelings, which found expression in the melody and lyrics, the rest of the music arising to realise further this 'idea'.

However, undertaking prolonged work on the song, U2 struggled to develop it into a satisfactory form and considered abandoning it. The impasse was only overcome by chance when The Edge was experimenting with a prototype of the 'infinite guitar', a device allowing the guitar to be played with an infinite degree of sustain. The Edge explains that while he was doing this,

> Gavin Friday and Bono were in the control room listening to the backing track [containing percussion and bass] of 'With or Without You' … [when] through an open door, they heard the sound of the infinite guitar combining with the bass and drums and just went: 'That's it!'. (The Edge in McCormick 2005: 172)

Immediately the band began to record The Edge's guitar part and the way was paved to completing the song. The key combination of the rhythm track and the infinite guitar arose by 'total accident', then, as The Edge puts it. That combination was not designed to realise the 'idea' of anguish and music-family conflict embodied in the melody and lyrics.

But perhaps, once it had arisen by accident, that combination of instrumental parts was still selected because it could be used and adapted to realise the song's organising 'idea' of music-family anguish. *Is* that what the infinite guitar does (together with the bass guitar)? To assess this, let's map out what the guitar does overall (see Figs. 7.1, 7.2, and 7.3 and Table 7.1).

I've described the song as having verses and choruses, but in fact this is only obviously true of Bono's vocals.[6] Allan Moore instead sees 'With or Without You' as an instance of 'bolero' form: the whole builds to a crescendo, drops away, then builds back more moderately (Moore 2012a: 175–176). This rise-fall-and-return is part of how the song moves through a narrative, above all through the guitar's contributions. Their varied character, with The Edge never playing a simple sequence of major or minor triads, creates a narrative progression. Roughly, that narrative begins with a schism between mind and body, causing a build up of tension that

Fig. 7.1   U2, 'With or Without You', first riff

Electric Guitar

Fig. 7.2   U2, 'With or Without You', second riff

Electric Guitar

Fig. 7.3   U2, 'With or Without You', third riff

eventually gives way to an outburst of formerly repressed passion; finally the passion is assuaged, leading to tranquillity; the passion then begins to build again, but now this inevitable tension is accepted. Thus, a movement occurs from conflict to simple resolution to more complex resolution. This is not a logical development that unfolds the implications of a motive and generates emotional qualities along the way. Rather, the narrative of emotional development is created texturally above all, by the interweaving of the guitar tracks and their changing relations to one another.

We could regard this course of emotional development as realising Bono's 'idea' of the song: the anguish of conflicting emotions, the problem of repressed passions resurfacing, and the need to accept emotional conflict. That 'idea' does map quite well onto the narrative that the guitar charts. But it would be implausible to see that idea as being all along embodied in the vocal melody and words so that the guitar merely elaborates it further. For the vocal melody on its own is expressive of anguish without reaching a resolution. Bono's vocal climaxes with an outpouring of passion——'and you give yourself away'——but then he reiterates 'I can't live with or without you': the conflict remains. In his remarks, too, Bono stresses the anguish more than the resolution. That resolution is narrated not by the words or melody but by the guitar. Thus, rather than elaborating on an idea already embodied in the melody or words, the guitar adds its *own* contribution to the song's meaning.

It is not that Bono's description of the song's meaning is incorrect. It *is* substantially correct——but what is incorrect is to see the vocal melody and words as embodying the song's entire meaning on which the other instrumental parts merely expand. Rather, their contributions interact with those initially supplied by the vocal melody, generating a combined

Table 7.1 U2, 'With or Without You', guitar, structure

Timing	Section	Measures	Guitar one	Guitar two (and three)	Emotional quality
00:00–00:27	Intro	12	After some false starts that stop when the bass guitar enters, the infinite guitar——very high-pitched (around F♯₅)——rises slightly to hold the dominant (A) over eight measures,		The slight rising motion and unfeasibly long sustain build tension; the quietness adds to the guitar's eerie, seemingly disembodied sound. There is a great distance in register and pace from the faster-moving bass guitar, which plays eight eighth-notes for the root of each (implied) chord in succession. All this suggests a gulf between mind and body, with bodily desire suppressed (down in the bass) but pushing forward in need of release
00:27–01:02	Verse	16	then it continues (still on A₅) into this first verse, before dropping down to a sustained F♯₅,	Near the end a second infinite guitar track enters, moving within the octave below that of the first track,	An initial wave of tension recedes slightly,
01:02–01:11	Chorus	4	then to E₅, held for much of this half-length chorus, then beginning to rise again,	held on A₄, but finally moving up near the first track	but then the tension reasserts itself, through the long sustain and the upward rise of the second guitar track
01:11–01:28	Verse	8	now becoming notably louder, arching up (by a fourth) and back down	Having dropped out, towards the end of this section the second infinite guitar returns,	Again, a rising wave of tension,

(continued)

Table 7.1 (continued)

Timing	Section	Measures	Guitar one	Guitar two (and three)	Emotional quality
01:28–01:45	Chorus	8	Still gaining in volume, the guitar largely stays level on a very sustained F#$_5$, lasting into the next section,	again moving below the first,	persisting and so building up,
01:45–01:54	Bridge	4	at the end of which a loud, jagged arpeggiated guitar riff (Fig. 7.1), played with digital delay, breaks in,	now rising into the same register as the first track, then dropping out in favour of the riff	finally reaching a point where the tension breaks and gives way to an outbreak of pent-up passion
01:54–02:12	Refrain ('and you give yourself away…')	8	and is repeated		The guitar is now lower-pitched (around G$_4$) moving at the same eighth-note pace as the bass; they have converged——what was suppressed is finding expression
02:12–02:29	Verse	8	This riff continues to be repeated,	The second infinite guitar returns, occupying the higher register formerly occupied by the first track, again arching up by a fourth,	Tension continues to be expressed, but also to build up again
02:29–02:46	Refrain ('and you give yourself away…')	8	for two measures, then after a brief interlude the riff is reasserted more loudly and forcefully,	finally closing back to D$_5$ A third track of guitar enters playing harmonics	The tension conveyed by the second track recedes, through the outpouring expressed by the first track / A potential state of equilibrium or harmony now comes into view

02:46–03:04	Chorus	8	which continues, rising towards a crescendo (along with all the instruments),		Emotional energy is bursting through, the rise in volume suggesting an unstoppable momentum
03:04–03:21	Interlude ('whoa, whoa…')	8	which is reached now, and the first guitar changes very briefly to playing a second riff, still arching but more smoothly and gently (Fig. 7.2), based on an arpeggiated D suspended chord. It rapidly gives way to successive, quite high-pitched forms of the tonic chord	The second guitar plays harmonics	The change to a smoother riff and then to forms of the tonic chord suggest a continuing outflow of passion but one that is more comfortable than before, suggesting a more emotionally rounded state. The continued harmonics suggest an ongoing movement towards mental harmony
03:21–03:39	Chorus	8	The crescendo continues then begins gradually to drop away; while this happens, the guitar continues to play various chords, mostly forms of the tonic, and finally		The passion seems more 'accepted' by virtue of the transition from the jagged riff to chords,
03:39–03:48	Bridge	4	a straightforward D major chord rings out, just as much of the instrumentation falls away		And the sustained tonic chord suggests that resolution has been reached, along with the peace or rest suggested by the crescendo dying away

(continued)

Table 7.1 (continued)

Timing	Section	Measures	Guitar one	Guitar two (and three)	Emotional quality
03:48–04:05	Interlude	8		The high-pitched infinite guitar comes back, and remains, then on measure six it goes over to playing the first riff, quietly then more prominently than the new (third) riff. As this happens, everything builds back to another brief crescendo, but then immediately begins to fade out	But tension begins to return…
04:05–04:56	Coda	22	A third riff comes in (Fig. 7.3). It cycles repeatedly through four variations on the tonic chord, none of them a straightforward major triad. Its steady shape contrasts to the jagged arch of the first riff		…and finds expression again (in the third riff), but this time the outflow of passion is accepted, this third riff having a more steady and resolved character (the tonic is present throughout it). The interplay between the first and third riffs suggests that passion is still felt and is not entirely comfortable. But the tension itself can now be accommodated—hence the two intertwining riffs, more settled and more tempestuous

meaning that depends on the co-operation of these intersecting parts. It is as a result of this process that the vocal melody and words acquire their meaning as Bono articulates it, as expressing anguished feelings, where that meaning is embedded in the broader overall meaning that conflicting feelings become worked through and reach resolution. That meaning grows from the 'bottom up'——from the coalescence of manifold musical elements——rather than being imposed from the top down. This is only one example, but I suggest that 'With or Without You' typifies how multiple instrumental parts contribute to popular songs' meanings.

3   Lyrics: Sound and Content

If lyrics do not state organising ideas that regulate song construction, then how *do* lyrics contribute to songs' meanings? Are lyrics just one musematic component of songs among others? Lyrics, though, have explicit meaning, as songs' non-verbal components do not. It therefore seems that lyrics must at least contribute to songs' meanings in a different way from the non-verbal components.

A qualification, though. Not all popular music has lyrics: many albums spanning many genres contain instrumental tracks, and some musicians' entire output is instrumental——Dick Dale, for example, and Link Wray.[7] Some genres are largely instrumental, such as many kinds of electronic dance music. This does not mean that songs in these genres have no melodies: house tracks often have a central synthesiser riff that comes and goes and falls away in volume during the 'breakdown' while the percussion stops, with the riff then building back up in volume until the drums resume (a structure clearly instantiated in, say, Darude's trance track 'Sandstorm'). Just as melodies can be non-verbal, conversely words can be non-melodic, when they are rapped (although rap songs have evolved so that their vocal parts now often combine rapped and melodic elements, or have choruses that are fairly straightforwardly melodic——a pattern going back at least to tracks such as the Fugees' 'Ready Or Not', on *The Score*, or, even earlier, to the 1983 track 'The Crown' by Gary Byrd and the GB Experience). To say that rapped vocals are non-melodic or partly non-melodic is no criticism of them. Even when they are entirely non-melodic, rap vocals remain *musical*, for they function rhythmically and expressively, they vary dynamically, and they contribute to a track's timbre and texture.[8] In any case, rap only takes further the tendency in much popular music for vocals to be semi-spoken (or shouted, growled, whispered, etc.), precise pitch being sacrificed in favour of continuity with the expressive vocal behaviours of everyday life.

The net result is that vocals, lyrics, and melody can come apart. Still, when vocals with lyrics *are* present, as in most popular songs, the question remains: What distinct contribution do lyrics make to songs' meanings by virtue of being explicitly meaningful as songs' instrumental layers are not? And how can that contribution take place without the lyrics effectively governing what the other layers signify so that conceptual understanding is privileged?

One way to consider lyrics' contribution is to scrutinise their semantic content in its own right, using content analysis to identify themes and preoccupations in lyrics and trace how their changes over time reflect wider social trends. Not surprisingly, content analysts have found that most lyrics deal with romantic relationships, at least in the chart hits on which these analysts tend to concentrate. Thomas Scheff (2011), for example, estimates that since 1930 a steady 75 % of lyrics has concerned romance.[9] Nonetheless, over time notable shifts have occurred in these broadly romance-centred lyrics. James Carey (1969) found that lyrics had changed since the 1950s in ways that mirrored changes in gender relations, more liberal attitudes towards sex, and greater regard for individual autonomy. Scheff, less favourably, takes changes in lyrics to reflect growing social atomisation, with lyrics becoming increasingly preoccupied with the feelings of single individuals rather than with loving relationships (2011: 138–9).

Anyway, at least two problems beset content-analytic approaches. First, in looking only at semantic content we fail to consider how lyrics function musically and how those musical functions may affect what the lyrics mean. Second, those analysing lyrical content often presume that popular music lyrics are formulaic and banal. After all, it is the very presence of formulae——of words and phrases clustered into fixed patterns and idioms at given periods——which enables theorists to pinpoint how lyrics reflect broader social currents.[10] Hence, another strand of writing on lyrics condemns them for being standardised, trite, and unimaginative——as with Dave Harker (1980), who gives a socialist slant to this complaint. Ultimately, these critiques reflect the influence of expressivist and modernist aesthetic values. The charge that most lyrics are trite and unimaginative is that they fail to express any personal vision or genuinely felt emotions; the charge that lyrics are formulaic is that they fail to break from prevailing conventions.

One response has been to raise lyrics in status by re-positioning them as poetry.[11] For example, in his anthology *The Poetry of Rock*, Richard Goldstein traced how rock-'n'-roll had 'evolved into a full-fledged art-form' (1969: 1). His collection was part of the broader effort to elevate rock music to art status (Astor 2010), and shares its problems. Some lyrics can be categorised as poetry more readily than others: those that are more formulaic or plain-spoken will fall short. Lyrics by white women and by black men and women tend to be viewed in the latter way——and people from these groups are more likely to be pushed by record company personnel to write on conventional themes, partly because of their relative lack of power within the industry, partly because of constraints stemming from prejudiced expectations on the part of radio stations and audiences. Nile Rodgers commented in 1999:

> In the black-music world in America, if you go against the grain, chances are, you will not get on the radio and people won't hear you. I always hear a lot of criticism of black artists saying the lyrics are shallow, they only write about sex, and you say to yourself, there's a reason for it. It's not because there isn't interesting intellectual subject matter for black artists to delve into, it's the fact that you won't get played. ... [Bowie] had a demo of 'China Girl', and my first reaction was, 'God, it's damn good to be white!' You can write an esoteric song with hidden meanings, whereas in black music if you have a song called 'China Girl' it had damn better convey some message about a girl you met in China or something. It has to be a lot more literal! (Buckley 2005: 337–8)[12]

The resulting biases about which lyrics count as 'poetic' are exemplified in Goldstein's anthology. He does not exclude lyrics by women or black people. Chuck Berry, Little Richard, Willie Dixon, and the Holland-Dozier-Holland team are included, as are Zelda Sanders and Lona Stevens (the writers of 'Sally Go Round the Roses' by the 1960s girl group the Jaynetts) among others. Yet Goldstein divides the evolution of lyrics into four historical phases, beginning with the pre-artistic phase of 'Raunch and roots', supposedly kicked off by Chuck Berry's 'simplistic and primitive' lyrics (1969: 15). By no coincidence, the vast majority of the black and female song-writers featured in the anthology are found in this section. For Goldstein, they wrote poetry of a sort——but inferior poetry, not properly artistic, unlike the lyrics featured in his final phase, 'Allegory and beyond'. The museum of rock-lyrical poetry harbours similar racial and gender biases to that of rock-as-art.

In any case, resolving which lyrics count as poetry is near-impossible because poetry is a contested and heterogeneous class. The vagueness and openness of the concept *poetry* means that discussion of whether lyrics are poetry usually falls back on whether lyrics display a personal vision or use commonplace language. Griffiths (2003) proposes an alternative classification scheme on which lyrics are on a continuum from the more poetic——making greater use of rhyme, assonance, and alliteration——to the more prosaic ('anti-lyrical')——more given to direct statements. Even the most 'poetic' lyrics so understood, though, are not straightforwardly po*ems*, for reasons pithily put by critic Robert Christgau: 'Poems are read or said. Songs are sung' (1967). Rap complicates Christgau's point. But rapped vocals too are sung in the broad sense that their musical qualities are of paramount importance, albeit that in rap these qualities are rhythmic, expressive, textural, and timbral more than melodic. So if we broaden the meaning of 'song' beyond that of melody, we may stick with Christgau's point. What, then, does it mean to say that lyrics are distinctive in being sung (in this expanded sense)?

For Frith, the fact that lyrics are sung entails that they never mere statements of explicit meaning but are always signs of a speaker, embodying the unique sound of his or her voice and vocal style (Frith 1996: 229). This leads us into a manifold of variables that bear on lyrics as sung. They include:

(i) The 'grain' of the musician's voice. As Barthes initially used 'grain' (it is from Barthes that the term has entered popular music theory), it picked out singing styles that allow more of the materiality of a singer's body to come through, contrary to styles that subordinate that materiality in the name of precise pitch and phrasing.[13] But all vocalising has some level of 'grain', and its materiality is not a single thing: different vocal styles manifest different body organs—head, stomach, chest, nose—to varying degrees.

(ii) A vocalist's individual style also reflects her pitch range; the nuances under which she realises pitches; how she combines melodic and non-melodic sounds, and how far she incorporates everyday expressive vocal behaviours (stuttering, shouting, sneering, etc.);[14] nuances and micro-variations in her rhythms and her timing of vocal lines; and her accent and habits of articulation.

(iii) Groups of words exhibit phonetic patterns such as rhyme, assonance, and alliteration (Salley 2011: 409). Affecting these patterns, in any single phrase of song vocalisation usually unfolds in a continuous stream, and so additional consonants regularly creep in to ease transitions between syllables—Salley mentions how 'I am the egg-man' in the Beatles' 'I Am the Walrus' (on *Magical Mystery Tour*) effectively becomes 'I am the *y*egg-man' (Salley 2011: 414). Consonants can 'migrate' between words, moving from the end of one word to the start of the next; or consonants may drop out ('Baby please *don'* go') or be softened. For example, the chorus of 'I Told Her on Alderaan' by Neon Neon (on *Stainless Style*) runs 'I told her on Alderaan /that nothing else was going on'. But phonetically something like the following is uttered (Fig. 7.4).[15]

To map out the rhymes and phonetic patterns in these two lines:

I<u>te</u> <u>ol de ron olderon</u>
<u>That nuh thi nelse was go wi non</u>

Thus, many more alliterative and rhyming patterns overlap here than we would see from the lyrics when written down.

Alliterative and rhyming patterns depend on how words are enunciated and so different vocalists will tend to produce specific kinds of pattern. Styles of enunciation have expressive import too. For example, Bernard Sumner gives a fairly harsh articulation to the words of 'Blue Monday', stressing the consonants more than the vowels to convey coldness and distance——perhaps because the consonants hold the syllables apart from one another, conveying distance through resemblance.

(iv) Syllables need to be matched up with notes of melody, if vocals are melodic. This is most often achieved syllabically in popular music, with one syllable set to each note. But some degree of melisma is

Fig. 7.4 Neon Neon, 'I Told Her on Alderaan', vocal melody, timing ca. 01:11–01:18

also reasonably widespread, especially in soul music and genres influenced by it. If vocals are rapped, each syllable needs to be matched up with a point in the subdivision of the beat. That said, rapped syllables can flow across beat and measure divisions and can be voiced in unexpected places relative to the subdivision of the beat that other layers of sound spell out, thus dividing up musical time in different ways to those other layers.

(v) Lines of lyric need to be matched up with phrases of song. Those phrases can be demarcated on a purely rhythmic basis, as sometimes occurs in rap, or by rhythm and pitch together when vocals are melodic. In both cases it is typical for grammatical sentences or clauses to end at the same point as the phrases do. Consider the opening lines of 'Orgasm Addict' by Buzzcocks (included on their *Singles: Going Steady*). Its first and second lines are set to phrases of melody that both end—on 'kicks' and 'sticks'—by descending conclusively from dominant (F#) to tonic (B). The end of the first phrase is also demarcated rhythmically by the longer note on 'kicks' and the brief pause after it (see Fig. 7.5).

The second phrase, though, is foreshortened: 'sticks' rolls straight into a rapid 'and you're an' segment that leads into the chorus. This shortened second phrase contributes to the song's hurried rhythm: the vocal seems so urgent and impatient as to tumble over itself in haste, in keeping with the narrative: the protagonist (addressed as 'you') cannot control his sexual urges and descends through worsening stages of addiction. Anyway, overall, these opening lines are fitted to the phrases of melody in that each line contains a clause that reaches a point of grammatical closure where the phrase ends. It would be anomalous, although not impossible, for (say) the first line to end on 'for', not 'kicks', and the second on 'that', not 'sticks'.

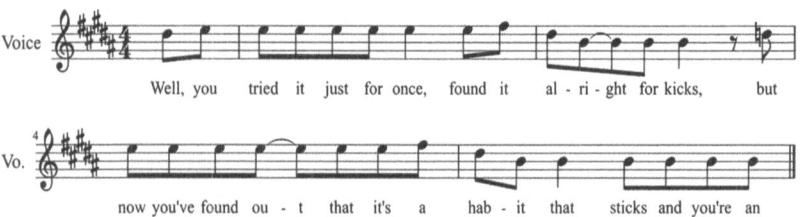

Fig. 7.5   Buzzcocks, 'Orgasm Addict', vocal melody, timing ca. 00:01–00:06

(vi) These Buzzcocks lyrics exemplify another standard practice: use of rhyming couplets—for example *kicks/sticks*—to mark where clauses and phrases end. These can be 'rhymes' in a broad and extended sense, that is 'near'-rhymes or imperfect rhymes (Griffiths 2003: 50–51; Hirjee and Brown 2009). Rhyming couplets highlight how a vocal part is divided up, in turn sign-posting divisions between song sections and thus a song's formal organisation. But rhymes can be used *within* clauses too, most conspicuously in rap. Over time, rappers have progressively increased the amount of rhymes used within each clause, so that rap lyrics now include on average twice as many rhymes as rock lyrics and considerably more rhymes involving multi-syllable words (Hirjee and Brown 2009: 715). All this augments the rhythmic function of rap vocals.

(vii) Clauses need to contain regularly recurring points of emphasis which fit in with the rhythms of vocal phrases and relate to the rhythmic patterns presented by other layers of sound. Against this background a further norm is for words to be used with their normal, everyday emphases, which therefore need to be calibrated with the emphases that the vocal rhythm demands. That is, sentences need to be used in which the emphases fall in the right places *both* for the vocal rhythm *and* to preserve the normal emphases of everyday speech. Exceptions do occur, in which words are given unusual emphases: in 'desolate' 'des-' is normally emphasised, but in The Smiths' 'This Charming Man' Morrissey instead stresses '-o-' and the '-lay-' of 'late' by elongating these syllables and beginning them on the beats that are rhythmically emphasised, that is the backbeats (Fig. 7.6).

The opening lines of 'Orgasm Addict' are more typical insofar as they retain everyday speech emphases: the usual emphasis in 'habit' falls on 'hab-', which Pete Shelley indeed stresses, partly by placing 'hab-' on the first, metrically accented beat of the measure.

Fig 7.6 The Smiths, 'This Charming Man', vocal melody, timing ca. 00:16–00:19

But is 'Orgasm Addict' unusual in putting the stress on syllables that fall on metrically accented beats? David Temperley maintains that normally in popular song stressed syllables do *not* fall on metrically strong beats: 'there is a norm of stressed events occurring *against* some continuing metrical structure' (1999: 35; my emphasis). But although stressed syllables can fall on the backbeat (as in Fig. 7.6), I am not convinced that that is the norm. Consider the chorus line of The Manic Street Preachers' 'A Design for Life' (on *Everything Must Go*). Contrary to the usual emphasis in speech, the stresses in this phrase are on 'a' and 'for', whereas ordinarily one would stress '-sign' and 'life'. Yet 'a' and 'for' fall on the metrically accented beats——the first beat of the measures in which they appear.

Consider also the verse of Lily Allen's 'The Fear' (on *It's Not Me, It's You*), in which Allen's vocal is semi-spoken and conversational. It is based around a very clearly defined repeated phrase, set to an eighth-note subdivision of the 4/4 beat but with the phrases overlapping rather than coinciding with the divisions between measures. Taking a short excerpt, I've underlined the stressed syllables (Fig. 7.7).

As these measures illustrate, Allen generally begins each phrase ('And...', 'and...') on beat four of the eighth-note subdivision. But she stresses the syllables that fall on beat five, which is metrically accented as marking the half-measure (albeit less strongly accented than beat one). She also stresses the syllables that span measure divisions, extending from beat eight of one measure into beat one of the next. But this means that she basically stresses the syllables on the first, accented beats of each measure but with a degree of anticipation. Overall, then, Allen stresses the metrically accented beats. 'The Fear' and 'A Design for Life' illustrate that there is no shortage of vocal lines that *do* emphasise syllables that coincide with metrically strong beats. Besides 'Orgasm Addict', other instances include the Beatles' 'Lucy in the Sky with Diamonds' and Pulp's 'Babies', mentioned below. In this way, the vocals often pull against the backbeat that is stressed by the percussion, and so contribute to songs' rhythmic tension, insofar as this arises from playing overt rhythm and metre off against one another, in the way I analysed in Chap. 5.

(fi)nd the-m.   And I'll take my clo - thes off,   and it will be sha - me-less,   '

Fig. 7.7   Lily Allen, 'The Fear', vocal melody, timing ca. 00:21–00:25

However, 'The Fear' also epitomises the fact that it would be unusual for a vocal rhythm to fit in slavishly with metric accent (or indeed with the backbeat). More commonly, vocal lines include more-or-less slight divergences from beat divisions in respect of their timings or stresses, thereby again adding to rhythmic dynamism. This happens when Allen stresses the syllables that cross the measure-lines, specifically starting the stressed syllables slightly early——a common strategy in popular singing (heard also in 'Babies', below). Divergences of this kind help to give vocals a connotation of authenticity: they will not conform to beat divisions but insist on going at their own flow and pace.

The Lily Allen example also clarifies what it means for stressed syllables to fit in with the rhythm of vocal phrases. When a single phrase repeated under variations provides the basis of a melody, the emphases must fall at roughly the same places in each iteration, and the words must comply with this or be adjusted to do so (extra occurrences of 'and' or contractions as of 'because' to 'cause' can help). Similar sets of constraints obtain when phrases follow more varied patterns (ABCB, ABAC, etc.): that is, the emphases in the B-phrases or A-phrases, respectively, must always fall in similar places.

Possibly excepting (i), all of factors (ii)–(vii) that bear on lyrics-as-sung are rhythmic, at least in part. How timing and rhythmic nuance contribute to vocal style; which syllables or words are stressed in relation to backbeat, metre, beat divisions, and other sources of rhythmic tension; how grammatical clauses are aligned temporally with vocal phrases and how syllables are lined up with notes or beat subdivisions; how alliteration and rhyme are used; how clauses mark out divisions between phrases, measures, and sections of song——all these involve rhythm. This confirms rhythm's central importance in popular music.

When so many variables bear on words-as-sung, perhaps it follows that 'in rock music most lyrics don't matter very much' (Gracyk 1996: 63). But there is an ambiguity here. The lyrics' content in purely semantic terms might matter little, but it is the *same* words that have semantic content that also have rhythmic, melodic and other sensory qualities, so that it could still matter in *those* respects which words are used. That is, the lyrics might matter for their sound, not their explicit meaning. Further, because the same words contribute both as sounds and in their semantic content, there may be constraints on what semantic content can be used consistently with words having the desired sonic qualities.

How extensive are such constraints? We might reply: not very extensive. Yes, rhythmic, melodic, and other sensory considerations establish certain general constraints or norms, for example to place rhyming couplets where pairs of vocal phrases end. But one can still use any rhyming couplet one chooses, even one that rhymes only inexactly. And, yes, having said 'alright for kicks', Pete Shelley had to end his next clause with a word ending in '-icks'——*or* go back and change 'kicks'——indicating that couplings can be altered endlessly until suitable pairs are found. Additional constraints might follow from genre——the harsh '*icks*' sound in 'sticks' and 'kicks' suits punk's aggressiveness, possibly more so than would 'fun' and 'numbs'——then again, the blankness and alienation of 'numb' fit punk too. Even with the norm to give words their ordinary emphases, a vocalist can always deviate and pronounce words unusually. The constraints that sensory factors impose on word choices seem so loose as to rule little out.

This does not mean that constraints do not exist, though, only that lyricists have indefinitely many options for negotiating them. But we might wonder whether the constraints are reciprocal, so that the need to use meaningful sentences on a given theme constrains how a vocal line is to be phrased and structured and, given the thematic words to be used, where the emphases can fall. Thus, Walter Everett suggests that melodies tend to be phrased to match grammatical constructions (2008: 134–5). By implication, a sentence's explicit meaning perhaps constrains its sensory materiality as much as its materiality constrains its explicit meaning. Or do the constraints run more one way than the other? To answer this question I want to return to Kristeva's distinction between semiotic and symbolic.

4   Semiotic and Symbolic in Words and Music

As we saw earlier, for Kristeva, language always has symbolic and semiotic aspects, where the symbolic encompasses semantics and the syntactical rules that underpin it by enabling phonemes to be united into sentences. In contrast the semiotic is a bodily kind of meaning, rooted in infancy. We do not jettison the semiotic on entering the symbolic. We remain beings of body and affect throughout our lives, and the semiotic always remains the precondition of explicit symbolic meaning, which we could not understand if semiotic processes did not first generate meanings and make them available for explication and articulation.

Nonetheless, once it has arisen the symbolic dominates the semiotic, as it '"takes charge of" the semiotic and binds it into syntax and phonemes' (A. White, quoted in Hebdige 1979: 164). Kristeva holds that in many cultures, such as that of pre-modern Christian Europe, that dominance was counter-balanced by the power vested in non-linguistic modes of representation, in that case Christian iconography, especially that of the Virgin Mary. Yet Kristeva thinks that in modernity the symbolic's dominance has grown——and problematically so——because large-scale institutions of government, commerce, and production require highly bureaucratised, codified, and specialised kinds of thought. The precision and specialisation of the concepts used in these kinds of thinking leave diminishing room for the tacit, processual, musical, and affective realm of the semiotic. But it is just when we participate in the semiotic field that our bodily being finds expression and outlet, whereas the more the symbolic prevails, the more our bodies and their affective energies undergo repression. Hence Kristeva, like Adorno, is unhappy about the growing dominance of the intellect in modernity.

Kristeva therefore champions the 'revolution in poetic language' effected by avant-garde literary writers such as Lautréamont and Mallarmé. For her, they re-orientate language towards the semiotic by allowing words' sensory qualities and affective connotations to course into and diffuse through symbolic constructions. Consider these lines from Rimbaud's 1871 poem 'Le Bateau Ivre'——my example rather than Kristeva's, using Martin Sorrell's English translation (Rimbaud 2001: 126–7):

Et dès lors, je me suis baigné dans le Poème De la Mer, infusé d'astres, et lactescent, Dévorant les azurs verts; où, flottaison blême Et ravie, un noyé pensif parfois descend; Où, teignant tout à coup les bleuités, délires Et rhythmes lents sous les rutilements du jour, Plus fortes que l'alcool, plus vastes que nos lyres, Fermentent les rousseurs amères de l'amour!	From that time on I bathed in the Poem Of the Sea, lactescent and steeped in stars, Devouring green azures; where a drowned man Like bleached flotsam sometimes sinks in a trance; Where, suddenly tinting the bluities, Slow deliriums in shimmering light, Fiercer than alcohol, vaster than lyres, The bitter rednesses of love ferment.

The narrator——who is actually the boat——tells of its submergence in the 'poem of the sea', a field of semiotic currents in which human beings drown and dream, a realm of rhythm, music, and affect far more powerful than ordinary life. These words explicate what is enacted in the sensory qualities of Rimbaud's words: their many alliterations (e.g. '*pensif parfois*', '*rhythmes*' ... '*rutilements*'), regular patterns of emphasis ('plus *fortes* que l'alcool, plus *vastes* que nos lyres'), rhymes ('Poème/blème', '...*escent*'/'*descend*', etc.), and near-rhymes ('amères de l'amour'). The many colours evoked——green, azure, blueness, redness——blur together synaesthetically, seeming to generate an interconnected realm prior to sharp symbolic and conceptual distinctions——a re-creation of infantile experience, perhaps. Rimbaud thus brings the semiotic realm *into* the symbolic, crafting new meanings and constructions at the symbolic level so as to remodel it after the less highly articulated patterns of meaning that emerge in the semiotic. For instance, he transforms the adjective *bleu* first into the noun *bleuité* and then from singular to plural, so that we move from the everyday sphere in which properties belong to objects ('X is blue') to a vaguer field where qualities migrate and are indefinitely many in number, thereby blurring into processes. For Kristeva, such literary experiments are a much-needed corrective to the symbolic's dominance in modernity.

We can now come back to the music-words relation in popular music. The lyrics——as words joined in clauses and sentences that have explicit meanings——comprise the symbolic aspect of popular song. Then there are *two* semiotic layers that impact on lyrics: the semiotic connotations embodied in songs by their non-verbal stylistic components and their interactions; *and* the semiotic qualities and connotations that the words themselves have on account of their sensory aspect. The two semiotic layers co-operate, because words' semiotic qualities contribute to songs' overall semiotic meanings——as when the harsh sounds of 'kicks' and 'sticks' in 'Orgasm Addict' reinforce the song's connotations of aggression and its genre location in punk.

Generally, then, how do the two semiotic layers impact upon the symbolic one in popular music? One might reply: not as much as they ought to do. After all, popular song lyricists rarely aim for the kind of revolutionary transformation of meaning attempted by avant-gardists such as Rimbaud. There are exceptions: one is the nonsense language adopted by Elizabeth Frazer of the Cocteau Twins, for example 'It's the droplets, it's the droplet on my truth. ... It's the spangle, it's that spangle maker', from 'The Spangle Maker'. Other exceptions include the word-play in 'I Am the Walrus'——'Yellow matter custard dripping from a dead dog's eye'——which Lennon deliberately intended as an assault on reason and common-sense. But these exceptions prove the rule just by the fact that they are unusual.

Instead of venturing into non-sense, popular song lyrics tend to '*work on ordinary language*', as Simon Frith remarks (2007b: 231). 'Woke up, fell out of bed', 'dragged a comb across my head'; McCartney's language here is everyday, prosaic, and immediately intelligible; he straightforwardly refers to certain objects and situations (bed, head, comb); he is conversational, describing his hasty early morning routine. This kind of continuity with everyday speech——in all its dialects, slang, idioms, and so on——is central to popular music (Lacasse 2010: 227).

Again typically, McCartney speaks in the first person (albeit leaving the 'I' presumed but unspoken in 'woke up', etc.). Likewise, popular music lyrics are usually addressed by an 'I' to a 'you', often referring to 'he', 'she', or 'they'. The lyrics are presented as communications, inviting the listener to equate him- or herself with the 'you' who is addressed.[16] Apparently, then, lyrics normally conform to the 'thetic function', as Kristeva calls it, whereby subjects make statements about objects to other subjects.

Popular music lyrics also seem to operate squarely in a symbolic mode in that, as far as practically possible, stresses are placed on syllables that express nouns, adjectives or verbs (or parts of these), rather than pronouns or conjunctive elements. Thus McCartney stresses 'woke', 'bed', 'comb', and 'head' (which form one rhyming and another near-rhyming pair). Thus, a key semiotic aspect of the words——the placement of stresses—— is organised so as to highlight the meaningful, semantic aspect of the sentences and not their syntax. There are exceptions——one being 'A Design for Life', mentioned earlier——but these stand out as being unusual. And anyway they do not necessarily disprove the rule that emphasising meaningful sentence constituents is desirable, other things being equal——in this case, that rule is overridden by the song's overarching message that the 'design' at issue is hollow and empty, and the unusual placement of the stresses reinforces that meaning.

Finally, popular music lyrics usually seem to place the symbolic at the helm in that the patterns of emphasis typical of ordinary speech are preserved. Unusual emphases highlight the sensory qualities of the words in question, by bringing them to our attention; normal emphases downplay the same qualities because they are expected and so pass unnoticed.

The fact that the sensory qualities of the words are thus usually down-played in this respect seems to confirm that the words are being used as bearers of symbolic content.

The symbolic, then, may seem to dominate the semiotic in popular music, at least with respect to the semiotic aspect of the words. Those words, it seems, are used in and for their ordinary meanings. Of course, it does not follow that the symbolic also dominates the other semiotic aspect of songs, that is their non-verbal musical components. That would follow if the explicit meanings stated in the lyrics regulated the production of those other components, but I argued against that view in Sect. 2. Even so, if the symbolic dominates the semiotic within the words of songs, then this would still compromise my claim that popular music affirms that the semiotic has priority to the symbolic.

However, the considerations that have suggested that the symbolic might hold sway in popular song words are off-set by the many ways in which lyrical content is constrained by sonic features of the words, features that have semiotic significance. As we've seen, there are constraints for words to have specific rhythmic, melodic, and other sensory qualities. Further constraints derive from the relation of vocal lines to the other layers of sound, for those layers embody particular semiotic meanings, which exerts a pressure to use words that have semiotic qualities congru-ent with those of the non-vocal layers. Ironically, it is precisely the semiotic constraints on song words which militate *against* popular song-writers attempting any revolutionary transformation of symbolic meaning. Let me explain.

For one thing, these constraints push popular musicians towards using short words and short clauses, with a heavy presence of short conjunc-tive elements. One-syllable words are most easily accommodated to the rhythms of a song, because in this case the lyricist need not try to ensure that the emphasis falls on the 'correct' syllable (the one normally stressed in everyday speech). In turn two-syllable words can be accommodated more easily than three-syllable words, and so on. It is easier to make one-syllable words rhyme than two-syllable words, which in turn are more eas-ily rhymed than three-syllable words.[17] Short clauses tend to fit best with vocal phrases, since those in turn tend to be short, lasting for four mea-sures or less. Thus, it is with clauses that last for just a few words that one can most easily achieve a degree of grammatical closure within the length of a phrase. But if one is using short clauses, then long words are liable to occupy nearly the whole clause, whereas short words leave more room

Fig. 7.8 Pulp, 'Babies', vocal melody, timing 00:37–00:47

for manoeuvre, giving lyricists more scope to take words in and out until suitable rhymes or patterns of emphasis are found. Lily Allen's words in 'The Fear' exemplified this, but so do those of Pulp's 'Babies' (Fig. 7.8):

As this excerpt indicates, each line in the first verse contains seven syllables (except line four with six) making up a clause, and each clause subdivides into a four-syllable group then a three-syllable group (two-syllable in line four). The opening clauses, as with those that follow, exemplify not only the norm to be conversational and prosaic but also the norm to use many short words. This makes sense given the constraints at work: (i) the space constraints that clauses need to be short enough to coincide with phrases of melody that align temporally with the other repeated instrumental elements; (ii) the need for the words to fit the regular rhythms of these phrases, in which singer Jarvis Cocker emphasises the last eighth-note in the measure, extending into the first note of the next measure on clause endings; (iii) the desirability of maintaining the emphases of ordinary speech (e.g. 'happened', 'ago'); (iv) the norm to mark phrase endings with rhymes or near-rhymes, in this verse patterned AABCBC (e.g. '-go'/'road', 'sister', 'school'/'older', 'room'); (v) and the desirability of including pleasurable patterns of alliteration and near-rhyme (e.g. 'Well' and 'when', 'hap-' and '-hope').

To be sure, it is possible to craft lyrics that incorporate longer and more unusual words while successfully accommodating their usual emphases. John Lennon did so in 'Lucy in the Sky with Diamonds' (on *Sgt. Pepper*). In the verse, each phrase lasts for (approximately) four measures (see Fig. 7.9):

Here the usual emphases in such relatively unwieldy words as 'tangerine', 'marmalade' and 'kaleidoscope' are neatly fitted to a regular emphasis on the first beat of each measure in 3/4 time. And it is possible in principle

...tan-ger-ine   trees   and   mar-ma-lade   skies.   Some-bo-dy   calls   you. You

an-swer quite   slow-ly,   the   girl   with   ka-lei-do-scope   ey-es....

Fig. 7.9   The Beatles, 'Lucy in the Sky with Diamonds', vocal melody, timing ca. 00:11–00:27

to include clauses with relatively complicated grammatical constructions, such as 'why pamper life's complexity when the leather runs smooth on the passenger seat' in The Smiths' 'This Charming Man'.

Yet the fact remains that the musical constraints in force make it difficult for musicians to accommodate complicated grammar or include the sort of rich and evocative vocabulary of 'Lucy in the Sky with Diamonds'. They can do so, and many insist on retaining unwieldy words even when they do not fit with their musical setting. But the risk is that this will diminish the coherence of songs. So it is understandable that for the most part musicians focus on making sure that their lyrics 'work' musically—— and, in particular, rhythmically——rather than probing the boundaries of what can be achieved in strictly verbal terms. After all, lyricists are making *music* first and foremost.

Thus, it is precisely the semiotic constraints that music imposes upon lyrics which push against musicians attempting to transform language radically. Indeed, to refer back to the ways in which popular song words seemed to foreground the symbolic, we can now see the following. Prosaic, everyday language featuring many short words, conjunctions, and phrases is most easily adapted to rhythmic requirements. The same goes for sentences containing frequent uses of 'I', 'you', 'she', 'it', 'we', and so on. Thus, these kinds of language are used because of the primacy of the *semiotic*, not the symbolic as it seemed earlier. Admittedly, musicians do tend to stick with words' usual emphases and not to stress conjunctive elements. But this is because their primary goal is to find words and sentences that satisfy the musical constraints under which they are operating. Accordingly their attention is directed away from experimenting with everyday speech and its usual placements of emphasis in their own right. Instead attention goes towards finding ways to adapt everyday language to music. The language thus adapted remains largely everyday, prosaic, and conversational just because it is not itself the direct object of transformation.

As to whether popular song language privileges the symbolic over the semiotic, we may now conclude that it does not. Actually popular music prioritises the *semiotic*, for the semiotic qualities of the music *and* the words combine to impose limits on what meanings can be stated and on what *kind* of meanings these are: those expressible in everyday language. It is not that popular song employs this language because musicians accept the dominance of the symbolic. Rather, popular music is primarily a semiotic practice: that of making music that embodies meanings semiotically in material details of style. Likewise the words in popular music function semiotically above all——embodying connotations through their rhythmic, expressive, and other sensory qualities. It is *because* the focus is so firmly on the semiotic and not the symbolic that popular song-writing is inclined away from the revolutionary transformation of the symbolic.

5   TWO APPROACHES TO LYRICS

Musicians clearly differ in how concerned they are about lyrical content. Some are content to redeploy stereotypical formulations skilfully; others endeavour to craft lyrics that are unique and individual——and, as Nile Rodgers's comments attest, not all musicians have equal freedom to choose between these options. Still, along such lines we can identify a continuum of kinds of lyric ranging from the more formulaic——found in much 'pop'——to the more serious, where lyrics do more to diverge from stereotypical formulations. This is a continuum: most songs exemplify both approaches to some degree. But if lyrical content *is* taken to matter insofar as lyrics exemplify the more 'serious' approach, doesn't that mean that words and their meanings regularly *are* treated as important objects of creative practice in their own right? That is, that the symbolic *is* a focus of popular music practice after all? To explore this, let me for clarification purposes identify the two approaches to lyrics in abstraction from one another, even though they often entwine within individual songs.

To begin with the 'pop' approach, the use of fairly stereotypical, formulaic language embodies a judgement that the content of words is not very important. It may be deemed so unimportant that the words are reduced to bare meaningless syllables, as in the 'la la la, /la la la la la, /la la la, /la la la la la' refrain in Kylie Minogue's 'Can't Get You Out of My Head' (on *Fever*, of 2001). The monotonous, robotic sound of the syllables and their rhythmic groupings are all-important, their meaning so negligible in importance that it can be dispensed with altogether (in the refrain). On similar grounds stereotypical and bland lyrics may be positively favoured, as being so familiar and inconspicuous that they recede from the listener's attention in favour of the music's sonic materiality, including that of the vocal line.[18] This 'pop' approach is not confined to songs of the metagenre *pop*. When electronic dance music has lyrics these often exemplify this approach, being very minimal and repetitive and shading into wordless melody. The lyrics of the Prodigy's 1997 single 'Smack My Bitch Up' (on *The Fat of the Land*) are illustrative: they largely alternate between just two repeated phrases, 'Change my pitch up', 'Smack my bitch up'. Although the words drew condemnation from the US National Organisation for Women, song-writer Liam Howlett stressed that the words were used for their sound, not their meaning (Goldberg 1997).

That popular music lyrics are often formulaic to some degree, then, is not a reason to disparage the form. For there is a good reason why lyrics often have a formulaic quality: this reflects the primary importance of the musical (rhythmic, melodic, timbral) qualities of the words uttered as well as of the instrumental layers. Having said this, the more formulaic lyrics are, the more potential they have to fail to draw out the *specific* meanings expressed in the songs that use them. This is because stock phrases and expressions are ones used across a range of songs, even though those songs' musical qualities can vary greatly. This can result in lyrics that diverge in meaning from the attendant music.

Take The Supremes' 'My World is Empty Without You', written by Motown's Holland-Dozier-Holland song-writing team (and included on the band's 1966 album *I Hear a Symphony*). Eddie Holland's lyrics describe the narrator's desolation after a relationship has ended: 'I find it hard for me to carry on', 'Inside this cold and empty house I dwell'. These lyrics are fairly openly formulaic: countless other pop songs describe abandonment in similar terms. Musically, though, 'My World is Empty Without You' conveys something quite different. Fast-paced, at around 164 beats per minute, the track has a lively and infectious rhythm, established by the bass guitar above all: it plays a bouncy pattern, duplicated at times by a horn section. The bass guitar repeats this pattern on the root notes of each chord in turn for most of the song, with only occasional departures. Tying in closely with the bass-drum and pulling against the snare-drum, the bass guitar sets up a counter-pull against the backbeat, the two opposing forces virtually compelling the listener to dance. For its part the rhythm guitar plays the chords in a highly percussive, typically Motown 'choppy' style, heavily emphasising the strokes that coincide with the snare-drum and thus pulling against the bass guitar rhythmically. Along with the presence of the horns, strings, and backing vocals, all this adds up to a quite cluttered and urgent-sounding texture——something, again, that is typical of the Motown sound (see Borthwick and Moy 2004: 14). The busy texture and bouncy rhythm largely override the sadness described in the lyrics and expressed by the song's B minor key. That sadness is not totally eradicated, but it persists as a note of longing within an overall bright, lively mood, perhaps suggesting sadness remembered but overcome.

The sound of Diana Ross's lead vocal melody is in keeping with this. Rather than being slow and subdued in line with the desolation narrated in the lyrics, her vocal moves along in a quick, sprightly manner, making a light arching movement in the chorus and traversing series of shorter arches in the verse, consonant with the bouncy bass-line. Ross sounds calm and at ease, not overwhelmed by emotion but in control of herself, as if recalling old pains——reflected in the ups and downs in the melody line——at a calm distance. This is not to say that Ross's voice sounds old and wise; rather the effortlessness with which she navigates the melody conveys youthful agility and optimism.

The meaning of the music, then, is out of step with the content of the lyrics, and this illustrates that when lyrics are relatively formulaic they can come apart from the individual meanings that a given song expresses stylistically.[19] This need not happen——sometimes stereotypical formulations can nonetheless draw out those meanings in their particularity—— but it is possible. Are songs whose lyrical and musical meanings come apart deficient? That is, perhaps they fail to coalesce? Not necessarily; it may well be that lyrics are more formulaic just because less importance is given to their semantic meaning rather than their sound in the first place. But if the words' content is not treated as contributing significantly to the song's meaning, then the divergence of that content from the rest of the music need not prevent the songs' other parts from coalescing into a meaningful whole. That said, there are cases where people find that a song's trite lyrics spoil the entire way that it sounds; stereotypical content can, but need not, diminish a song.

At the less 'pop' and more 'serious' end of the spectrum, lyrics are used to articulate and make explicit the particular affects and meanings that a song embodies. We have already encountered several songs that fall under this heading. The words of 'With or Without You' speak about the anguish of which the melody and instrumentation is expressive. Or songs can be expressive of a lack of or flight from emotion, as in 'Blue Monday', the lyrics of which refer to that lack: 'how do I feel?', 'how does it feel when your heart grows cold?'. In 'Losing My Religion' the lyrics refer, albeit opaquely, to feelings of unrequited love alternating with hope, an alternation of which the chord progression is expressive. In all these cases the lyrics articulate qualities expressed by the combined instrumental layers and by the vocal lines in respect of their melodic shape, style of articulation, and other sonic features. The same applies when vocals are non-melodic: for instance, in the chorus of 'The Message' by Grandmaster Flash, the rapped words——'Don't push me 'cause I'm close to the edge, /I'm tryin' not to lose my head'——are uttered very slowly and deliberately compared to those of the faster-flowing verse. This change in pace and articulation expresses the narrator's determination to retain his self-control against the forces that threaten to push him over the edge—— the same determination to which the lyrics refer.

Making explicit reference to the emotional and other qualities expressed in music is only one of a plurality of ways in which lyrics may articulate those qualities. An alternative is to tell stories, possibly in the third person——an approach associated with Bob Dylan——or to use images or metaphors that crystallise certain meanings, as when the ambiguous lyrics of 'Paparazzi'——paparazza/star or lover/beloved——distil the ambivalence about fame *versus* love of which the music is expressive.

When lyrics articulate the meanings and emotional qualities of which songs are expressive, this does not entail that the lyrics must be written after the other parts of songs in time: any order of composition is possible. Lyrics might be written first, as with those of Ian Curtis, but be adapted subsequently to articulate the significance conveyed by other instrumental parts. Alternatively, lyrics and vocal might be written as a piece, as with 'With or Without You', so that the lyrics all along articulate the meanings that are expressed in the vocal melody. Or lyrics, melody, and other instrumental parts can be written separately and subsequently combined.

Lyrics that exemplify this more 'serious' approach usually remain couched in representational and communicative language. To articulate songs' meanings lyrics need to function representationally, to tell us what the narrator's emotions are or describe situations that carry suitable connotations. That said, lyricists may well want to voice hitherto neglected feelings by employing unique formulations, images, or narratives——ones that are not formulaic and can therefore articulate feelings that existing formulae do not capture. Hence Morrissey's 'punctured bicycle/on a hill-side desolate'. Literary merit can then be claimed for such lyrics on account of their originality. Nonetheless, the 'serious'——articulatory——purpose of such lyrics presses towards representational, communicative language. And so it is common for lyrics of this kind to achieve originality not through the opacity of their language but rather through the particularity of the contexts, situations, and feelings that they nonetheless describe in fairly plain-spoken language.

6   Meaning and Materiality

I have distinguished 'pop' from 'serious' approaches to clarify the grounds on which lyrical content is taken to matter, or not, within popular music. But, to reiterate, 'serious' and 'pop' approaches are only poles of a spectrum. A vast middle ground spans the two poles: here stereotypical lyrics can rise to capture familiar experience in pithy, vivid, and poignant ways; while musicians who aspire to articulate neglected feelings may fall back upon stereotypical idioms. And most songs do both to a degree: 'Paparazzi', for example, draws out the music's ambivalence through its ambiguous imagery, yet much of that imagery is fairly stereotypical (e.g., 'this photo of us, it don't have a price'). It is because most lyrics serve the purpose of articulating song meaning to at least some degree that we can use these lyrics to help us to identify what a song means. I have done so at various points in this book. But the lyrics guide us *not* because they state the idea that regulates a song's production but to the extent that they articulate meanings that the song already conveys through semiotic processes.

Furthermore, 'serious' need not mean 'better'. *Both* approaches have value, on my terms, in that they accord priority to the semiotic, although they do this in different ways. Inasmuch as lyrical content is taken not to matter, this is because the music and the words' musical qualities are judged all-important——the semiotic is valorised, not the symbolic. Conversely when lyrical content *is* treated as important, this is on the grounds that lyrics can articulate the meanings conveyed in the music. In that case the symbolic is granted importance just inasmuch it draws out connotations conveyed by the music at a semiotic level. Either way the semiotic is given primary importance.

On both approaches, though, typical popular-music practice is *not* to try to infuse semiotic qualities and energies through the symbolic——the mission of the literary avant-garde. Rather in popular music the symbolic is typically allowed to operate in its familiar, everyday manner. But this is not because the symbolic's dominance is accepted. On the contrary, the semiotic's primacy is *re-affirmed*. Sometimes this is so in that stock (symbolic) formulae and phrases are used as empty vessels within which desired semiotic qualities are at work; sometimes it is so in that the symbolic is employed to articulate semiotic connotations. But different as they are from avant-garde literary practices, popular-musical approaches nevertheless challenge the dominance of the symbolic over the semiotic and so, too, of the intellect over the body.

In Chap. 6 I identified another way that popular music affirms materiality in addition to its typical matter-form configuration and rhythmic intensity, namely that the meanings embodied in popular songs' combined musical elements arise in a semiotic way. That is: these meanings have an affective dimension; they are implicit rather than stated; and they arise from the manifold kinds of relations within which these elements stand, including their interactions with one another——relations and interactions in which pitch and rhythm figure centrally. In that popular music embodies these material processes of meaning-generation, it presents the truth that meaning emerges first and foremost at a semiotic and bodily-based level. However, that argument left unexplained the place of lyrics in popular music. I have now addressed this issue, showing——I hope——that in its typical handling of lyrics popular music still does affirm the priority of the semiotic. For lyrics are used either to articulate semiotic meanings, or for their sounds and semiotic qualities rather than their symbolic content, or a mixture of the two. Indeed, popular music's characteristic way of affirming the priority of the semiotic is to do so *by* using lyrics——but in ways that make their symbolic content secondary to semiotic meaning. By so using lyrics popular music presents the symbolic as depending on the semiotic, and thereby also presents the truth that explicit understanding depends on the prior affective processes of the body.

NOTES

1. The books on music in Open Court's *Philosophy and Popular Culture* series provide evidence that many people subscribe to this overall picture: the contributors focus overwhelmingly either on

lyrics or on what ideas musicians wish to convey, where in fact 'musicians' nearly always means 'lyricists'. The contributors to the U2 volume, for instance, focus almost entirely on Bono.

2. '*Joy Division* ... were very much a product of time and place. *Ian Curtis* ... became a driven writer trying to find a way out' (Savage 2008; my emphasis). That is, Savage clarifies what Joy Division 'meant' with reference to Curtis's state of mind. Greil Marcus reports that Hook was dissatisfied with the 'Dance to the radio' lyric, thinking it too pro-radio, but Curtis reassured him that the song was a 'call to arms' against the radio. Marcus in turn reassures us: 'It wasn't that Hook ever missed the black hole of the song' (2014: 46). Marcus implies that Curtis wrote a song that was a 'black hole', a meaning that other band members might have missed——despite Hook's bass-line being the core of the song.

3. However, vocalists tends to be the focus of biographical interest more than writers (Frith 1996: 185), because vocalists are taken to 'pour out' their emotions in how they realise a melody, and their emotional life therefore garners interest. As with Depeche Mode's lead vocalist Dave Gahan, in contrast to song-writer Martin Gore, this pattern of reception can exacerbate tensions between the two personae. Vocalists want more recognition that they actually contribute to songs' meanings, while song-writers want more of the media attention that stays focused on singers.

4. Ruth Finnegan speaks of the 'rock mode of collective prior composition' (Finnegan, quoted in Zak 2001: 32; see also Wicke 1982, Middleton 1990: 39–40, Warner 2003: 35). Studying two Liverpool bands, Sara Cohen found that one produced songs more collectively while the other built on compositions supplied by the group's 'leader'. His reluctance to accommodate the other band members' contributions was criticised (1991: 155–6). This testifies, on the one hand, to the democratic and collaborative ethos that exists widely in popular music making. On the other hand, it testifies to musicians' persistent if contested *belief* in the primary role of the vocalist-cum-lead-songwriter.

5. Moore says that most often the first part of a track to be written, chronologically, is the series of chords (Moore 2012a: 21), although he notes that other musicians may begin by developing a melody (91). As we saw regarding Joy Division, there are also cases where bass-lines come first. Albin Zak documents instances of

these and other possibilities: chords first (*Pet Sounds*); riff first (Bowie's 'Fashion'); backing tracks first (Roxy Music's *Stranded*); jamming first (U2 on *Zooropa*); rhythmic groove first (many Peter Gabriel recordings) (Zak 2001: 29–31). In all those cases melodies and lyrics came later on, being 'evaluated from the beginning in terms of their suitability to the track as a whole' (29). Percussion rhythms or samples of these can come first too: in rap, they usually provide a track's 'structural foundation' (Williams 2013: 2).

6. For alternative accounts of the song's form, see Endrinal (2008: 112) and Moore (1998: 15, 29).

7. John Covach remarks: 'It is some measure of how much the music business had changed in the fifteen years since the end of World War II that instrumental records by [Dick] Dale, … [and others] in the early 1960s could be considered a novelty. During the Big Band era, many records were instrumental, and often when singing did occur, it was secondary to the playing of the band' (Covach 2006: 140). That situation changed with the rise of solo singers, which Frank Sinatra spearheaded. By the rock-'n'-roll era vocals were standard.

8. Krims distinguishes 'sung' (old-school) rap vocals from those that are 'percussion-' and 'speech-effusive' (Krims 2000: 49ff). By 'sung', Krims means not 'melodic' but rather that these raps have rhythmic profiles similar to those of rock and pop, whereas in 'speech-effusive' styles——represented by Chuck D and Ice Cube——vocals are more of a continuous, rapid flow of everyday speech, over-running metric boundaries. While in 'percussion-effusive' styles——represented by B-Real of Cypress Real——the voice is used more as a percussion instrument (taken further in beatboxing).

9. Other common themes include trains and cars, rebellion, school, death, and Christmas——see B. Lee Cooper (1991). Looking at 50 best-selling UK singles of 1976, Dave Laing found that 60 % of their lyrics concerned romance and sexual relationships (Laing 1985: 39).

10. Donald Horton (1990: 14) states this reasoning explicitly.

11. Various lyrics continue to be published under the banner of poetry, for example the massive Bob Dylan compendium *The Lyrics: Since 1962* (Dylan 2014) and the *Mother, Lover, Brother* anthology by former Pulp vocalist Jarvis Cocker (2012).

12. Thanks to Brian Garvey for alerting me to this quotation.

13. Barthes himself did not link grain with popular music; rather, he associated the suppression of grain with 'mass' or 'average' culture (1977: 185).

14. Lacasse describes these everyday vocal behaviours as the 'paralinguistic' aspects of speech (or singing)——for example sighing, drawing one's breath in, groaning, speeding up or slowing down the pace of one's speech——all of which are important to communication (2010: 226; see also Thompson and Balkwill 2010).

15. For accessibility's sake I have not used the phonemic symbols codified by the International Phonetic Association. These can be found on the British Council's website at http://www.teachingenglish. org.uk/article/phonemic-symbols

16. Horton notes that normally popular song language is conversational (1957: 14). Several theorists have examined how listeners are invited to identify with those addressed as 'you' as their positions are constructed in songs through lyrics and music. Thus lyrics can interpellate listeners into particular positions in social power relations, say that of the 'inconstant' woman who ought to be loyal to her man. Instances of such analyses include Bradby (1990), Brady and Torode (2000), and Dibben (2001).

17. As I remarked earlier, Brown and Hirjee have found that rap has evolved to include more multi-syllable rhymes than rock. One of their instances is from Pharoahe Monch's 'Behind Closed Doors': 'How I made it: you salivated over my calibrated raps that validated...' (his 'ghetto credibility'). See Hirjee and Brown (2009: 712).

18. Walter Hughes makes this point about the often empty and vacuous lyrics in disco (1994: 149).

19. In terms of their working methods, Lamont Dozier and Brian Holland would first write songs' melodies and basic formal structures on piano then work with Motown's house band the Funk Brothers (or sometimes other musicians) to produce a studio recording. Then they would 'give the track to Eddie [Holland], who would go off and write the lyrics'——which Holland did rather piecemeal, often re-using unused lyrics from one song in another. So Brian Holland reports (see Kawashima 2005).

Conclusion: Popular Music, Aesthetic Value, and Materiality

Popular music has been accused of being formulaic, homogeneous, manufactured, trite, vulgar, trivial, ephemeral, and so on. These condemnations have roots in aspects of the Western aesthetic tradition, especially its modernist and expressivist branches, according to which great art innovates, breaks and re-makes the rules, expresses the artist's personal vision or unique emotions, or all these. Popular music has its defenders. But they have tended to appeal to the same inherited aesthetic criteria, defending some branches of popular music at the expense of others——valorising its artistic, expressive, innovative, or authentic branches against mere 'pop'. These evaluations are problematic, because they presuppose all along a set of criteria that are slanted against the popular field. We therefore need new frameworks for the evaluation of popular music. These frameworks need to enable us to evaluate pieces of popular music by the standards proper to this particular cultural form——to judge how well these pieces work *as* popular music, not how successfully they rise above the popular condition.

To devise such frameworks we need an account of popular music's standard features and of the further organising qualities and typical values to which these features give rise. Popular music normally has four layers of sound——melody, chords, bass, and percussion——and each layer is normally made up of repetitions of short elements, these repetitions being aligned temporally with one another, with whole sections of repeated material then being repeated in turn to constitute song sections.

© The Author(s) 2016
A. Stone, *The Value of Popular Music*,
DOI 10.1007/978-3-319-46544-9

This repetitive mode of construction means that the elements of popular songs are not generated out of one another by a logical development. Not being so generated, the elements are relatively independent of one another, leaving popular musicians with considerable scope as to which of numerous possible combinations of elements to adopt. That lee-way is expanded further by popular music's constitutive pluralism——it works with a range of harmonic systems and sets of norms, for example for which chords can follow which other chords. In sum, the elements of any particular song come together contingently: this particular combination is just one of many possibilities, and may be literally stumbled upon by chance. But this doesn't reduce popular songs to being mere sums or aggregates. Typically a popular song *is* a whole——but its wholeness arises from how its elements coalesce, something that——beyond satisfying certain minimal harmonic and rhythmic constraints——they do insofar as their connotations qualify and interact productively with one another to generate higher-level structures of meaning. These structures bind songs together into meaningful wholes. In this way, popular songs are typically so configured that their materials generate their forms.

Popular music is also structured in ways that intensify its rhythmic dimension. Each element of each layer of sound has a rhythmic quality, and these qualities are enhanced by their relations with the percussion layer, as they pull either with the latter (i.e. normally to stress the backbeat) or against it (i.e. normally to stress the metrically accented beats). When these patterns of pull and counter-pull are repeated many times over, their rhythmic momentum builds up, and the tension between metric accent and rhythmic stress on the backbeat becomes intensified. As a result the music makes a palpable appeal to our bodies, affording us the opportunity to move in time with the music in ways that realise our bodies' inherent intelligence and creativity, as we make sense of the music's rhythms by directly mapping them in our bodily movements.

Furthermore, popular music has characteristic ways of handling meaning. Songs' meanings arise in a semiotic way: they are implicit, have an affective dimension, and emerge from the relations among stylistic elements and between these elements and extra-musical phenomena, including through their pitched and rhythmic aspects. This makes popular music continuous with the bodily-based realm of human infancy, in which the semiotic first obtains. The typical popular-musical approach to lyrics is consistent with this. Although popular songs usually have words, their semantic content is heavily constrained by their semiotic qualities, that is, their rhythmic, pitched and other sensory qualities as these carry specific connotations that relate to those embodied by the non-verbal layers of sound. The constraints run from semiotic to symbolic more than they do the other way around. Furthermore, most popular song lyrics are located on a continuum from the formulaic to the unique. At both ends of this spectrum, lyrics' symbolic aspect——their semantic content——is treated as secondary to semiotic processes of meaning-making. This is either in that the content is treated as unimportant——only the sound and its qualities matter——or in that the content is treated as being important just in articulating meanings conveyed at the music's semiotic level. While including lyrics, then, popular music not only remains fundamentally continuous with the semiotic realm, but also treats the symbolic as being dependent on the semiotic.

Flowing from these organising dimensions of popular music are several ways that it presents us with truths about the importance of materiality in human life. By deriving form from materials, popular music presents form as dependent on materials and materials as capable of generating form, having a kind of agency in their own right. By giving salience to rhythm, popular music appeals to our bodies and takes on a bodily, energetic character. It thereby presents the truth that our bodies are creative and intelligent agencies in their own right, and that it is good for our bodies to achieve self-realisation, as they can when we move creatively to music. By giving priority to semiotic meaning, popular music presents the truth that bodily-based meaning is prior to symbolic meaning, and thus again that material, bodily processes are the root source of explicit meaning and intellectual understanding.

This gives popular music aesthetic value in a sense that derives from Hegel, for whom phenomena have aesthetic value when they present us with truth in a sensory form. Specifically, for Hegel, aesthetic phenomena do this when their materials are so organised as to embody the truth and make it available to be apprehended. Hegel has in mind the truth that the idea, as a rational structure, organises the material world, as in a beautiful aesthetic object its form organises the distribution, shape and make-up of its materials. Reversing that form-matter relation, a popular song's materials typically generate the song's form as a meaningful whole, thereby presenting the truth that matter is the source of form. And because that whole is meaningful in a semiotic way, with lyrics in secondary place, the truth is also embodied that bodily-based meaning precedes and preconditions explicit understanding. Finally, because the materials are so organised that their rhythmic aspects are heightened, the truth is presented that intelligence has somatic roots, as when we make sense of the rhythmic dimension of the music in bodily movement.

This has been my account of the positive aesthetic value of popular music. To be sure, it is only one of many possible accounts of popular music's aesthetic value. I intend it not to be definitive or exhaustive, but to open up consideration of other possible senses in which popular music might have aesthetic value, and of how to understand that value without presupposing that popular culture ranks below art.

On my account, the value of the form *popular music* is multi-faceted——it derives from several interrelated sources: the material-formal, rhythmic, and semiotic——and different songs and genres realise this form and its attendant values in varied ways. Not all popular songs and genres have aesthetic value, nor do those that have that value do so equally or in identical respects. For example, I criticised progressive rock for distancing itself from materiality, compared to many other popular music genres, through its usual approach to rhythm, form, and sound. Nonetheless, prog conveys this distance primarily through stylistic devices——that is semiotically——and as such it does embody one typical source of value in popular music. Some might argue that prog does so to such a high degree that it has just as much aesthetic worth as other genres that, say, are stronger on danceable rhythms but are let down by trite meanings. Others might argue that these meanings are trite because the primacy of the semiotic is being affirmed. The point is, there is still ample scope for discussion about which songs and genres have greater or lesser value and why, matters on which listeners are unlikely ever to reach any stable consensus.

Popular songs can also have value by participating in other musical forms, as with folk-rock or jazz-rock, or by sharing in some features and values of classical music, in the case of some prog. The popular music form need not be the only source of value in popular songs. Still, insofar as songs belong to the popular music field, this form is a potential source of their value, which, crucially, means that these songs can have value at least in part *because* they are popular music.

My aim, then, has not been to argue that certain popular songs or genres have or lack value, but rather to suggest a framework within which such arguments can be conducted and popular songs judged by the standards of the form to which they belong. Songs need not be judged *only* by those standards——if they hybridise with, for example, jazz or folk. But insofar as songs are part of the popular music field, the standards proper to this form should normally be central in these songs' evaluation, and these standards need to be articulated in their own right. Once we have an account of popular music's aesthetic value, we can assess popular songs by the standards of the cultural form to which they belong——not by inappropriate standards that enshrine prejudices against popular music at the outset.

BIBLIOGRAPHY

Abel, Mark. 2014. *Groove: An aesthetic of measured time*. Leiden: Brill.

Adorno, Theodor W. 1976. *Introduction to the sociology of music*. Trans. E.B. Ashton. New York: Seabury. Original German publication in 1962.

———. 1982. Subject and object. In *The essential Frankfurt School reader*, ed. Andrew Arato, and Eike Gebhardt, 497–511. New York: Continuum. Original German publication in 1969.

———. 1990. *Negative dialectics*. Trans. E.B. Ashton. London: Routledge. Original German publication in 1966.

———. 1991. *The culture industry: Selected essays on mass culture*. London: Routledge.

———. 1997. *Aesthetic theory*. Trans. Robert Hullot-Kentor. Minneapolis: University of Minnesota Press. Original German publication in 1970.

———. 1998. *Beethoven: The philosophy of music,* ed. Rolf Tiedemann. Trans. E. Jephcott. Cambridge: Polity.

———. 2002. *Essays on music,* ed. Richard Leppert. New translations by Susan H. Gillespie. Berkeley: University of California Press.

———. 2006. *Philosophy of new music*. Trans. Robert Hullot-Kentor. Minneapolis: University of Minnesota Press. Original German publication in 1949.

Adorno, Theodor W., and Max Horkheimer. 1997. *Dialectic of enlightenment*. Trans. John Cumming. London: Verso. Original German publication in 1944.

Ahlkvist, Jarl. 2011. What makes rock music 'Prog?' Fan evaluation and the struggle to define progressive rock. *Popular Music and Society 34*(5): 639–660.

Albiez, Sean, and David Pattie (ed). 2011. *Kraftwerk: Music non-stop*. New York: Continuum.

Anderton, Chris. 2010. A many-headed beast: Progressive rock as European meta-genre. *Popular Music 29*(3): 417–435.

© The Author(s) 2016
A. Stone, *The Value of Popular Music*,
DOI 10.1007/978-3-319-46544-9

Ansell-Pearson, Keith. 2016. Why I write such excellent songs: David Bowie, 1947–2016. *Radical Philosophy 196*: 2–5.

Astor, Pete. 2010. The poetry of rock: Song lyrics are not poems but the words still matter: Another look at Richard Goldstein's collection of rock lyrics. *Popular Music 29*(1): 143–148.

Attali, Jacques. 1985. *Noise: The political economy of music*. Trans. Brian Massumi. Minneapolis: University of Minnesota Press. Original French publication in 1977.

Atton, Chris. 2001. 'Living in the past'?: Value discourses in progressive rock fanzines. *Popular Music 20*(1): 29–46.

Bangs, Lester. 1980. *Blondie*. New York: Simon & Schuster.

Bannister, Matthew. 2006. *White boys, white noise: Masculinities and 1980s indie guitar rock*. Farnham/Surrey: Ashgate.

Barthes, Roland. 1972. *Mythologies*. Trans. Annette Lavers. London: Paladin. Originally published in French in 1957.

———. 1977. *Image-music-text*. Trans. Stephen Heath. New York: Hill and Wang.

Battersby, Christine. 1994. *Gender and genius: Towards a feminist aesthetics*. London: The Women's Press.

Baugh, Bruce. 1990. Left-wing elitism: Adorno on popular culture. *Philosophy and Literature 14*(1): 65–78.

———. 1993. Prolegomena to any aesthetics of rock music. *Journal of Aesthetics and Art Criticism 51*(1): 23–29.

Beauvoir, Simone. 1988. *The second sex*. Trans. H.M. Parshley. London: Picador. Original French publication in 1949. English translation originally published in 1953.

Beethoven, Ludwig van. 2001. *Symphonie Nr. 5 in C. Op. 67*. Urtext. Ed. Jonathan Del Mar. Kassel: Bärenreiter.

Berry, Chuck. 2005. Excerpts from *The autobiography*. In *The pop, rock, and soul reader*, ed. David Brackett, 83–87. New York: Oxford University Press. Originally published in 1987.

Bewarp, Anders, and Henrik Crona, dir. 2013. The story of Blue Monday [film]. Nordvision. https://www.youtube.com/watch?v=qseAVl9ikxQ. Accessed 8 Apr 2015.

Bicknell, Jeanette. 2015. *Philosophy of song and singing: An introduction*. New York: Routledge.

Björnberg, Alf. 1984. On aeolian harmony in contemporary popular music. With editorial comments by Philip Tagg. http://www.tagg.org/others/othxpdfs/bjbgeol.pdf. Accessed 28 Jan 2015.

———. 2000. Structural relationships of music and images in music video. In *Reading pop*, ed. Richard Middleton, 347–378. Oxford: Oxford University Press.

Blacking, John. 1981. Making artistic popular music: The goal of true folk. *Popular Music 1*: 9–14.

Bloom, Allan. 1987. *The closing of the American mind*. New York: Simon & Schuster.

Borthwick, Stuart, and Ron Moy. 2004. *Popular music genres: An introduction*. Edinburgh: Edinburgh University Press.

Bourdieu, Pierre. 1984. *Distinction: A social critique of the judgement of taste*. Trans. Richard Nice. Cambridge, MA: Harvard University Press. Originally published in French in 1979.

BPI. 2014. Rock turns the tables on pop. Press release. 11 Feb. https://www.bpi.co.uk/assets/files/rock%20turns%20the%20tables%20on%20pop.pdf. Accessed 23 Oct 2014.

Brackett, David. 2002. (In search of) musical meaning: Genres, categories and crossover. In *Popular music studies*, ed. David Hesmondhalgh, and Keith Negus, 65–83. London: Arnold.

——— (ed). 2005. *The pop, rock, and soul reader*. New York: Oxford University Press.

Bradby, Barbara. 1990. Do-talk and don't-talk: The division of the subject in girl-group music. In *On record*, ed. Simon Frith, and Andrew Goodwin, 291–314. London: Routledge.

Bradley, Dick. 1992. *Understanding rock 'n' roll: Popular music in Britain 1955–1964*. Milton Keynes: Open University Press.

Brady, Barbara, and Brian Torode. 2000. Pity Peggy Sue. In *Reading pop*, ed. Richard Middleton, 203–227. Oxford: Oxford University Press.

Brady, Emily. 2003. *Aesthetics of the natural environment*. Edinburgh: Edinburgh University Press.

Brody, Michael, and James Campbell. 1999. *Rock and roll: An introduction*. New York: Schirmer.

Brown, Lee B. 2000. Phonography, rock records, and the ontology of recorded music. *Journal of Aesthetics and Art Criticism* 58(4): 361–373.

Bryson, Bethany. 1996. 'Anything but heavy metal': Symbolic exclusion and musical dislikes. *American Sociological Review* 61(5): 884–899.

Buchenau, Stephanie. 2013. *The founding of aesthetics in the German enlightenment: The art of invention and the invention of art*. Cambridge, UK: Cambridge University Press.

Buckley, David. 2002. *R.E.M./fiction: An alternative biography*. London: Virgin Books.

———. 2005. *Strange fascination: David Bowie – the definitive story*. Revised edn. London: Virgin Books. Originally published 1999.

Burns, Gary. 1987. A typology of 'Hooks' in popular records. *Popular Music* 6(1): 1–20.

Burns, Lori, and Marc Lafrance. 2014. Celebrity, spectacle, and surveillance: Understanding Lady Gaga's "Paparazzi" and "Telephone" through music, image, and movement. In *Lady Gaga and popular music*, ed. Martin Iddon, and Melanie L. Marshall, 117–147. London: Routledge.

Buskin, Richard. 2010. Classic tracks: Human League: Don't You Want Me. *Sound on Sound*. July. http://www.soundonsound.com/sos/jul10/articles/classictracks_0710.htm. Accessed 26 Feb 2015.

Butler, Mark J. 2006. *Unlocking the groove: Rhythm, meter, and musical design in electronic dance music*. Bloomington: Indiana University Press.

Carey, James T. 1969. Changing courtship patterns in the popular song. *American Journal of Sociology* 74(6): 720–731.

Carpenter, Alexander. 2012. The 'Ground Zero' of goth: Bauhaus, 'Bela Lugosi's Dead' and the origins of gothic rock. *Popular Music and Society* 35(1): 25–52.

Carroll, Noël. 1998. *A philosophy of mass art*. Oxford: Clarendon Press.

Cateforis, Theo. 2011. *Are we not new wave?: Modern pop at the turn of the 1980s*. Ann Arbor: University of Michigan Press.

Caygill, Howard. 2011. He preferred not to…. *Radical Philosophy* 165: 42–45.

Chang, Jeff. 2006. *Can't stop, won't stop: A history of the hiphop generation*. New York: Picador.

Chapple, Steve, and Reebee Garofalo. 1977. *Rock'n'roll is here to pay*. Chicago: Nelson Hall.

Chester, Andrew. 1970a. For a rock aesthetic. *New Left Review* 59: 83–96.

———. 1970b. Second thoughts on a rock aesthetic: The Band. *New Left Review* 62: 75–82.

Christgau, Robert. 1967. Rock lyrics are poetry (Maybe). http://www.robert-christgau.com/xg/music/lyrics-che.php. Accessed 10 Jan 2015.

Cocker, Jarvis. 2012. *Mother, brother, lover: Selected lyrics*. London: Faber & Faber.

Cohen, Sara. 1991. *Rock culture in liverpool: Popular music in the making*. Oxford: Oxford University Press.

Collingwood, R.G. 1958. *The principles of art*. Oxford: Oxford University Press. Originally published in 1938.

Cook, Deborah. 1996. *The culture industry revisited: Theodor W. Adorno on mass culture*. Lanham: Rowman & Littlefield.

———. 2014. *Adorno on nature*. Cheshunt, Bucks: Acumen.

Cook, Nicholas. 1989. Music theory and 'Good Comparison': A Viennese perspective. *Journal of Music Theory* 33(1): 117–141.

Cook, Nicholas, and Nicola Dibben. 2010. Emotion in culture and history: Perspectives from musicology. In *Handbook of music and emotion: Theory, research, applications*, ed. Patrick N. Juslin, and John A. Sloboda, 45–70. Oxford: Oxford University Press.

Cooke, Deryck. 1959. *The language of music*. Oxford: Oxford University Press.

Cooper, B. Lee. 1991. *Popular music perspectives: Ideas, themes and patterns in contemporary lyrics*. Bowling Green: Popular Press of Bowling Green State University.

Cooper, Grosvenor W., and Leonard B. Meyer. 1960. *The rhythmic structure of music*. Chicago: University of Chicago Press.

Covach, John. 1997. Progressive rock, 'Close to the Edge', and the boundaries of style. In *Understanding rock: Essays in musical analysis*, ed. John Covach, and Graeme M. Boone, 3–32. New York: Oxford University Press.

———. 2005. Form in rock music: A primer. In *Engaging music: Essays in musical analysis*, ed. Deborah Stein, 65–76. New York: Oxford University Press.

———. 2006. *What's that sound?: An introduction to rock and its history*. New York: Norton.

Cowie, Jefferson R., and Lauren Boehm. 2006. Dead man's town: 'Born in the U.S.A.', social history, and working-class identity. *American Quarterly 58*(2): 353–378.

Coyle, Michael, and Jon Dolan. 1999. Modeling authenticity, authenticating commercial models. In *Reading rock and roll: Authenticity, appropriation, aesthetics*, ed. Kevin J.H. Dettmar, and William Richey, 17–36. New York: Columbia University Press.

Cunningham, David. 2014. Rock as minimal modernism. *Radical Philosophy 183*: 69–72.

Curtis, Meagin E., and Jamshed J. Bharucha. 2010. The minor third communicates sadness in speech, mirroring its use in music. *Emotion 10*: 335–348.

Daly, Steven. 2005. Hip-hop happens. *Vanity Fair* Nov. http://www.vanityfair.com/culture/2005/11/hiphop200511. Accessed 23 Feb 2015.

Danto, Arthur. 1986. The end of art. In *The philosophical disenfranchisement of art*, 81–116. New York: Columbia University Press.

Darby, Derrick, and Tommie Shelby (ed). 2005. *Hip-hop and philosophy: Rhyme 2 reason*. La Salle: Open Court.

Davies, Stephen. 1999. Rock versus classical music. *Journal of Aesthetics and Art Criticism 57*(2): 193–204.

———. 2001. *Musical works and performances: A philosophical exploration*. Oxford: Oxford University Press.

———. 2011. *Musical understandings: And other essays on the philosophy of music*. Oxford: Oxford University Press.

De Clercq, Trevor, and David Temperley. 2011. A corpus analysis of rock harmony. *Popular Music 30*(1): 47–70.

DeNora, Tia. 2000. *Music in everyday life*. Cambridge, UK: Cambridge University Press.

———. 2003. *After Adorno: Rethinking music sociology*. Cambridge, UK: Cambridge University Press.

Deruty, Emmanuel. 2011. 'Dynamic range' and the loudness war. *Sound on Sound*. Sept. http://www.soundonsound.com/sos/sep11/articles/loudness.htm. Accessed 13 Jan 2015.

Dettmar, Kevin J.H., and William Richey (ed). 1999. *Reading rock and roll: Authenticity, appropriation, aesthetics*. New York: Columbia University Press.

Dibben, Nicola. 2001. Pulp, pornography and spectatorship: Subject matter and subject position in Pulp's album 'This is Hardcore'. *Journal of the Royal Musicological Association 126*: 83–106.

———. 2009. Vocal performance and the projection of emotional authenticity. In *The Ashgate research companion to popular musicology*, ed. Derek B. Scott, 317–334. Farnham, Surrey: Ashgate.

Duffett, Mark. 2010. Average white band: Kraftwerk and the politics of race. In *Kraftwerk: Music non-stop*, ed. David Pattie, and Sean Albiez, 194–213. New York: Continuum.

Duncombe, Stephen, and Maxwell Tremblay (ed). 2011. *White riot: Punk rock and the politics of race*. London: Verso.

Durant, Alan. 1984. *Conditions of music*. Albany: SUNY Press.

Dyer, Richard. 1995. In defence of disco. In *The Faber book of pop*, ed. Hanif Kureishi, and Jon Savage, 518–527. London: Faber & Faber. Essay originally published in 1979.

Dylan, Bob. 2014. *The lyrics: Since 1962*. New York: Simon & Schuster.

Eagleton, Terry. 1988. *The ideology of the aesthetic*. Oxford: Blackwell.

Ealham, Chris. 2015. Review of *Rhymin' and Stealin': Musical borrowing in hip-hop* by Justin A Williams. *Popular Music 34*(1): 140–142.

Echols, Alice. 2010. *Hot stuff: Disco and the remaking of American culture*. New York: Norton.

Editors of Rolling Stone. 1994. *U2: The Rolling Stone files*. New York: Hyperion Press.

Ehrenreich, Barbara. 2007. *Dancing in the streets: A history of collective joy*. London: Granta.

Eliot, Marc. 1996. *Rockonomics: The money behind the music*. New York: Citadel Press.

Endrinal, Christopher James Scott. 2008. *Form and style in the music of U2*. PhD dissertation, Florida State University DigiNole Commons, 2-25-2008.

Erlewine, Stephen Thomas. 2014. Review of Katy Perry *Teenage Dream*. Allmusic. com. http://www.allmusic.com/album/teenage-dream-mw0002011446. Accessed 15 Jan 2015.

Everett, Walter. 1999. *The Beatles as musicians: Revolver through the Anthology*. New York: Oxford University Press.

———. 2000a. Confessions from Blueberry Hill: Or, pitch can be a sticky substance. In *Expression in pop-rock music*, ed. Walter Everett, 269–346. New York: Garland.

——— (ed). 2000b. *Expression in pop-rock music: A collection of critical and analytical essays*. New York: Garland.

———. 2004. Making sense of rock's tonal systems. *Music Theory Online* 10(4). http://www.mtosmt.org/issues/mto.04.10.4/mto.04.10.4.w_everett.html. Accessed 12 Feb 2015.

————. 2008. *The foundations of rock.* Oxford: Oxford University Press.

Fabbri, Franco. 1982. What kind of music? Trans. Iain Chambers. *Popular Music* 2: 131–143.

Fast, Susan. 2000. Music, contexts, and meaning in U2. In *Expression in pop-rock music,* ed. Walter Everett, 33–58. New York: Garland.

Fisher, John Andrew. 1998. Rock 'n' recording: The ontological complexity of rock music. In *Musical worlds: New directions in the philosophy of music,* ed. Philip Alperson, 109–123. University Park, PA: Penn State Press.

————. 2011. Popular music. In *The Routledge companion to philosophy and music,* ed. Theodore Gracyk, and Andrew Kania, 405–415. New York: Routledge.

Fletcher, Tony. 2002. *Remarks remade: The story of R.E.M.* New York: Omnibus Press.

Fricke, David. 1999. The Ramones … Loud and fast. Booklet accompanying *Ramones: Anthology: Hey Ho Let's Go!* Warner Bros.

Frith, Simon. 1981. *Sound effects: Youth, leisure, and the politics of rock.* New York: Pantheon.

————. 1996. *Performing rites: Evaluating popular music.* Oxford: Oxford University Press.

————. 2001. Pop music. In *The Cambridge companion to pop and rock,* ed. Simon Frith, Will Straw, and John Street, 93–108. Cambridge, UK: Cambridge University Press.

————. 2004. What is bad music? In *Bad music: The music we love to hate,* ed. Christopher J. Washburne, and Maiken Derno, 15–38. New York: Routledge.

————. 2005. The real thing: Bruce Springsteen. In *The rock, pop and soul reader,* ed. David Brackett, 356–359. New York: Oxford University Press. Originally published in 1988.

————. 2007a. *Taking popular music seriously: Selected essays.* Aldershot: Ashgate.

————. 2007b. Why do songs have words? In *Taking popular music seriously: selected essays,* 209–238 . Aldershot: Ashgate. Essay originally published in 1987.

Frith, Simon, and Andrew Goodwin (ed). 1990. *On record: Rock, pop, and the written word.* London: Routledge.

Frith, Simon, and Howard Horne. 1987. *Art into pop.* London: Methuen.

Frith, Simon, and Lee Marshall (ed). 2004. *Music and copyright,* 2nd edn. Edinburgh: Edinburgh University Press.

Frith, Simon, and Angela McRobbie. 2007. Rock and sexuality. In *Taking popular music seriously,* 41–58. Aldershot: Ashgate. Essay originally published in 1978/9.

Frith, Simon, Will Straw, and John Street (ed). 2001. *The Cambridge companion to pop and rock.* Cambridge, UK: Cambridge University Press.

Garnett, Robert. 1999. Too low to be low: Art pop and the Sex Pistols. In *Punk rock: So what?: The cultural legacy of punk,* ed. Roger Sabin, 17–30. London: Routledge.

Garofalo, Reebee. 2010. *Rockin' out: popular music in the USA*, 5th edn. New York: Pearson.

Gates, Henry Louis, Jr. 1988. *The signifying monkey: A theory of African-American literary criticism*. Oxford: Oxford University Press.

Gendron, Bernard. 1986. Theodor Adorno meets the Cadillacs. In *Studies in entertainment*, ed. Tania Modleski, 18–38. Bloomington: Indiana University Press.

———. 2002. *From Montmartre to the Mudd club: Popular music and the avant-garde*. Chicago: University of Chicago Press.

Gilbert, Jeremy. 2014. Britpop and Blairism. http://jeremygilbertwriting.files. wordpress.com/2014/05/white-noise.pdf. Accessed 14 Jan 2015.

Gilbert, Jeremy, and Ewan Pearson. 1999. *Discographies: Dance music, culture and the politics of sound*. London: Routledge.

Gillett, Charlie. 1983. *The sound of the city*, Revised edn. London: Souvenir Press. Original publication in 1970.

Goehr, Lydia. 1992. *The imaginary museum of musical works*. Oxford: Clarendon Press.

Goldberg, Michael. 1997. Prodigy defense of 'Smack My Bitch Up'. *MTV News* 12 May. www.mtv.com/news/2096/prodigy-defense-of-smack-my-bitch-up/. Accessed 18 Jan 2015.

Goldstein, Richard. 1969. *The poetry of rock*. New York: Corgi.

Goodwin, Andrew. 1990. Sample and hold: Pop music in the digital age of reproduction. In Simon Frith and Andrew Goodwin, ed. *On Record*, 258–273. London: Routledge.

Gracyk, Theodore. 1996. *Rhythm and noise: An aesthetics of rock*. Durham: Duke University Press.

———. 2001. *I wanna be me: Rock music and the politics of identity*. Philadelphia: Temple University Press.

———. 2007. *Listening to popular music, or how I learned to stop worrying and love Led Zeppelin*. Lansing: University of Michigan Press.

———. 2008. The aesthetics of popular music. *Internet Encyclopedia of Philosophy*. ISSN 2161-0002. http://www.iep.utm.edu/. Accessed 5 Feb 2015.

Gracyk, Theodore, and Andrew Kania (ed). 2011. *The Routledge companion to philosophy and music*. New York: Routledge.

Gracyk, Theodore. 2013. *On music*. New York: Routledge.

Graham, Stephen. 2014. Too loud & it all sounds the same? Why researchers were wrong on pop. *The Quietus* 5 Dec. http://thequietus.com/articles/10904-scientific-reports-pop-music-flaw. Accessed 10 Jan 2015.

Green, Lucy. 2008. *Music on deaf ears: Musical meaning, ideology and education*, 2nd edn. Suffolk: Arima. First edn published in 1988.

Greenberg, Clement. 1939. Avant-garde and kitsch. *Partisan Review* 6(5): 34–49.

———. 1982. Modernist painting. In *Modern art and modernism: A critical anthology*, ed. Francis Frascina, and Charles Harrison. New York: Sage. Essay originally published in 1961.

Greenfield, Steve, and Guy Osborn. 2004. Copyright law and power in the music industry. In *Music and copyright*, 2nd edn, ed. Simon Frith, and Lee Marshall, 89–102. Edinburgh: Edinburgh University Press.

Gribin, Anthony J., and Matthew M. Schiff. 1992. *Doo-wop: The forgotten third of rock 'n' roll*. Iola: Krause Publications.

Griffin, Brendon. 2002. Sleeve notes to *The Message: The Best of Grandmaster Flash & The Sugarhill Gang*. BMG. [CD]

Griffiths, Dai. 2003. From lyric to anti-lyric: Analyzing the words in pop song. In *Analyzing popular music*, ed. Allan F. Moore, 39–59. Cambridge, UK: Cambridge University Press.

———. 2010–11. What was, or is, critical musicology? *Radical Musicology* 5. http://www.radical-musicology.org.uk. Accessed 2 June 2015.

Grossberg, Lawrence. 1990. Is there rock after punk? In *On record*, ed. Simon Frith, and Andrew Goodwin, 110–123. London: Routledge. Essay originally published in 1986.

———. 1992. *We gotta get out of this place: Popular conservatism and postmodern culture*. New York: Routledge.

Guest, Katy. 2012. Name that tune. *The Independent* 29 July. http://www.independent.co.uk/voices/commentators/katy-guest-why-dont-men-take-a-stand-against-wearing-a-tie-7984904.html. Accessed 13 Jan 2015.

Guralnick, Peter. 1988. *Sweet soul music: Rhythm and blues and the southern dream of freedom*. New York: Harper Collins.

Hamilton, Andy. 2007. *Aesthetics and music*. London: Continuum.

Han-Pile, Béatrice. 2006. 'This music changed the shape of the world': U2 and the phenomenological understanding of music. In *U2 and philosophy*, ed. Mark A. Wrathall, 149–162. La Salle: Open Court.

Hanslick, Eduard. 1986. *On the musically beautiful*. Trans. Geoffrey Payzant. Indianapolis: Hackett. Original German publication of the eighth edition in 1891.

Harker, Dave. 1980. *One for the money: Politics and popular song*. London: Hutchinson.

———. 1985. *Fakesong: The manufacture of British folk song, 1700 to the present day*. Maidenhead: Open University Press.

Harris, James F. 1993. *Philosophy at 33$\frac{1}{3}$ RPM: Themes of classic rock music*. La Salle: Open Court.

Hatherley, Owen. 2011. *Uncommon*. London: Zero Books.

Hebdige, Dick. 1979. *Subculture: The meaning of style*. London: Routledge.

Hegel, G. W. F. 1970. *Aesthetics: Lectures on fine art*. 2 vols. Trans. T.M. Knox. Oxford: Clarendon Press.

Hesmondhalgh, David. 2013. *Why music matters*. Oxford: Wiley-Blackwell.

Hesmondhalgh, David, and Keith Negus (ed). 2002. *Popular music studies*. London: Arnold.

Hibbert, Ryan. 2005. What is indie rock? *Popular Music and Society* 28(1): 55–77.

Hirjee, Hussein, and Daniel G. Brown. 2009. Automatic detection of internal and imperfect rhymes in rap lyrics. *Proceedings of the tenth International Society for Music Information Retrieval conference.* http://ismir2009.ismir.net/proceedings/OS8-1.pdf. Accessed 10 Jan 2015.

Hodgkinson, Will. 2007. *Song man: One man's mission to write the perfect pop song.* London: Bloomsbury.

Holt, Greg. 2006–11. Little Feat. http://gregholt.co.uk/littlefeat.htm. Accessed 16 Mar 2015.

Hook, Peter. 2012. *Unknown pleasures: Inside Joy Division.* London: Simon & Schuster.

Horton, Donald. 1990. The dialogue of courtship in popular song. In *On record,* ed. Simon Frith, and Andrew Goodwin, 11–21. London: Routledge Article originally published in 1957.

Howes, Frank. 1962. A critique of folk, popular and 'Art' music. *British Journal of Aesthetics* 2(3): 239–248.

Hughes, Walter. 1994. In the empire of the beat: Discipline and disco. In *Microphone fiends: Youth music and youth culture,* ed. Andrew Ross, and Tricia Rose, 147–157. New York: Routledge.

Huhn, Tom, and Lambert Zuidervaart (ed). 1997. *The semblance of subjectivity: Essays on Adorno's aesthetic theory.* Cambridge, MA: MIT Press.

Hullot-Kentor, Robert. 2006. Translator's introduction to *Philosophy of new music,* ed. Theodor W. Adorno. Minneapolis: University of Minnesota Press.

Irvin, Sherri. 2008. The pervasiveness of the aesthetic in ordinary experience. *British Journal of Aesthetics* 48(1): 29–44.

James, William. 1890. *The principles of psychology.* http://psychclassics.yorku.ca/James/Principles/prin25.htm. Accessed 16 May 2016.

Johnson, Julian. 2002. *Who needs classical music?: Cultural choice and musical values.* Oxford: Oxford University Press.

Johnson, Paul. 1964. The menace of Beatlism. *New Statesman.* Reprinted 28 August 2014. http://www.newstatesman.com/culture/2014/08/archive-menace-beatlism. Accessed 6 Apr 2016.

Jourdain, Robert. 1997. *Music, the brain, and ecstasy: How music captures our imagination.* New York: Harper Perennial.

Juslin, Patrick N., and John A. Sloboda (ed). 2010. *Handbook of music and emotion: Theory, research, applications.* Oxford: Oxford University Press.

Kania, Andrew. 2006. Making tracks: The ontology of rock music. *Journal of Aesthetics and Art Criticism* 64(4): 401–414.

———. 2014. The philosophy of music. In *The Stanford encyclopedia of philosophy.* Spring 2014 Edition, ed. Edward N. Zalta. http://plato.stanford.edu/archives/spr2014/entries/music/. Accessed 13 Jan 2015.

Kant, Immanuel. 1987. *Critique of judgement.* Trans. Werner S. Pluhar. Indianapolis: Hackett. Original German publication in 1790 (first edn) and 1793 (second edn).

Katz, Mark. 2012. *Groove music: The art and culture of the hip-hop DJ*. Oxford: Oxford University Press.

Kawashima, Dale. 2005. Legendary trio Holland-Dozier-Holland talk about their Motown hits, and new projects (2005 Interview). http://www.songwriteruniverse.com/hdh.htm. Accessed 18 Jan 2015.

Keil, Charles, and Steven Feld. 1994. *Music grooves*. Chicago: University of Chicago Press.

Keil, Charles. 1966. *Urban blues*. Chicago: University of Chicago Press.

Kivy, Peter. 2002. *Introduction to a philosophy of music*. Oxford: Oxford University Press.

Knightley, Keir. 2001. Reconsidering rock. In *The Cambridge companion to pop and rock*, ed. Simon Frith, Will Straw, and John Street, 109–142. Cambridge, UK: Cambridge University Press.

Korsmeyer, Carolyn. 2004. *Gender and aesthetics*. New York: Routledge.

——— (ed). 1998. *Aesthetics: The big questions*. Malden: Blackwell.

Krims, Adam. 2000. *Rap music and the poetics of identity*. Cambridge, UK: Cambridge University Press.

Kristeller, Paul Oskar. 1951. The modern system of the arts: A study in the history of aesthetics (I). *Journal of the History of Ideas* 12(4): 496–527.

Kristeva, Julia. 1984. *Revolution in poetic language*. Trans. Margaret Waller. New York: Columbia University Press. Original French publication in 1974.

———. 2002. *Revolt, she said*. New York: Semiotext(e).

Lacasse, Serge. 2010. The phonographic voice: Paralinguistic features and phonographic staging in popular music singing. In *Recorded music: Performance, culture, and technology*, ed. Amanda Bayley, 227–251. Cambridge, UK: Cambridge University Press.

Laing, Dave. 1985. *One chord wonders: Power and meaning in punk rock*. Milton Keynes: Open University Press.

Lariviere, Aaron. 2013. The 10 best New Order songs. At Stereogum.com, Jan 25. http://www.stereogum.com/1244332/the-10-best-new-order-songs/franchises/10-best-songs/. Accessed 6 Apr 2015.

Leach, Elizabeth Eva. 2001. Vicars of 'Wannabe': Authenticity and the Spice Girls. *Popular Music* 20(2): 143–167.

———. 2009. Popular music. In *An introduction to music studies*, ed. J.P.E. Harper-Scott, and Jim Samson, 188–199. Cambridge: Cambridge University Press.

Leahey, Andrew. 2012. Behind the song: Satisfaction. *American Songwriter* March 9. http://www.americansongwriter.com/2012/03/behind-the-song-i-cant-get-no-satisfaction/. Accessed 17 Jan 2015.

Lee, Stephen. 1995. Re-examining the concept of the 'Independent' record company: The case of Wax Trax! records. *Popular Music* 14(1): 13–31.

Leonard, Tom. 2014. The singalong revolutionary the White House couldn't crush. *Daily Mail* 29 Jan. http://www.dailymail.co.uk/news/article-e2547793/Pete-Seeger-Singalong-revolutionary-White-House-crush.html. Accessed 14 Jan 2015.

Lerdahl, Fred, and Ray Jackendoff. 1983. *A generative theory of tonal music.* Cambridge, MA: MIT Press.

Leppert, Richard. 2002. Commentary (music and mass culture). In *Essays on music*, ed. Richard Leppert, 327–372. Berkeley: University of California Press.

Lester, Paul. 2008. Steel crazy: The Human League, ABC, Heaven 17. In *The Scotsman* 13 Nov. http://www.scotsman.com/what-s-on/music/steel-crazy-the-human-league-abc-heaven-17-1-1146635. Accessed 26 Feb 2015.

Levinson, Jerrold. 1980. What a musical work is. *The Journal of Philosophy LXXVII* 1: 5–28.

———. 2015. *Musical concerns: Essays in philosophy of music.* Oxford: Oxford University Press.

London, Justin. 2015. Rhythm. *Grove music online. Oxford music online.* Oxford: Oxford University Press. http://www.oxfordmusiconline.com/libezproxy. open.ac.uk/subscriber/article/grove/music/45963. Accessed 30 Apr 2015.

Lyotard, Jean-François. 1984. *The postmodern condition: A report on knowledge.* Trans. Geoff Bennington and Brian Massumi. Manchester: Manchester University Press. Original French publication in 1979.

Macan, Edward. 1997. *Rockin' the classics: English progressive rock and the counter-culture.* New York: Oxford University Press.

Macdonald, Ian. 2005. *Revolution in the head: The Beatles' records and the sixties,* 2nd revised edn. London: Pimlico.

Machin, David. 2010. *Analysing popular music: Image, sound, text.* London: Sage.

Maconie, Stuart. 2013. *The people's songs: The story of modern Britain in 50 records.* London: Ebury.

Macrae, Fiona. 2012. All the songs DO sound the same. *Daily Mail* 26 July. http://www.dailymail.co.uk/sciencetech/article-2179432/All-songs-DO-sound-Modern-pop-louder-uses-chords-classic-albums-Fifties-Sixties.html. Accessed 13 Jan 2015.

Madell, Geoffrey. 2002. *Music, philosophy and emotion.* Edinburgh: Edinburgh University Press.

Madonnatribe. 2014. Madonnatribe meets Billy Steinberg. 4 Nov. http://www.madonnatribe.com/interviews/madonnatribe-meets-billy-steinberg/. Accessed 23 Jan 2015.

Malins, Steve. 2001. Liner notes to *Replicas*, by Gary Numan and Tubeway Army. Re-release and remaster with extra tracks. Beggars Banquet. [CD]

Manuel, Peter. 1995. Music as symbol, music as simulacrum: Postmodern, pre-modern, and modern aesthetics in subcultural popular musics. *Popular Music* 14(2): 227–239.

Marcus, Greil. 1978. Wire, 'Pink Flag'. *Rolling Stone* 20 April. http://greilmarcus.net/2014/10/14/wire-pink-flag-042078/. Accessed 23 Feb 2015.

———. 2011. *Lipstick traces: A secret history of the twentieth century.* Twentieth anniversary edn. London: Faber & Faber. Originally published in 1989.

———. 2014. *The history of rock 'n' roll in ten songs*. New Haven: Yale University Press.

Mauch, Matthias, Robert M. MacCallum, Mark Levy, and Armand M. Leroi. 2015. The evolution of popular music: USA 1960–2010. *Royal Society Open Science 2*: 150081.

McCartney, Paul, John Lennon, George Harrison, Ringo Starr, Tetsuya Fujita, Yuji Hagino, et al. 1993. *The Beatles: Complete scores*. London: Wise Publications.

McCormick, Neil (ed). 2005. *U2 by U2*. London: HarperCollins.

Merleau-Ponty, Maurice. 2002. *The phenomenology of perception*. Trans. Colin Smith. Reprint edn. London: Routledge. Original French publication in 1945.

Meyer, Leonard. 1956. *Emotion and meaning in music*. Chicago: University of Chicago Press.

Michaels, Sean. 2012. Pop music these days: It all sounds the same, survey reveals. *The Guardian* 27 July. http://www.theguardian.com/music/2012/jul/27/pop-music-sounds-same-survey-reveals. Accessed 1 Apr 2017.

Middleton, Richard. 1990. *Studying popular music*. Milton Keynes: Open University Press.

——— (ed). 2000. *Reading pop: Approaches to textual analysis in popular music*. Oxford: Oxford University Press.

———. 2006. *Voicing the popular: On the subjects of popular music*. London: Taylor and Francis.

Mill, John Stuart. 1859. Bentham. In *Dissertations and discussions: Political, philosophical and historical*, vol 1, 330–392. London: John W. Parker and Son.

Milner, Greg. 2010. *Perfecting sound forever: The story of recorded music*. London: Granta.

Moon, Tony, ed. 1977. *Sideburns* 1. Jan. Available to download at URL: http://daveo-musicandstuff.blogspot.co.uk/2011/03/sideeburns-no1-this-is-chord--this-is.html. Accessed 27 Feb 2015.

Moore, Allan F. 1992. Patterns of harmony. *Popular Music 11*(1): 73–106.

———. 1995. The so-called 'Flattened Seventh' in rock. *Popular Music 14*(2): 185–201.

———. 1997. *The Beatles: Sgt. Pepper's Lonely Hearts Club Band*. Cambridge, UK: Cambridge University Press.

———. 1998. U2 and the myth of authenticity in rock. *Popular Musicology 3*(6): 5–33. http://www.allanfmoore.org.uk/U2myth.pdf. Accessed 30 Jan 2015.

———. 2001. *Rock: The primary text: Developing a musicology of rock*. Farnham: Ashgate.

———. 2012a. *Song means: Analysing and interpreting recorded popular song*. Farnham: Ashgate.

———. 2012b. The track. In *Recorded music: Performance, culture, and technology*, ed. Amanda Bayley, 252–267. Cambridge, UK: Cambridge University Press.

——— (ed). 2003. *Analyzing popular music*. Cambridge, UK: Cambridge University Press.

Morelle, Rebecca. 2015. Pop music marked by three revolutions in 50 years. BBC News 6 May 2015. http://www.bbc.co.uk/news/science-environment-32599916. Accessed 2 Jun 2015.

Morley, Paul. 2014. Pop belongs to the last century. *The Guardian* 21 September. http://www.theguardian.com/music/2014/sep/21/pop-belongs-last-century-classical-music-relevant-future-paul-morley. Accessed 15 Jan 2015.

Mowitt, John. 2002. *Percussion: Beating, drumming, striking.* Durham: Duke University Press.

Moy, Ron. 2007. *Kate Bush and the Hounds of Love.* Farnham: Ashgate.

Navarez, Leonard. 2013. How Joy Division came to sound like Manchester. *Journal of Popular Music Studies* 25(1): 56–76.

Neate, Wilson. 2009. *Pink Flag.* London: Continuum.

Negus, Keith. 1992. *Producing pop: Culture and conflict in the popular music industry.* London: Edward Arnold.

———. 1996. *Popular music in theory: An introduction.* Cambridge, UK: Polity.

Negus, Keith, and Michael Pickering. 2002. Creativity and musical experience. In *Popular music studies*, ed. David Hesmondhalgh, and Keith Negus, 178–190. London: Arnold.

Newton, Francis [Eric Hobsbawm]. 2007. Beatles and before. Selections by Robert Taylor. *New Statesman* 28 June. http://www.newstatesman.com/society/2007/06/beatles-music-blues-1963. Accessed 26 Jan 2015. Originally published in 1963.

Niimi, J. 2005. *Murmur.* New York: Continuum.

Northcutt, William M. 2006. The spectacle of alienation: Death, loss and the crowd in *Sgt. Pepper's Lonely Hearts Club Band.* In *Reading the Beatles*, ed. Kenneth Womack, and Todd F. Davis, 129–146. Albany: SUNY Press.

Numan, Gary, with Steve Malins. 1997. *Praying to the aliens: An autobiography.* London: André Deutsch.

Ott, Chris. 2004. *Unknown pleasures.* New York: Continuum.

Oxford English Dictionary. 2013. *Rock. Full entry.* 2nd, revised edn. Oxford: Oxford University Press.

Paddison, Max. 1982. The critique criticised: Adorno and popular music. *Popular Music 2*: 201–218.

———. 1993. *Adorno's aesthetics of music.* Cambridge, UK: Cambridge University Press.

———. 2004. Authenticity and failure in Adorno's aesthetics of music. In *The Cambridge companion to Adorno*, ed. Tom Huhn, 198–221. Cambridge, UK: Cambridge University Press.

Partridge, Christopher. 2011. Popular music, affective space, and meaning. In *Religion, media, and culture: A reader*, ed. Gordon Lynch, Jolyon Mitchell, and Anna Strhan, 182–193. London: Routledge.

———. 2014. *The lyre of Orpheus: Popular music, the sacred, and the profane.* New York: Oxford University Press.

Pedler, Dominic. 2003. *The songwriting secrets of the Beatles.* London: Omnibus.

Peterson, Richard. 1997. The rise and fall of highbrow snobbery as a status marker. *Poetics* 25(2): 75–92.

Railton, Diane, and Paul Watson. 2011. *Music video and the politics of representation.* Edinburgh: Edinburgh University Press.

Reynolds, Simon. 2005. *Rip it up and start again.* London: Faber & Faber.

Rifai, Ayah. 2010. Gaga in Oz: Hearing the woman behind the camera in Lady Gaga's 'Paparazzi'. *Gaga Stigmata.* Nov 10. http://gagajournal.blogspot. co.uk/2010/11/gaga-in-oz-hearing-woman-behind-camera.html. Accessed 13 Jan 2015.

Rimbaud, Arthur. 2001. *Collected poems.* Ed. and trans. Martin Sorrell. Oxford: Oxford University Press.

Robinson, Jenefer. 2005. *Deeper than reason: Emotion and its role in literature, music, and art.* Oxford: Oxford University Press.

Roholt, Tiger C. 2014. *Groove: A phenomenology of rhythmic nuance.* New York: Bloomsbury.

Rose, Tricia. 1994. *Black noise: Rap music and black culture in contemporary America.* Middletown: Wesleyan University Press.

Rosen, Craig. 1997. *R.E.M. inside out: The stories behind every song.* New York: Thunder's Mouth Press.

Rudinow, Joel. 2010. *Soul music: Tracking the spiritual roots of pop from Plato to Motown.* Ann Arbor: University of Michigan Press.

Runowicz, John Michael. 2010. *Forever doo-wop.* Amherst: University of Massachusetts Press.

Sabin, Roger. 1999a. 'I won't let that dago go by': Rethinking punk and racism. In *Punk rock: So what?: The cultural legacy of punk*, 199–218. London: Routledge.

——— (ed). 1999b. *Punk rock: So what?: The cultural legacy of punk.* London: Routledge.

Saito, Yuriko. 2010. *Everyday aesthetics.* Oxford: Oxford University Press.

Salley, Keith. 2011. On the interaction of alliteration with rhythm and metre in popular music. *Popular Music* 30(3): 409–432.

Sartre, Jean-Paul. 1993. *Being and nothingness.* Trans. Hazel E. Barnes. London: Routledge. Original French publication in 1943.

Savage, Jon. 1989. Sleeve notes to *Wire: On returning (1977-1979).* EMI. [LP].

———. 2008. Controlled chaos. *The Guardian* 10 May. http://www.theguardian.com/books/2008/may/10/popandrock.joydivision. Accessed 10 Apr 2015.

Savage, Mike, and Modesto Gayo. 2011. Unravelling the omnivore: A field analysis of contemporary musical taste in the United Kingdom. *Poetics* 39: 337–357.

Scheff, Thomas. 2011. *What's love got to do with it?: Emotions and relationships in pop songs.* Boulder, CO: Paradigm.

Schindler, Anton. 1996. *Beethoven as I knew him*. Trans. Constance S. Jolly. Translation originally published in 1966 based on the third German edn. of 1860. New York: Dover Press.

Schlegel, Friedrich. 1971. *Lucinde and the Fragments*. Trans. Peter Firchow. Minneapolis: Minnesota University Press.

Schopenhauer, Arthur. 1966. *The world as will and representation*. 2 vols. Trans. E.F.J. Payne. Mineola: Dover Press. Original German publication in 1819 (first edn) and 1844 (second edn).

Schuker, Lauren A. E. 2009. The artist and the director. *The Wall Street Journal* Oct 2. http://www.wsj.com/articles/SB10001424052748704471504577444 5603670923492. Accessed 15 Jan 2015.

Schuller, Gunther. 1986. *Early jazz: Its roots and musical development*. Oxford: Oxford University Press.

Scott, Derek B. 2008. *Sounds of the metropolis: The 19th-century popular music revolution in London, New York, Paris, and Vienna*. Oxford: Oxford University Press.

Scruton, Roger. 1997. *The aesthetics of music*. Oxford: Oxford University Press.

———. 1998. *An intelligent person's guide to modern culture*. South Bend: St. Augustine's Press.

———. 2007. Thoughts on rhythm. In *Philosophers on music*, ed. Kathleen Stock, 226–255. Oxford: Oxford University Press.

———. 2011. Rhythm, melody, and harmony. In *The Routledge companion to philosophy and music*, ed. Theodore Gracyk, and Andrew Kania, 24–37. New York: Routledge.

Serrà, J., A. Corral, M. Boguñá, M. Haro, and J.Ll. Arcos. 2012. Measuring the evolution of contemporary western popular music. *Scientific Reports* 2(521): 1–6. doi:10.1038/srep00521.

Shaw, Arnold. 1978. *Honkers and shouters: The golden years of rhythm and blues*. New York: Crowell-Collier Press.

Shiner, Larry. 2001. *The invention of art*. Chicago: University of Chicago Press.

Shuker, Roy. 2001. *Understanding popular music*, 2nd edn. London: Routledge.

Shusterman, Richard. 1991. Form and funk: The aesthetic challenge of popular art. *British Journal of Aesthetics* 31(3): 203–213.

———. 2000. *Performing live: Aesthetic alternatives for the ends of art*. Ithaca: Cornell University Press.

Sibley, Frank. 1959. Aesthetic concepts. *Philosophical Review* 68(4): 421–450.

Simpson, Dave. 2013. How we made Blue Monday. Interview with Gillian Gilbert and Peter Saville. *The Guardian* 11 February. http://www.theguardian.com/culture/2013/feb/11/how-we-made-blue-monday. Accessed 2 Apr 2015.

———. 2014. How we made Are 'Friends' Electric? Interview with Gary Numan and Mary Vango. *The Guardian* 18 February. http://www.theguardian.com/music/2014/feb/18/how-we-made-are-friends-electric-gary-numan. Accessed 28 Jan 2015.

Sinclair, John. 2011. Liner notes to MC5's Kick Out the Jams! Reprinted in *White Riot*, ed. Duncombe, and Tremblay, 28–29. London: Verso.

Sinnreich, Aram. 2011. *Mashed up: Music, technology and the rise of configurable culture*. Amherst: University of Massachusetts Press.

Slomowicz, Ron. 2008. Lady Gaga interview. http://dancemusic.about.com/od/artistshomepages/a/LadyGagaInt_2.htm. Accessed 12 Jan 2015.

Small, Christopher. 1998. *Musicking: The meanings of performing and listening*. Middletown: Wesleyan University Press.

———. 1999. *Music of the common tongue: Survival and celebration in Afro-American music*. Middletown: Wesleyan University Press. Originally published in 1987.

Spicer, Mark. 2004. (Ac)cumulative form in pop-rock music. *Twentieth Century Music* 1(1): 29–64.

Stanley, Bob. 2013. *Yeah yeah yeah: The story of modern pop*. London: Faber & Faber.

Starr, Larry, and Christopher Waterman. 2006. *American popular music: The rock years*. Oxford: Oxford University Press.

Stecker, Robert. 2006. Aesthetic experience and aesthetic value. *Philosophy Compass* 1(1): 1–10.

Stephenson, Ken. 2002. *What to listen for in rock: A stylistic analysis*. New Haven: Yale University Press.

Stevens, Rachael. 2013. The Human League and a vision of the future. *Creative review: Advertising, design and visual culture*. CR Blog. 11 October. http://www.creativereview.co.uk/cr-blog/2013/october/travelogue. Accessed 25 Feb 2015.

Stock, Kathleen (ed). 2007. *Philosophers on music: Experience, meaning, and work*. Oxford: Oxford University Press.

Stone, Alison. 2006. Adorno and the disenchantment of nature. *Philosophy and Social Criticism* 32(2): 231–253.

Strang, Fay. 2013. My intention was to put art culture into pop music. *Daily Mail* November 4. http://www.dailymail.co.uk/tvshowbiz/article-2486872/Lady-Gaga-reveals-aimed-reverse-Warhol-new-album-ARTPOP.html#ixzz2yUQtEIiH. Accessed 14 Jan 2015.

Street, Stephen, William Orbit, and Ben Hillier. 2009. Blur – Album by album. *Uncut* July, Take 146. http://www.uncut.co.uk/blur/blur-album-by-album-by-stephen-street-william-orbit-and-ben-hillier-feature. Accessed 28 Jan 2015.

Stubbs, David. 2014a. *Future days: Krautrock and the building of modern Germany*. London: Faber & Faber.

———. 2014b. How Motorik infected the mainstream. *The Quietus* 7 August. http://thequietus.com/articles/15929-david-stubbs-krautrock-motorik. Accessed 25 Mar 2015.

Sweers, Britta. 2005. *Electric folk: The changing face of English traditional music*. Oxford: Oxford University Press.

Subotnik, Rose Rosengard. 1991. *Developing variations: Style and ideology in Western music.* Minneapolis: University of Minnesota Press.

———. 1995. *Deconstructive variations: Music and reason in Western society.* Minneapolis: University of Minnesota Press.

Tagg, Philip. 1982. Analysing popular music: Theory, method and practice. *Popular Music 2*: 37–65.

———. 1989. Open letter about 'Black Music', 'Afro-American Music' and 'European Music'. *Popular Music 8*(3): 285–298.

———. 1994. From refrain to rave: The decline of figure and the rise of ground. *Popular Music 13*(2): 209–222.

———. 1997. Understanding musical time sense – Concepts, sketches and consequences. http://tagg.org/articles/xpdfs/timesens.pdf. Accessed 15 Apr 2015. Revised, expanded version of a 1984 article.

———. 2000. *Fernando the flute.* New York/Huddersfield: The Mass Media Music Scholars' Press.

———. 2012. *Music's meanings: A modern musicology for non-musos.* New York/Huddersfield: The Mass Media Music Scholars' Press.

Taylor, Charles. 1975. *Hegel.* Cambridge, UK: Cambridge University Press.

———. 1989. *Sources of the self.* Cambridge, MA: Harvard University Press.

Temperley, David. 1999. Syncopation in rock: A perceptual perspective. *Popular Music 18*(1): 19–40.

———. 2007. The melodic-harmonic 'Divorce' in rock. *Popular Music 26*(2): 323–342.

Temperley, David, and Trevor de Clercq. 2013. Statistical analysis of harmony and melody in rock music. *Journal of New Music Research 42*(3): 187–204.

Théberge, Paul. 2001. 'Plugged In': Technology and popular music. In *The Cambridge companion to pop and rock*, ed. Simon Frith, Will Straw, and John Street, 3–25. Cambridge, UK: Cambridge University Press.

———. 2004. Technology, creative practice and copyright. In *Music and copyright*, second edn, ed. Simon Frith, and Lee Marshall, 139–156. Edinburgh: Edinburgh University Press.

Thompson, William Forde, and Laura-Lee Balkwill. 2010. Cross-cultural similarities and differences. In *Handbook of music and emotion*, ed. Patrik N. Juslin, and John A. Sloboda, 755–788. Oxford: Oxford University Press.

Tilden, Imogen. 2013. What pop music owes to the classical masters. *The Guardian* 24 January. http://www.theguardian.com/music/2013/jan/24/what-pop-music-owes-classical-masters. Accessed 6 Apr 2016.

Toynbee, Jason. 2004. Musicians. In *Music and copyright*, 2nd edn, ed. Simon Frith, and Lee Marshall, 123–138. Edinburgh: Edinburgh University Press.

Trehub, Sandra E., Erin E. Hannon, and Adena Schachner. 2010. Perspectives on music and affect in the early years. In *Handbook of music and emotion*, ed. Patrik N. Juslin, and John A. Sloboda, 645–668. Oxford: Oxford University Press.

Turino, Thomas. 2008. *Music as social life: The politics of participation.* Chicago: University of Chicago Press.

Venrooij, Alex van. 2009. The aesthetic discourse space of popular music: 1985–86 and 2004–05. *Poetics 37*(4): 315–332.

Waksman, Steve. 1999. *Instruments of desire: The electric guitar and the shaping of musical experience.* Cambridge, MA: Harvard University Press.

———. 2003. The turn to noise: Rock guitar from the 1950s to the 1970s. In *The Cambridge companion to the guitar*, ed. Victor Anand Coelho, 109–121. Cambridge, UK: Cambridge University Press.

Wald, Elijah. 2009. *How the Beatles destroyed rock 'n' roll: An alternative history of American popular music.* Oxford: Oxford University Press.

———. 2012. *The dozens: A history of rap's mama.* New York: Oxford University Press.

Walser, Robert. 1993. *Running with the devil: Power, gender and madness in heavy metal music.* Middletown: Wesleyan University Press.

———. 2003. Popular music analysis: Ten apothegms and four instances. In *Analyzing popular music*, ed. Allan F. Moore, 16–38. Cambridge, UK: Cambridge University Press.

Walser, Robert, and Susan McClary. 1990. Start making sense! Musicology wrestles with rock. In *On Record*, ed. Simon Frith and Andrew Goodwin, 237–249. London: Routledge.

Walton, Kendall. 1970. Categories of art. *Philosophical Review 79*(3): 334–367.

Warner, Timothy. 2003. *Pop music – technology and creativity.* Farnham, Surrey: Ashgate.

Washburne, Christopher J., and Maiken Derno (ed). 2004. *Bad music: The music we love to hate.* New York: Routledge.

Weinberg, Norman. 1998. *Guide to standardized drum notation.* Lawton: Percussive Arts Society.

Wicke, Peter. 1982. Rock music: A musical aesthetic study. *Popular Music 2*: 219–243.

Wickham, Chris. 2012. Pop music too loud and all sounds the same: Official. *Reuters* July 26. http://www.reuters.com/article/2012/07/26/us-science-music-idUSBRE86P0R820120726. Accessed 12 Jan 2015.

Williams, Justin A. 2013. *Rhymin' and stealin': Musical borrowing in hip-hop.* Ann Arbor: University of Michigan Press.

Williams, Raymond. 1983. *Keywords.* Revised edn. London: Fontana.

Williamson, Victoria. 2014. *You are the music: How music reveals what it means to be human.* London: Icon.

Witkin, Robert W. 1998. *Adorno on music.* London: Routledge.

———. 2003. *Adorno on popular culture.* London: Routledge.

Wittgenstein, Ludwig. 1958. *The blue and brown books.* Oxford: Blackwell.

Wrathall, Mark A. (ed). 2006. *U2 and philosophy.* La Salle: Open Court.

Young, James O. 1995. Between rock and a harp place. *Journal of Aesthetics and Art Criticism* 53(1): 78–81.

———. 2015. The ancient and modern system of the arts. *British Journal of Aesthetics* 55(1): 1–17.

Youorski, Joe. 2014. Six rock/electro musicians you didn't know were classically trained. *Paste Monthly.* August 9. http://www.pastemagazine.com/articles/2014/08/five-indie-stars-you-didnt-know-were-classically-t.html. Accessed 6 Apr 2014.

Zak, Albin J. 2001. *The poetics of rock: Cutting tracks, making records.* Berkeley: University of California Press.

Zentner, Marcel, and Tuomas Eerola. 2010. Self-report measures and models. In *Handbook of music and emotion: theory, research, applications,* ed. Patrick N. Juslin, and John A. Sloboda, 187–221. Oxford: Oxford University Press.

Zuidervaart, Lambert. 1990. The social significance of autonomous art: Adorno and Bürger. *Journal of Aesthetics and Art Criticism* 48(1): 61–77.

DISCOGRAPHY

Allen, Lily. 2009. *It's Not Me, It's You*. Regal.

Axis of Awesome. 2011. Four Chords 2011 Official Music Video. URL: https://www.youtube.com/watch?v=oOIDewpCfZQ. Accessed 15 Jun 2015.

Bambaataa, Afrika, and The Soulsonic Force. 1982. Planet Rock. Warner Bros.

Beatles, The. 1963. She Loves You. Parlophone.

———. 1965. *Rubber Soul*. Apple.

———. 1966. *Revolver*. EMI.

———. 1967a. *Magical Mystery Tour*. EMI.

———. 1967b. *Sgt. Pepper's Lonely Hearts Club*. EMI.

———. 1996. *Anthology 2*. Apple.

Berry, Chuck. 1957. Rock and Roll Music. Chess.

———. 1958. *One Dozen Berrys*. Chess.

Blur. 1997. *Blur*. Food.

Bowie, David. 1971. *Hunky Dory*. RCA.

———. 1990. *The Rise and Fall of Ziggy Stardust and the Spiders from Mars*. Re-issue with extra tracks. RCA. Album originally released in 1972.

Breeders, The. 1993. *Last Splash*. 4AD.

Brown, James. 1970. Funky Drummer (Part 1). King.

———. 1971. Make It Funky (Part 1). Polydor.

Bruce Springsteen. 1984. *Born in the U.S.A.* Columbia.

Buzzcocks. 1977. *Spiral Scratch* EP. New Hormones.

———. 1979. *Singles: Going Steady*. Liberty-United Records.

Byrd, Gary, and the GB Experience. 1983. The Crown. Motown.

Chic. 1979. *Risqué*. Atlantic.

Chords, The. 1954. Sh-Boom. Cat.

© The Author(s) 2016
A. Stone, *The Value of Popular Music*,
DOI 10.1007/978-3-319-46544-9

Clinton, George. 1982. Atomic Dog. On *Computer Games*. Capitol. [MP3]

Cocteau Twins, The. 1984. *The Spangle Maker* EP. 4AD.

Darude. 2000. Sandstorm. Robbins.

Del Rey, Lana. 2012. *Born to Die*. Polydor.

Denver, John. 2001. *Poems, Prayers, and Promises*. Reissued together with *Farewell Andromeda*. BMG. Album originally released in 1971.

Dizzee Rascal. 2003. *Boy in da Corner*. XL.

Duran Duran. 1985. A View to a Kill. EMI.

Eric B and Rakim. 1987. *Paid in Full*. 4th and B'way.

Felt. 1985. *Ignite the Seven Cannons*. Cherry Red.

Frankie Goes to Hollywood. 1983. Relax. ZTT.

Frankie Lymon and The Teenagers. 1956. Why Do Fools Fall in Love? Gee.

Fugees, The. 1996. *The Score*. Ruffhouse.

Heaven 17. 1981. Penthouse and Pavement. Virgin.

Human League, The. 1978. Being Boiled. Fast Product.

———. 1981. *Dare!* Virgin.

Jackson, Michael. 2003. *Number Ones*. Epic.

Jaynetts, The. 1990. Sally Go Round the Roses. On *The Best of the Girl Groups* vol. 1. Rhino. Single originally released in 1963.

John, Elton. 1997. *Something About the Way You Look Tonight/Candle in the Wind 1997 EP*. Mercury.

Joy Division. 1979. *Unknown Pleasures*. Factory.

———. 1988. *Substance: 1977-1980*. CentreDate.

King Crimson. 1969. *In the Court of the Crimson King*. Atlantic.

———. 1974. *Red*. Island.

Kraftwerk. 1975. *Radio-Activity*. Kling Klang.

———. 1977. *Trans-Europe Express*. Kling Klang.

Lady Gaga. 2008. *The Fame*. Interscope.

Led Zeppelin. 1975. *Physical Graffiti*. Swan Song.

M.A.R.S.S. 1987. Pump Up the Volume. 4AD.

M.I.A. 2007. *Kala*. XL.

Madonna. 1984. *Like a Virgin*. Sire.

Manic Street Preachers, The. 1996. *Everything Must Go*. Epic.

Minogue, Kylie. 2001. *Fever*. Parlophone.

Monch, Pharaohe. 1999. *Internal Affairs*. Rawkus.

Moonglows, The. 1954. Sincerely. Chess.

Neon Neon. 2008. *Stainless Style*. Lex.

New Order. 1987. *Substance*. CentreDate.

Numan, Gary, and Tubeway Army. 2001. *Replicas*. Re-released remastered version with extra tracks. Beggars Banquet. Album originally released in 1979.

Orange Juice. 1982. *Rip It Up*. Polydor.

Patti Smith Group. 1978. *Easter*. Arista.

Penguins, The. 1954. Earth Angel. Dootone.

Perry, Katy. 2010. *Teenage Dream*. Capitol.

Pink Floyd. 1973. Money. On *The Dark Side of the Moon*. Harvest.

Prince. 1984. *Purple Rain*. Warner Bros.

Prodigy, The. 1997. *The Fat of the Land*. XL.

Pulp. 1993. *Intro: The Gift Recordings*. Island.

R.E.M. 1983. *Murmur*. I.R.S.

———. 1991. *Out of Time*. Warner Bros.

Radiohead. 1997. *OK Computer*. Parlophone.

Ramones. 1976. *Ramones*. Sire.

Reddy, Helen. 1972. I Am Woman (single version). Capitol.

Reed, Lou. 1972. *Transformer*. RCA.

Richman, Jonathan and The Modern Lovers. 1972. Roadrunner. Beserkley.

Rolling Stones, The. 1965. (I Can't Get No) Satisfaction. London.

Smiths, The. 1983. This Charming Man. Rough Trade.

Steeleye Span. 1973. *Parcel of Rogues*. Chrysalis.

Sugarhill Gang, The. 1979. Rapper's Delight. Sugar Hill.

Summer, Donna. 1979. *Bad Girls*. Casablanca.

Supremes, The. 1966. *I Hear a Symphony*. Motown.

Sylvester. 1978. You Make Me Feel (Mighty Real). Fantasy.

Temptations, The. 1972. Papa was a Rolling Stone. Gordy.

U2. 1980. *Boy*. Island.

———. 1983. *War*. Island.

———. 1987. *The Joshua Tree*. Island.

Vapors, The. 1980. Turning Japanese. Parlophone.

Visage. 1980. Fade to Grey. Polydor.

Who, The. 1965. My Generation. Brunswick.

Winstons, The. 1969. Color Him Father. Metromedia.

Wire. 1989. *On Returning (1977-1979)*. EMI.

———. 1994. *Pink Flag*. EMI. Digital remaster with bonus tracks. Album originally released in 1977.

Wynette, Tammy. 1968. Stand By Your Man. BMG.

Index

Note: Page numbers followed by "n" denote notes.

© The Author(s) 2016   279
A. Stone, *The Value of Popular Music,*
DOI 10.1007/978-3-319-46544-9

The manufacturer's authorised representative in the EU is Springer
Nature Customer Service Centre GmbH, Europaplatz 3, 69115 Heidelberg,
Germany. If you have any concerns regarding our products, please
contact ProductSafety@springernature.com

Printed and bound by CPI Group (UK) Ltd, Croydon, CR0 4YY
27/04/2026
02097560-0005